Indian Pharmacy Laws
Foundations and Applications

Indian Pharmacy Laws

Foundations and Applications

Muralidhar Rao Akkaladevi
Principal, St. Mary's College of Pharmacy
Secunderabad, Telangana, India

Prabhakar Reddy Veerareddy
Head, University College of Pharmaceutical Sciences
Palamuru University
Mahabubnagar, Telangana, India

PharmaMed Press
An imprint of BSP Books Pvt. Ltd.
4-4-309/316, Giriraj Lane,
Sultan Bazar, Hyderabad - 500 095.

Indian Pharmacy Laws: Foundations and Applications
***by* Muralidhar Rao Akkaladevi and Prabhakar Reddy Veerareddy**

Disclaimer: The authors and publishers have taken due care to provide authentic, reliable and up-to-date information related to the subject. However, neither the authors nor the publisher shall be responsible for any liability for any damage caused because of the use of this book. The respective users must check the accuracy from other sources too.

Published by

PharmaMed Press
An imprint of BSP Books Pvt. Ltd.
4-4-309/316, Giriraj Lane, Sultan Bazar, Hyderabad - 500 095.
Phone: 040-23445688; Fax: 91+40-23445611
E-mail: info@pharmamedpress.net
www.bspbooks.net/www.pharmamedpress.net

ISBN: 978-93-49562-89-9 (Hardback)

Preface

The pharmaceutical industry in India plays a crucial role in global healthcare by providing affordable and high-quality medicines. However, navigating the intricate web of laws and regulations governing this industry can be overwhelming. From drug manufacturing and licensing to marketing, distribution, and exports, every step is guided by comprehensive rules aimed at ensuring safety, quality, and efficacy. This book, **Indian Pharmacy Laws: Foundations and Applications**, is designed to bring all these topics together under one umbrella. While many books focus on specific aspects of pharmacy laws, there is a lack of a single, unified resource that covers all key areas in a structured and accessible manner. This book fills that gap by addressing every important law and regulation relevant to the pharmaceutical sector in India. It includes detailed discussions on laws related to the manufacture, licensing, import, export, and sale of medicines, as well as other critical areas such as intellectual property rights, e-pharmacy, consumer protection, and environmental sustainability. Written in simple and easy-to-understand language, this book is intended for a wide range of readers. Whether you are a pharmacy student, a professional working in the pharmaceutical industry, or someone planning to start a business in the pharma sector, this book will serve as an essential reference. It provides a clear understanding of the legal framework that governs pharmaceutical operations in India and offers practical insights for compliance. Each chapter has been carefully crafted to provide not only theoretical knowledge but also practical applications. Case studies, real-world examples, and detailed explanations make this guide comprehensive and useful. The book also highlights emerging trends, global harmonization efforts, and the impact of evolving technologies and regulations on the industry. By bringing together all relevant topics under one roof, this book aims to empower its readers with the knowledge needed to succeed in the dynamic and highly regulated field of pharmaceuticals. It is our hope that this guide will become a valuable resource for anyone involved in or aspiring to be a part of India's thriving pharmaceutical landscape. We invite you to explore the pages ahead and gain a deeper understanding of the laws that shape one of India's most significant and impactful industries.

Dr. Muralidhar Rao Akkaladevi

Dr. Veerareddy Prabhakar Reddy

Contents

Chapter 7

E-Pharmacy

Chapter 8

Regulatory Affairs

Chapter 9

Health Insurance

Chapter 10

Consumer Protection Laws

Chapter 11

Imports and Exports

Chapter 12

Food Safety and Standards Authority of India (FSSAI)

About the Authors

Dr. Muralidhar Rao Akkaladevi is the National Head for APP Pharmaceutical Technology and Development Division , Principal of St. Mary's College of Pharmacy and ex- President of Association of Pharmacy Professionals (APP) for Telangana State. With over 27 years of teaching experience, he has made significant contributions to pharmacy education and research. He holds a B.Pharm, M.Pharm, and Ph.D. from the prestigious Kakatiya University and secured an impressive All India Rank of 126 in GATE 1995. Dr. Rao has authored 15 books on various pharmacy topics and published numerous research papers. He is a Fellow of the Association of Pharmacy Professionals (APP) and the Indian Science Congress Association (ISCA). He is also a life member of several esteemed organizations, including the Association of Pharmaceutical Teachers of India (APTI), the Indian Pharmacy Graduates' Association (IPGA), and the Indian Pharmacological Society (IPS).Dr. Rao is an eminent speaker who has shared his expertise at numerous national and international conferences, inspiring both professionals and students with his knowledge and experience. He is also a key resource person for Faculty Development Programs (FDPs) conducted nationwide.

Dr. Prabhakar Reddy Veerareddy is an accomplished researcher, eminent teacher in Pharmaceutical Sciences. He has been Head/Principal at University College of Pharmaceutical Sciences, Palamuru University, Mahabubnagar, Telangana State, India since November 2013. He did his B.Pharm from University College of Pharmaceutical Sciences (UCPS), Kakatiya University, Warangal; M.Pharm from University College of Pharmaceutical Sciences (UCPS), Andhra University, Visakhapatnam; Ph.D from University College of Pharmaceutical Sciences (UCPS), Kakatiya University, Warangal and Post Doctoral Fellowship (PDF) from Butler University, Indianapolis, Indiana, United States of America (USA). In addition, he has also received his LLB from Kakatiya University, Warangal. **Dr.Reddy** received Senior Research Fellowship (SRF) from Council of Scientific and Industrial Research (CSIR), New Delhi; DST (India)-DAAD (Germany) Fellowship as Research Fellow, Department for Craniomaxillofacial and Plastic Surgery, University of Cologne, Germany; CSIR International Travel Grant to attend Controlled Release Society Conference (CRS), Honolulu, Hawaii, USA; AICTE International Travel Grant to attend Federation of International Pharmacists (FIP), New Orelans, USA; DST International Travel Grant to attend The 3rd International Conference and Exhibition On Pharmaceutics & Novel Drug Delivery Systems at Chicago, USA; Best Industrial Poster Award, USA by Federation of International Pharmacists (FIP), New Orelans, USA; Travel Scholarship Award by InPharm, Bangalore, India; Elected as Industrial

Pharmacy Section (IPS) Membership Manager; Best Presentation (Oral) Award in IPC, Mumbai; Association of Biotechnology and Pharmacy Fellowship Award; Rashtriya Vidya Saraswati Puraskar Award by IIEM, New Delhi; Broomfield Foundation Award to Attend FIP Pharma bridge Programme on Pharm. D in Michigan, USA and inclusion in 2013 Marquis Who's Who publication, USA. Name inclusion in Top 2% World Scientist Rankings 2023, 2024, 2025 by The AD Scientific Index "World Scientist and University Rankings", USA. Best Oral Presentation award in 73rd IPC, Hyderabad from 4-7 July 2024. Association of Pharmaceutical Teachers of India (APTI) Fellowship Award 2024 in 27th Annual Convention of APTICON 2024, Bhubaneswar from 27-28 September 2024. **Dr.Reddy** has 29 h-index with more than 2700 citations, published eight books, received two research grants, one patent, Editorial Board member in national and international Journals, reviewer in national and international journals. Dr.Reddy is a Resource Person for UGC, AICTE Sponsored Seminars; Expert Committee Member for Research Review Meetings and Evaluation of M.Pharm/Ph.D Thesis; Speaker/Poster Evaluator/Chairman for local, regional, national and international conferences. **Dr.Reddy** has an extensive research experience in Nanoparticles, Solid Lipid Nanoparticles, Sublingual Tablets, Fast Disintegrating Tablets, Solid Dispersions, Mouth Dissolving Tablets, Sustained Release Systems, Controlled Release Systems, Transdermal, Colon Specific and Gastro retentive drug delivery systems. He has delivered more than 80 invited talks on drug delivery systems. He is a visiting professor in Kathmandu University, Nepal. He has attended many symposiums and workshops at the national and international level. He has more than 80 research publications in several international and national journals and guided 120 M. Pharm and 8 PhD students. **Dr.Reddy** has extensively travelled to USA, Germany, Switzerland, Rome, Canada, France, Egypt, Dubai, Thailand, China, Nepal, Turkey and Portugal. He has Life memberships in Indian Pharmaceutical Association (IPA), Indian Pharmacological Society (IPS), Indian Pharmacy Graduate Association (IPGA), Association of Pharmaceutical Teachers of India (APTI), Fellow of the Institution of Chemists (India), Ex-Member in Board of Studies, Kakatiya University and Palamuru University; Ex-General Secretary in Kakatiya University Alumni Association; Ex-President for Association of Pharmaceutical Teachers of India (APTI), Telangana State; President, Telangana Registered Pharmacist Association (TRPhA); Secretary for Indian Pharmacy Graduates Association (IPGA), Telangana State and Central Council Member-Pharmacy Council of India, New Delhi.

CHAPTER 1

Pharmacy Council of India (PCI)

Introduction to the Pharmacy Council of India (PCI)

The **Pharmacy Council of India (PCI)** is an essential regulatory body within India's healthcare ecosystem. It serves as a cornerstone for the country's pharmacy education and professional standards, shaping the way pharmacy is practiced and ensuring that it aligns with national health priorities.

The Pharmacy Council of India (PCI) is a statutory body established under the **Pharmacy Act of 1948**. Its primary mandate is to regulate the **education and practice of pharmacy in India**. As a central authority, it ensures that pharmacists across the country are trained to meet the highest professional and ethical standards. This regulation not only protects public health but also upholds the integrity of the pharmacy profession.

- **Core Functions**:
    - Setting **minimum standards** for pharmacy education at various levels, including Diploma in Pharmacy (D. Pharm.), Bachelor of Pharmacy (B. Pharm.), and Doctor of Pharmacy (Pharm.D.).
    - Granting **approval** to institutions offering pharmacy courses.
    - Registering qualified pharmacists to enable them to practice legally in India.
    - Issuing a **Code of Ethics** to guide pharmacists in their professional duties.

Pharmacy, as a field, sits at the intersection of **medicine, chemistry, and biology**, requiring rigorous training and regulation to ensure its safe practice. The PCI plays a critical role in achieving this balance.

Objectives: Regulation of Pharmacy Education and Practice in India

At its core, the PCI seeks to harmonize the diverse aspects of pharmacy education and professional practice. Let's explore its objectives in detail:

1. **Regulating Pharmacy Education**: The PCI sets academic standards for pharmacy programs across the country. These standards include syllabi, practical training requirements, and faculty qualifications, ensuring that pharmacy graduates are well-prepared for their roles.
   - Example: The introduction of the **Pharm.D. program in 2008** was a significant step to align India with global standards in clinical pharmacy education.
2. **Standardizing Professional Practice**: The PCI maintains a central register of pharmacists and collaborates with state pharmacy councils to ensure compliance with the legal framework. This safeguards the public from unqualified practitioners.
3. **Ensuring Ethical Conduct**: Through its **Code of Ethics**, the PCI fosters a culture of professionalism and accountability among pharmacists.

Historical Background

Establishment Under the Pharmacy Act, 1948

The origins of the PCI are rooted in India's early attempts to standardize pharmacy practice. Prior to independence, pharmacy education and practice were largely unregulated, leading to inconsistencies in training and service delivery. Recognizing the need for a national regulatory body, the Indian government enacted the **Pharmacy Act of 1948**, which laid the foundation for the establishment of the PCI.

- **Key Provisions of the Pharmacy Act, 1948**:
  - Creation of the PCI to oversee pharmacy education and maintain professional standards.
  - Establishment of state pharmacy councils to manage the registration and licensing of pharmacists.
  - Introduction of legal requirements for individuals and institutions involved in pharmacy practice.

Key Milestones in PCI's Evolution

Over the decades, the PCI has evolved in response to the changing demands of the healthcare sector. Several milestones highlight its growth and adaptability:

1. **1953**: The first set of **Education Regulations (ER 1953)** was introduced, specifying the syllabus and practical training requirements for the Diploma in Pharmacy.
2. **1984**: Revisions to the Pharmacy Act strengthened the PCI's role in regulating pharmacy education and expanded its scope to include emerging healthcare needs.
3. **2008**: Launch of the **Pharm.D. program**, marking India's entry into advanced clinical pharmacy education. This program was designed to meet global standards and improve patient care through better-trained clinical pharmacists.

Significance in Healthcare

Role in Standardizing Pharmacy Education

One of the PCI's most critical contributions is its role in creating a standardized framework for pharmacy education. By ensuring uniformity across institutions, the PCI guarantees that all pharmacy graduates possess the knowledge and skills necessary to meet the demands of modern healthcare.

- **Key Areas of Focus**:
    - **Theoretical Knowledge**:
        - Subjects like medicinal chemistry, pharmacology, and pharmaceutics form the foundation of pharmacy education.
    - **Practical Training**:
        - Laboratory work and internships in hospitals or industries bridge the gap between theory and practice.
- **Impact**:
    - Graduates from PCI-recognized institutions are recognized for their competence both nationally and internationally.

Contribution to Professional Development and Public Health

The PCI's influence extends beyond education to professional practice and public health.

1. **Professional Development**:
    - The PCI promotes continuous learning through workshops, seminars, and training programs.
    - Example: Recent workshops on **Good Manufacturing Practices (GMP)** help pharmacists stay updated on regulatory requirements.
2. **Public Health**:
    - By ensuring the quality of pharmacy services, the PCI indirectly enhances public health outcomes.
    - Example: During the **COVID-19 pandemic**, pharmacists trained under PCI guidelines played a pivotal role in vaccine distribution and patient education.
3. **Bridging Gaps**:
    - The PCI's efforts to introduce the **Pharm.D. program** have improved the integration of pharmacists into clinical settings, enabling better patient care.

1.1 Legal Framework of the Pharmacy Council of India (PCI)

The **Pharmacy Council of India (PCI)** operates within a well-defined legal framework established by the **Pharmacy Act, 1948**, which provides the foundation for regulating pharmacy education and professional standards in India. Understanding this framework is essential to appreciate the PCI's authority, its responsibilities, and how it interacts with other regulatory bodies.

Pharmacy Act, 1948

The **Pharmacy Act of 1948** is a landmark piece of legislation that formalized the regulation of pharmacy education and practice in India. It marked a significant step in standardizing pharmaceutical services, safeguarding public health, and ensuring ethical practices in the profession.

---

1. Objectives and Provisions Relevant to PCI

The primary goal of the Pharmacy Act, 1948, was to establish a structured system for regulating the pharmacy profession. The Act introduced several provisions that remain relevant today:

1. **Objectives**:
   - To standardize pharmacy education across India by prescribing minimum educational qualifications.
   - To regulate the practice of pharmacy to ensure safe and effective drug dispensing and counseling.
   - To maintain a central register of pharmacists to ensure that only qualified individuals are allowed to practice.
2. **Provisions**:
   - **Creation of the Pharmacy Council of India (PCI)**:
     - The Act established the PCI as a central body to oversee and regulate pharmacy education and professional conduct.
   - **Establishment of State Pharmacy Councils (SPCs)**:
     - SPCs were created to register pharmacists at the state level and coordinate with PCI for enforcement of the Act.
   - **Recognition of Pharmacy Education**:
     - The Act mandates that only institutions approved by the PCI can offer pharmacy courses, ensuring uniformity and quality.
   - **Definition of "Pharmacist"**:
     - Only individuals registered under the Act are recognized as pharmacists, empowering them to practice legally.

---

2. Key Sections Related to Education, Registration, and Practice

The Act consists of several sections that outline the roles and responsibilities of the PCI and define the regulatory landscape of pharmacy in India:

1. **Section 3**:
   - Establishes the Pharmacy Council of India (PCI) as the central regulatory body.

  - Details the composition of the Council, including members from various stakeholder groups such as academia, government, and industry.

2. **Section 10**:
   - Empowers the PCI to frame **Education Regulations (ERs)**, which set the minimum standards for pharmacy education.
3. **Section 12**:
   - Recognizes qualifications awarded by institutions approved by the PCI.
   - Ensures that only PCI-accredited programs are valid for registration as a pharmacist.
4. **Section 26**:
   - Mandates the creation of a central register of pharmacists.
   - Provides guidelines for the registration and renewal of practicing pharmacists.
5. **Section 42**:
   - Prohibits individuals without proper registration from engaging in the profession of pharmacy.
   - Ensures public safety by barring unqualified individuals from dispensing drugs.

Regulatory Authority

The Pharmacy Act, 1948, empowers the PCI with regulatory authority over pharmacy education and practice. This authority extends to various aspects of the profession, ensuring adherence to high standards and ethical conduct.

---

1. Empowerment of PCI to Oversee Education and Professional Standards

The PCI's regulatory authority encompasses the following areas:

1. **Approval of Pharmacy Institutions**:
   - The PCI inspects institutions offering pharmacy programs to verify compliance with its **Education Regulations (ERs)**.
   - Institutions that fail to meet these standards may have their recognition revoked.

2. **Curriculum Design**:
    - The PCI periodically updates the curriculum to incorporate advancements in pharmaceutical sciences and address emerging healthcare challenges.
    - Example: The introduction of topics like **pharmacovigilance**, **clinical pharmacy**, and **biotechnology** reflects the evolving needs of the profession.
3. **Professional Conduct**:
    - The PCI issues a **Code of Ethics** for pharmacists, promoting accountability and professionalism.
4. **Monitoring and Enforcement**:
    - The PCI conducts audits and inspections to ensure compliance with standards and regulations.

Pharmacy Council of India (PCI):

- **Focus**: Exclusively regulates pharmacy education and practice in India.
- **Authority**:
    - Approves institutions offering pharmacy programs such as D. Pharm., B. Pharm., M. Pharm., and Pharm.D.
    - Ensures compliance with the standards set under the Pharmacy Act, 1948.
    - Monitors the curriculum, faculty qualifications, and infrastructure for pharmacy education.
- **Legal Mandate**:
    - Derived from the Pharmacy Act, 1948, which overrides AICTE's jurisdiction in pharmacy education.

1.2 Structure and Organization of the Pharmacy Council of India (PCI)

The **Pharmacy Council of India (PCI)** operates within a well-defined organizational structure that ensures its functions are carried out efficiently. Its hierarchical and functional setup is designed to facilitate decision-making, regulatory oversight, and collaboration with other stakeholders in pharmacy education and practice.

Administrative Framework

Composition of the Council

The governing body of the PCI consists of members from various professional and administrative backgrounds. This diversity ensures balanced representation and expertise in decision-making.

1. **President and Vice President**:
    - The President serves as the head of the Council, overseeing all activities and providing strategic direction.
    - The Vice President assists in administrative and regulatory functions and acts in the President's stead when necessary.
2. **Members**: The Council comprises representatives from multiple sectors:
    - **Ex-officio Members**:
        - The **Director General of Health Services (DGHS)**.
        - The **Drug Controller General of India (DCGI)**.
    - **Elected Members**:
        - Representatives elected from state pharmacy councils.
    - **Nominated Members**:
        - Individuals nominated by the Central Government for their expertise in pharmacy education and practice.
    - **Academic Representatives**:
        - Representatives from academic institutions involved in pharmacy education.

This multi-stakeholder structure ensures that decisions are well-informed and reflective of the diverse needs of the pharmacy profession.

Election and Nomination Processes

The election and nomination processes for PCI members are outlined in the **Pharmacy Act, 1948**, ensuring transparency and inclusivity:

1. **Elections**:
    - State pharmacy councils elect their representatives to the PCI. These members bring state-specific insights and priorities to the national body.

2. **Nominations**:
    - The Central Government nominates members with expertise in pharmacy education, practice, or related fields. This ensures the inclusion of eminent professionals who can contribute valuable perspectives.
3. **Term Duration**:
    - Members typically serve for a term of **five years**, after which new elections or nominations are conducted.

Committees and Subcommittees

To streamline its activities, the PCI has established specialized committees and subcommittees that focus on specific aspects of its mandate.

1. Education Regulations Committee:

- This committee is responsible for drafting, reviewing, and updating the **Education Regulations (ERs)**, which set the minimum standards for pharmacy education.
- Tasks include:
    - Designing curricula for D. Pharm., B. Pharm., M. Pharm., and Pharm.D programs.
    - Introducing new topics to keep pace with advancements in pharmaceutical sciences, such as **clinical pharmacy** and **pharmacovigilance**.

2. Ethics Committee:

- This committee ensures the promotion of ethical conduct among pharmacy professionals.
- Responsibilities:
    - Drafting and enforcing the **Code of Ethics for Pharmacists**.
    - Addressing cases of professional misconduct reported by state pharmacy councils or other stakeholders.

3. Examination and Accreditation Committee:

- This committee oversees the accreditation of institutions offering pharmacy programs.
- Core functions include:
    - Conducting inspections to assess compliance with PCI standards.

- Evaluating examination systems to ensure uniformity and fairness.
- Accrediting institutions that meet the prescribed criteria.

By delegating these tasks to specialized committees, the PCI ensures focused attention and expertise in each area of its operations.

1.3 Pharmacy Education and Curriculum Standards

Pharmacy education is the cornerstone of professional practice in the pharmaceutical sciences. The **Pharmacy Council of India (PCI)**, as the regulatory body, ensures that the standards of pharmacy education in India align with the evolving demands of healthcare and pharmaceutical industries. This section delves into the **minimum standards of education**, **examinations and assessments**, and the promotion of **research and development** within pharmacy education.

Minimum Standards of Education

The PCI prescribes stringent educational standards to ensure that pharmacy graduates possess the necessary theoretical knowledge and practical skills to contribute effectively to healthcare and pharmaceutical industries.

Detailed Syllabus for D. Pharm., B. Pharm., and Pharm.D Courses

1. **Diploma in Pharmacy (D. Pharm.)**:
    - A **two-year program** designed as an entry-level qualification for pharmacists.
    - **Syllabus Highlights**:
        - **Pharmaceutics**: Basics of drug formulation and preparation.
        - **Pharmacology**: Understanding drug action and uses.
        - **Hospital and Clinical Pharmacy**: Practical aspects of dispensing and patient counseling.
    - **Objective**: Equip students with skills for community pharmacy and hospital settings.
2. **Bachelor of Pharmacy (B. Pharm.)**:
    - A **four-year undergraduate program** focusing on the scientific foundations of pharmacy.

- **Syllabus Highlights**:
    - **Medicinal Chemistry**: Design and synthesis of pharmaceuticals.
    - **Pharmacognosy**: Study of drugs derived from natural sources.
    - **Pharmaceutics and Pharmacology**: Advanced understanding of dosage forms and drug interactions.
    - **Biopharmaceutics**: Drug absorption, distribution, metabolism, and elimination (ADME).
- **Objective**: Prepare students for careers in research, production, marketing, and regulatory affairs.

3. **Doctor of Pharmacy (Pharm.D)**:
    - A **six-year program** emphasizing clinical pharmacy and patient care.
    - **Syllabus Highlights**:
        - **Clinical Pharmacy and Therapeutics**: Management of diseases through pharmacotherapy.
        - **Pharmacovigilance**: Monitoring adverse drug reactions (ADRs).
        - **Internship**: Mandatory one-year internship in hospital settings.
    - **Objective**: Develop clinical pharmacists capable of optimizing patient outcomes.

Focus on Theoretical Knowledge and Practical Skills

- The curriculum balances **classroom instruction** with **practical training**, ensuring students gain:
    - In-depth understanding of drug design, production, and regulation.
    - Hands-on experience in laboratories, hospitals, and community pharmacies.
- **Real-World Example**: Students in Pharm.D programs often assist in **therapeutic drug monitoring (TDM)** during their hospital rotations, bridging the gap between academics and clinical practice.

Examinations and Assessments

To maintain uniformity and high standards in pharmacy education, the PCI has established clear guidelines for evaluating student performance.

Guidelines for Internal and External Evaluations

1. **Internal Assessments**:
    - Conducted periodically by the institution to gauge students' progress.
    - Include **written tests, practical examinations, and project submissions**.
    - Encourage continuous learning and regular engagement with course material.
2. **External Assessments**:
    - Final examinations are conducted under PCI guidelines to ensure uniform evaluation.
    - Consist of:
        - **Theory Exams**: Assessing conceptual knowledge.
        - **Practical Exams**: Evaluating laboratory skills and problem-solving abilities.
    - External examiners are appointed by the PCI to uphold impartiality and objectivity.

PCI's Role in Ensuring Uniformity in Examinations

- The PCI provides standardized question banks and evaluation criteria to ensure consistency across institutions.
- **Audit Mechanisms**:
    - Periodic inspections to verify the examination process.
    - Feedback loops to identify and rectify discrepancies in assessment methods.

Outcome-Based Assessments

- Focus on **skill acquisition and application** rather than rote memorization.
- Example: Evaluating a student's ability to recommend appropriate therapy in simulated patient scenarios.

Research and Development

Recognizing the importance of innovation, the PCI promotes a **research-oriented approach** in pharmacy education.

Promotion of Research-Oriented Education

1. **Incorporation into Curricula**:
    - Research methodologies and biostatistics are integral components of B. Pharm. and M. Pharm. programs.
    - Final-year projects require students to undertake original research, fostering critical thinking.
2. **Encouragement of Student Research**:
    - Students are encouraged to publish research findings in reputed journals.
    - Example: Research on novel drug delivery systems (NDDS) by pharmacy students has led to significant advancements in controlled drug release technologies.

Collaborations with Research Institutions

1. **Partnerships with Academic and Industrial Organizations**:
    - PCI facilitates collaborations between pharmacy colleges and research organizations like the **Indian Council of Medical Research (ICMR)** and **Council of Scientific and Industrial Research (CSIR)**.
    - These partnerships provide students with exposure to cutting-edge research.
2. **Funding for Research Initiatives**:
    - PCI advocates for funding from government bodies like the **Department of Science and Technology (DST)** to support institutional research projects.
3. **Focus Areas**:
    - Drug discovery and development.
    - Pharmacovigilance and adverse drug reaction monitoring.
    - Biotechnology and biosimilar development.

Impact of Research Orientation

- Enhances the employability of pharmacy graduates by equipping them with practical research skills.

- Contributes to the growth of the pharmaceutical industry through the development of **cost-effective therapies** and **innovative drug delivery systems**.

1.4 PCI's Role in Global Pharmacy Standards

In an increasingly interconnected world, the Pharmacy Council of India (PCI) has a critical role in aligning Indian pharmacy education and practice with global standards. Through collaboration and harmonization, the PCI aims to elevate the global recognition of Indian pharmacy professionals.

Harmonization with International Bodies

Collaboration with FIP (International Pharmaceutical Federation) and WHO

The PCI works closely with global organizations to align its standards with international benchmarks:

1. **FIP (International Pharmaceutical Federation)**:
    - The PCI collaborates with FIP to adopt best practices in pharmacy education and practice.
    - Areas of focus include promoting clinical pharmacy and integrating technology into pharmacy education.
2. **World Health Organization (WHO)**:
    - PCI's partnership with WHO emphasizes pharmacovigilance, ensuring the safe use of medicines.
    - Example: Training programs for healthcare professionals on adverse drug reaction (ADR) reporting.

Adoption of Global Best Practices in Education and Practice

The PCI regularly updates its curriculum to reflect global advancements:

1. **Inclusion of Advanced Topics**:
    - Subjects like pharmacovigilance, biotechnology, and regulatory affairs are integrated to prepare students for global challenges.
2. **Outcome-Based Education**:
    - Emphasis on competency-based learning ensures graduates are industry-ready.

Facilitating Mobility

PCI's Efforts to Align with Global Pharmacy Curricula

The PCI has taken significant steps to harmonize Indian pharmacy programs with international standards:

1. **Curriculum Updates**:
    - Aligning the Pharm.D curriculum with global models, particularly the US and EU.
2. **Licensing Support**:
    - Workshops and preparatory courses for international licensing exams (e.g., FPGEE, PEBC).

Recognition of Indian Pharmacists

Efforts to Enhance the Credibility of Indian Pharmacy Professionals Abroad

The PCI has initiated efforts to promote Indian pharmacists as skilled professionals:

1. **Global Advocacy**:
    - Highlighting India's contribution to global healthcare, particularly in pharmaceutical manufacturing and supply chains.
2. **Accreditation and Exchange Programs**:

   Collaborations with international universities to offer dual-degree programs and research opportunities.

CHAPTER 2

The Drugs, Cosmetics and Medical Devices Act

The **Drugs, Cosmetics, and Medical Devices Act** represents a cornerstone of India's regulatory framework, governing the manufacturing, distribution, sale, and quality of drugs, cosmetics, and medical devices. This legislation serves as a critical instrument in ensuring the safety, efficacy, and quality of products consumed or utilized by millions of people, directly impacting public health and safety.

Overview of the Act

The **Drugs and Cosmetics Act, 1940**, initially enacted as the **Drugs Act, 1940**, has undergone significant transformations to accommodate evolving healthcare and industry needs. It is now widely recognized as one of the most comprehensive regulatory frameworks in India.

Purpose and Scope of the Legislation

The primary objectives of the Act include:

1. **Ensuring Product Quality**:
    - Safeguard the public by ensuring drugs, cosmetics, and medical devices meet established safety and efficacy standards.
2. **Preventing Malpractices**:
    - Prohibit the sale of spurious, adulterated, or misbranded products.
3. **Promoting Accountability**:
    - Regulate the processes of manufacturing, labeling, and marketing to ensure transparency and adherence to ethical practices.

Importance in Regulating Drugs, Cosmetics, and Medical Devices in India

1. **Drugs**:
   - Covers both allopathic and traditional medicines like **Ayurveda, Siddha, and Unani** under specific provisions.
   - Sets guidelines for testing, clinical trials, and production.
2. **Cosmetics**:
   - Ensures products used for personal care and beautification are safe and free from harmful substances.
3. **Medical Devices**:
   - Incorporates a structured approach to regulate a wide array of devices, from diagnostic tools to surgical equipment, following global norms.

This broad scope underscores the Act's pivotal role in protecting consumer health and ensuring industry accountability.

Historical Context

Pre-Independence Drug Regulations

Before the enactment of this legislation, drug regulation in India was virtually non-existent. Key challenges included:

1. **Import of Substandard Drugs**:
   - India was flooded with subpar and often dangerous medicines imported from other countries.
2. **Lack of Domestic Oversight**:
   - No framework existed to regulate the manufacturing, sale, or distribution of pharmaceutical products.

The dire need for a structured regulatory system gained prominence after the publication of the **Health Survey and Development Committee Report (1921)**, which highlighted the public health risks associated with unregulated drugs.

Enactment of the Drugs and Cosmetics Act, 1940

The initial version of the Act, called the **Drugs Act, 1940**, was passed to address these pressing issues. Key features included:

1. **Regulation of Drug Quality**:
   - Set standards for drug manufacturing and sale.

2. **Licensing System**:
    - Introduced mandatory licensing for manufacturers, distributors, and sellers.
3. **Establishment of Testing Laboratories**:
    - Emphasized the need for drug testing to ensure quality.

In 1960, the Act was renamed the **Drugs and Cosmetics Act**, reflecting its expanded focus on cosmetic products.

Amendments and Evolution Over the Years to Include Medical Devices

1. **Early Amendments**:
    - Various amendments were introduced to strengthen regulatory oversight, such as the addition of provisions for Ayurveda and Unani medicines.
2. **Major Revisions in 1982 and Beyond**:
    - Expanded the scope to include **medical devices** under drug regulations, a step driven by the increasing use of technology in healthcare.
3. **2020 Medical Devices Rules**:
    - Introduced a detailed regulatory framework specifically for medical devices, classifying them based on risk (Classes A to D) and ensuring adherence to global standards like ISO certifications.

These changes demonstrate the Act's adaptability to address emerging challenges in healthcare and technology.

Significance

The Act is crucial in creating a robust framework that protects public health while supporting industry growth.

Role in Safeguarding Public Health

1. **Ensuring Consumer Safety**:
    - Prevents the circulation of unsafe or ineffective products through stringent quality checks.
2. **Regulating Clinical Trials**:
    - Mandates ethical practices in clinical research to minimize risks to trial participants.

3. **Monitoring Post-Market Safety**:
   - Establishes mechanisms for adverse event reporting and product recalls.

Aligning Indian Standards with Global Regulatory Frameworks

1. **Harmonization with International Norms**:
   - Aligns Indian regulations with global benchmarks, such as those set by the **World Health Organization (WHO)** and **International Council for Harmonisation (ICH)**.
2. **Promoting Exports**:
   - Enhances the credibility of Indian pharmaceuticals and medical devices in global markets, aiding the country's reputation as the "**Pharmacy of the World**."

2.1 Objectives of the Drugs, Cosmetics, and Medical Devices Act

The **Drugs, Cosmetics, and Medical Devices Act** is a pivotal legislation designed to safeguard public health by regulating the manufacturing, sale, distribution, and quality of drugs, cosmetics, and medical devices. The objectives of the Act are comprehensive and address both consumer protection and industry regulation. Let's explore these objectives in detail.

Ensuring the Quality, Safety, and Efficacy of Drugs, Cosmetics, and Medical Devices

One of the Act's foremost goals is to establish stringent standards for products that directly impact public health.

1. **Quality Assurance**:
   - The Act prescribes clear benchmarks for the manufacturing process, materials used, and final product evaluation.
   - For example:
     - Drugs must meet **pharmacopeial standards** (as outlined in the Indian Pharmacopoeia) regarding identity, purity, and strength.
     - Medical devices are required to adhere to **ISO and other global standards** for functionality and safety.

2. **Safety Measures**:
   - By mandating pre-market testing and post-market surveillance, the Act minimizes risks associated with unsafe products.
   - Cosmetics are evaluated for the absence of harmful substances, ensuring their safety for human use.
3. **Efficacy Standards**:
   - Drugs and medical devices must demonstrate therapeutic efficacy through rigorous clinical trials or equivalent evidence.
   - Example: Antiviral drugs developed during pandemics undergo expedited yet stringent efficacy testing under the Act's provisions.

Preventing the Sale of Substandard, Spurious, and Misbranded Products

The Act actively combats malpractices in the manufacturing and distribution of drugs, cosmetics, and medical devices to protect consumers from harm.

1. **Substandard Products**:
   - These are products that fail to meet prescribed quality standards, potentially leading to ineffective or harmful treatments.
   - Example: A drug that contains less active ingredient than labeled would fall under this category.
2. **Spurious Products**:
   - Fake or counterfeit products that imitate branded items but lack the proper formulation or efficacy.
   - The Act imposes severe penalties, including imprisonment, to deter the production and sale of counterfeit drugs.
3. **Misbranded Products**:
   - Items that are falsely labeled or fail to meet labeling requirements.
   - For example:
     - Incorrect claims about a drug's benefits.
     - Absence of critical information such as usage instructions or side effects.

By addressing these issues, the Act protects consumers from unsafe products and ensures trust in the healthcare system.

Regulating Clinical Trials and Manufacturing Practices

Clinical Trials

The Act provides a framework for conducting clinical trials, emphasizing participant safety and ethical practices.

1. **Approval Process**:
   - Clinical trials require prior approval from the **Central Drugs Standard Control Organization (CDSCO)**.
   - Ethical oversight is ensured through Institutional Ethics Committees (IECs).
2. **Safety Monitoring**:
   - Adverse events during trials must be reported to regulatory authorities, and corrective actions are mandated when necessary.
3. **Ethical Considerations**:
   - Informed consent from participants is a non-negotiable requirement.
   - Trials must comply with **Good Clinical Practice (GCP)** guidelines.

Manufacturing Practices

1. **Good Manufacturing Practices (GMP)**:
   - The Act mandates adherence to GMP guidelines to ensure uniformity, quality, and safety in production processes.
   - These guidelines cover:
     - Facility standards.
     - Staff training and hygiene.
     - Documentation and record-keeping.
2. **Inspection and Monitoring**:
   - Regular inspections by drug inspectors ensure compliance with GMP.
   - Violations may result in suspension or revocation of manufacturing licenses.

Establishing a Framework for Inspections, Enforcement, and Penalties

The Act outlines mechanisms for enforcing its provisions through systematic inspections, legal actions, and penalties.

1. **Inspections**:
   - Authorized officers, such as drug inspectors, conduct surprise inspections of manufacturing facilities, retail outlets, and distribution centers.
   - Inspectors are empowered to:
     - Seize substandard or spurious products.
     - Collect samples for testing.
2. **Enforcement**:
   - Offenders are prosecuted under the relevant sections of the Act.
   - Examples of enforcement include raids on counterfeit drug manufacturing units and legal actions against violators.
3. **Penalties**:
   - The Act imposes strict penalties to deter non-compliance:
     - **Monetary Fines**: For minor infractions such as labeling errors.
     - **Imprisonment**: For severe offenses like the production of spurious drugs.
   - These penalties reinforce accountability across the supply chain.

2.2 Key Provisions of the Drugs, Cosmetics, and Medical Devices Act

The **Drugs, Cosmetics, and Medical Devices Act** establishes a comprehensive regulatory framework that ensures the quality, safety, and efficacy of products impacting public health. Its key provisions are designed to address critical aspects such as definitions and classifications, licensing, manufacturing standards, and the import-export framework. These provisions form the foundation for effective regulation and compliance.

Definition and Classification

Definitions of "Drug," "Cosmetic," and "Medical Device"

To provide clarity and ensure accurate regulation, the Act defines key terms:

1. **Drug**:
   - Includes allopathic medicines, substances used for diagnosis, treatment, or prevention of diseases, and items intended to affect bodily functions (e.g., vaccines, diagnostic agents).
   - Extends to Ayurvedic, Siddha, and Unani medicines under specific provisions.
2. **Cosmetic**:
   - Products intended for external application for beautification, cleansing, or improving appearance.
   - Examples: Soaps, shampoos, creams, and makeup products.
3. **Medical Device**:
   - Equipment, instruments, implants, or software used for diagnosis, prevention, or treatment.
   - Examples: Stents, pacemakers, diagnostic kits, and surgical tools.
   - Expanded to include digital health technologies under the **Medical Devices Rules, 2020**.

Categories and Schedules Under the Act

1. **Categorization of Products**:
   - Drugs, cosmetics, and medical devices are grouped into categories for efficient regulation.
   - Risk-based classification for medical devices:
     - **Class A (low risk)**: Surgical gloves.
     - **Class B (moderate risk)**: Blood pressure monitors.
     - **Class C & D (high risk)**: Implants and pacemakers.
2. **Schedules**:
   - The Act introduces **Schedules** to specify rules for manufacturing, labeling, storage, and distribution.
   - **Key Schedules**:
     - **Schedule M**: Good Manufacturing Practices (GMP) for drugs.

- **Schedule Y**: Clinical trial regulations.
- **Schedule S**: Standards for cosmetics.

Licensing

Licensing provisions under the Act ensure that only authorized entities engage in the manufacturing, distribution, and sale of regulated products.

Licensing Requirements for Manufacturers, Importers, and Sellers

1. **Manufacturing License**:
   - Mandatory for drug, cosmetic, or medical device production.
   - Includes site inspections to verify compliance with GMP.
2. **Importer's License**:
   - Required for importing products into India.
   - Must demonstrate adherence to Indian standards or equivalent global benchmarks.
3. **Retail and Wholesale License**:
   - Ensures that sellers meet storage and distribution requirements.
   - Retailers must employ qualified pharmacists to handle drug dispensing.

Types of Licenses and Their Renewal Processes

1. **Provisional vs. Full Licenses**:
   - **Provisional Licenses**: Issued temporarily for product launch, pending full compliance.
   - **Full Licenses**: Granted after thorough inspection and documentation review.
2. **Renewal**:
   - Licenses require periodic renewal to confirm continued adherence to standards.
   - Failure to renew results in suspension of operations.

Manufacturing Standards

Good Manufacturing Practices (GMP) for Drugs and Cosmetics

1. **Compliance Requirements**:
    - Defined under **Schedule M** for drugs and **Schedule S** for cosmetics.
    - Include specifications for:
        - Facility design.
        - Equipment maintenance.
        - Documentation and quality control procedures.
2. **Objectives of GMP**:
    - Prevent contamination during manufacturing.
    - Ensure uniformity across batches.
    - Maintain detailed records for traceability.

Quality Standards for Medical Devices

1. **Regulatory Framework**:
    - Governed under the **Medical Devices Rules, 2020**.
    - Emphasis on risk management and compliance with **ISO standards**.
2. **Post-Market Surveillance**:
    - Monitoring devices in use to identify and mitigate risks.
    - Manufacturers are required to report adverse events and product recalls.

Import and Export

Regulatory Provisions for Importing and Exporting Drugs, Cosmetics, and Medical Devices

1. **Import Requirements**:
    - Import licenses are granted by the **Central Drugs Standard Control Organization (CDSCO)**.
    - Importers must ensure products meet Indian regulatory standards.

2. **Export Requirements**:
    - Drugs and medical devices intended for export must comply with the regulatory standards of the importing country.
    - Exporters often rely on certifications such as **WHO-GMP** to gain market access.

Role of the Act in Promoting Global Trade Compliance

1. **Facilitating Exports**:
    - By aligning Indian standards with global benchmarks, the Act strengthens the credibility of Indian pharmaceutical and medical device exports.
    - India's adherence to international frameworks, such as **ICH guidelines**, boosts its status as a global supplier.
2. **Supporting Domestic Manufacturers**:
    - Provides incentives for quality manufacturing, fostering competitiveness in international markets.

2.3 Amendments and Updates

The **Drugs, Cosmetics, and Medical Devices Act** has undergone significant amendments over the years to address emerging challenges, adapt to technological advancements, and align with international standards. These amendments have modernized the regulatory framework and reinforced its ability to ensure the safety, efficacy, and quality of drugs, cosmetics, and medical devices in India.

Major Amendments

Drugs and Cosmetics (Amendment) Act, 1964

1. **Background**:
    - Triggered by the global tragedy of **thalidomide** and its teratogenic effects, this amendment was introduced to ensure stricter control over drug safety.
2. **Key Changes**:
    - **Introduction of Clinical Trial Oversight**:
        - Mandated clinical trials to establish drug safety and efficacy before marketing.

- **Penalties for Spurious Drugs**:
  - Enhanced penalties for manufacturing or selling substandard and spurious drugs.
- **Creation of Schedules**:
  - Added detailed guidelines for drug quality standards, labeling, and storage.

3. **Impact**:
   - Strengthened consumer protection and instilled greater accountability among manufacturers.

Inclusion of Medical Devices Under the 2020 Rules

1. **Background**:
   - Previously, medical devices were loosely regulated as "drugs." Recognizing the growing complexity and significance of medical technology, specific rules were introduced in **2020** to regulate medical devices.
2. **Key Provisions**:
   - **Classification Based on Risk**:
     - Devices were categorized into **Class A (low risk)** to **Class D (high risk)** for focused regulation.
   - **Mandatory Registration**:
     - All medical devices were required to be registered with the **Central Drugs Standard Control Organization (CDSCO)**.
   - **Adoption of ISO Standards**:
     - Established quality benchmarks aligned with international standards.
   - **Post-Market Surveillance**:
     - Emphasis on monitoring adverse events and ensuring timely recalls if needed.
3. **Impact**:
   - Improved safety and performance of medical devices.
   - Boosted the credibility of Indian medical device manufacturers in global markets.

Impact of Amendments

Strengthening of Regulatory Frameworks

1. **Increased Stringency**:
   - Amendments like the 1964 Act introduced strict penalties and oversight mechanisms, enhancing the deterrent against malpractices.
2. **Broader Scope**:
   - Expanded coverage to include a wider range of products, such as **traditional medicines** and **medical devices**.
3. **Improved Accountability**:
   - Established detailed guidelines for clinical trials, licensing, and manufacturing standards.

Modernization of the Act to Include Emerging Technologies and Products

1. **Inclusion of Advanced Healthcare Products**:
   - Regulation of biologics, biosimilars, and advanced therapies, such as **cell and gene therapy**.
2. **Streamlining Processes**:
   - Introduction of digital platforms for licensing and monitoring, reducing paperwork and delays.

Need for Further Updates

Despite its advancements, the Act requires further modernization to address emerging challenges in the healthcare and pharmaceutical sectors.

Regulatory Gaps in Digital Health Products

1. **Challenges**:
   - The rise of **telemedicine** and **wearable health devices** lacks a specific regulatory framework.
   - Data privacy and cybersecurity concerns related to health apps and digital platforms.
2. **Proposed Solutions**:
   - Integration of digital health products under the regulatory ambit.

- Collaboration with the **Ministry of Electronics and Information Technology (MeitY)** to address data security.

AI-Driven Medical Devices

1. **Challenges**:
   - Absence of guidelines for AI algorithms used in diagnostics and decision-making tools.
   - Difficulty in ensuring the transparency and accountability of machine learning models.
2. **Proposed Solutions**:
   - Development of specific regulations for **AI-driven devices** to ensure explainability and fairness.
   - Introduction of standards for validating AI algorithms.

2.4 Drugs

Drugs, as defined under the **Drugs, Cosmetics, and Medical Devices Act**, encompass a broad range of pharmaceutical products intended for human and veterinary use. These products are subject to stringent regulations to ensure their safety, efficacy, and quality. The Act sets clear standards for the production, distribution, and monitoring of drugs to safeguard public health.

Definition and Scope

Overview of Pharmaceutical Products Covered Under the Act

1. **Definition**:
   - **A drug is defined as any substance or combination of substances intended for use in:**
     - Diagnosis, treatment, mitigation, or prevention of disease.
     - Altering physiological functions in humans or animals.
   - **This definition extends to:**
     - **Allopathic medicines**.
     - **Ayurvedic, Siddha, and Unani medicines**.
     - **Diagnostic agents**, such as contrast media.
     - **Vaccines and biologics**, including biosimilars.

2. **Scope**:
    - **The Act applies to:**
        - Prescription drugs (Schedule H and X).
        - Over-the-counter (OTC) medicines.
        - Biologicals and advanced therapies like cell and gene treatments.
        - Traditional medicines, with separate provisions for their quality control.

Quality Standards

Testing Parameters and Analytical Techniques for Ensuring Efficacy and Safety

1. **Standards Set by the Indian Pharmacopoeia (IP)**:
    - Drugs must conform to the standards of identity, purity, and strength specified in the **Indian Pharmacopoeia (IP)**.
    - Testing covers:
        - **Potency**: Ensurestheactiveingredient's effectiveness.
        - **Purity**: Detects impurities or contaminants.
        - **Dissolution and disintegration**: Verifies the drug's release mechanism.
2. **Analytical Techniques**:
    - **High-Performance Liquid Chromatography (HPLC)** for potency testing.
    - **Gas Chromatography (GC)** for impurity profiling.
    - **Spectrophotometry** for UV-visible and infrared analysis.
    - **Microbiological Testing** for sterile products like injectables.
3. **Batch Testing**:
    - Every batch of drugs must undergo rigorous quality control to ensure consistency and reliability.

Labeling Requirements

Mandatory Details

The Act prescribes specific labeling requirements to ensure consumer safety and informed usage:

1. **Key Information**:
   - Name of the drug (brand and generic).
   - Composition and strength of the active ingredient.
   - Batch number, manufacturing date, and expiration date.
   - Directions for use and dosage instructions.
   - Storage conditions (e.g., "Store in a cool, dry place").
2. **Special Warnings**:
   - Schedule H drugs: "To be sold by retail on the prescription of a Registered Medical Practitioner only."
   - Schedule X drugs: Additional requirements for controlled substances.
3. **Tamper-Proof Packaging**:
   - Ensures product integrity and minimizes the risk of counterfeit drugs.

Prohibited Practices

Penalties for Manufacturing or Selling Spurious, Adulterated, or Unapproved Drugs

1. **Spurious Drugs**:
   - Defined as drugs that are falsely labeled or manufactured without authorization.
   - Penalties include:
     - Up to **life imprisonment**.
     - Fines up to **₹10 lakh or three times the drug's market value**.
2. **Adulterated Drugs**:
   - Drugs contaminated with harmful substances or degraded over time.
   - Example: Antibiotics with reduced potency.
   - Strict penalties are imposed to deter such practices.

3. **Unapproved Drugs**:
   - Any drug sold or marketed without prior approval from the **Central Drugs Standard Control Organization (CDSCO)**.
   - Includes experimental drugs not cleared for public use.

Clinical Trials

Guidelines for Conducting Clinical Trials in India

1. **Approval Process**:
   - Clinical trials require approval from the **Central Drugs Standard Control Organization (CDSCO)**.
   - The sponsor must submit a detailed protocol outlining:
     - Objectives.
     - Methodology.
     - Risk assessment.
     - Expected outcomes.
2. **Good Clinical Practices (GCP)**:
   - Trials must adhere to **GCP guidelines**, ensuring that the rights and safety of participants are protected.
3. **Phases of Clinical Trials**:
   - **Phase I**: Testing safety in a small group of healthy volunteers.
   - **Phase II**: Assessing efficacy and dose optimization in patients.
   - **Phase III**: Large-scale testing for therapeutic benefits and side effects.
   - **Phase IV**: Post-marketing surveillance to monitor long-term effects.

Ethical Considerations and Informed Consent

1. **Ethical Oversight**:
   - Institutional Ethics Committees (IECs) ensure trials are ethically conducted.
   - Regular audits and inspections are mandated.

2. **Informed Consent**:
   - Participants must be informed about:
     - The trial's purpose and procedures.
     - Potential risks and benefits.
     - Their right to withdraw at any time.
   - Consent must be documented and signed.
3. **Compensation**:
   - Participants injured during trials are entitled to compensation under the Act.

2.5 Cosmetics

The regulation of cosmetics under the **Drugs, Cosmetics, and Medical Devices Act** ensures that products used for personal care and beautification are safe, effective, and free from harmful substances. With the increasing demand for cosmetics, it is crucial to regulate their production, labeling, and usage to protect consumers.

Definition and Scope

Products Covered Under the Cosmetics Category

1. **Definition of Cosmetics**:
   - According to the Act, a cosmetic is any article intended for:
     - Cleansing, beautifying, promoting attractiveness, or altering appearance.
     - This includes lotions, creams, powders, perfumes, shampoos, and makeup products.
2. **Scope**:
   - Covers a wide range of products, including:
     - **Skincare**: Moisturizers, sunscreens, and anti-aging creams.
     - **Haircare**: Shampoos, conditioners, and hair dyes.
     - **Oral care**: Toothpaste and mouthwashes.
     - **Fragrances**: Perfumes, deodorants, and body sprays.

3. **Traditional Cosmetics**:
    - Ayurvedic and herbal cosmetics, widely used in India, are also regulated under specific provisions of the Act.

Quality Control

Safety Testing for Ingredients and Formulations

1. **Pre-Market Safety Assessments**:
    - Manufacturers must test ingredients and formulations for:
        - **Dermal toxicity**: Ensuring no irritation or allergic reactions occur.
        - **Eye irritation**: Particularly for products like kajal or eyeliners.
        - **Long-term safety**: Testing for carcinogenic or endocrine-disrupting properties.
2. **Use of Global Standards**:
    - India aligns with **ISO standards** for cosmetic safety assessments, ensuring compatibility with international markets.
3. **Stability Testing**:
    - Products must undergo stability testing to ensure safety and effectiveness over their shelf life under various conditions.
4. **Role of CDSCO**:
    - The **Central Drugs Standard Control Organization (CDSCO)** oversees the quality control of cosmetics and ensures compliance with regulations.

Labeling and Packaging

Requirements for Packaging, Warnings, and Usage Directions

1. **Mandatory Labeling Information**:
    - Name and address of the manufacturer.
    - Batch number, manufacturing date, and expiration date.
    - List of ingredients, particularly active components and allergens.
    - Instructions for use and storage conditions.

2. **Special Warnings**:
   - Specific warnings for certain products:
     - Hair dyes must carry the warning: "Caution: This product contains ingredients that may cause skin irritation."
     - Sunscreens must indicate **SPF levels** and whether they are water-resistant.
3. **Tamper-Proof Packaging**:
   - Required for products like lipsticks and eyeliners to ensure product integrity.
4. **Recyclable and Sustainable Packaging**:
   - Encouraged to align with environmental norms and consumer preferences.

Prohibited Substances

Banned and Restricted Substances in Cosmetic Products

1. **Banned Substances**:
   - The Act specifies a list of substances prohibited in cosmetics to prevent harm. Examples include:
     - **Lead and mercury compounds** in skin-lightening creams.
     - **Chloroform** in skincare products.
     - **Vinyl chloride** in aerosol sprays.
2. **Restricted Substances**:
   - Some ingredients are allowed but with restrictions on concentration or usage. Examples:
     - **Hydroquinone** in skin-lightening products, limited to 2%.
     - **Formaldehyde** in hair-straightening treatments.
3. **Continuous Monitoring**:
   - The list of banned and restricted substances is updated regularly based on new scientific evidence and global trends.

Adverse Reaction Reporting

Role of CDSCO in Monitoring Adverse Effects from Cosmetic Products

1. **Cosmetic Vigilance**:
   - The CDSCO monitors adverse reactions associated with cosmetics through a robust reporting system.
   - Consumers, healthcare professionals, and manufacturers can report adverse effects via designated portals.
2. **Investigation and Recall**:
   - Reported cases are investigated to identify the cause, whether due to contamination, formulation errors, or misuse.
   - Products found to be unsafe are recalled from the market, with manufacturers facing penalties.
3. **Public Awareness Campaigns**:
   - Educating consumers about the safe use of cosmetics, potential side effects, and how to identify counterfeit products.

2.6 Medical Devices

Medical devices are an integral part of healthcare delivery, ranging from simple tools like thermometers to advanced technologies like pacemakers and imaging systems. Recognizing their critical role, the **Drugs, Cosmetics, and Medical Devices Act** has incorporated provisions for their regulation, with significant updates introduced through the **2020 Medical Devices Rules**. This ensures safety, efficacy, and quality while fostering innovation and global competitiveness.

Inclusion Under the Act

Overview of the 2020 Medical Devices Rules

1. **Historical Context**:
   - Initially, medical devices were loosely regulated as "drugs" under the Act. However, their complexity necessitated distinct regulatory provisions.
   - The **Medical Devices Rules, 2020**, established a comprehensive framework for regulation.

2. **Key Features of the Rules**:
   - **Comprehensive Coverage**:
     - Applies to all medical devices used for diagnosis, prevention, monitoring, and treatment.
   - **Device-Specific Oversight**:
     - Focuses on device performance, safety, and risk mitigation.
   - **Alignment with International Norms**:
     - Adopts global standards to ensure competitiveness in international markets.
3. **Central Regulatory Authority**:
   - The **Central Drugs Standard Control Organization (CDSCO)** acts as the primary regulator, with oversight delegated to **Notified Bodies** for certain categories.

Classification of Medical Devices

Risk-Based Categorization: Class A, B, C, and D

1. **Purpose of Categorization**:
   - Risk-based classification ensures proportional regulation, with higher-risk devices subjected to stricter scrutiny.
2. **Categories**:
   - **Class A (Low Risk)**:
     - Examples: Surgical gloves, bandages, thermometers.
   - **Class B (Moderate Risk)**:
     - Examples: Blood pressure monitors, infusion pumps.
   - **Class C (High Risk)**:
     - Examples: Dialysis machines, ventilators.
   - **Class D (Very High Risk)**:
     - Examples: Pacemakers, implantable defibrillators, and heart valves.
3. **Impact of Classification**:
   - Determines the level of pre-market testing, certification, and post-market surveillance required for each device.

Quality Standards

ISO and Other International Standards for Device Safety and Performance

1. **ISO Standards**:
   - **ISO 13485**: Specifies requirements for quality management systems in medical device manufacturing.
   - **ISO 14971**: Focuses on risk management for medical devices.
2. **Safety and Performance Testing**:
   - Devices must meet stringent performance benchmarks, including:
     - **Electrical safety** for powered devices.
     - **Biocompatibility testing** for implants.
3. **Harmonization with Global Practices**:
   - Indian regulations align with standards from organizations like the **USFDA** and **European Medicines Agency (EMA)** to facilitate global trade.

Licensing and Registration

Processes for Domestic Manufacturing and Imports

1. **Domestic Manufacturing**:
   - Manufacturers must obtain a license from the **CDSCO** for devices in Classes B, C, and D.
   - Class A devices require simple registration with minimal oversight.
2. **Import Licensing**:
   - Importers must register devices with the CDSCO and demonstrate compliance with Indian standards.
   - Certifications such as **CE marking** or **USFDA approval** may expedite the process.
3. **Regulatory Approvals**:
   - Licenses are granted only after site inspections and verification of compliance with **Good Manufacturing Practices (GMP)**.

4. **Renewal and Maintenance**:
   - Licenses require periodic renewal, with non-compliance leading to penalties or revocation.

Post-Market Surveillance

Monitoring Adverse Events and Recalls

1. **Adverse Event Reporting**:
   - Manufacturers, distributors, and healthcare providers must report adverse events to the **Materiovigilance Programme of India (MvPI)**.
   - Examples of adverse events:
     - Device malfunction during surgery.
     - Unexpected side effects from implants.
2. **Risk Mitigation**:
   - Reported issues trigger investigations by the CDSCO, which may lead to corrective actions, including product redesign or labeling updates.
3. **Recalls**:
   - Unsafe devices are recalled to prevent further harm. For instance:
     - Faulty heart valves may lead to a nationwide recall.
   - The CDSCO oversees the recall process, ensuring accountability from manufacturers.
4. **Public Awareness**:
   - Alerts are issued to healthcare professionals and the public about identified risks.

2.7 Penalties and Enforcement

The **Drugs, Cosmetics, and Medical Devices Act** is a cornerstone of public health protection in India, designed to regulate the safety, quality, and efficacy of pharmaceuticals, cosmetics, and medical devices. The Act enforces compliance through a structured framework of penalties for violations and an enforcement mechanism that includes inspections, legal actions, and judicial oversight. These measures aim to deter malpractices and ensure accountability in the healthcare and pharmaceutical sectors.

Offenses and Penalties

Categories of Violations

The Act outlines specific categories of offenses with corresponding penalties to address malpractices:

1. **Manufacturing or Selling Spurious Drugs**:
   - **Spurious Drugs**: Products falsely labeled or deliberately manufactured to mislead consumers.
   - **Penalty**:
     - Imprisonment: Up to **life imprisonment** for severe violations.
     - Fine: Up to **₹10 lakh** or three times the value of the spurious product.
2. **Adulterated Drugs and Cosmetics**:
   - **Definition**: Products contaminated or prepared under unsanitary conditions, posing health risks.
   - **Penalty**:
     - Imprisonment: Up to **10 years**.
     - Fine: Not less than **₹1 lakh**.
3. **Non-Compliance with Labeling Norms**:
   - **Examples**: Missing batch numbers, manufacturing/expiry dates, or storage instructions.
   - **Penalty**:
     - Fine: Up to **₹5,000** for minor infractions.
4. **Violation of Licensing Terms**:
   - **Definition**: Operating without a valid license or breaching license conditions.
   - **Penalty**:
     - Imprisonment: Up to **5 years**.
     - Fine: Varies based on the severity of the violation.
5. **Unlawful Clinical Trials**:
   - **Examples**: Conducting trials without approval or failing to adhere to ethical guidelines.
   - **Penalty**:
     - Imprisonment: Up to **3 years**.
     - Fine: Up to **₹20 lakh**.

Monetary Fines and Imprisonment Terms

The Act provides a graded system of penalties to deter violations:

1. **Minor Offenses**:
   - Typically result in monetary fines and warnings.
2. **Major Offenses**:
   - Attract severe penalties, including substantial fines and imprisonment.
3. **Repeat Violations**:
   - Lead to harsher penalties and possible cancellation of licenses.

Enforcement Mechanisms

Role of Inspectors and Regulatory Officers in Ensuring Compliance

1. **Drug Inspectors**:
   - Appointed by the government to enforce provisions of the Act.
   - Responsibilities include:
     - Conducting inspections of manufacturing facilities, pharmacies, and warehouses.
     - Collecting samples for testing.
     - Ensuring adherence to **Good Manufacturing Practices (GMP)**.
2. **Regulatory Officers**:
   - Oversee compliance with licensing, labeling, and quality standards.
   - Investigate complaints and initiate legal actions for non-compliance.

Procedures for Raids, Sampling, and Legal Actions

1. **Raids and Inspections**:
   - Conducted to identify and prevent the sale of spurious or adulterated products.
   - Example: Raids on unlicensed medical stores distributing counterfeit drugs.

2. **Sampling**:
    - Inspectors collect product samples for laboratory analysis to verify compliance with quality standards.
    - Non-compliant products are seized, and reports are filed for further legal action.
3. **Legal Actions**:
    - Offenders are prosecuted under the provisions of the Act.
    - Penalties are determined based on the gravity of the offense.

Judicial Precedents

Landmark Cases Shaping the Enforcement of the Act

1. **Cipla Ltd. vs. Union of India (2005)**:
    - Issue: Allegations of manufacturing substandard drugs.
    - Outcome: Highlighted the importance of adhering to GMP and set stricter inspection standards.
2. **State of Maharashtra vs. Suresh Ganpat Kankar (2014)**:
    - Issue: Sale of spurious drugs resulting in fatalities.
    - Outcome: Imposed the maximum penalty, reinforcing the deterrent effect of the Act.
3. **Novartis AG vs. Union of India (2013)**:
    - Issue: Granting of compulsory licenses for lifesaving drugs.
    - Outcome: Established that public interest overrides patent protection in specific cases.

2.8 Harmonization with Global Standards

The global pharmaceutical and medical device industries operate within a framework of international standards to ensure the quality, safety, and efficacy of products. To remain competitive and foster trade, the **Drugs, Cosmetics, and Medical Devices Act** incorporates provisions to harmonize India's regulatory practices with global standards. This alignment not only enhances consumer safety but also bolsters India's position as a leading hub for pharmaceuticals and medical devices.

Alignment with International Guidelines

Adopting WHO and ICH Standards

1. **World Health Organization (WHO) Guidelines**:
   - India aligns its regulatory practices with **WHO Good Manufacturing Practices (GMP)** to:
     - Ensure consistency in drug manufacturing.
     - Maintain high standards of safety and efficacy for domestic and exported products.
2. **International Council for Harmonisation (ICH)**:
   - India's participation in ICH enables it to adopt best practices in:
     - **Quality guidelines (ICH Q-series)**: Addressing aspects like pharmaceutical development and stability testing.
     - **Safety guidelines (ICH S-series)**: Managing toxicological assessments.
     - **Efficacy guidelines (ICH E-series)**: Standardizing clinical trial requirements.
3. **Global Recognition**:
   - By adhering to these standards, Indian pharmaceutical and medical device manufacturers gain credibility in global markets.

Participation in Global Regulatory Forums

1. **Membership in Global Initiatives**:
   - India actively participates in international regulatory forums, such as:
     - **International Medical Device Regulators Forum (IMDRF).**
     - **Pharmaceutical Inspection Co-operation Scheme (PIC/S).**
2. **Collaborative Efforts**:
   - These platforms facilitate:
     - Exchange of regulatory intelligence.
     - Development of harmonized policies for quality control and surveillance.

3. **India's Role as a Contributor**:
   - The **Central Drugs Standard Control Organization (CDSCO)** contributes to global discussions on emerging challenges, such as:
     - Regulating AI-driven medical devices.
     - Addressing antimicrobial resistance.

Facilitating Exports

Ensuring Compliance with US FDA and European EMA Requirements

1. **US FDA Standards**:
   - Indian manufacturers exporting to the US must meet **Current Good Manufacturing Practices (cGMP)** outlined by the **US Food and Drug Administration (FDA)**.
   - Regular FDA audits of Indian facilities underscore the importance of maintaining compliance.
2. **European Medicines Agency (EMA)**:
   - Products exported to Europe must adhere to **EU GMP guidelines**.
   - Additional certifications, such as **CE marking** for medical devices, validate product safety and performance.
3. **Bridging Regulatory Gaps**:
   - The Indian government supports manufacturers in aligning with these stringent requirements through:
     - Training programs.
     - Regulatory guidance documents.
4. **Success Stories**:
   - Indian pharmaceutical companies, such as **Sun Pharmaceuticals** and **Dr. Reddy's Laboratories**, have successfully gained approvals for complex generics and biosimilars in the US and EU markets.

Impact on Global Trade

Enhancing India's Reputation as a Pharmaceutical and Medical Device Hub

1. **Growth in Exports**:
   - India is the **world's largest supplier of generic medicines**, accounting for nearly **20% of global generic drug exports**.
   - The country is also emerging as a leader in the production of **low-cost medical devices**.
2. **Improved Market Access**:
   - Harmonized standards reduce regulatory bottlenecks, enabling Indian products to enter diverse markets more efficiently.
3. **Trust and Credibility**:
   - Compliance with global standards strengthens India's reputation, attracting:
     - Foreign direct investment (FDI).
     - International collaborations for research and development.

Contributing to Global Public Health

1. **COVID-19 Response**:
   - India supplied **vaccines** and essential medicines to over 150 countries during the pandemic, demonstrating the global relevance of its pharmaceutical sector.
   - Harmonized standards facilitated swift approvals and distribution.
2. **Affordable Healthcare Solutions**:

   India's ability to produce high-quality, affordable drugs and devices has positioned it as a key player in improving healthcare access in low- and middle-income countries.

CHAPTER 3

Central Drugs Standard Control Organization (CDSCO)

Introduction to CDSCO

The **Central Drugs Standard Control Organization (CDSCO)** serves as India's apex regulatory authority for pharmaceuticals, cosmetics, and medical devices. It is the backbone of India's regulatory framework, ensuring that products entering the market meet stringent safety, efficacy, and quality standards. This chapter explores the definition, role, historical background, and significance of CDSCO in the Indian healthcare ecosystem.

The **CDSCO**, under the aegis of the **Ministry of Health and Family Welfare**, is the regulatory body responsible for:

- Approving new drugs and clinical trials.
- Licensing and monitoring drug manufacturing, distribution, and marketing.
- Regulating medical devices and overseeing their compliance with established standards.
- Enforcing provisions under the **Drugs and Cosmetics Act, 1940**, and its related rules.

In essence, CDSCO operates as India's **National Regulatory Authority (NRA)**, much like the **US Food and Drug Administration (FDA)** or the **European Medicines Agency (EMA)**.

Primary Functions in Drug Regulation and Public Health

The CDSCO's role extends across several domains:

1. **Product Approvals**:
    - New drugs, vaccines, and biosimilars.
    - Medical devices, including risk-based classifications.

2. **Clinical Trials**:
    - Approving clinical trial protocols and ensuring ethical compliance.
    - Monitoring trials to ensure participant safety and data integrity.
3. **Post-Market Surveillance**:
    - Monitoring adverse drug reactions (ADRs) through programs like the **Pharmacovigilance Programme of India (PvPI)**.
    - Investigating complaints and taking corrective actions like recalls.
4. **Standard Setting**:
    - Collaborating with bodies like the **Indian Pharmacopoeia Commission (IPC)** to set drug quality standards.

Importance of CDSCO in India's Healthcare System

Role as the National Regulatory Authority (NRA)

The CDSCO acts as a gatekeeper for public health by ensuring that only safe, effective, and high-quality drugs and devices reach consumers. Key aspects of its importance include:

- **Safeguarding Public Health**:
    - Ensuring that substandard or spurious products are kept out of the market.
    - Monitoring and mitigating adverse effects of pharmaceutical products.
- **Supporting Industry Growth**:
    - Streamlining regulatory processes to encourage innovation.
    - Enhancing India's position as a global hub for pharmaceuticals and medical devices.

Ensuring Safety, Efficacy, and Quality

CDSCO's work ensures that:

- Drugs and devices comply with stringent quality standards.
- Clinical trials are conducted ethically, adhering to **Good Clinical Practices (GCP)**.
- Manufacturers adopt **Good Manufacturing Practices (GMP)** for consistent product quality.

Historical Background

Establishment and Evolution of CDSCO

1. **Origins**:
    - Established in 1940 under the **Drugs and Cosmetics Act**, the CDSCO initially focused on regulating drugs and cosmetics.
    - Over time, its scope expanded to include medical devices and clinical trials, reflecting advancements in healthcare technologies.
2. **Growth and Milestones**:
    - **1970s**: Introduction of the **Drug Controller General of India (DCGI)** as the head of CDSCO.
    - **1990s**: Expansion of responsibilities to include monitoring imported drugs and devices.
    - **2019**: Implementation of the **New Drugs and Clinical Trials Rules**, streamlining clinical trial approvals.
    - **2020**: Introduction of the **Medical Devices Rules**, formally bringing devices under a risk-based regulatory framework.

Significant Milestones in its Development

1. **Establishment of Zonal Offices**:
    - To decentralize regulatory oversight, zonal offices were set up across the country to inspect facilities, sample drugs, and ensure compliance.
2. **Digital Initiatives**:
    - Launch of online portals like **Sugam** for drug and device applications, making processes more transparent and efficient.
3. **International Collaboration**:
    - CDSCO's participation in global initiatives like the **Pharmaceutical Inspection Co-operation Scheme (PIC/S)** and **ICH** has bolstered India's regulatory alignment with international standards.

3.1 Structure and Organization of CDSCO

The Central Drugs Standard Control Organization (CDSCO) operates as a complex and multifaceted regulatory body responsible for ensuring the safety, efficacy, and quality of drugs, cosmetics, and medical devices in India. Its organizational structure reflects a robust framework designed to address the diverse regulatory needs of a vast country with a growing healthcare sector. This section explores the administrative setup, regional coordination, and specialized committees that enable CDSCO to perform its functions effectively.

Administrative Framework

Central and Zonal Offices

1. **Central Office**:
   - The central office of CDSCO is located in **New Delhi** and serves as the headquarters.
   - It houses the office of the **Drug Controller General of India (DCGI)**, who oversees the organization's functions, including:
     - Approving new drugs and clinical trials.
     - Regulating the import of drugs and medical devices.
     - Formulating policies and guidelines in collaboration with government bodies.
2. **Zonal Offices**:
   - To decentralize operations and ensure regional coverage, CDSCO has established **six zonal offices** in major cities such as Mumbai, Kolkata, Chennai, Hyderabad, Ahmedabad, and Ghaziabad.
   - Functions of zonal offices include:
     - Conducting inspections of manufacturing facilities.
     - Sampling drugs for quality assurance.
     - Assisting in training and capacity-building programs.

Role of the Drug Controller General of India (DCGI)

- The **DCGI** is the apex authority within CDSCO, appointed by the **Ministry of Health and Family Welfare**.
- Key Responsibilities:
  1. **Policy Formulation**:
     - Establishing regulations for drugs, cosmetics, and medical devices.
     - Ensuring compliance with national and international standards.
  2. **Regulatory Oversight**:
     - Granting approvals for new drugs, biosimilars, and vaccines.
     - Reviewing clinical trial protocols and monitoring their implementation.

3. **Coordination**:
    - Acting as a liaison between the central and state drug control authorities.
    - Representing India in global regulatory forums like the **World Health Organization (WHO)** and **International Council for Harmonisation (ICH)**.

Regional and State Coordination

Collaboration with State Drug Control Organizations

- **Dual Regulatory System**:
    - CDSCO operates alongside **state drug regulatory authorities**, with clearly defined responsibilities under the **Drugs and Cosmetics Act, 1940**.
    - States oversee the regulation of:
        - Retail drug licenses.
        - Monitoring of small-scale drug manufacturing units.
    - CDSCO focuses on higher-level approvals and interstate issues.
- **Training and Capacity Building**:
    - CDSCO conducts workshops and training sessions to ensure state authorities are well-equipped to handle local regulatory challenges.

Functions of Zonal, Sub-Zonal, and Port Offices

1. **Zonal Offices**:
    - Function as extensions of the central office to provide localized regulatory oversight.
    - Conduct inspections and verify compliance with **Good Manufacturing Practices (GMP)**.
2. **Sub-Zonal Offices**:
    - Smaller offices under zonal jurisdictions to manage local regulatory tasks.
3. **Port Offices**:
    - Located at key entry points such as ports and airports.
    - Responsibilities:

  - Inspecting and clearing imported drugs, cosmetics, and medical devices.
  - Preventing the entry of substandard or unapproved products into the country.

Committees and Panels

Drugs Technical Advisory Board (DTAB)

1. **Purpose**:
   - DTAB is the highest advisory body on technical matters related to drug regulation in India.
2. **Composition**:
   - Includes experts from the medical, pharmaceutical, and legal fields.
   - Representatives from organizations like **Indian Council of Medical Research (ICMR)** and **Medical Council of India (MCI)**.
3. **Functions**:
   - Advises the central government on amendments to drug laws.
   - Recommends guidelines for the approval of new drugs and clinical trials.

Drugs Consultative Committee (DCC)

1. **Purpose**:
   - Acts as a platform for collaboration between CDSCO and state drug regulatory authorities.
2. **Composition**:
   - Representatives from state drug control organizations and CDSCO.
3. **Functions**:
   - Ensures uniform enforcement of drug laws across states.
   - Discusses challenges in implementation and proposes solutions.

New Drug Advisory Committees (NDACs)

1. **Purpose**:
    - Specialized committees that evaluate applications for new drug approvals.
2. **Composition**:
    - Comprised of subject matter experts in pharmacology, medicine, and toxicology.
3. **Functions**:
    - Reviewing data from preclinical and clinical studies.
    - Recommending approval or rejection based on safety and efficacy.

3.2 Functions and Responsibilities of CDSCO

The Central Drugs Standard Control Organization (CDSCO) plays a pivotal role in regulating India's pharmaceutical, medical device, and cosmetic industries. Its responsibilities encompass the entire lifecycle of these products, from development to post-marketing surveillance, ensuring they meet the highest standards of safety, efficacy, and quality. This section delves into the specific functions and responsibilities that define CDSCO's role in safeguarding public health.

Regulation of Drugs and Medical Devices

Licensing and Approval Processes

- **Drug Licensing**:
    - CDSCO oversees the **licensing of manufacturing units, importers, and sellers** for drugs and medical devices.
    - For new drugs, manufacturers are required to:
        - Submit preclinical and clinical data.
        - Obtain marketing authorization following CDSCO's evaluation.
    - Types of licenses:
        - **Form 25**: For manufacturing drugs.
        - **Form 10**: For importing drugs into India.
- **Medical Device Licensing**:
    - Under the **Medical Devices Rules, 2020**, devices are categorized based on risk (Class A to D).

  - High-risk devices (Class C and D) require thorough regulatory scrutiny.

Oversight of Manufacturing, Marketing, and Distribution

- CDSCO ensures adherence to **Good Manufacturing Practices (GMP)** to maintain consistent product quality.
- It regulates the marketing of pharmaceuticals to prevent false claims and misleading advertisements.
- Distribution networks are monitored to prevent the sale of **spurious or substandard products**.

Clinical Trial Oversight

Approvals for Clinical Trial Protocols

- Before a clinical trial can commence in India, CDSCO evaluates:
  - **Trial design** to ensure scientific rigor.
  - **Safety measures** for participants.
  - Ethical compliance with guidelines issued by **Good Clinical Practices (GCP)**.
- The regulatory process involves:
  - Submission of the protocol and investigational product dossier.
  - Approval by an **Institutional Ethics Committee (IEC)** and the DCGI.

Monitoring Compliance with Good Clinical Practice (GCP)

- CDSCO conducts **site inspections** to ensure adherence to GCP.
- It mandates that trials:
  - Prioritize patient safety.
  - Report adverse events promptly to both CDSCO and IECs.
- Non-compliance can lead to suspension or cancellation of trial approval.

Pharmacovigilance and Safety Monitoring

Role in Adverse Drug Reaction (ADR) Reporting

- CDSCO actively monitors the safety of marketed drugs and devices through:

    - **Spontaneous ADR reporting systems** where healthcare providers and consumers report adverse events.
    - Databases that collate and analyze safety data.
- Tools for ADR monitoring:
    - The **VigiFlow** system in collaboration with the **World Health Organization (WHO)**.

Coordination with the Pharmacovigilance Programme of India (PvPI)

- PvPI, operated by the **Indian Pharmacopoeia Commission (IPC)**, is the primary framework for pharmacovigilance.
- CDSCO's role includes:
    - Establishing PvPI guidelines for adverse event reporting.
    - Reviewing PvPI's findings and taking regulatory action, such as issuing warnings or recalling products.

Inspection and Compliance

Routine and Surprise Inspections

- **Planned Inspections**:
    - Regular audits of manufacturing facilities to verify GMP compliance.
    - Inspection of imported drug consignments at port offices.
- **Surprise Inspections**:
    - Conducted to investigate complaints of non-compliance or quality concerns.
    - May lead to suspension of licenses or product recalls if violations are found.

Ensuring Adherence to Good Manufacturing Practices (GMP)

- GMP ensures that:
    - Drugs and devices are consistently produced and controlled according to quality standards.
    - Key aspects inspected include:
        - Cleanliness and hygiene in manufacturing facilities.
        - Proper documentation of manufacturing processes.
- Non-adherence to GMP can result in penalties, including the cancellation of manufacturing licenses.

Training and Capacity Building

Workshops and Programs for Regulatory Staff

- To keep up with emerging technologies and global standards, CDSCO organizes:
  - **Training sessions for inspectors** on new regulations, GMP updates, and advanced analytical techniques.
  - Collaborations with international regulatory bodies like the **US FDA** and **EMA** for capacity building.

Programs for Industry Professionals

- CDSCO conducts workshops to educate pharmaceutical and medical device manufacturers on:
  - Changes in regulatory requirements.
  - Best practices for quality assurance and compliance.
- Topics often covered include:
  - **eCTD submissions** for regulatory approvals.
  - **Pharmacovigilance obligations**.

3.3 Key Regulations Overseen by CDSCO

The Central Drugs Standard Control Organization (CDSCO) operates within the framework of several critical regulations that govern the pharmaceutical, cosmetic, and medical device industries in India. These regulations ensure that products meet stringent safety, quality, and ethical standards while facilitating innovation and global trade compliance. This section provides a detailed overview of the primary regulations overseen by CDSCO, highlighting their significance and impact.

Drugs and Cosmetics Act, 1940

Provisions Relating to Drug Safety

- The **Drugs and Cosmetics Act, 1940**, is the cornerstone of pharmaceutical regulation in India, providing a legal framework for the manufacture, import, sale, and distribution of drugs and cosmetics.
- **Safety Standards**:
  - Ensures that all drugs are free from harmful substances and meet predefined safety benchmarks.

- Mandates preclinical and clinical testing for new drugs to establish safety before they are approved for marketing.

Provisions Relating to Drug Quality

- **Good Manufacturing Practices (GMP)**:
  - The Act requires adherence to GMP for all pharmaceutical manufacturing facilities to ensure consistent product quality.
  - Regular inspections are conducted by CDSCO to enforce GMP compliance.
- **Testing Standards**:
  - Establishes parameters for identity, purity, potency, and efficacy of drugs, often in collaboration with the **Indian Pharmacopoeia Commission (IPC)**.

Provisions Relating to Labeling

- **Mandatory Labeling Requirements**:
  - Labels must include critical details such as:
    - Drug name (brand and generic).
    - Batch number and expiration date.
    - Dosage instructions and storage conditions.
  - Specific warnings (e.g., "Schedule H Drug: To be sold by retail on the prescription of a Registered Medical Practitioner only").
- **Misbranded or Spurious Drugs**:
  - Strict penalties for manufacturing or selling drugs that are misbranded, adulterated, or spurious.

Medical Devices Rules, 2020

Framework for Risk-Based Classification

- The **Medical Devices Rules, 2020**, brought medical devices under a structured regulatory framework, aligning with global best practices.
- **Risk-Based Classification**:
  - Devices are categorized into four classes based on risk:
    - **Class A**: Low risk (e.g., surgical gloves).
    - **Class B**: Low-to-moderate risk (e.g., blood pressure monitors).
    - **Class C**: Moderate-to-high risk (e.g., ventilators).
    - **Class D**: High risk (e.g., implantable defibrillators).

Regulation of Medical Devices

- **Registration and Licensing**:
    - Mandatory registration for manufacturers and importers.
    - CDSCO grants licenses based on compliance with quality and safety standards.
- **Quality Assurance**:
    - Adherence to international standards such as ISO certifications for safety and performance.
- **Post-Market Surveillance**:
    - Continuous monitoring of adverse events and recalls to ensure device safety and effectiveness.

Clinical Trial Rules, 2019

Streamlining Approval Processes

- Introduced to simplify and standardize the approval of clinical trials in India.
- **Accelerated Approvals**:
    - Expedited pathways for drugs addressing unmet medical needs or for life-threatening diseases.
    - Fast-track approval for global clinical trial protocols submitted by pharmaceutical sponsors.
- **Single-Window Clearance**:
    - Simplifies trial approvals by integrating CDSCO's processes with ethics committees.

Ensuring Ethical Compliance

- **Good Clinical Practice (GCP)**:
    - Mandates that trials adhere to GCP guidelines to ensure participant safety, data integrity, and ethical conduct.
- **Informed Consent**:
    - Sponsors and investigators must ensure participants are fully informed about the trial's purpose, risks, and benefits.
- **Compensation for Injury**:
    - Requires sponsors to provide compensation for trial-related injuries or deaths, strengthening participant rights.

- **Inspections and Audits**:
  - CDSCO monitors compliance through regular inspections of trial sites and auditing of clinical data.

3.4 Clinical Trial Regulation

Clinical trials are a critical phase in drug development, providing evidence for the safety and efficacy of new pharmaceutical products. In India, the Central Drugs Standard Control Organization (CDSCO) is the primary authority regulating clinical trials, ensuring that they are conducted ethically and meet global standards. This section explores the approval processes, ethical considerations, and monitoring mechanisms that govern clinical trials in India.

Approval Processes

Protocol Evaluation

- The **clinical trial protocol** is a document that outlines the objectives, design, methodology, and ethical considerations of a clinical study. It is a key component of the approval process.
- **Steps in Protocol Evaluation**:
  1. **Submission**:
     - Sponsors submit the protocol and relevant documentation, including investigational drug data, informed consent forms, and details of study sites.
  2. **Review by CDSCO**:
     - The **New Drug Advisory Committees (NDACs)** review the protocol for scientific validity and participant safety.
  3. **Approval by Ethics Committees**:
     - The protocol must also be approved by an **Institutional Ethics Committee (IEC)** for each participating site.

Timelines for Clinical Trials in India

- **Streamlined Approvals**:
  - The **Clinical Trial Rules, 2019**, introduced clear timelines:
    - 30 days for processing applications for local trials.
    - 90 days for global clinical trial applications involving foreign sponsors.

- **Accelerated Approvals**:
  - Trials for drugs addressing unmet medical needs, such as those for rare diseases or pandemics, are fast-tracked.

Ethical Considerations

Role of Institutional Ethics Committees (IECs)

- **Composition of IECs**:
  - IECs must include a diverse group of experts, such as:
    - A medical scientist.
    - A legal expert.
    - A social worker or layperson.
  - This diversity ensures balanced decision-making and participant protection.
- **Functions of IECs**:
  - Reviewing the ethical aspects of trial protocols.
  - Monitoring ongoing trials to ensure compliance with ethical standards.

Adherence to National and International GCP Guidelines

- **National Guidelines**:
  - The **Indian Good Clinical Practice (GCP) Guidelines**, issued by CDSCO, align with global standards to ensure participant safety and data reliability.
- **International Guidelines**:
  - India follows the **ICH-GCP Guidelines** to maintain consistency with global practices, facilitating international collaborations.
- **Key Ethical Principles**:
  - **Informed Consent**:
    - Participants must be fully informed about the trial's purpose, risks, and benefits.
    - Consent forms must be written in simple, local language.
  - **Voluntary Participation**:
    - Participants have the right to withdraw from the trial at any time without repercussions.

Monitoring and Audits

Inspection of Trial Sites

- **Purpose**:
  - Ensure compliance with GCP guidelines and the approved protocol.
  - Verify data integrity and participant safety.
- **Inspection Types**:
  - **Routine Inspections**:
    - Conducted periodically to ensure ongoing compliance.
  - **For-Cause Inspections**:
    - Triggered by complaints, suspected non-compliance, or adverse events.

Compliance Checks

- CDSCO and IECs jointly monitor compliance at trial sites. Key activities include:
  - **Data Verification**:
    - Ensuring the accuracy and completeness of clinical trial data.
  - **Adverse Event Reporting**:
    - Sponsors and investigators must report adverse events to CDSCO and IECs.
  - **Participant Safety**:
    - Monitoring mechanisms are in place to address any trial-related harm immediately.

3.5 Collaboration with Other Regulatory Bodies

The Central Drugs Standard Control Organization (CDSCO) plays a vital role in safeguarding public health, which often requires collaboration with other regulatory bodies, both nationally and internationally. These partnerships enable CDSCO to harmonize regulatory practices, enhance compliance, and keep pace with global advancements in pharmaceuticals, medical devices, and clinical research. This section explores CDSCO's collaborative efforts within India and across international borders.

National Collaboration

Coordination with State Drug Regulatory Authorities

- **Dual Regulatory System**:
  - India operates under a dual regulatory framework where CDSCO oversees central functions, while state drug regulatory authorities manage local-level responsibilities, such as licensing retail drug outlets and monitoring small-scale manufacturing units.
  - Effective coordination between these entities ensures uniform enforcement of drug laws across the country.
- **Key Collaborative Efforts**:
  1. **Training Programs**:
     - CDSCO organizes workshops and seminars for state regulatory staff to ensure consistent interpretation and enforcement of drug regulations.
  2. **Joint Inspections**:
     - State authorities and CDSCO collaborate on inspections of manufacturing units to verify compliance with **Good Manufacturing Practices (GMP)**.
  3. **Data Sharing**:
     - Regular communication channels facilitate the exchange of data on substandard drugs, spurious medicines, and adverse events.

Interaction with Indian Pharmacopoeia Commission (IPC)

- **Defining Drug Standards**:
  - CDSCO collaborates with IPC to establish and update standards for drugs listed in the **Indian Pharmacopoeia (IP)**.
  - These standards ensure the quality, safety, and efficacy of pharmaceutical products in India.
- **Pharmacovigilance Programme of India (PvPI)**:
  - CDSCO works closely with IPC, which operates PvPI, to monitor adverse drug reactions (ADRs) and improve post-marketing surveillance.

Collaboration with Other National Bodies

- CDSCO interacts with several other organizations, including:
    - **Ministry of Health and Family Welfare**: For policy formulation.
    - **Indian Council of Medical Research (ICMR)**: For clinical trial guidelines and health research initiatives.
    - **Bureau of Indian Standards (BIS)**: For standardization of medical devices.

International Collaboration

Membership in Global Initiatives

- **World Health Organization (WHO)**:
    - CDSCO's membership in WHO initiatives ensures alignment with global health standards.
    - **Collaborative Projects**:
        - Contributing to the **Prequalification Program** for essential medicines and vaccines.
        - Participating in global campaigns to combat substandard and falsified medicines.
- **International Council for Harmonisation (ICH)**:
    - India, through CDSCO, adheres to ICH guidelines for drug registration, ensuring international compatibility of clinical trial data and manufacturing standards.

Partnerships with Foreign Regulatory Agencies

- **United States Food and Drug Administration (US FDA)**:
    - Regular collaboration to streamline the approval of Indian pharmaceutical exports to the U.S.
    - Joint inspections of Indian manufacturing units supplying drugs to the U.S. market.
- **European Medicines Agency (EMA)**:
    - Harmonization of drug approval processes to facilitate exports to the European Union.
    - Sharing of data on pharmacovigilance and clinical trials.
- **Other Partnerships**:
    - Collaborations with regulatory authorities in Japan (PMDA), Canada (Health Canada), and Australia (TGA) to:

  - Enhance compliance with global standards.
  - Promote mutual recognition of inspection reports.

Global Harmonization Efforts

- **Standardization of Medical Devices**:
  - CDSCO aligns its medical device regulations with international standards, such as ISO certifications.
- **Clinical Trial Data Sharing**:
  - Participation in global clinical trial registries to enhance transparency and reduce duplication of research efforts.
- **Combating Counterfeit Drugs**:
  - Joint efforts with WHO and INTERPOL to address the global challenge of counterfeit medicines.

CHAPTER 4

State Drug Regulatory Authorities

State Drug Regulatory Authorities (SDRAs) are integral components of India's healthcare regulatory framework. They operate at the state level to implement and enforce drug laws, ensuring that medicines, cosmetics, and medical devices available in the market meet safety, quality, and efficacy standards. This chapter delves into the definition, purpose, and significance of SDRAs, highlighting their critical role in public health and their relationship with central regulatory bodies like the Central Drugs Standard Control Organization (CDSCO).

Definition and Purpose

What are State Drug Regulatory Authorities (SDRAs)?

State Drug Regulatory Authorities are state-level bodies established under the **Drugs and Cosmetics Act, 1940**. They are tasked with enforcing drug laws within their jurisdiction, ensuring compliance with manufacturing, distribution, and retail regulations. Each state has its own SDRA, typically headed by a **State Drug Controller**, supported by a team of inspectors, analysts, and administrative staff.

Role of SDRAs in Implementing and Enforcing Drug Laws

1. **Licensing and Registration**:
    - Granting licenses to manufacturers, wholesalers, and retailers of drugs and cosmetics.
    - Renewing and revoking licenses based on compliance with regulations.
2. **Inspection and Monitoring**:
    - Conducting regular inspections of manufacturing units, storage facilities, and retail outlets.
    - Ensuring adherence to **Good Manufacturing Practices (GMP)** and **Good Distribution Practices (GDP)**.

3. **Quality Assurance**:
    - Sampling and testing drugs to detect substandard or spurious products.
    - Collaborating with state drug testing laboratories to ensure product quality.
4. **Consumer Protection**:
    - Addressing complaints and taking legal action against violators.
    - Penalizing those involved in the manufacture or sale of counterfeit drugs.

Importance in Public Health

Ensuring Drug Safety and Quality in Local Markets

- SDRAs play a frontline role in protecting public health by ensuring that medicines sold in the market are safe, effective, and of high quality.
- They enforce standards outlined in the **Indian Pharmacopoeia**, ensuring that drugs meet prescribed specifications for identity, purity, potency, and performance.

Addressing Region-Specific Issues in Pharmaceutical Regulation

- Each state has unique healthcare needs and challenges. SDRAs tailor their regulatory efforts to address:
    - Specific health concerns prevalent in the region (e.g., vector-borne diseases in tropical states).
    - Local manufacturing practices and distribution networks.
    - Accessibility of essential medicines in rural and remote areas.

Supporting Pharmacovigilance

- SDRAs contribute to the **Pharmacovigilance Programme of India (PvPI)** by reporting adverse drug reactions (ADRs) and monitoring the safety of medicines post-marketing.
- They collaborate with healthcare professionals, pharmacists, and consumers to identify and address safety concerns promptly.

Relation with Central Regulatory Bodies

Coordination with the Central Drugs Standard Control Organization (CDSCO)

- **Unified Regulatory Framework**:
    - The CDSCO, as the central authority, sets overarching guidelines and policies, while SDRAs execute these at the state level.
    - This dual regulatory framework ensures consistency in enforcing drug laws across the country.
- **Joint Initiatives**:
    - SDRAs collaborate with CDSCO for:
        - Conducting inspections of large-scale manufacturing units.
        - Investigating cases of counterfeit or substandard drugs that have interstate implications.
        - Approving new drugs and clinical trial protocols that require both state and central oversight.
- **Data Sharing**:
    - Regular exchange of information between SDRAs and CDSCO helps in tracking:
        - Non-compliance by manufacturers and distributors.
        - Adverse drug events and recalls.

Bridging National and Local Priorities

- SDRAs act as a bridge between national policies and local implementation, ensuring that central guidelines are adapted to meet state-specific needs.
- For instance:
    - While CDSCO regulates large-scale manufacturers, SDRAs focus on small-scale units and retail outlets within the state.
    - SDRAs enforce regional policies for ensuring the availability of essential drugs in underserved areas.

4.1 Structure and Organization of State Drug Regulatory Authorities (SDRAs)

The effectiveness of State Drug Regulatory Authorities (SDRAs) lies in their structured organization and hierarchical framework, which enables them to enforce drug regulations efficiently at the state level. This section explores the administrative composition, regional divisions, and committees that constitute the backbone of SDRAs, ensuring comprehensive regulatory oversight.

Administrative Framework

Composition of SDRAs

- SDRAs are structured with a well-defined hierarchy to ensure smooth regulatory functioning. The key components include:
    1. **State Drug Controller**:
        - Acts as the head of the SDRA.
        - Responsible for overall decision-making and implementation of state drug laws.
        - Represents the state in national-level regulatory discussions and collaborations with the CDSCO.
    2. **Drug Inspectors**:
        - Operate under the supervision of the State Drug Controller.
        - Conduct inspections of manufacturing units, retail outlets, and storage facilities.
        - Collect drug samples for quality testing and ensure compliance with Good Manufacturing Practices (GMP) and Good Distribution Practices (GDP).
    3. **Analysts and Technical Staff**:
        - Work in state drug testing laboratories.
        - Perform analytical testing to identify substandard, spurious, or counterfeit drugs.
    4. **Support and Administrative Staff**:
        - Provide logistical and clerical support to ensure the smooth operation of the authority.

Appointment and Reporting Structure

- **Appointment**:
  - The State Drug Controller is typically appointed by the state government, often based on extensive experience in pharmaceuticals or regulatory affairs.
  - Drug Inspectors and technical staff are recruited through competitive examinations and interviews conducted at the state level.
- **Reporting**:
  - The State Drug Controller reports to the state health department or directly to the Health Secretary.
  - Drug Inspectors report to their respective zonal or district offices, which in turn coordinate with the central office of the SDRA.

Regional Divisions

District-Level Offices

- **Operational Scope**:
  - SDRAs often have district offices to decentralize regulatory activities and address local concerns more effectively.
  - These offices oversee licensing, inspections, and enforcement within their respective districts.
- **Responsibilities**:
  - Monitoring retail pharmacies, wholesalers, and small-scale manufacturing units.
  - Addressing consumer complaints related to drug quality or safety.
  - Conducting awareness programs for local healthcare providers and consumers.

Coordination with State Health Departments

- SDRAs work closely with state health departments to align regulatory efforts with public health policies.
- **Collaborative Efforts**:
  - Joint initiatives for ensuring the availability of essential medicines during health crises or epidemics.

    - Implementation of state health schemes that involve drug distribution or subsidized medications.
- **Communication Channels**:
    - Regular meetings between the State Drug Controller and health department officials.
    - Periodic reporting on inspections, compliance issues, and quality assurance outcomes.

Key Committees

Advisory Committees

- **Purpose**:
    - Provide policy recommendations to enhance the regulatory framework.
    - Address complex issues, such as licensing disputes or the approval of innovative pharmaceutical products.
- **Composition**:
    - Experts in pharmaceuticals, medicine, and regulatory affairs.
    - Representatives from academia, the pharmaceutical industry, and legal professionals.
- **Functions**:
    - Advising on amendments to state-specific drug laws.
    - Reviewing cases of non-compliance and recommending penalties or corrective actions.

Role of Technical and Legal Experts

- **Technical Experts**:
    - Provide guidance on quality control, testing methodologies, and emerging challenges in drug manufacturing.
    - Review and refine standards for licensing and inspections.
- **Legal Experts**:
    - Ensure that all regulatory actions are compliant with the **Drugs and Cosmetics Act, 1940**, and other applicable laws.
    - Represent SDRAs in legal disputes and enforcement actions.

4.2 Licensing Processes

Licensing is one of the core functions of State Drug Regulatory Authorities (SDRAs) and ensures that all entities involved in the manufacture, sale, and distribution of drugs, cosmetics, and medical devices operate in compliance with established regulations. This section provides a detailed exploration of the licensing processes for retail and wholesale outlets, manufacturing units, and the challenges faced in ensuring efficiency and compliance.

Retail and Wholesale Licenses

Application and Documentation Requirements

- **Eligibility Criteria**:
  - For retail outlets: The applicant must have a qualified pharmacist registered under the State Pharmacy Council.
  - For wholesale outlets: The applicant must employ a competent person with experience in pharmaceutical sales.
- **Documentation**:
  - Application form (specific to the state's regulatory framework).
  - Proof of premises (ownership or lease agreement) compliant with regulatory standards for storage and safety.
  - Pharmacist or competent person's qualification certificates and registration details.
  - Details of products to be sold or distributed.
  - Fee receipt for application submission.

Process Overview:

1. **Submission**:
   - The application is submitted to the district or zonal SDRA office.
2. **Inspection**:
   - A Drug Inspector visits the premises to verify compliance with storage and safety requirements.
3. **Approval**:
   - Upon satisfactory inspection and document verification, a license is granted.
4. **Timeframe**:
   - The process typically takes 30-60 days, depending on the state and complexity of the application.

Renewal and Conditions for Revocation

- **Renewal Process**:
  - Licenses are generally valid for 1-5 years and must be renewed before expiration.
  - Renewal applications require an updated set of documents, including an annual turnover declaration and any changes in ownership or personnel.
- **Revocation**:
  - Licenses may be revoked for:
    - Selling substandard or spurious drugs.
    - Non-compliance with storage conditions.
    - Operating without a qualified pharmacist or competent person.
  - In cases of revocation, the entity can appeal to the State Drug Controller for reconsideration.

Manufacturing Licenses

Procedures for Obtaining Licenses

- **Eligibility Requirements**:
  - Premises must comply with **Good Manufacturing Practices (GMP)** outlined in **Schedule M** of the Drugs and Cosmetics Act.
  - The applicant must have access to qualified technical staff (e.g., manufacturing chemist, analytical chemist) and proper equipment for production and quality control.
- **Application Process**:
  1. **Submission**:

     The manufacturer submits an application to the SDRA, specifying the type of products (e.g., drugs, cosmetics) and dosage forms (e.g., tablets, injectables).
  2. **Document Verification**:

     Documents required include:

     Site master file detailing facilities, equipment, and manufacturing processes.

     Quality assurance and quality control protocols.

     Environmental clearances, where applicable.

3. **Inspection**:

   The SDRA conducts a thorough inspection of the facility to assess compliance with GMP standards.

4. **Grant of License**:

   Upon successful inspection and verification, a manufacturing license is granted, typically valid for five years.

Compliance with State-Specific and National Guidelines

- **State-Level Requirements**:
  - States may impose additional conditions, such as adherence to local pollution control norms.
- **National Guidelines**:
  - Licensing must comply with central regulations under the Drugs and Cosmetics Act, 1940, and the **Medical Devices Rules, 2020**, where applicable.
  - The manufacturer must also ensure that products meet the standards outlined in the **Indian Pharmacopoeia** or other recognized standards.

Challenges in Licensing

Delays in Processing Applications

- **Causes of Delays**:
  - Insufficient manpower within SDRAs to handle application volumes.
  - Complex documentation requirements leading to incomplete submissions by applicants.
  - Inefficient communication between zonal and central offices.
- **Impact**:
  - Delays can hinder timely market entry for new businesses and products, impacting public health and economic growth.

Addressing Gaps in State-Level Infrastructure

- **Lack of Digital Platforms**:
  - Many SDRAs rely on manual processes for application reviews, leading to inefficiencies and errors.

- **Inadequate Inspectorate Resources**:
  - A shortage of trained inspectors hampers timely inspections of premises.
- **Solutions**:
  - Adopting digital licensing systems for online application submissions and tracking.
  - Training programs to increase the capacity and expertise of inspectors.
  - Streamlining documentation requirements to reduce administrative burdens on applicants.

4.3 Drug Testing and Quality Control

Ensuring the quality of drugs available in the market is a cornerstone of the regulatory responsibilities of State Drug Regulatory Authorities (SDRAs). This is achieved through robust testing and quality control mechanisms managed by state drug testing laboratories, systematic sampling, and stringent actions against substandard products. This section explores the structure and functioning of state drug testing laboratories, sampling and testing procedures, and measures taken to address quality issues.

State Drug Testing Laboratories

Role and Capacity of State Laboratories in Ensuring Drug Quality

- **Primary Role**:
  - State drug testing laboratories are dedicated facilities that test drug samples collected by SDRAs to ensure compliance with quality standards. These labs play a crucial role in detecting substandard, spurious, or adulterated drugs that may pose risks to public health.
- **Functions**:
  - Analyze drug samples for compliance with prescribed standards of **potency, purity, and safety**.
  - Evaluate cosmetics and medical devices as mandated by the **Drugs and Cosmetics Act, 1940**.
  - Assist in the investigation of complaints or suspected quality issues raised by healthcare professionals or consumers.

- **Capacity**:
    - The capacity of these laboratories varies by state, depending on resources, infrastructure, and workforce. Advanced states may have multiple laboratories with specialized equipment, while resource-constrained states may rely on central facilities for complex analyses.

Accreditation and Compliance with National Standards

- **Accreditation**:
    - Laboratories must be accredited by bodies like the **National Accreditation Board for Testing and Calibration Laboratories (NABL)**, ensuring adherence to international quality standards such as ISO/IEC 17025.
- **Compliance**:
    - Labs must operate in alignment with national standards outlined in the **Indian Pharmacopoeia**, which specifies testing protocols and benchmarks for pharmaceutical products.
    - Periodic audits by SDRAs and central agencies, such as the **Central Drugs Standard Control Organization (CDSCO)**, ensure continued compliance.

Sampling and Testing Procedures

Random and Targeted Sampling Methods

- **Random Sampling**:
    - SDRAs routinely collect drug samples from various stages of the supply chain, including manufacturing facilities, wholesalers, and retail outlets.
    - Random sampling ensures broad surveillance of the market and helps detect non-compliance across a wide range of products.
- **Targeted Sampling**:
    - In response to specific complaints, reports of adverse drug reactions (ADRs), or intelligence on spurious drugs, SDRAs conduct targeted sampling.
    - This approach focuses on specific manufacturers, products, or distribution channels suspected of non-compliance.

Parameters Tested: Potency, Purity, and Safety

- **Potency**:
    - Measuring the active ingredient's strength to ensure it meets therapeutic requirements.
    - Example: Testing the potency of antibiotics to verify their efficacy in treating infections.
- **Purity**:
    - Assessing the absence of contaminants or impurities that could compromise safety or effectiveness.
    - Example: Detecting heavy metals or microbial contamination in formulations.
- **Safety**:
    - Ensuring products are free from harmful substances or adverse effects.
    - Example: Conducting stability studies to ensure drugs remain safe under prescribed storage conditions.

Testing Techniques

- Laboratories employ advanced techniques, including:
    - **Chromatography** (HPLC, GC) for assessing chemical composition.
    - **Spectroscopy** (UV-Vis, IR) for identifying substances and their concentrations.
    - **Microbial testing** for sterile products to detect bacterial or fungal contamination.

Addressing Quality Issues

Actions Taken for Substandard or Spurious Drugs

- **Issuance of Notices**:
    - If a product fails quality tests, the SDRA issues a show-cause notice to the manufacturer, requiring an explanation and corrective action.
- **Seizure and Recall**:
    - Substandard or spurious drugs are immediately seized from the market, and a recall process is initiated to remove them from the supply chain.

- **Penalties and Legal Action**:
  - SDRAs may impose fines, suspend licenses, or prosecute manufacturers under the provisions of the **Drugs and Cosmetics Act**.

Reporting and Recalls Initiated by SDRAs

- **Reporting**:
  - SDRAs report quality issues to the **Central Drugs Standard Control Organization (CDSCO)** for nationwide alerts if the affected product is distributed across multiple states.
- **Recall Mechanism**:
  - Manufacturers are required to follow established recall procedures, ensuring that substandard products are effectively removed from all points of sale and distribution.
  - Example: A large-scale recall of contaminated paracetamol syrups detected through routine state testing.
- **Follow-Up Actions**:
  - Post-recall investigations assess the root cause of the quality failure and mandate corrective actions to prevent recurrence.

4.4 Enforcement Mechanisms

Enforcement mechanisms are at the core of the regulatory responsibilities of State Drug Regulatory Authorities (SDRAs). These mechanisms ensure compliance with laws governing drugs, cosmetics, and medical devices. This section explores the structured protocols for inspections, penalties for non-compliance, and strategies to combat spurious drugs, emphasizing the role of SDRAs in safeguarding public health.

Inspection Protocols

Guidelines for Routine and Surprise Inspections

- **Routine Inspections**:
  - Conducted regularly to verify compliance with Good Manufacturing Practices (GMP), Good Distribution Practices (GDP), and Good Storage Practices (GSP).
  - Focus on licensed entities, such as manufacturers, wholesalers, and retailers, to ensure adherence to quality standards.

  - Inspectors examine facilities, storage conditions, record-keeping practices, and the authenticity of products.
- **Surprise Inspections**:
  - Conducted without prior notice, typically triggered by complaints, intelligence reports, or adverse findings during routine inspections.
  - Aim to identify illegal activities, such as the sale of unapproved drugs, non-compliance with labeling norms, or unauthorized manufacturing.
  - Provide a real-time assessment of compliance, reducing the chance of pre-inspection manipulations.

Use of Technology in Inspection Processes

- **Digital Record-Keeping**:
  - SDRAs leverage digital platforms to maintain records of licenses, inspection reports, and compliance histories.
  - Enables real-time tracking of inspection schedules and outcomes.
- **Inspection Tools**:
  - Use of portable devices for on-the-spot quality testing, such as spectrophotometers for checking drug composition.
  - Barcode scanning for verifying product authenticity and tracing supply chain origins.
- **Automation and AI**:
  - Implementation of artificial intelligence (AI) for analyzing inspection data to identify high-risk entities.
  - Use of predictive analytics to prioritize facilities for inspections based on historical non-compliance trends.

Penalties and Legal Actions

Fines and Imprisonment for Violations

- The **Drugs and Cosmetics Act, 1940**, prescribes stringent penalties for regulatory breaches, categorized as follows:
  - **Minor Offenses**:
    - Failure to comply with labeling or storage requirements.
    - Fines ranging from ₹1,000 to ₹10,000.

  - **Major Offenses**:
    - Manufacturing or selling spurious or adulterated drugs.
    - Punishable by imprisonment ranging from 5 years to life, along with hefty fines.
  - **Repeat Violations**:
    - Escalated penalties and suspension or cancellation of licenses.

Role of SDRAs in Prosecuting Offenders

- SDRAs initiate legal proceedings against violators by:
  - Filing complaints in courts based on evidence gathered during inspections.
  - Collaborating with legal experts to ensure cases are prosecuted effectively.
  - Testifying in court to substantiate findings from inspections and investigations.

Handling Spurious Drugs

Investigations and Raids to Combat Counterfeit Drug Networks

- **Identification**:
  - SDRAs receive intelligence on counterfeit drug operations through consumer complaints, pharmacist reports, or whistleblower tips.
  - High-risk areas are identified based on past incidents or market trends.
- **Planning Raids**:
  - Raids are planned in coordination with law enforcement agencies to ensure maximum impact.
  - Teams include drug inspectors, law enforcement officers, and forensic experts.
- **Execution**:
  - Raids focus on suspected manufacturing units, warehouses, or distribution networks.
  - Seized products are sent to drug testing laboratories for analysis to confirm counterfeit or substandard quality.

- **Post-Raid Actions**:
  - Based on findings, legal notices are issued, licenses may be suspended, and offenders are prosecuted.

Collaboration with Law Enforcement Agencies

- **Coordinated Efforts**:
  - SDRAs work closely with police departments, customs authorities, and intelligence agencies to dismantle counterfeit drug networks.
  - Example: Joint operations with customs authorities to intercept shipments of counterfeit drugs at ports.
- **National and International Networks**:
  - SDRAs collaborate with central authorities like the **Central Drugs Standard Control Organization (CDSCO)** and international bodies such as the **World Health Organization (WHO)** to combat transnational counterfeit drug operations.
- **Awareness Campaigns**:
  - Educating stakeholders, including pharmacists and consumers, to recognize and report counterfeit drugs.
  - Public outreach programs on the dangers of spurious drugs and the importance of buying medicines from licensed retailers.

4.5 Collaboration with CDSCO and Other Bodies

The collaborative framework between State Drug Regulatory Authorities (SDRAs), the Central Drugs Standard Control Organization (CDSCO), and other regulatory bodies is essential for ensuring uniform enforcement of drug laws and maintaining the quality and safety of pharmaceutical products. This section explores the dual regulatory framework, state-level coordination, and data-sharing mechanisms that enable efficient regulation across the country.

Dual Regulatory Framework

Responsibilities Shared Between CDSCO and SDRAs

- **Central Role of CDSCO**:
  - As the apex regulatory body, the CDSCO oversees the approval of new drugs, clinical trials, and the regulation of medical devices.

    - CDSCO ensures compliance with national and international regulatory standards and coordinates efforts across states.
- **State-Level Role of SDRAs**:
    - SDRAs are responsible for granting retail and wholesale licenses, inspecting local manufacturing units, and enforcing drug laws at the state level.
    - They ensure the implementation of Good Manufacturing Practices (GMP) and Good Distribution Practices (GDP) within their jurisdictions.
- **Overlap and Collaboration**:
    - For critical operations like clinical trial site inspections and post-marketing surveillance, CDSCO and SDRAs work together to avoid duplication and ensure efficiency.
    - Example: Joint inspections for high-risk drug categories or in cases of complaints regarding drug safety.

Joint Initiatives for Inspections and Compliance Monitoring

- **National Campaigns**:
    - Periodic nationwide inspections targeting spurious drugs or substandard manufacturing units, jointly conducted by CDSCO and SDRAs.
    - Example: A country-wide crackdown on unlicensed pharmaceutical manufacturers in collaboration with law enforcement agencies.
- **Specialized Audits**:
    - Focused audits for sensitive product categories like vaccines, biologics, and critical care drugs, coordinated between the central and state authorities.

State-Level Coordination

Interaction with State Health Departments for Policy Alignment

- **Policy Implementation**:
    - SDRAs coordinate with state health departments to implement national policies such as the **National List of Essential Medicines (NLEM)** and public health schemes.

- **Health Crisis Management**:
  - During emergencies like disease outbreaks or pandemics, SDRAs liaise with health departments to ensure the availability of critical medicines and medical devices.
  - Example: Ensuring rapid distribution of antiviral drugs during the COVID-19 pandemic.
- **Legislative Inputs**:
  - SDRAs provide feedback to state health departments on regulatory gaps and challenges, contributing to amendments in state-specific health laws.

Role in State-Specific Health Programs and Initiatives

- **Promoting Access to Medicines**:
  - SDRAs ensure the availability of quality medicines in rural and underserved areas by monitoring supply chains and pricing.
- **Awareness Campaigns**:
  - Collaborating with state governments to organize campaigns on drug safety, counterfeit medicines, and the responsible use of antibiotics.

Data Sharing

Reporting Quality Issues and ADRs to CDSCO

- **Adverse Drug Reactions (ADRs)**:
  - SDRAs monitor ADRs reported within their jurisdictions and share this data with the CDSCO as part of the **Pharmacovigilance Programme of India (PvPI)**.
  - Real-time reporting enables swift regulatory action, including recalls or safety warnings.
- **Quality Control Data**:
  - Testing results from state drug testing laboratories are communicated to CDSCO for national-level analyses and alerts.
  - Example: Sharing findings of substandard drugs that may affect multiple states.
  - Collaborating with Indian Pharmacopoeia Commission (IPC) for Standard-Setting

- **Standard Development**:
    - SDRAs contribute to the development and revision of monographs in the **Indian Pharmacopoeia (IP)** by providing data on commonly used drugs and regional market trends.
- **Training and Guidance**:
    - IPC provides training to SDRAs on implementing new testing methodologies and adhering to updated pharmacopoeial standards.

CHAPTER 5

Indian Pharmacopoeia Commission (IPC)

Introduction to the Indian Pharmacopoeia Commission (IPC)

The Indian Pharmacopoeia Commission (IPC) stands as a cornerstone institution in India's healthcare and pharmaceutical landscape, dedicated to ensuring the quality, safety, and efficacy of medicines. This introduction explores its definition, historical evolution, and critical role in public health and the pharmaceutical industry.

Definition and Purpose

What is the Indian Pharmacopoeia Commission?

The **Indian Pharmacopoeia Commission (IPC)** is an autonomous institution under the **Ministry of Health and Family Welfare, Government of India**. Established to set standards for drugs manufactured and marketed in India, IPC serves as the authoritative body for the development, maintenance, and publication of the **Indian Pharmacopoeia (IP)**, which is the official compendium of drug standards in the country.

Objectives of IPC

The IPC's primary objectives are:

1. **Standardizing Drugs**:
    - Establishing scientifically validated standards for the identity, purity, strength, and quality of drugs.
2. **Ensuring Quality and Safety**:
    - Preventing the distribution of substandard or counterfeit drugs in the market.
    - Assuring the safety and efficacy of medicines used in healthcare.
3. **Facilitating Regulatory Compliance**:
    - Supporting drug regulatory authorities by providing reliable standards for enforcement.

4. **Global Harmonization**:
    - Aligning Indian standards with international norms to facilitate the export of Indian pharmaceuticals.

Historical Evolution

Establishment of IPC

The IPC was formally established in **1948** as part of India's post-independence efforts to create self-reliant healthcare infrastructure. Before its inception, Indian drug standards relied heavily on the **British Pharmacopoeia (BP)**, reflecting the colonial influence on the nation's regulatory framework.

Transition from British Pharmacopoeia to Indian Pharmacopoeia

The shift from British standards to an indigenous pharmacopoeia marked a significant milestone:

- The first edition of the **Indian Pharmacopoeia (IP)** was published in **1955**, under the guidance of the **Indian Pharmacopoeia Committee**.
- It focused on incorporating modern scientific methods and addressing the unique pharmaceutical needs of India, covering both traditional and modern medicine.
- Over the years, subsequent editions of IP have evolved to include cutting-edge analytical methods, reflecting advancements in pharmaceutical sciences.

Milestones in the Evolution of IPC

1. **Introduction of Monographs**:
    - The early editions featured monographs on essential drugs widely used in India.
2. **Inclusion of Biopharmaceuticals**:
    - The recent editions incorporated standards for complex biopharmaceuticals like monoclonal antibodies and vaccines.
3. **Integration with Pharmacovigilance**:
    - IPC became the **National Coordination Centre (NCC)** for the **Pharmacovigilance Programme of India (PvPI)** in 2010, expanding its mandate to include drug safety monitoring.

Role in Healthcare

Contribution to Public Health by Ensuring Drug Quality

- **Prevention of Substandard Medicines**:
  - IPC's rigorous standards act as a safeguard against the proliferation of substandard or counterfeit drugs, ensuring the integrity of India's healthcare system.
  - Example: Routine testing by IPC has flagged non-compliant drug batches, leading to their withdrawal from the market.
- **Protecting Patients**:
  - Reliable standards for drug safety minimize the risk of adverse drug reactions and therapeutic failures.

IPC's Role in Supporting the Pharmaceutical Industry

- **Facilitating Export Growth**:
  - By aligning with global pharmacopoeial standards like the **United States Pharmacopoeia (USP)** and the **European Pharmacopoeia (EP)**, IPC ensures that Indian pharmaceutical products meet international regulatory requirements, boosting exports.
- **Supporting Innovation**:
  - IPC's research initiatives help the pharmaceutical industry develop innovative formulations while adhering to stringent quality norms.
- **Training and Capacity Building**:
  - The IPC conducts workshops and training sessions for industry professionals and regulators, enhancing their understanding of drug standards and compliance mechanisms.

5.1 Structure and Organization of the Indian Pharmacopoeia Commission (IPC)

The organizational structure of the Indian Pharmacopoeia Commission (IPC) reflects its critical role in establishing and maintaining drug standards in India. The IPC's well-defined administrative framework, its regional and national coordination mechanisms, and its expert committees ensure efficient operations and adherence to global pharmaceutical norms.

Administrative Framework

1. Governing Body and Leadership Roles

The IPC operates under the Ministry of Health and Family Welfare, Government of India, and is governed by a robust leadership team that ensures its objectives are met effectively.

- **Governing Body**:
    - The apex decision-making body responsible for formulating policies and overseeing the IPC's operations.
    - Includes representatives from the Ministry of Health, the pharmaceutical industry, academic institutions, and regulatory authorities.
- **Leadership Roles**:
    - **Chairperson**:
        - Provides strategic direction and leadership to the commission.
        - Acts as the key decision-maker on policy matters.
    - **Secretary-Cum-Scientific Director**:
        - Manages the day-to-day operations and execution of the IPC's vision.
        - Oversees research, publication, and coordination activities.
    - **Controller of Publications**:
        - Responsible for the timely publication of the Indian Pharmacopoeia and related documents.

---

2. Key Divisions and Their Responsibilities

The IPC is organized into specialized divisions, each tasked with critical functions to support its mandate.

- **Standards Development Division**:
    - Prepares and updates monographs for the Indian Pharmacopoeia.
    - Ensures that standards are scientifically validated and aligned with international benchmarks.
- **Pharmacovigilance Division**:
    - Manages the Pharmacovigilance Programme of India (PvPI), which monitors adverse drug reactions (ADRs) to improve patient safety.

- **Research and Analysis Division**:
    - Conducts research on drug formulations, analytical methods, and bioequivalence studies.
    - Collaborates with academic and industrial partners for innovation.
- **Quality Assurance Division**:
    - Ensures the accuracy and reliability of published pharmacopoeial standards.
    - Audits and certifies the performance of collaborating laboratories.

Regional and National Coordination

1. Collaboration with State Drug Control Laboratories

The IPC works closely with state drug control laboratories to ensure the uniform implementation of pharmacopoeial standards across India.

- **Role of State Laboratories**:
    - Test drug samples for compliance with pharmacopoeial standards.
    - Report findings to the IPC for updates or corrective actions.
- **Impact**:
    - Strengthens drug quality surveillance at the state level, ensuring consistency in enforcement.

---

2. Network of Pharmacopoeial Laboratories

The IPC has established a network of national and regional laboratories to enhance its reach and efficiency.

- **Central Indian Pharmacopoeial Laboratory (CIPL)**:
    - Serves as the central hub for pharmacopoeial testing and analysis.
    - Supports the development of reference standards and validation studies.
- **Regional Pharmacopoeial Laboratories**:
    - Provide localized support for testing and capacity building.
    - Help maintain uniformity in drug quality across different regions.

- **Public-Private Partnerships**:
  - Collaborations with private laboratories accredited by the National Accreditation Board for Testing and Calibration Laboratories (NABL).
  - Example: Partnering with private labs to expedite the analysis of complex drug formulations.

Expert Committees

1. Role of Scientific Experts in Developing Standards

The IPC relies on a network of scientific experts to ensure the scientific rigor and relevance of its pharmacopoeial standards.

- **Composition**:
  - Includes professionals from academia, research institutions, pharmaceutical companies, and regulatory bodies.
  - Draws on diverse expertise in pharmacology, analytical chemistry, biotechnology, and related fields.
- **Responsibilities**:
  - Review and approve monographs for inclusion in the Indian Pharmacopoeia.
  - Recommend updates to analytical methods and quality parameters.

---

2. Advisory Boards and Working Groups

- **Central Advisory Board**:
  - Provides strategic guidance on long-term goals and priorities.
  - Advises on policy issues related to the Indian Pharmacopoeia and its implementation.
- **Technical Working Groups**:
  - Tasked with specialized functions such as developing monographs for biopharmaceuticals or traditional medicines.
  - Conduct in-depth reviews of emerging trends and global best practices.
- **Impact of Committees**:
  - Ensures that the Indian Pharmacopoeia reflects the latest scientific advancements and industry needs.

  - Example: The inclusion of monographs for biosimilars and gene therapies resulted from expert committee recommendations.

5.2 Functions and Objectives of the Indian Pharmacopoeia Commission (IPC)

The Indian Pharmacopoeia Commission (IPC) performs a wide range of functions that are critical to ensuring the quality, safety, and efficacy of drugs in India. Its objectives revolve around developing the **Indian Pharmacopoeia (IP)**, standardizing pharmaceuticals, strengthening pharmacovigilance, building capacity within the healthcare sector, and promoting research and innovation.

Development and Publication of the Indian Pharmacopoeia

The IPC's flagship activity is the creation and periodic updating of the **Indian Pharmacopoeia**, which sets the official drug standards in the country.

---

1. Process of Compiling and Updating the Indian Pharmacopoeia

- **Data Collection and Review**:
  - The IPC collects scientific data on drugs and their formulations from manufacturers, research institutions, and regulatory authorities.
  - A detailed review of the data ensures that the standards are evidence-based and reflective of current pharmaceutical practices.
- **Expert Consultation**:
  - Committees comprising industry experts, academicians, and regulators review the data.
  - Suggestions for monographs, analytical methods, and test parameters are incorporated.
- **Public Feedback**:
  - Draft standards are made available for public consultation.
  - Feedback from stakeholders, including pharmaceutical companies and healthcare professionals, is considered before finalization.

- **Publication**:
  - The finalized standards are compiled into the **Indian Pharmacopoeia** and published.
  - Supplementary updates are issued periodically to include new drugs or update existing standards.

---

2. Inclusion Criteria for Drugs and Formulations

- **Relevance and Utility**:
  - Drugs must be widely used and relevant to public health.
  - Example: Antibiotics, antivirals, and vaccines for diseases prevalent in India.
- **Innovation**:
  - New drugs and formulations demonstrating significant therapeutic advancements are prioritized.
  - Example: Inclusion of biosimilars and gene therapies in recent editions.
- **Safety and Efficacy**:
  - Only drugs meeting stringent safety and efficacy criteria are included.

Standardization of Pharmaceuticals

Standardization ensures uniform quality across all drugs manufactured and marketed in India, building trust among healthcare providers and patients.

---

1. Defining Quality Benchmarks for Drugs

The IPC defines quality benchmarks to ensure drugs meet essential standards for safety and effectiveness.

- **Identity**:
  - Establishes the chemical and physical characteristics of a drug.
  - Example: Spectral identification using infrared or UV-visible spectroscopy.
- **Purity**:
  - Specifies permissible levels of impurities, ensuring safety.
  - Example: Setting limits for heavy metals or residual solvents in formulations.

- **Potency**:
    - Ensures that drugs contain the declared amount of active ingredient.
    - Example: Assay methods using high-performance liquid chromatography (HPLC).
- **Performance**:
    - Tests such as dissolution and disintegration assess the drug's behavior in biological conditions.

---

2. Parameters for Standardization

- **Analytical Methods**:
    - Validated methods for quantifying drug components.
    - Example: Chromatographic techniques for complex formulations.
- **Reference Standards**:
    - Official reference materials are used to calibrate testing methods.

Pharmacovigilance

Pharmacovigilance is integral to the IPC's mission, focusing on drug safety through monitoring and reporting systems.

---

1. Monitoring Adverse Drug Reactions (ADRs)

- **Pharmacovigilance Programme of India (PvPI)**:
    - The IPC acts as the **National Coordination Centre (NCC)** for PvPI.
    - Collects ADR data from hospitals, healthcare professionals, and patients.
- **ADR Reporting Mechanisms**:
    - Encourages reporting via mobile apps, online portals, and toll-free numbers.
    - Example: The "ADR Monitoring Centres" (AMCs) collect data for analysis.
- **Outcome**:
    - Identification of safety signals leading to regulatory actions, such as drug recalls or label modifications.

---

2. Role in Materiovigilance and Haemovigilance Programs

- **Materiovigilance**:
  - Focuses on monitoring adverse events related to medical devices.
  - Example: Reports on faulty implants or diagnostic kits leading to safety alerts.
- **Haemovigilance**:
  - Tracks adverse events in blood transfusion and its components.
  - Example: Reporting cases of transfusion reactions to improve blood safety.

Capacity Building

The IPC actively conducts training and workshops to enhance the skills of healthcare professionals, regulators, and industry personnel.

---

1. Training Programs for Healthcare Professionals

- **Topics Covered**:
  - Drug testing methods, pharmacovigilance reporting, and regulatory compliance.
- **Beneficiaries**:
  - Pharmacists, doctors, and quality assurance personnel.

---

2. Workshops for Regulatory Authorities and Pharmaceutical Companies

- **Objective**:
  - To familiarize stakeholders with updated pharmacopoeial standards and methodologies.
- **Example**:
  - Workshops on analytical techniques like mass spectrometry for regulators and manufacturers.

Research and Development

The IPC supports innovation to keep pace with advancements in pharmaceutical sciences.

---

1. Supporting Innovation in Analytical Methodologies

- **Development of New Methods**:
    - Research focuses on more accurate and efficient methods for drug analysis.
    - Example: Spectroscopic techniques for non-invasive testing.
- **Validation Studies**:
    - Ensures methods meet global standards for precision and reliability.

---

2. Collaborations with Academic and Research Institutions

- **Partnerships**:
    - Collaborates with universities and research labs to advance pharmaceutical science.
    - Example: Joint research projects on biopharmaceuticals or herbal formulations.
- **Knowledge Sharing**:
    - Publishes research findings in journals and conferences to disseminate knowledge.

5.3 Indian Pharmacopoeia (IP)

The **Indian Pharmacopoeia (IP)** serves as the official compendium of drug standards in India, ensuring the quality, safety, and efficacy of medicines. It plays a pivotal role in public health and the pharmaceutical industry, providing essential guidelines for regulatory compliance and drug development.

Overview of the Indian Pharmacopoeia

1. Definition and Purpose

The **Indian Pharmacopoeia (IP)** is a legally recognized book of standards that provides the specifications for the identity, purity, strength, and performance of drugs and pharmaceutical products.

- **Purpose**:
    - To ensure drugs meet defined quality benchmarks before they are approved for sale.
    - To safeguard public health by preventing the distribution of substandard medicines.

- **Scope**:
  - Covers modern drugs, traditional medicines, and biologicals.
  - Serves as a reference for testing and quality assurance in regulatory and industrial settings.

---

2. Significance in Ensuring Drug Quality and Regulatory Compliance

- **Quality Assurance**:
  - Establishes minimum standards that all drugs must meet to be marketed in India.
  - Example: Assay limits for active pharmaceutical ingredients (APIs).
- **Regulatory Compliance**:
  - Mandatory for drug manufacturers, importers, and regulators.
  - Facilitates uniform enforcement of drug quality laws across India.
- **Consumer Trust**:
  - Ensures that medicines reaching patients are safe, effective, and of high quality.

Editions and Updates

1. History and Evolution of IP Editions

The evolution of the Indian Pharmacopoeia reflects the progress of the pharmaceutical industry and advancements in scientific knowledge.

- **Initial Edition (1955)**:
  - Marked the transition from reliance on the **British Pharmacopoeia (BP)** to an independent Indian standard.
  - Focused primarily on essential medicines for public health needs.
- **Subsequent Editions**:
  - Each edition introduced updates reflecting technological advancements and the addition of new drugs.
  - Example: The inclusion of vaccines and antibiotics in response to emerging public health challenges.

---

2. Recent Updates and Key Changes in the Latest Edition

The latest edition of the Indian Pharmacopoeia demonstrates a commitment to modernity and global harmonization.

- **Key Updates**:
  - Addition of monographs for biologicals, biosimilars, and advanced drug delivery systems.
  - Revision of existing standards for accuracy and relevance.
- **Innovations**:
  - Incorporation of advanced analytical techniques like **mass spectrometry** and **nuclear magnetic resonance (NMR)**.
  - Enhanced focus on safety parameters, such as limits for impurities and contaminants.
- **Inclusion of Herbal Medicines**:
  - Increased recognition of traditional medicines with monographs for Ayurvedic, Siddha, and Unani formulations.

Components of the IP

The Indian Pharmacopoeia is structured into various sections, each addressing a specific aspect of drug quality and testing.

---

1. Monographs for Drugs and Formulations

- **Definition**:
  - Detailed descriptions of individual drugs, including their chemical composition, purity requirements, and assay methods.
- **Applications**:
  - Used by manufacturers and laboratories to ensure the quality of drugs during production and testing.

---

2. General Chapters on Analytical Techniques

- **Purpose**:
  - Provide standardized methods for testing drugs and formulations.
- **Examples**:
  - Chromatographic methods (HPLC, GC).
  - Spectroscopic techniques (UV-visible, IR, NMR).

---

3. Appendices Covering Test Methods and Specifications

- **Content**:
  - Guidelines for specialized tests such as dissolution, disintegration, and sterility testing.
  - Specifications for reagents, reference materials, and equipment.
- **Example**:
  - Appendices include methods for microbial limit testing and pyrogen testing.

Global Relevance

1. Harmonization with International Standards

The Indian Pharmacopoeia aligns with global pharmacopoeial standards to facilitate trade and regulatory acceptance.

- **International Standards**:
  - Draws on benchmarks set by the **United States Pharmacopeia (USP)**, **British Pharmacopoeia (BP)**, and **European Pharmacopoeia (EP)**.
- **Harmonization Initiatives**:
  - Incorporates globally recognized guidelines, such as those from the **International Council for Harmonisation (ICH)**.

---

2. Role of IP in Facilitating Exports

- **Global Acceptance**:
  - Indian pharmaceutical products are exported to over 200 countries, and adherence to IP standards ensures regulatory approval in international markets.
- **Support for Generics**:
  - IP standards play a critical role in the export of affordable generics, particularly to developing countries.
- **Case Example**:
  - Indian vaccines meeting IP standards have achieved global recognition through agencies like WHO and UNICEF.

5.4 Pharmacovigilance Programme of India (PvPI)

The **Pharmacovigilance Programme of India (PvPI)** is a flagship initiative aimed at ensuring the safety of drugs and protecting public health through the systematic monitoring and evaluation of adverse drug reactions (ADRs). Administered by the **Indian Pharmacopoeia Commission (IPC)** as the **National Coordination Centre (NCC)**, PvPI plays a vital role in strengthening India's healthcare infrastructure.

Introduction to PvPI

1. Definition and Objectives

Pharmacovigilance is the science of detecting, assessing, understanding, and preventing adverse effects or any other drug-related problems.

- **PvPI Definition**:
  - PvPI is India's national pharmacovigilance program launched in **2010** under the aegis of the Ministry of Health and Family Welfare.
  - Its mission is to ensure that the benefits of pharmaceutical products outweigh their risks.
- **Objectives**:
  - To collect, collate, and analyze ADR reports from across the country.
  - To improve patient safety by identifying drug-related risks.
  - To provide feedback to regulatory authorities for informed decision-making on drug safety.

---

2. Role of IPC as the National Coordination Centre (NCC)

The **Indian Pharmacopoeia Commission (IPC)** serves as the pivotal hub for PvPI operations.

- **Responsibilities**:
  - Coordinating activities across the country's ADR monitoring centers (AMCs).
  - Maintaining the National ADR database.
  - Providing training and technical support to healthcare professionals and institutions.
- **Key Functions**:
  - Evaluating ADR reports and identifying safety signals.

  - Collaborating with international pharmacovigilance programs such as the **WHO Programme for International Drug Monitoring**.

Operational Framework

PvPI operates through a structured framework that ensures the effective monitoring of ADRs and their integration into the healthcare system.

---

1. **Reporting Systems for Adverse Drug Reactions (ADRs)**
   - **Methods of Reporting**:
     - **Manual Reporting**:
       - Healthcare professionals and patients can report ADRs using physical ADR reporting forms available at AMCs.
     - **Digital Platforms**:
       - Mobile apps like the **ADR PvPI App** and online portals make it easier for users to report ADRs in real time.
       - Example: The app supports simplified reporting with features like dropdown menus for drug names and symptoms.
     - **Toll-Free Helpline**:
       - A dedicated helpline number allows patients and professionals to report ADRs directly.
   - **ADR Monitoring Centres (AMCs)**:
     - Over 350 AMCs across India are responsible for collecting and submitting ADR data to the IPC.
     - These centers are often located in major hospitals and academic institutions.

---

2. **Integration with Healthcare Providers and Pharmaceutical Companies**
   - **Collaboration with Healthcare Providers**:
     - Training programs for doctors, nurses, and pharmacists to recognize and report ADRs.
     - Regular awareness campaigns to highlight the importance of pharmacovigilance in clinical practice.

- **Engagement with Pharmaceutical Companies**:
  - Mandatory reporting of ADRs as part of post-marketing surveillance (PMS).
  - Pharmaceutical firms are required to submit periodic safety update reports (PSURs) for marketed drugs.
- **Data Flow**:
  - ADRs reported by AMCs and pharmaceutical companies are analyzed by IPC.
  - Insights from the data are shared with regulatory authorities, such as the **Central Drugs Standard Control Organization (CDSCO)**, for action.

Success Stories

The impact of PvPI can be best illustrated through examples of drugs flagged for safety concerns and the resulting regulatory actions.

---

1. Examples of Drugs Flagged for Safety Concerns

- **Nimesulide**:
  - An anti-inflammatory drug extensively used in India was flagged by PvPI due to reports of hepatotoxicity (liver damage).
  - **Outcome**:
    - Restrictions were imposed on its use in pediatric populations to minimize risks.
- **Ranitidine**:
  - Reports of contamination with **NDMA (N-nitrosodimethylamine)**, a probable carcinogen, led to global recalls.
  - **PvPI Contribution**:
    - Indian ADR data contributed to the regulatory decision to withdraw the drug from the market.
- **Antibiotics**:
  - Overuse and misuse of certain antibiotics flagged as contributing to antimicrobial resistance.
  - **Outcome**:
    - Strengthened guidelines for antibiotic prescriptions in hospitals.

---

2. Impact on Regulatory Actions and Patient Safety

- **Regulatory Decisions**:
  - PvPI findings have led to drug label updates, market withdrawals, and the introduction of stricter post-marketing surveillance.
- **Improved Safety**:
  - Patients benefit from better-informed prescribing practices and safer drugs.
- **Global Recognition**:
  - India's contributions to the WHO's global pharmacovigilance database highlight PvPI's growing credibility and importance in drug safety.

5.5 Role of IPC in Drug Regulation

The **Indian Pharmacopoeia Commission (IPC)** plays an essential role in regulating drugs in India by collaborating with regulatory authorities, ensuring compliance with quality standards, and harmonizing Indian drug standards with global benchmarks. Its efforts ensure that drugs in India meet stringent safety, efficacy, and quality requirements, safeguarding public health and promoting the growth of the pharmaceutical industry.

Collaboration with Regulatory Authorities

1. **Coordination with the Central Drugs Standard Control Organization (CDSCO)**

The IPC works closely with the **Central Drugs Standard Control Organization (CDSCO)**, which is the national regulatory body responsible for the approval, monitoring, and enforcement of drug standards in India.

- **Coordination Mechanisms**:
  - The IPC provides scientific and technical expertise to support CDSCO's regulatory functions.
  - Joint efforts in evaluating and approving new drug applications (NDAs) and abbreviated new drug applications (ANDAs).
- **Policy Guidance**:
  - IPC's pharmacopoeial standards form the foundation for CDSCO's regulatory policies.

- Example: IPC's standards for APIs and finished drug formulations are mandatory benchmarks during drug approval processes.

- **Post-Marketing Surveillance**:
  - IPC's **Pharmacovigilance Programme of India (PvPI)** collaborates with CDSCO to monitor adverse drug reactions (ADRs) and ensure the safety of drugs in the market.

---

2. Contributions to Policy-Making and Drug Approvals

- **Policy Formulation**:
  - The IPC provides scientific input during the drafting of policies related to drug regulation, including amendments to the Drugs and Cosmetics Act and the implementation of Good Manufacturing Practices (GMP).
- **Drug Approval Process**:
  - IPC plays a consultative role in evaluating the quality and analytical data submitted during drug approval processes.
  - Example: Analytical methods and reference standards developed by IPC are used to verify the quality of drugs during approval.
- **Advisory Role**:
  - IPC advises the government on the inclusion or exclusion of drugs from the **National List of Essential Medicines (NLEM)**, ensuring affordability and access to quality medicines.

Ensuring Compliance

1. Role of IPC in Conducting Inspections and Audits

- **Inspections**:
  - IPC supports regulatory authorities in inspecting manufacturing units, ensuring adherence to pharmacopoeial standards.
  - Example: Inspectors use IPC's monographs and test methods to verify drug quality during site visits.
- **Audits**:
  - IPC collaborates with state and central drug regulatory agencies to audit drug testing laboratories.

  - Ensures that these labs meet the quality benchmarks outlined in the Indian Pharmacopoeia.
- **Capacity Building**:
  - Conducts training programs for inspectors and auditors to enhance their understanding of pharmacopoeial standards and analytical methods.

---

2. Standard-Setting to Ensure Quality Control

- **Establishing Quality Standards**:
  - IPC sets mandatory quality standards for drugs, including specifications for identity, purity, strength, and performance.
- **Periodic Updates**:
  - Regularly updates standards in the **Indian Pharmacopoeia (IP)** to reflect advancements in science and technology.
  - Example: Recent updates include guidelines for biopharmaceuticals and advanced delivery systems.
- **Testing Methods**:
  - IPC develops validated analytical methods to ensure that drugs meet pharmacopoeial specifications.
  - Example: HPLC and spectrophotometric methods for API and excipient testing.

Global Harmonization

1. IPC's Participation in International Forums

The IPC actively engages with global organizations to harmonize Indian drug standards with international norms.

- **World Health Organization (WHO)**:
  - IPC collaborates with WHO on initiatives like the **International Pharmacopoeia** and prequalification of medicines.
  - Contributes to the WHO's database on essential medicines and pharmacovigilance.
- **International Council for Harmonisation (ICH)**:
  - IPC adopts guidelines from the ICH on the quality, safety, and efficacy of pharmaceuticals.
  - Example: Implementation of ICH Q3 guidelines on impurities in drug substances.

- **Pharmacopoeial Discussion Group (PDG)**:
    - IPC participates in discussions with global pharmacopoeias like the **USP**, **BP**, and **EP** to align standards and minimize differences.

---

2. Aligning Indian Drug Standards with Global Benchmarks

- **Harmonized Monographs**:
    - IPC ensures that Indian Pharmacopoeia monographs align with international pharmacopoeias for APIs and formulations.
    - Example: Standards for widely used antibiotics like amoxicillin are harmonized to facilitate global trade.
- **Facilitating Exports**:
    - Harmonization enhances the acceptance of Indian pharmaceuticals in regulated markets like the US, EU, and Japan.
    - Example: IPC's standards ensure that Indian generic drugs meet the stringent requirements of the USFDA and EMA.
- **Global Recognition**:
    - IPC's efforts have earned India a reputation for producing high-quality generics, positioning the country as the "Pharmacy of the World."

CHAPTER 6

Patents Act

Introduction to the Patents Act

Definition and Purpose of Patents

At its core, a **patent** is a form of intellectual property (IP) that grants an inventor exclusive rights to their invention. These rights allow the inventor to make, use, sell, or distribute their invention without unauthorized interference for a specified period. The primary purpose of patents is twofold:

1. **Encourage Innovation**: By offering legal protection, patents incentivize individuals and organizations to invest time, resources, and creativity in developing new technologies and solutions.
2. **Promote Knowledge Sharing**: Patent systems require inventors to publicly disclose detailed information about their inventions, fostering a culture of learning and further innovation.

Key Features of a Patent:

- Must be **novel**, meaning it has not been disclosed publicly anywhere in the world.
- Should involve an **inventive step** (non-obviousness) that is not easily deduced by someone skilled in the relevant field.
- Must have **industrial applicability**, ensuring it can be produced or used practically.

Historical Context and Evolution of Patent Laws Globally

The concept of protecting intellectual creations dates back centuries. Patent laws have evolved globally to balance the interests of inventors, the public, and the broader economy.

Early Beginnings:

- The origins of patents can be traced to **Venice, Italy, in 1474**, where the first patent statute was enacted to protect inventors for a fixed period.

- In **England**, the Statute of Monopolies (1624) established a legal foundation for granting patents.

Modern Patent Systems:

- The **United States Patent Act of 1790** formalized patent protection in the U.S., emphasizing innovation as a driver of economic growth.
- The **Paris Convention for the Protection of Industrial Property (1883)** was one of the first international agreements to establish uniform patent protections across member nations.
- **Post-World War II Developments**: The establishment of the **World Intellectual Property Organization (WIPO)** in 1967 and the **Trade-Related Aspects of Intellectual Property Rights (TRIPS) Agreement** in 1995 significantly harmonized patent laws globally, ensuring that inventors' rights were respected across borders.

Importance of Patent Protection in Fostering Innovation

Patents play a pivotal role in driving economic development and societal progress. The importance of patent protection is particularly evident in industries such as pharmaceuticals, technology, and manufacturing, where significant investments are made in R&D.

1. Incentivizing Research and Development:

- Innovators and companies are more likely to invest in R&D if assured of exclusive rights to reap the rewards of their efforts.
- Example: The pharmaceutical industry relies on patents to recover the substantial costs of drug development, which can exceed billions of dollars per drug.

2. Encouraging Knowledge Sharing:

- Patents require detailed disclosure of the invention, enabling others to learn from and build upon the innovation.
- This system fosters a culture of incremental advancements, driving overall progress.

3. Economic Benefits:

- Countries with strong patent systems often attract greater foreign direct investment (FDI), as investors seek environments that protect intellectual assets.
- Patents also stimulate job creation in high-tech industries.

4. Consumer Benefits:

- Patents lead to the development of new products and technologies, enhancing quality of life.
- From smartphones to life-saving drugs, many innovations owe their existence to the patent system.

Overview of the Patents Act in India

India's journey with patent laws reflects its unique socioeconomic and industrial needs, balancing the interests of innovators and the public.

1. The Patents Act, 1970:

- Before 1970, India followed the **British Patents and Designs Act, 1911**, which was not well-suited to the country's needs.
- The **Patents Act, 1970**, was a landmark law aimed at fostering domestic innovation while ensuring accessibility to essential technologies.

2. Key Features:

- Emphasized process patents in critical sectors like pharmaceuticals and agriculture, allowing multiple companies to manufacture the same product using different processes.
- Aimed to reduce monopolies in essential industries, ensuring affordability and accessibility.

3. TRIPS Compliance and Amendments:

- In response to India's obligations under the **TRIPS Agreement**, the Patents Act was amended in **1999**, **2002**, and **2005** to introduce product patents in sectors like pharmaceuticals and chemicals.
- These amendments aligned Indian patent law with global standards, ensuring better protection for innovators while balancing public interest.

4. Current Relevance:

- Today, the Indian patent system is a robust framework that supports innovation, attracts global investment, and addresses national priorities like public health and sustainability.
- The **Controller General of Patents, Designs, and Trade Marks (CGPDTM)** oversees the administration of patents in India, ensuring compliance with the law.

6.1 Understanding Patents

Patents are one of the most critical components of intellectual property rights, designed to foster innovation and protect inventors. This section explores the definition and scope of patents, types of patents, and the criteria for patentability, alongside exclusions under patent law.

Definition and Scope

Patents are legal rights granted by a government to an inventor for a specific period, giving them exclusive control over the use, production, and sale of their invention. The purpose of this exclusivity is to encourage innovation by allowing inventors to benefit financially from their creations.

What Constitutes a Patent?

A patent is a grant for an invention, which could be a product or a process. To qualify, the invention must meet specific criteria:

1. **Newness (Novelty)**: The invention must not have been disclosed or used publicly before the filing date.
2. **Inventiveness (Non-Obviousness)**: It must involve an inventive step, meaning it is not obvious to someone skilled in the relevant field.
3. **Industrial Applicability**: The invention should be capable of practical use in industry or commerce.

Patents are granted for a fixed term (usually 20 years), after which the invention enters the public domain, allowing unrestricted use.

Types of Patents

Patents can be categorized based on their subject matter and the scope of protection they offer:

1. **Utility Patents**:
    - Protect inventions with a functional aspect, such as machines, processes, or manufactured articles.
    - Example: The patent for the telephone by Alexander Graham Bell.
2. **Design Patents**:
    - Cover the ornamental or aesthetic aspects of a product, not its functionality.
    - Example: The unique shape of a Coca-Cola bottle.

3. **Plant Patents**:
   - Granted for new and distinct varieties of plants that are asexually reproduced.
   - Example: A patent for a hybrid rose plant.

Each type of patent serves a distinct purpose, ensuring comprehensive protection for different kinds of intellectual endeavors.

Patentable and Non-Patentable Subject Matter

Not every idea or discovery qualifies for a patent. Patent laws outline specific criteria that inventions must meet, as well as exclusions.

Criteria for Patentability

To be eligible for a patent, an invention must satisfy the following:

1. **Novelty**:
   - The invention must be new and not part of the prior art (existing knowledge or publicly available information).
   - Example: A new method of producing renewable energy that has not been disclosed in scientific literature or used commercially.
2. **Inventive Step**:
   - The invention must involve a step that is not obvious to someone skilled in the relevant field.
   - Example: Modifying an existing drug delivery system to make it more efficient.
3. **Industrial Applicability**:
   - The invention must have practical utility and be capable of being manufactured or used in industry.
   - Example: A new type of biodegradable plastic with applications in packaging.

Exclusions Under the Patents Act

Certain categories of discoveries or inventions are excluded from patent protection to balance innovation with ethical, scientific, and societal considerations. The **Indian Patents Act, 1970**, outlines these exclusions:

1. **Scientific Theories and Abstract Ideas**:
   - Laws of nature, mathematical formulas, and fundamental scientific principles cannot be patented.
   - Example: $E=mc^2$ is not patentable.

2. **Natural Processes and Biological Discoveries**:
   - Products of nature or biological processes occurring naturally are not patentable.
   - Example: A naturally occurring gene sequence cannot be patented, though a synthetically modified version might qualify.
3. **Inventions Contrary to Public Morality**:
   - Inventions that promote harm to society or contradict ethical norms are excluded.
   - Example: A machine designed for illegal activities.
4. **Business Methods and Software (without technical application)**:
   - Purely business-related methods or standalone software programs are not eligible unless they demonstrate a technical advancement.
   - Example: A method for calculating tax savings is not patentable, but software automating this calculation integrated into a device may qualify.
5. **Medical Procedures and Treatments**:
   - Processes for diagnosing, treating, or curing diseases in humans or animals are excluded.
   - Example: A surgical technique cannot be patented, though the equipment used in the surgery may be.
6. **Agricultural Processes**:
   - Processes essential to agriculture or horticulture are excluded from patentability.
   - Example: Methods for growing crops or breeding animals.

6.2 The Indian Patents Act, 1970

The Indian Patents Act, 1970, is a landmark legislation that marked the beginning of a structured intellectual property framework in India. It has evolved over time to balance the needs of public welfare, innovation, and compliance with international standards. This section delves into the historical background, objectives, and significant amendments to the Act.

Historical Background

Pre-1970 Patent Laws in India

Before the introduction of the Indian Patents Act, 1970, India operated under the **British Patents and Designs Act, 1911**. While this legislation provided a framework for patent protection, it was ill-suited to India's socio-economic landscape.

- **Key Issues**:
    - Focused predominantly on product patents, including pharmaceuticals, leading to monopolistic practices by foreign companies.
    - Resulted in high drug prices and limited access to essential medicines.
    - Did not encourage domestic innovation or manufacturing.

Introduction of the Patents Act, 1970

The shortcomings of the British-era law, coupled with India's developmental priorities post-independence, led to the formulation of the **Patents Act, 1970**. This Act was a direct outcome of recommendations made by the **Ayyangar Committee** in 1959.

- **Salient Features of the 1970 Act**:
    - Shifted focus to **process patents** in key industries like pharmaceuticals and food.
    - Reduced the patent term for process patents to 7 years and for others to 14 years.
    - Excluded inventions related to atomic energy from patentability.
    - Established the **Controller General of Patents, Designs, and Trademarks (CGPDTM)** to oversee patent administration.

The Act aimed to make essential goods affordable while fostering an environment conducive to domestic research and development.

Key Objectives

The Patents Act, 1970, was designed with clear objectives that aligned with India's socio-economic priorities.

1. Balancing Innovation with Public Interest

- **Affordability of Essential Goods**:
  - By granting process patents instead of product patents in critical sectors, the Act allowed domestic companies to manufacture drugs using alternative processes, leading to reduced prices.
  - Example: India became a leading supplier of affordable generic medicines globally.
- **Encouraging Access to Technology**:
  - The Act facilitated technology transfer and discouraged monopolies, ensuring widespread availability of innovations.

2. Encouraging Domestic R&D

- **Focus on Indigenous Innovation**:
  - The limited scope of product patents incentivized Indian companies to invest in **process innovations**.
  - Result: A thriving generic drug industry, with companies like Cipla, Sun Pharma, and Dr. Reddy's Laboratories emerging as global leaders.
- **Building Research Ecosystems**:
  - The Act fostered collaboration between industry and academia, laying the foundation for robust R&D capabilities in pharmaceuticals, agriculture, and technology.

Amendments to the Act

The Indian Patents Act has undergone significant amendments to adapt to changing global standards and domestic requirements. These amendments were particularly crucial for compliance with the **TRIPS Agreement** under the World Trade Organization (WTO).

1. The 1999 Amendment

- **Objective**:
  - Established a transitional framework for TRIPS compliance.
- **Key Provisions**:
  - Allowed **Exclusive Marketing Rights (EMRs)** for pharmaceutical and agricultural chemical products until a full-fledged product patent regime could be implemented.

  - Introduced provisions for the filing of **mailbox applications**, ensuring that patent claims filed during the transitional period could be reviewed once the product patent regime was established.

2. The 2002 Amendment

- **Objective**:
  - Strengthened the procedural framework for patent protection.
- **Key Changes**:
  - Extended the patent term uniformly to **20 years** for all patents.
  - Introduced the concept of a **patent of addition**, allowing incremental innovations to be patented.
  - Expanded the definition of "invention" to include software in combination with hardware, encouraging innovation in emerging fields like IT and electronics.
  - Enhanced provisions for opposition, enabling public and competitors to challenge frivolous or invalid patents.

3. The 2005 Amendment

- **Objective**:
  - Fully aligned Indian patent laws with TRIPS, introducing a product patent regime in pharmaceuticals, chemicals, and biotechnology.
- **Key Changes**:
  - Allowed **product patents** in previously restricted sectors, such as pharmaceuticals and food.
  - Introduced **compulsory licensing** provisions, enabling generic production of patented products under specific conditions (e.g., affordability and public health emergencies).
  - Strengthened opposition mechanisms with **pre-grant and post-grant opposition** options to enhance scrutiny of patent applications.

Impact of TRIPS Compliance

- **Global Integration**:
  - Brought India's patent laws in line with international standards, facilitating trade and attracting foreign direct investment (FDI).

- **Balancing Act**:
    - The amendments maintained provisions like compulsory licensing and patent exclusions to address public health concerns, earning India a reputation as the "pharmacy of the world."

6.3 Key Provisions of the Patents Act

The Indian Patents Act outlines the essential processes and regulations for patent protection. This section explores the application and filing process, the granting of patents, the rights conferred by a patent, and the term of patent protection, providing a comprehensive understanding of how the law facilitates and regulates innovation.

Application and Filing Process

The patent application process is the first step in securing legal protection for an invention. It is critical to ensure accuracy and compliance with the procedural requirements outlined in the Patents Act.

1. Types of Applications

- **Provisional Application**:
    - Filed when the invention is in a developmental stage and the applicant requires more time to refine or complete it.
    - **Benefits:**
        - Establishes a **priority date**, which can be crucial in case of disputes.
        - Provides a window of **12 months** to file the complete specification.
    - Example: An inventor may file a provisional application for a new drug formula while awaiting clinical trial results.
- **Complete Application**:
    - Filed with detailed specifications and claims that define the invention.
    - **Must include:**
        - A detailed description of the invention.
        - Claims outlining the scope of protection sought.
        - Drawings or models, if necessary.

2. Timeline and Fees Associated with Patent Filing

- **Timeline**:
    - Filing a complete specification (after a provisional application): Within **12 months**.
    - Publication of the application: Typically occurs after **18 months** from the filing date unless an early publication request is made.
    - Examination request: Must be filed within **48 months** from the priority date.
- **Fees**:
    - Filing fees vary based on the applicant type (individual, small entity, or large entity).
    - Additional costs include fees for patent examinations, claims beyond a specified limit, and renewals.

Grant of Patent

Securing a patent involves a rigorous process to ensure compliance with the criteria for patentability.

1. Examination Process

- After filing, the application undergoes a **formal examination** to verify compliance with procedural requirements.
- **Substantive Examination**:
    - Determines if the invention meets the criteria of novelty, inventive step, and industrial applicability.
    - The examiner may issue a **First Examination Report (FER)**, highlighting deficiencies or objections.

2. Opposition Mechanisms

The Patents Act provides mechanisms to challenge patent applications to ensure the system is not exploited for frivolous claims.

- **Pre-Grant Opposition**:
    - Can be filed by any person within **6 months** of the application's publication or before the grant of the patent.
    - Grounds: Lack of novelty, prior disclosure, or insufficient disclosure.
- **Post-Grant Opposition**:
    - Can be filed within **1 year** of the grant by any interested party.

   - Grounds: Fraudulent claims, violation of patentability criteria, or wrongful obtainment.

3. Role of the Patent Office and Controller General

- The **Indian Patent Office**, under the **Controller General of Patents, Designs, and Trade Marks (CGPDTM)**, oversees the examination, grant, and maintenance of patents.
- **Functions:**
   - Assess applications and grant patents.
   - Resolve disputes during opposition proceedings.
   - Maintain patent records and ensure transparency.

Rights Conferred by a Patent

A granted patent provides the inventor with exclusive rights, but these rights come with limitations to balance public and private interests.

1. Exclusive Rights

- The patentee has the right to:
   - **Make** the invention.
   - **Use** it for commercial or industrial purposes.
   - **Sell** or **distribute** it in any jurisdiction where it is patented.
   - **License** or **assign** rights to others.
- Example: A pharmaceutical company with a patent for a new drug can license its production to multiple manufacturers while retaining ownership.

2. Limitations and Exceptions

- **Compulsory Licensing**:
   - In cases of public health emergencies or when the patented product is unaffordable or unavailable, the government can issue a compulsory license.
   - Example: Generic versions of expensive life-saving drugs.
- **Fair Use Provisions**:
   - Experimental use for educational or research purposes is permitted without infringing the patent.
   - Use of a patented process for private, non-commercial purposes is also allowed.

Term of a Patent

The duration of patent protection is finite, ensuring inventors benefit from their creations while eventually allowing public access.

1. Duration of Patent Protection

- Patents in India are granted for a period of **20 years** from the date of filing the application.
- For international applications filed under the **Patent Cooperation Treaty (PCT)**, the term starts from the international filing date.

2. Renewal and Maintenance

- **Annual Fees**:
  - To keep a patent active, the patentee must pay **annual renewal fees** starting from the 3rd year.
  - Non-payment results in the patent **lapsing**.
- **Restoration**:
  - Lapsed patents can be restored within a specific period, provided the delay in renewal was unintentional.

6.4 Patents in Pharmaceutical and Biotech Industries

The pharmaceutical and biotechnology industries are highly reliant on innovation and intellectual property protection. Patents in these sectors play a critical role in safeguarding new discoveries, ensuring return on investment, and balancing innovation with public health needs.

Significance of Patents in Pharma

The pharmaceutical and biotech industries involve substantial investments in research and development (R&D), with long development cycles and high failure rates. Patents serve as a cornerstone for protecting innovations and driving advancements.

---

1. Protecting Innovations in Drug Development

- **Exclusive Rights**:
  - A patent provides the innovator with exclusive rights to manufacture, use, and sell their invention for a specified period (20 years in India).
  - This exclusivity allows companies to recoup the significant costs associated with drug development, including preclinical trials, clinical testing, and regulatory approvals.

  - Example: The patent on Lipitor (atorvastatin) by Pfizer allowed the company to maintain exclusivity, generating billions in revenue before it became generic.
- **Incentivizing Innovation**:
  - Patents encourage pharmaceutical companies to invest in high-risk projects, such as developing treatments for rare diseases or complex conditions.
  - Example: Biotech companies often rely on patent portfolios to attract funding for cutting-edge technologies like gene therapies and biologics.

---

2. Promoting Investment in R&D

- **High R&D Costs**:
  - The average cost of developing a new drug is estimated at $2.6 billion, considering the expenses of failed projects.
  - Patents offer a pathway to recover these investments through market exclusivity.
- **Attracting Investors**:
  - Robust patent portfolios enhance the valuation of pharmaceutical and biotech companies, making them attractive to investors and venture capitalists.
  - Example: Startups in biotechnology often secure patents for innovative drug delivery systems or monoclonal antibodies to secure funding for commercialization.
- **Global Competitiveness**:
  - Patents help Indian pharmaceutical companies compete globally by fostering innovation in generic drugs, biosimilars, and new formulations.
  - Example: Dr. Reddy's Laboratories and Biocon have leveraged patents to establish their presence in international markets.

Compulsory Licensing

Compulsory licensing is a mechanism under the Indian Patents Act that allows the government or a third party to produce a patented product without the patent holder's consent under specific conditions.

---

1. Definition and Conditions Under the Patents Act

- **What is Compulsory Licensing?**
    - It permits the use of a patented invention without the authorization of the patent holder, typically to address public health concerns or supply shortages.
- **Conditions for Granting Compulsory Licenses**:

  The patented product is not reasonably affordable to the public.

    1. The invention is not available in sufficient quantities to meet public demand.
    2. The patented invention is not being worked on in the territory of India.
- **Section 84 of the Indian Patents Act** governs the criteria and application for compulsory licenses.

---

2. Case Studies

- **Natco Pharma vs. Bayer (2012)**:
    - Bayer held a patent for Nexavar, a cancer drug priced at INR 2.8 lakh per month.
    - Natco Pharma applied for a compulsory license, arguing the drug was unaffordable and not sufficiently available in India.
    - Outcome:
        - The Indian Patent Office granted Natco the license to produce a generic version at INR 8,800 per month, making it accessible to a broader population.
        - Bayer received 6% of Natco's sales as royalty.
- **Global Implications**:
    - This case positioned India as a proponent of balancing patent protection with public health needs, earning both praise and criticism internationally.

Evergreening of Patents

Evergreening refers to strategies employed by pharmaceutical companies to extend the exclusivity period of their patents, often delaying the entry of generics into the market.

---

1. Strategies Used by Pharmaceutical Companies

- **Minor Modifications**:
  - Filing secondary patents for slight modifications, such as new formulations, dosing regimens, or delivery methods.
  - Example: Reformulating a tablet into a sustained-release version and patenting it anew.
- **Combination Patents**:
  - Patenting combinations of existing drugs to claim a new invention.
  - Example: A fixed-dose combination of two well-known drugs.
- **Patenting Polymorphs**:
  - Securing patents for different crystalline forms of the same chemical compound.

---

2. Legal and Ethical Implications

- **Legal Challenges**:
  - Courts worldwide, including India, have questioned the legitimacy of evergreening tactics.
  - Section 3(d) of the Indian Patents Act explicitly prevents patenting of incremental innovations unless they demonstrate enhanced efficacy.
  - Landmark Case:
    - **Novartis vs. Union of India (2013)**:
      - Novartis sought a patent for a new form of its cancer drug Gleevec.
      - The Indian Supreme Court denied the patent, stating the new form did not demonstrate significantly enhanced efficacy over the original.
- **Ethical Concerns**:
  - Critics argue that evergreening keeps drug prices artificially high, restricting access to life-saving medications.
  - Advocates claim it incentivizes continued R&D to improve existing drugs.

6.5 International Framework and Indian Compliance

The Indian patent system operates within a global framework that harmonizes intellectual property (IP) rights across countries. International agreements and organizations such as the **TRIPS Agreement**, **World Intellectual Property Organization (WIPO)**, and the **Paris Convention** play pivotal roles in shaping India's patent policies and ensuring compliance with global standards.

TRIPS Agreement

The **Agreement on Trade-Related Aspects of Intellectual Property Rights (TRIPS)**, established under the **World Trade Organization (WTO)** in 1995, is one of the most significant international agreements governing IP rights. TRIPS sets minimum standards for the protection and enforcement of IP rights, including patents.

---

1. Overview and Significance in Global IP Laws

- **Global Standardization**:
  - TRIPS created a uniform framework for IP rights across member nations, promoting fair trade and innovation while reducing disparities in IP protection levels.
  - Key Features:
    - Minimum protection standards for patents, trademarks, copyrights, and trade secrets.
    - Enforcement mechanisms to address IP violations.
- **Patents under TRIPS**:
  - Member countries must provide patent protection for inventions across all fields of technology.
  - The minimum duration of patent protection is **20 years** from the date of filing.
- **Flexibilities**:
  - TRIPS includes provisions for **compulsory licensing** and **exceptions** to patent rights, allowing countries to address public health needs and other critical issues.

---

2. India's Obligations Under TRIPS

India, as a WTO member, was required to align its IP laws with TRIPS standards. This process significantly influenced amendments to the **Indian**

Patents Act, 1970.

- **Timeline for Compliance**:
    - India utilized the **transitional period** (1995–2005) provided to developing countries for implementing product patents in sectors like pharmaceuticals and agriculture.
    - Measures during the transitional period included the introduction of **Exclusive Marketing Rights (EMRs)** and a **mailbox system** to protect patent applications filed during this phase.
- **Key Amendments**:
    - **1999 Amendment**: Allowed filing of product patent applications under the mailbox system.
    - **2002 Amendment**: Strengthened procedural aspects of patent applications and extended the patent term to 20 years.
    - **2005 Amendment**: Introduced product patents for pharmaceuticals, chemicals, and food, fully complying with TRIPS.
- **Impact on India**:
    - Enhanced India's integration into the global IP ecosystem.
    - Maintained provisions such as **Section 3(d)** to safeguard public health by preventing the patenting of incremental innovations without significant efficacy.

WIPO (World Intellectual Property Organization)

Established in 1967, **WIPO** is a specialized agency of the United Nations dedicated to promoting innovation and creativity through effective IP protection.

---

1. Role in Facilitating Global Patent Cooperation

- **Patent Cooperation Treaty (PCT)**:
    - Administered by WIPO, the PCT simplifies the process of filing patent applications in multiple countries.
    - Features:
        - A single international application filed under the PCT is recognized in over 150 member countries.
        - Provides an **international search report** and a preliminary examination to assess patentability.

- **Capacity Building**:
  - WIPO conducts training programs, workshops, and knowledge-sharing initiatives to help countries strengthen their IP systems.
  - Example: WIPO's collaboration with India to support startups and small businesses in navigating the patent process.
- **Global Databases**:
  - WIPO offers access to patent databases like **PATENTSCOPE**, enabling inventors to conduct prior art searches and identify existing patents.

Paris Convention

The **Paris Convention for the Protection of Industrial Property (1883)** was one of the first international treaties to establish principles for IP protection across member nations.

---

1. Principles of National Treatment and Priority Rights

- **National Treatment**:
  - Member countries must treat foreign applicants equally to their own nationals regarding IP rights.
  - Example: An Indian inventor filing a patent in the United States under the Paris Convention receives the same rights as a U.S. citizen.
- **Right of Priority**:
  - Allows an applicant to file for patent protection in multiple member countries using the original filing date as a priority date.
  - Priority Period:
    - Patents: 12 months.
    - Trademarks: 6 months.
  - Example: An Indian inventor filing a patent in India can claim the same priority date when applying in Germany within 12 months.
- **Provisions for IP Enforcement**:
  - The Paris Convention requires member countries to provide legal frameworks for protecting industrial property, including patents, trademarks, and trade secrets.

India's Compliance with International Frameworks

India's participation in global IP agreements reflects its commitment to fostering innovation while safeguarding public welfare.

- **Integration with WIPO and PCT**:
  - India became a member of WIPO in 1975 and joined the PCT in 1998, enabling Indian inventors to file patents internationally with greater ease.
- **TRIPS-Plus Measures**:
  - India has resisted adopting TRIPS-Plus provisions, such as extending patent terms or limiting compulsory licensing, to maintain a balance between innovation and accessibility.
- **Leveraging the Paris Convention**:
  - Indian inventors and companies frequently use the priority rights offered by the Paris Convention to expand their patent protection internationally.

6.6 Patent Infringement and Enforcement

Patent infringement occurs when an unauthorized party uses, makes, sells, or distributes a patented invention without the patent holder's consent. This section explores the types of infringement, legal remedies available to patent holders, and defenses against infringement claims.

Types of Infringement

Understanding the various forms of patent infringement is critical to enforcing patent rights effectively.

---

1. Direct Infringement

- **Definition**:
  - Occurs when an entity directly uses, produces, sells, or distributes a patented invention without authorization.
- **Example**:
  - A company manufacturing a patented drug without obtaining a license from the patent holder.
- **Key Characteristics**:
  - Does not require intent or knowledge of the patent's existence.
  - Considered a strict liability offense.

---

2. Indirect Infringement

- **Definition**:
  - Involves encouraging or aiding another party to commit direct infringement.
- **Example**:
  - A supplier providing components specifically designed to be used in a patented invention, knowing their intended use infringes on the patent.
- **Key Characteristics**:
  - Requires proof that the party had knowledge of the patent and intended to facilitate infringement.

---

3. Contributory Infringement

- **Definition**:
  - A subset of indirect infringement, where a party supplies a non-staple product or component specifically for use in a patented invention.
- **Example**:
  - A company selling a specialized part that has no substantial non-infringing use other than in a patented invention.
- **Key Characteristics**:
  - Requires the infringing component to be integral to the patented invention.

Legal Remedies

Patent holders can seek legal recourse to protect their rights and mitigate losses from infringement.

---

1. Injunctions

- **Definition**:
  - A court order that prevents the infringer from continuing the infringing activity.
- **Types**:
  - **Preliminary Injunction**: Issued during litigation to stop infringement until the case is resolved.
  - **Permanent Injunction**: Granted after the court rules in favor of the patent holder.

- **Example**:
  - A court halting the production of counterfeit versions of a patented drug.

---

2. Damages

- **Definition**:
  - Monetary compensation awarded to the patent holder for losses caused by infringement.
- **Types**:
  - **Compensatory Damages**: Cover actual financial losses, such as lost profits.
  - **Punitive Damages**: Imposed to penalize willful infringement and deter future violations.
- **Example**:
  - A company paying damages for selling unlicensed products that competed with the patent holder's offerings.

---

3. Accounts of Profits

- **Definition**:
  - An order requiring the infringer to pay the profits earned from the infringing activity to the patent holder.
- **Example**:
  - A court ruling that a company must surrender profits earned from manufacturing a patented product without authorization.

---

4. Criminal Penalties

- **Definition**:
  - In cases of willful infringement, criminal penalties may be imposed, including fines or imprisonment.
- **Scope**:
  - Typically applies to large-scale counterfeiting or deliberate violation of patent rights.
- **Example**:
  - A company found guilty of mass-producing counterfeit patented goods.

Defenses Against Infringement

An accused infringer may present defenses to avoid liability, provided they meet specific legal criteria.

---

1. Prior Use Defense

- **Definition**:
  - A defense used when the accused party can prove that they were using the patented invention commercially before the patent was filed.
- **Legal Basis**:
  - Recognized under Section 104 of the Indian Patents Act.
- **Example**:
  - A company demonstrating that they had already been producing a patented product for commercial purposes before the patent holder filed their application.

---

2. Experimental Use Exception

- **Definition**:
  - An exception that allows the use of a patented invention for research or experimentation without constituting infringement.
- **Scope**:
  - Limited to non-commercial research aimed at improving or understanding the patented invention.
- **Example**:
  - A university conducting experiments to improve the efficiency of a patented solar panel design.

6.7 Filing and Managing Patents

Managing the lifecycle of a patent, from filing to maintenance, is a critical aspect of intellectual property management. This section explores the Indian Patent Office's structure and functions, the process of filing international patent applications under the Patent Cooperation Treaty (PCT), and the requirements for maintaining patents over their term.

Indian Patent Office

The Indian Patent Office, administered under the Office of the **Controller General of Patents, Designs, and Trademarks (CGPDTM)**, is the primary authority responsible for patent-related activities in India.

---

1. Structure and Jurisdiction

The Indian Patent Office operates through a decentralized structure with regional offices to cater to applicants from various parts of the country.

- **Regional Patent Offices**:
    - Located in **Delhi, Mumbai, Chennai, and Kolkata**.
    - Each office has jurisdiction over specific states and union territories.
    - Example: The Chennai Patent Office handles applications from southern states like Tamil Nadu and Karnataka.
- **Centralized Coordination**:
    - While each office manages filings within its jurisdiction, certain administrative tasks, such as international applications, are centralized under the CGPDTM.

---

2. Role of the Patent Controller

The **Patent Controller** is the authority overseeing patent administration in India, with several critical responsibilities:

- **Examination and Granting of Patents**:
    - Ensures that patent applications meet the criteria of **novelty, inventive step, and industrial applicability**.
    - Issues reports during the examination process and determines whether a patent should be granted.
- **Adjudication of Disputes**:
    - Handles oppositions to patent applications, both pre-grant and post-grant.
    - Resolves disputes regarding patent validity or infringement.
- **Maintenance of Patent Records**:
    - Ensures the accurate recording of patent grants, assignments, and licenses.
- **International Cooperation**:
    - Facilitates India's participation in global patent systems, including the PCT.

International Patent Applications

For innovators targeting global markets, international patent applications provide a streamlined way to secure protection in multiple jurisdictions.

---

1. Filing Under the Patent Cooperation Treaty (PCT)

The **Patent Cooperation Treaty (PCT)**, administered by the **World Intellectual Property Organization (WIPO)**, offers a unified system for filing patents in multiple countries.

- **Steps in PCT Filing**:
    1. **Filing the International Application**:
        - Applicants file a single application in one language at a receiving office (e.g., the Indian Patent Office for Indian applicants).
    2. **International Search Report**:
        - An examination identifies prior art relevant to the invention.
    3. **National Phase Entry**:
        - After the international phase, the applicant must proceed with the national patenting process in each designated country.
- **Timeline**:
    - PCT provides up to **30 months** from the filing date for the applicant to decide on entering the national phase, giving ample time to assess market potential.

---

2. Benefits of PCT for Indian Innovators

- **Cost-Effectiveness**:
    - A single application reduces the initial costs of filing in multiple countries, with national filing fees deferred to the national phase.
- **Strategic Decision-Making**:
    - The international search report helps inventors evaluate the patentability of their invention before committing to national filings.
- **Global Reach**:
    - The PCT is recognized by over **150 member countries**, simplifying global patent protection for Indian innovators.

Patent Maintenance

Securing a patent is only the beginning. Maintaining it requires adherence to procedural requirements, including fee payments and renewals.

---

1. Annual Fees and Penalties for Non-Payment

- **Annual Renewal Fees**:
  - Patentees must pay **annual fees** starting from the third year of the patent's life.
  - Fees increase progressively as the patent term progresses.
  - Example: A patent granted in 2023 will require renewal fees starting from 2026.
- **Penalties for Non-Payment**:
  - Failure to pay renewal fees results in the patent **lapsing**, rendering it unenforceable.
  - Example: A company unable to pay renewal fees for a patented drug may lose exclusivity, allowing competitors to produce it.

---

2. Restoration of Lapsed Patents

- **Procedure for Restoration**:
  - A lapsed patent can be restored if the patentee applies for restoration within **18 months** of the lapse, demonstrating that the failure to pay was unintentional.
  - The Patent Office reviews the application and may reinstate the patent with additional penalties.
- **Impact of Restoration**:
  - Restored patents regain full enforceability, though any actions taken by third parties during the lapse period may be exempt from infringement claims.

6.8 Patents and Public Interest

Patents are essential for fostering innovation, but their impact on public interest—especially in critical areas like healthcare and technology—raises important questions about accessibility, affordability, and ethics. This section explores the delicate balance between protecting intellectual property and addressing societal needs, with a focus on access to medicines, technology transfer, and ethical considerations.

Access to Medicines

Patents in the pharmaceutical industry have a profound impact on the pricing and availability of life-saving drugs. While patents incentivize innovation, they can also create barriers to affordable healthcare.

---

1. Impact of Patents on Drug Pricing and Availability

- **Exclusive Rights and Pricing Power**:
    - Patents grant companies exclusive rights to produce and sell their inventions, enabling them to set high prices to recoup R&D costs.
    - Example: New cancer drugs often debut at prices exceeding thousands of dollars per dose, placing them out of reach for many patients in low- and middle-income countries.
- **Challenges in Developing Countries**:
    - High drug prices disproportionately affect developing nations where healthcare infrastructure is limited, and out-of-pocket expenses dominate healthcare spending.
    - Example: The HIV/AIDS epidemic in Africa highlighted the tension between patented antiretroviral drugs and the urgent need for affordable treatment.
- **Generic Competition Post-Patent Expiry**:
    - Once a patent expires, generic manufacturers can produce cheaper versions, significantly lowering prices.
    - Example: The cost of antiretroviral therapy for HIV/AIDS dropped dramatically when generics became available.

---

2. Balancing Patent Rights with Public Health Needs

- **Compulsory Licensing**:
    - Governments can issue compulsory licenses to allow the production of patented drugs without the consent of the patent holder, particularly during public health emergencies.
    - Example: India's issuance of a compulsory license to Natco Pharma for producing a generic version of Bayer's cancer drug Nexavar.
- **TRIPS Flexibilities**:
    - The WTO's TRIPS Agreement includes provisions for balancing patent rights with public health, such as compulsory licensing and parallel imports.

  - Example: The Doha Declaration reaffirmed the right of WTO members to prioritize public health over patent enforcement.
- **Collaborative Models**:
  - Voluntary licensing and patent pools provide alternative solutions for improving drug access.
  - Example: The Medicines Patent Pool (MPP) facilitates licensing agreements between pharmaceutical companies and generic manufacturers to expand access to HIV, hepatitis, and tuberculosis treatments.

Technology Transfer

Patents not only protect inventions but also play a vital role in facilitating the sharing and commercialization of knowledge across borders and industries.

---

1. Role of Patents in Facilitating Knowledge Sharing

- **Encouraging Collaboration**:
  - Patents incentivize companies to share their innovations through licensing agreements, enabling other entities to build upon existing technologies.
  - Example: Biotechnology firms often license patented research tools, such as CRISPR gene-editing technology, to universities and startups for further development.
- **Promoting Industrial Growth**:
  - Technology transfer agreements facilitated by patents can drive industrial growth in developing countries by providing access to advanced technologies.
  - Example: India's pharmaceutical sector benefited from licensing agreements that enabled the production of generic drugs using patented processes.

---

2. Examples of Successful Technology Licensing Agreements

- **Agricultural Innovations**:
  - The Green Revolution in India was partly driven by the transfer of patented agricultural technologies, including high-yield crop varieties and advanced irrigation systems.

- **Pharmaceutical Breakthroughs**:
  - Gilead Sciences licensed its patents for hepatitis C drugs to generic manufacturers, enabling the production of affordable treatments in developing countries.
- **Clean Energy**:
  - Patent licensing in renewable energy technologies, such as solar panels and wind turbines, has facilitated global adoption of sustainable energy solutions.

Ethical Considerations

The expansion of patentable subject matter, particularly in life sciences, raises ethical questions about the boundaries of intellectual property rights.

---

1. Debate on Patenting Life Forms and Genetic Material

- **Patenting of Genes**:
  - The ability to patent isolated genetic material has sparked debates about whether genes, as natural entities, should be excluded from patent protection.
  - Example: The case of Myriad Genetics, where the U.S. Supreme Court invalidated patents on BRCA1 and BRCA2 genes linked to breast cancer, ruling that naturally occurring DNA cannot be patented.
- **Ethics of Life Form Patents**:
  - Patenting genetically modified organisms (GMOs) has been controversial, particularly in agriculture.
  - Supporters argue that patents incentivize innovation, while critics highlight concerns about corporate control over food supply and biodiversity.
  - Example: Monsanto's patents on genetically engineered seeds have led to legal disputes with farmers over seed reuse.
- **Impact on Developing Nations**:
  - The patenting of traditional knowledge, such as medicinal plants, raises ethical and economic concerns about exploitation without fair compensation.
  - Example: The patenting of neem and turmeric by foreign entities led to widespread opposition and eventual revocation of these patents.

6.9 Disputes and Litigation

Patent disputes are inevitable in a system that aims to balance innovation with public access. This section delves into notable patent disputes in India, alternative dispute resolution (ADR) mechanisms like mediation and arbitration, and the pivotal role of the judiciary in shaping Indian patent law.

Notable Patent Disputes in India

India has witnessed several high-profile patent disputes that have shaped its intellectual property landscape. These cases illustrate the complexities of enforcing patent rights while balancing public interest.

---

1. Novartis vs. Union of India (Gleevec Case)

- **Overview**:
    - Swiss pharmaceutical giant Novartis sought a patent in India for a beta-crystalline form of imatinib mesylate (marketed as Gleevec), a life-saving cancer drug.
    - The application was denied under **Section 3(d)** of the Indian Patents Act, which restricts patents for incremental innovations unless they demonstrate enhanced efficacy.
- **Legal Arguments**:
    - **Novartis**:
        - Claimed that the new form was more stable and absorbed better by the body.
    - **Indian Authorities**:
        - Argued that the new form did not show significantly enhanced therapeutic efficacy over the known substance.
- **Outcome**:
    - In 2013, the **Supreme Court of India** upheld the rejection, stating that granting a patent would hinder the availability of affordable generic versions.
- **Significance**:
    - Strengthened India's position as a global leader in affordable generics.
    - Set a precedent for applying Section 3(d) to prevent "evergreening" of patents.

---

2. Roche vs. Cipla (Tarceva Case)

- **Overview**:
    - Roche, a global pharmaceutical company, sued Cipla, an Indian generic manufacturer, for infringing its patent on **erlotinib**, a cancer drug marketed as Tarceva.
- **Legal Arguments**:
    - **Roche**:
        - Claimed that Cipla's generic version violated its patent rights.
    - **Cipla**:
        - Defended the case on grounds of public interest, arguing that affordable generics were essential for cancer patients in India.
- **Outcome**:
    - The **Delhi High Court** ruled in favor of Cipla, citing public interest as a key factor in denying Roche an injunction.
- **Significance**:
    - Highlighted the judiciary's role in balancing patent rights with the public's access to affordable medicines.
    - Demonstrated the importance of considering public health in patent litigation.

Mediation and Arbitration

Patent disputes can often be lengthy and costly. Alternative dispute resolution (ADR) mechanisms, such as mediation and arbitration, offer a quicker and more flexible approach to resolving conflicts.

---

1. Mediation

- **Definition**:
    - A non-binding process where a neutral mediator facilitates discussions between disputing parties to reach a mutually acceptable resolution.
- **Advantages**:
    - Cost-effective and time-efficient.
    - Preserves relationships between parties, making it ideal for licensing and collaborative agreements.

- **Example**:
  - Mediation can resolve licensing disputes between a pharmaceutical company and a generic manufacturer.

---

2. Arbitration

- **Definition**:
  - A binding process where an arbitrator reviews the evidence and makes a decision enforceable under law.
- **Advantages**:
  - Offers confidentiality, making it preferable for disputes involving sensitive trade secrets.
  - Enforceable globally under the **New York Convention** on Arbitration.
- **Example**:
  - Disputes over royalty payments in patent licensing agreements can be effectively resolved through arbitration.

Role of Judiciary

Indian courts have played a pivotal role in shaping patent law through landmark judgments that balance innovation, public health, and commercial interests.

---

1. Landmark Judgments Shaping Indian Patent Law

- **Bayer vs. Natco (Compulsory Licensing Case)**:
  - Bayer's cancer drug Nexavar was priced exorbitantly, limiting its accessibility.
  - In 2012, the Indian Patent Office granted Natco Pharma a compulsory license, reducing the price significantly.
  - **Significance**:
    - Reinforced the use of compulsory licensing for public health needs.
- **Merck vs. Glenmark (Sitagliptin Case)**:
  - Merck alleged patent infringement against Glenmark for producing a generic version of its diabetes drug, Januvia.
  - The Delhi High Court sided with Merck, emphasizing the importance of protecting valid patents.

- **Significance**:
    - Highlighted the judiciary's role in upholding patent exclusivity while ensuring fair market practices.

- **Enercon vs. Aloys Wobben**:
    - A dispute involving multiple patents for wind turbine technology.
    - The Supreme Court clarified procedural aspects for patent revocation and infringement suits.
    - **Significance**:
        - Strengthened procedural clarity in patent litigation.

---

2. Judicial Interpretation of Section 3(d)

- Indian courts have consistently used **Section 3(d)**, as seen in the Novartis case, to curb evergreening while promoting access to affordable medicines.
- This provision has positioned India as a model for balancing patent rights with societal needs.

6.10 Case Studies and Success Stories

Case studies and success stories offer valuable insights into the practical applications of patent laws, highlighting both the achievements and challenges faced by Indian companies in the global intellectual property landscape. This section explores successful patent portfolios, global collaborations, and lessons learned from patent rejections.

Successful Patent Portfolios

Indian companies have emerged as global leaders in patent filings, leveraging intellectual property to gain a competitive edge in industries like pharmaceuticals and biotechnology.

---

1. Dr. Reddy's Laboratories

- **Overview**:
    - Dr. Reddy's Laboratories is a prominent Indian pharmaceutical company known for its robust patent portfolio in generic drug development and novel therapeutics.

- **Key Achievements**:
  - Filed patents for innovative drug formulations, biosimilars, and active pharmaceutical ingredients (APIs).
  - Focused on creating complex generics, such as injectable and transdermal delivery systems, that require advanced R&D.
- **Impact**:
  - The company's patents have enabled it to penetrate regulated markets like the U.S., EU, and Japan.
  - Example: Its patent for an improved formulation of omeprazole (a proton-pump inhibitor) enhanced its market position in the gastrointestinal drug segment.

---

2. Biocon

- **Overview**:
  - Biocon, a pioneer in biotechnology, has built an impressive patent portfolio in biopharmaceuticals, particularly biosimilars and novel biologics.
- **Key Achievements**:
  - Patented several biosimilars, including those for insulin and monoclonal antibodies.
  - Secured global approvals for key products like **Trastuzumab** (a biosimilar for breast cancer treatment).
- **Impact**:
  - Its strong patent portfolio has facilitated partnerships with international firms like Mylan, enabling global market access.
  - Example: Biocon's patents in insulin glargine formulations have expanded access to affordable diabetes care.

Global Collaborations

Collaboration between Indian firms and international partners has been instrumental in leveraging patented technologies for mutual benefit.

---

1. Licensing of Technology

- **Example: Sun Pharma and Merck**:
  - Sun Pharmaceutical licensed its patented novel delivery system for a dermatological drug to Merck for global commercialization.

- Outcome:
  - Allowed Sun Pharma to focus on R&D while Merck handled global distribution, resulting in increased revenue and market penetration.
- **Example: Lupin and Eli Lilly**:
  - Lupin partnered with Eli Lilly to license and develop patented formulations for diabetes management.
  - Outcome:
    - Strengthened Lupin's presence in the metabolic disorders market while enabling Eli Lilly to expand its portfolio in emerging markets.

---

2. Joint Ventures

- **Example: Serum Institute of India and Oxford-AstraZeneca**:
  - During the COVID-19 pandemic, Serum Institute of India collaborated with Oxford University and AstraZeneca to produce Covishield, leveraging patented vaccine technology.
  - Outcome:
    - Enabled large-scale, affordable production of the vaccine, benefiting global health efforts.

Learning from Failures

Examining patent rejections and their implications provides critical lessons for innovators and companies navigating the complex patent landscape.

---

1. Rejected Patents

- **Case: Novartis' Gleevec in India**:
  - Rejection under Section 3(d) highlighted the importance of demonstrating significant efficacy improvements for incremental innovations.
  - Lesson:
    - Companies must invest in substantive advancements rather than relying on minor modifications to extend patent life.
- **Case: Pfizer's Patent for a Drug Formulation**:
  - The Indian Patent Office rejected Pfizer's patent application for a drug delivery system, citing prior art that rendered the invention obvious.

- Lesson:
    - Comprehensive prior art searches and clear articulation of inventive steps are crucial for patent success.

---

2. Implications of Rejections

- **Financial Impact**:
    - Patent rejections can lead to lost market exclusivity and increased competition from generics.
- **Strategic Adjustments**:
    - Companies often revise R&D strategies to focus on innovations that meet patentability criteria in multiple jurisdictions.

CHAPTER 7

E-Pharmacy

Introduction to E-Pharmacy

E-pharmacy, an intersection of healthcare and technology, is revolutionizing the way medicines and healthcare products are accessed and delivered. In today's world, where digital solutions dominate every sector, e-pharmacy has emerged as a vital player in ensuring convenient, efficient, and widespread access to medications. This section explores what e-pharmacy entails, its relevance in modern healthcare, and its historical evolution, setting the stage for understanding its transformative impact on the pharmaceutical landscape.

Definition and Scope of E-Pharmacy

What is E-Pharmacy?

E-pharmacy, or electronic pharmacy, refers to the practice of selling medicines, health supplements, and other pharmaceutical products through online platforms. Unlike traditional pharmacies, where customers visit physical outlets, e-pharmacies allow users to order medications digitally, which are then delivered to their doorstep.

But what makes e-pharmacy distinct? Beyond convenience, e-pharmacies often incorporate advanced technologies, such as artificial intelligence (AI), to personalize recommendations and streamline operations. They cater to both prescription medications and over-the-counter (OTC) drugs, and some platforms also provide value-added services like health consultations and chronic disease management programs.

Scope of E-Pharmacy

The scope of e-pharmacy extends far beyond mere convenience:

1. **Broad Product Range**:
    - Prescription drugs, OTC medications, health supplements, and wellness products.

2. **Comprehensive Services**:
    - Telemedicine integration, medication reminders, and subscription models for chronic care.
3. **Global Reach**:
    - Bridging geographical gaps, especially in rural and underserved regions.
4. **Data Analytics**:
    - Leveraging big data to analyze consumer trends and improve inventory management.

E-pharmacy is not just about medication delivery; it represents a comprehensive healthcare ecosystem that connects patients, providers, and pharmacies seamlessly.

Difference Between Traditional and E-Pharmacy Models

Traditional Pharmacy

A traditional pharmacy operates through physical stores where customers interact with pharmacists directly. While effective in providing personal advice, traditional pharmacies are often constrained by geographical reach, operating hours, and stock limitations.

- **Strengths**:
    - Personal interaction with a pharmacist.
    - Immediate access to medications for urgent needs.
- **Limitations**:
    - Restricted to local availability.
    - Limited operating hours.

E-Pharmacy Model

E-pharmacies, on the other hand, function entirely online. Users upload prescriptions, browse products, and place orders on a digital platform. These orders are verified, processed, and delivered via logistics networks.

- **Strengths**:
    - 24/7 accessibility.
    - Broader inventory and lower costs due to economies of scale.
    - Better documentation of purchase history.

- **Challenges**:
  - Dependence on internet connectivity.
  - Concerns about counterfeit drugs and data privacy.

The e-pharmacy model complements traditional pharmacies rather than replacing them, addressing gaps like accessibility and cost while relying on robust logistics and technology for seamless delivery.

Relevance in Modern Healthcare

The relevance of e-pharmacy lies in its ability to address critical challenges in the healthcare system, including accessibility, affordability, and quality of service. As healthcare ecosystems worldwide grapple with evolving consumer needs, e-pharmacies stand out as a dynamic solution.

Growing Demand for Online Healthcare Solutions

Healthcare delivery is no longer confined to hospitals and clinics; it has expanded into homes through telemedicine, wearable devices, and, of course, e-pharmacy platforms. Why is this demand growing?

1. **Lifestyle Shifts**:
   - The modern consumer seeks convenience and speed. Online pharmacies fit seamlessly into this paradigm, offering medications at the click of a button.
2. **COVID-19 Pandemic**:
   - The pandemic underscored the need for contactless healthcare solutions. E-pharmacies played a critical role in ensuring uninterrupted medicine supply during lockdowns.
3. **Technological Penetration**:
   - With widespread internet and smartphone adoption, even rural populations are increasingly accessing e-pharmacy platforms.
4. **Chronic Disease Management**:
   - E-pharmacies cater to patients requiring regular medications for conditions like diabetes, hypertension, and arthritis through subscription-based models and automated refills.

Role in Improving Access to Medicines

Accessibility is a cornerstone of healthcare equity. In many regions, especially rural and semi-urban areas, traditional pharmacies are sparse, and certain medicines may not be readily available.

- **Bridging Urban-Rural Gaps**:
  - E-pharmacies connect remote consumers with urban stockists, ensuring timely delivery.
- **Addressing Stock Shortages**:
  - Centralized inventory management enables e-pharmacies to fulfill demands for rare drugs more efficiently.
- **Cost-Effectiveness**:
  - Bulk purchasing and reduced operational costs allow e-pharmacies to offer competitive pricing, benefiting cost-conscious consumers.

Historical Evolution of E-Pharmacy

To truly appreciate the rise of e-pharmacy, one must examine its historical roots and evolution. From small beginnings to a multi-billion-dollar global industry, e-pharmacy has come a long way.

Origins of E-Pharmacy Globally

The concept of selling medicines online emerged in the late 1990s as e-commerce platforms began diversifying into various industries.

1. **Early Beginnings**:
   - In the United States, companies like **Drugstore.com** pioneered the model, offering OTC drugs and health products online.
   - However, these early ventures faced challenges such as lack of consumer trust and limited technological infrastructure.
2. **Growth Through Trust**:
   - Regulatory frameworks like the **Verified Internet Pharmacy Practice Sites (VIPPS)** accreditation in the U.S. boosted consumer confidence in online pharmacies.
3. **Global Expansion**:
   - Europe and Japan saw rapid adoption of e-pharmacies, particularly for chronic disease management and elderly care.

Evolution of E-Pharmacy in India

India's e-pharmacy journey began more recently but has grown exponentially, driven by the country's unique healthcare challenges and technological advancements.

1. **Emergence of Startups**:
   - Early players like **1mg**, **PharmEasy**, and **Netmeds** entered the market in the 2010s, capitalizing on the country's burgeoning e-commerce ecosystem.
2. **Regulatory Developments**:
   - Initially unregulated, the sector gained momentum with draft guidelines for e-pharmacies introduced by the **Central Drugs Standard Control Organization (CDSCO)**.
3. **COVID-19 as a Catalyst**:
   - During the pandemic, e-pharmacies became a lifeline for millions, with orders surging by over 200% in some cases.
4. **Collaborations and Investments**:
   - Partnerships with telemedicine providers and funding from venture capitalists have further strengthened the industry.

Milestones in Digital Transformation

1. **Integration with Telemedicine**:
   - Platforms now offer holistic solutions, from virtual consultations to doorstep delivery of prescribed medicines.
2. **Technological Innovations**:
   - Use of AI for personalized recommendations and blockchain for supply chain transparency.
3. **Adoption of Mobile Apps**:
   - User-friendly mobile applications have made e-pharmacies accessible to a larger demographic, including less tech-savvy users.

7.1 The E-Pharmacy Business Model

E-pharmacy business models represent a convergence of technology, healthcare, and logistics to provide a seamless experience for consumers seeking medicines and healthcare products online. This section explores how e-pharmacies operate, the different types of business models they employ, and the key components that enable them to function efficiently.

How E-Pharmacies Work

At the heart of every e-pharmacy lies a systematic workflow that ensures customers receive their medications safely, promptly, and with complete regulatory compliance.

---

1. Order Placement, Verification, and Fulfillment Process

1. **Order Placement**:
    - Customers access an e-pharmacy platform, either via a website or mobile app, to browse products, upload prescriptions, and place orders.
    - Features include:
        - Advanced search filters for medications by brand, generic name, or condition.
        - Subscription models for chronic medications.
2. **Prescription Verification**:
    - Uploaded prescriptions are reviewed by licensed pharmacists to ensure compliance with regulatory requirements.
    - Example:
        - If a customer orders antibiotics, a pharmacist verifies the prescription for authenticity and dosage.
3. **Order Fulfillment**:
    - Once verified, the order is processed through the e-pharmacy's inventory system.
    - Items are packed, labeled, and prepared for shipment following standard safety protocols, including temperature-controlled packaging for sensitive products.

---

2. Delivery Mechanisms and Logistics

The delivery mechanism is a critical component of e-pharmacy operations, ensuring that products reach customers efficiently and securely.

1. **Last-Mile Delivery**:
    - Orders are dispatched via courier partners or dedicated delivery fleets to customers' doorsteps.
    - Example: Urban areas may use real-time GPS tracking, while rural deliveries depend on local courier services.

2. **Cold-Chain Logistics**:
    - Medicines like insulin or vaccines require temperature-controlled transportation to maintain efficacy.
    - Specialized containers and monitoring devices are used to ensure compliance.
3. **Delivery Timelines**:
    - E-pharmacies typically offer multiple options:
        - Standard delivery (1–3 days).
        - Same-day or express delivery for urgent medications.
4. **Customer Communication**:
    - Real-time updates via SMS, email, or app notifications provide transparency regarding order status.

Types of E-Pharmacies

E-pharmacies operate under various models, catering to diverse customer and business needs. Each model has unique operational features and target audiences.

---

1. Business-to-Business (B2B) Platforms

B2B e-pharmacies facilitate transactions between wholesalers and retailers or hospitals and clinics.

1. **How It Works**:
    - Retail pharmacies or healthcare facilities place bulk orders for medicines directly from distributors via online platforms.
    - Example: A rural pharmacy might order stock from a central distributor through a B2B e-pharmacy.
2. **Advantages**:
    - Streamlined procurement for retailers.
    - Competitive pricing due to bulk transactions.
3. **Challenges**:
    - Dependence on efficient logistics networks to meet supply demands.

---

2. Business-to-Consumer (B2C) Platforms

B2C e-pharmacies cater directly to end consumers, providing medications and healthcare products via digital platforms.

1. **How It Works**:
   - Customers browse, order, and receive medications directly from the e-pharmacy.
   - Examples: Platforms like **Netmeds** or **PharmEasy** in India.
2. **Advantages**:
   - Convenience and accessibility for consumers.
   - Personalized services such as health reminders and consultations.
3. **Challenges**:
   - Maintaining regulatory compliance and ensuring prescription authenticity.

---

3. Hybrid Models

Hybrid models combine B2B and B2C functionalities, serving both retail pharmacies and end consumers.

1. **How It Works**:
   - A single platform caters to retail orders while also fulfilling individual consumer requirements.
   - Example: A platform might supply medicines to clinics while offering chronic care solutions to patients.
2. **Advantages**:
   - Diversified revenue streams.
   - Scalability across multiple customer bases.
3. **Challenges**:
   - Balancing inventory and managing varied logistics demands.

Key Components of the E-Pharmacy Model

The success of an e-pharmacy hinges on several core components that ensure smooth operations and a superior customer experience.

---

1. Digital Platforms and User Interfaces

A robust digital platform is the foundation of any e-pharmacy, enabling seamless interaction between users and the service.

1. **User-Friendly Interface**:
   - Simplified navigation, intuitive design, and responsive performance on both websites and mobile apps.
   - Features like voice search, product comparisons, and health blogs enhance user engagement.
2. **Secure Payment Gateways**:
   - Multiple payment options, including credit/debit cards, UPI, and cash on delivery.
   - Secure encryption protocols to protect sensitive financial data.
3. **Personalization**:
   - AI-powered recommendations based on purchase history, browsing behavior, and health profiles.

---

2. Back-End Inventory and Supply Chain Management

Efficient inventory management is crucial to meeting customer demands and maintaining product quality.

1. **Real-Time Inventory Tracking**:
   - Ensures products are in stock and minimizes the risk of overstocking or shortages.
   - Example: Systems automatically reorder stock when inventory falls below threshold levels.
2. **Centralized Warehousing**:
   - Strategically located warehouses to optimize delivery timelines and costs.
   - Temperature-controlled facilities for sensitive medicines.
3. **Supplier Integration**:
   - Partnerships with manufacturers and distributors to ensure timely restocking and authenticity of products.

---

3. Integration with Healthcare Providers

Collaboration with healthcare professionals adds value to e-pharmacy services and fosters trust.

1. **Prescription Verification**:
   - Pharmacists review prescriptions to ensure compliance and address any potential errors.

- Example: Flagging a prescription with a potentially harmful drug interaction.

2. **Telemedicine Integration**:
   - Platforms allow users to consult licensed doctors online, who can then issue e-prescriptions linked to the pharmacy.
3. **Chronic Disease Management**:
   - Subscription models for regular medication supplies.
   - Add-on services like diet consultations and wellness programs.

7.2 Benefits of E-Pharmacies

E-pharmacies have emerged as a transformative force in healthcare delivery, offering a range of benefits to consumers, businesses, and the healthcare ecosystem. Their seamless integration of technology, logistics, and customer service addresses critical challenges in traditional pharmacy systems. This section explores the multifaceted advantages of e-pharmacies, emphasizing their impact on convenience, cost-effectiveness, accessibility, and medication management.

Convenience for Consumers

One of the most significant advantages of e-pharmacies is the unparalleled convenience they offer. Traditional pharmacies, while effective, are often limited by operating hours, geographical reach, and stock availability. E-pharmacies bridge these gaps, enhancing the overall customer experience.

---

1. 24/7 Availability

E-pharmacies operate round the clock, providing consumers with the flexibility to place orders at any time, regardless of location.

- **No Time Constraints**:
  - Whether it's late at night or during holidays, e-pharmacies ensure uninterrupted access to medicines.
  - Example: A patient requiring emergency medication during odd hours can instantly order it from an e-pharmacy without waiting for physical stores to open.
- **Global Reach**:
  - Expats or travelers can use e-pharmacies to access medicines in a familiar language and format, avoiding local barriers.

---

2. Doorstep Delivery and Time Savings

E-pharmacies eliminate the need for consumers to visit physical stores, saving time and effort, particularly for individuals with mobility issues or packed schedules.

- **Doorstep Delivery**:
  - Medications are delivered directly to homes, often with real-time tracking options to keep consumers informed.
  - Example: Senior citizens can receive chronic care medications regularly without leaving their homes.
- **Efficient Processes**:
  - Automated order processing and quick verification reduce waiting times.
  - Urban consumers benefit from same-day delivery services, while rural areas enjoy access to previously unavailable medications.

Cost Effectiveness

E-pharmacies offer significant cost savings to both consumers and businesses, making healthcare more affordable and efficient.

---

1. Discounts and Competitive Pricing

Online pharmacies often provide discounts and promotional offers that traditional pharmacies struggle to match due to higher operational costs.

- **Bulk Purchasing Power**:
  - E-pharmacies leverage economies of scale to negotiate better deals with manufacturers and pass these savings on to customers.
  - Example: Discounts on chronic medications for conditions like diabetes or hypertension.
- **Loyalty Programs**:
  - Reward systems and subscription plans encourage repeat purchases while ensuring consistent savings for consumers.

---

2. Reduced Operational Costs for Businesses

For e-pharmacy businesses, digital platforms significantly lower expenses related to physical infrastructure and staffing.

- **No Retail Space Required**:
  - Centralized warehouses replace the need for multiple retail outlets, cutting rental and maintenance costs.
- **Streamlined Operations**:
  - Advanced inventory management systems reduce wastage and optimize supply chains.
  - Example: Automated stock replenishment systems ensure that high-demand drugs are always available, minimizing lost sales opportunities.

Improved Access to Medicines

In a country like India, where healthcare access is often limited by geography, e-pharmacies play a vital role in bridging gaps and ensuring equitable distribution of medicines.

---

1. Addressing Rural and Remote Healthcare Needs

Rural and remote areas often face challenges in accessing quality medicines due to a lack of pharmacies or logistical constraints.

- **Expanding Reach**:
  - E-pharmacies, through robust logistics networks, deliver medicines to even the most isolated locations.
  - Example: A tribal village in a hilly region receiving essential antibiotics via an e-pharmacy partner's delivery system.
- **Healthcare Equity**:
  - By addressing regional disparities, e-pharmacies support government initiatives aimed at universal healthcare access.

---

2. Availability of Rare or Less Commonly Stocked Medications

Traditional pharmacies may struggle to stock rare medications or those with limited demand. E-pharmacies, with centralized inventories, ensure that these drugs are readily available.

- **Centralized Warehousing**:
  - Enables stockpiling of niche medications that may not be economically viable for small pharmacies.
  - Example: A cancer patient accessing specialized chemotherapy drugs unavailable in their local pharmacy.

- **Quick Procurement**:
  - Partnerships with distributors and manufacturers allow e-pharmacies to fulfill orders for less common drugs in record time.

Enhanced Medication Management

E-pharmacies are not just about delivering medications; they also offer tools and services to help patients manage their treatments effectively.

---

1. Automated Prescription Reminders

Forgetfulness is a common challenge, particularly for patients managing chronic illnesses. E-pharmacies help address this with automated reminders.

- **Digital Alerts**:
  - Notifications via SMS or email inform patients when it's time to refill their prescriptions.
  - Example: A patient with high blood pressure receiving timely reminders to reorder their antihypertensive medications.
- **Subscription Models**:
  - Automatic reordering and doorstep delivery for regular medications, ensuring continuity of care without manual intervention.

---

2. Improved Patient Adherence to Treatment

Medication adherence is crucial for treatment efficacy. E-pharmacies contribute to better adherence through technology-driven solutions.

- **Detailed Information**:
  - Alongside medications, e-pharmacies often provide educational materials about dosage, side effects, and drug interactions.
  - Example: A digital guide on how to use an inhaler effectively for asthma patients.
- **Health Monitoring Integration**:
  - Some platforms integrate with wearable devices to monitor patient progress and adjust medication schedules accordingly.

7.3 Challenges Faced by E-Pharmacies

While e-pharmacies bring significant benefits to consumers and healthcare systems, they also face unique challenges that could hinder their growth and effectiveness. These challenges, spanning regulatory hurdles, data security concerns, quality assurance, and logistics, require robust strategies and solutions to ensure the sector's sustainable development.

Regulatory and Compliance Issues

E-pharmacies operate in a complex regulatory environment, often marked by ambiguities and enforcement challenges. Addressing these issues is critical for establishing trust and operational stability.

---

1. Lack of Clarity in E-Pharmacy Laws

The rapid emergence of e-pharmacies has outpaced the development of clear and comprehensive regulatory frameworks.

- **Current Gaps**:
    - In countries like India, the regulatory framework for e-pharmacies is still evolving, with draft guidelines often open to interpretation.
    - Example: The **Drugs and Cosmetics Act, 1940**, primarily governs traditional pharmacies and lacks specific provisions for online operations.
- **Impact**:
    - Uncertainty creates operational hurdles, deterring investment and innovation in the sector.
    - Smaller players struggle to navigate the regulatory landscape, while larger platforms may face delays in scaling up.
- **Proposed Solutions**:
    - Streamlined laws that explicitly address licensing, prescription verification, and cross-border sales can reduce ambiguity and foster growth.

---

2. Enforcement of Prescription-Only Sales

Ensuring compliance with laws that mandate prescriptions for certain medications is a persistent challenge for e-pharmacies.

- **Challenges**:
  - Verifying the authenticity of uploaded prescriptions is time-consuming and prone to error.
  - Instances of fraudulent or forged prescriptions exacerbate the issue.
- **Consequences**:
  - Non-compliance risks penalties, reputational damage, and regulatory scrutiny.
  - Over-the-counter availability of prescription drugs can lead to misuse or abuse, particularly for controlled substances.
- **Potential Mitigations**:
  - Leveraging AI and blockchain technologies for real-time prescription validation.
  - Partnering with certified healthcare providers for integrated teleconsultation and prescription services.

Data Privacy and Security

With vast amounts of sensitive patient data being stored and transmitted, e-pharmacies face significant responsibilities and risks related to data protection.

---

1. Protecting Patient Health Information (PHI)

The confidentiality of patient data is paramount for building consumer trust and complying with data protection laws.

- **Regulatory Requirements**:
  - Laws such as **HIPAA** (Health Insurance Portability and Accountability Act) in the U.S. and **GDPR** (General Data Protection Regulation) in the EU mandate strict data security protocols.
  - Example: Ensuring that platforms have secure log-in systems, encrypted transactions, and access controls.
- **Challenges**:
  - Ensuring compliance with evolving global and local data privacy regulations.
  - Managing third-party vendors who may have access to PHI.

---

2. Risks of Data Breaches and Cyberattacks

Cybersecurity threats are a growing concern for digital platforms, including e-pharmacies.

- **Potential Threats**:
    - Data breaches exposing sensitive patient information.
    - Ransomware attacks targeting operational disruptions.
- **High-Profile Incidents**:
    - Example: A leading e-pharmacy platform facing backlash after a data breach revealed customer purchase histories.
- **Mitigation Strategies**:
    - Investing in advanced cybersecurity solutions, such as firewalls, intrusion detection systems, and regular vulnerability assessments.
    - Educating employees on best practices for preventing phishing and social engineering attacks.

Quality Control and Counterfeit Drugs

Ensuring the authenticity and quality of medicines is a non-negotiable aspect of e-pharmacy operations, yet it remains one of the sector's biggest challenges.

---

1. Ensuring Authenticity and Safe Storage of Medicines

Medicines are sensitive products that require strict quality control measures throughout the supply chain.

- **Issues**:
    - Inadequate quality checks during procurement can lead to the distribution of substandard or expired drugs.
    - Improper storage conditions may compromise drug efficacy, especially for temperature-sensitive medications.
- **Solutions**:
    - Implementing robust supplier verification protocols.
    - Regular audits of storage facilities to ensure compliance with Good Distribution Practices (GDP).

---

2. Combating Counterfeit or Substandard Products

The global issue of counterfeit drugs poses a serious threat to patient safety and the credibility of e-pharmacies.

- **Extent of the Problem**:
  - Counterfeit drugs account for a significant percentage of medicines in developing countries, often entering supply chains through unauthorized distributors.
- **Impact**:
  - Loss of consumer trust.
  - Potential health hazards due to ineffective or harmful counterfeit products.
- **Preventive Measures**:
  - Use of **blockchain technology** to track medicines from manufacturer to consumer.
  - Collaboration with regulators to create centralized databases of verified medicines.

Logistics and Delivery

Efficient logistics and delivery systems are essential for ensuring timely and safe delivery of medications, yet they present unique challenges for e-pharmacies.

---

1. Cold-Chain Requirements for Certain Medicines

Medicines like vaccines, insulin, and biologics require temperature-controlled storage and transportation.

- **Challenges**:
  - Maintaining the integrity of cold-chain logistics during last-mile delivery.
  - High costs associated with specialized transportation infrastructure.
- **Innovative Solutions**:
  - Use of IoT-enabled temperature monitors to ensure compliance throughout the supply chain.
  - Partnerships with specialized logistics providers for cold-chain deliveries.

---

2. Delays in Delivery Due to Operational Challenges

Operational inefficiencies in logistics can lead to delays, affecting customer satisfaction and treatment adherence.

- **Common Issues**:
  - Traffic congestion in urban areas and poor road infrastructure in rural regions.
  - High delivery costs for remote locations.
- **Impact**:
  - Negative customer experiences and loss of repeat business.
  - Increased operational expenses due to failed deliveries or returns.
- **Optimization Strategies**:
  - Real-time tracking and route optimization using AI-powered logistics solutions.
  - Expanding local distribution hubs to minimize delivery times.

7.4 Regulatory Framework for E-Pharmacies

The regulatory framework for e-pharmacies is essential to ensuring their operations comply with national and international laws. These regulations safeguard public health, ensure the quality and authenticity of medicines, and foster trust in the e-pharmacy model. This section delves into the regulatory landscape in India, explores draft e-pharmacy rules, and provides a comparative view of global regulations.

India's Legal Landscape

India's regulatory framework for e-pharmacies is rooted in several key laws designed to ensure the safety, quality, and proper distribution of pharmaceutical products.

---

1. Drugs and Cosmetics Act, 1940

The **Drugs and Cosmetics Act, 1940**, is the cornerstone of pharmaceutical regulation in India, originally designed for traditional pharmacy operations. While it does not explicitly address e-pharmacies, its provisions still apply to their operations.

- **Key Provisions**:
  - Governs the manufacture, sale, and distribution of drugs in India.
  - Requires that all medicines sold, whether offline or online, comply with prescribed standards of safety, efficacy, and quality.
- **Relevance to E-Pharmacies**:
  - Prescription-only drugs (Schedule H and H1) must not be sold without a valid prescription.
  - Ensures proper storage and distribution of medicines, including temperature-sensitive products.
- **Challenges**:
  - Lack of explicit mention of e-pharmacy operations, leading to ambiguity.
  - Difficulty in enforcing rules for online sales across state borders.

---

2. Information Technology Act, 2000

The **Information Technology Act, 2000**, provides a legal framework for e-commerce activities, including e-pharmacies.

- **Key Provisions**:
  - Governs electronic transactions, data storage, and digital signatures.
  - Mandates secure practices for storing and transmitting sensitive data, including patient health information (PHI).
- **Implications for E-Pharmacies**:
  - Platforms must implement robust cybersecurity measures to protect customer data.
  - Digital prescriptions and payments must adhere to encryption and authentication standards.

---

3. E-Commerce Rules Under the Consumer Protection Act, 2019

The **Consumer Protection (E-Commerce) Rules, 2020**, introduced under the **Consumer Protection Act, 2019**, are designed to enhance transparency and accountability in online commerce.

- **Key Provisions**:
    - Mandates clear disclosure of seller details and product information on e-pharmacy platforms.
    - Requires mechanisms for consumer grievance redressal and dispute resolution.
- **Specific Requirements for E-Pharmacies**:
    - Display accurate drug information, including dosage, precautions, and expiration dates.
    - Implement a customer helpline for addressing complaints.
- **Challenges**:
    - Ensuring compliance across diverse e-pharmacy platforms.
    - Balancing consumer rights with operational flexibility for businesses.

Draft E-Pharmacy Rules

Recognizing the unique needs and challenges of e-pharmacies, the Indian government has proposed specific guidelines under the **Draft E-Pharmacy Rules**.

---

1. Key Provisions and Industry Impact

The draft rules aim to bring clarity and standardization to e-pharmacy operations.

- **Key Provisions**:
    - Mandatory registration of e-pharmacy platforms with the **Central Drugs Standard Control Organization (CDSCO)**.
    - Prohibition of narcotic drugs, psychotropic substances, and habit-forming medicines on e-pharmacy platforms.
    - Regular audits to ensure compliance with quality and safety standards.
- **Industry Impact**:
    - Promotes transparency and accountability.
    - Encourages trust among consumers and healthcare professionals.
    - Challenges smaller players due to increased compliance costs.

---

2. Requirements for Licensing, Data Storage, and Prescription Validation

- **Licensing**:
  - E-pharmacies must obtain a license to operate, valid across all states and union territories.
  - Periodic renewal and reporting are required to maintain compliance.
- **Data Storage**:
  - Sensitive patient data must be stored on servers located in India, ensuring adherence to data sovereignty laws.
  - Platforms must implement encryption and access control to prevent breaches.
- **Prescription Validation**:
  - Every order for prescription drugs must be accompanied by a valid prescription verified by a licensed pharmacist.
  - Use of AI and machine learning tools to detect forged or tampered prescriptions.

Global Regulations

While India's regulatory framework is evolving, established global markets offer valuable insights into managing e-pharmacies effectively.

---

1. FDA Guidelines for Online Pharmacies in the US

The **U.S. Food and Drug Administration (FDA)** has stringent rules for online pharmacies to ensure public safety.

- **Verified Internet Pharmacy Practice Sites (VIPPS)**:
  - Accreditation program to certify legitimate e-pharmacies.
  - Requires pharmacies to meet standards for prescription verification, data security, and quality control.
- **Prohibited Practices**:
  - Sale of prescription drugs without a valid prescription.
  - Cross-border shipping of drugs without FDA approval.
- **Enforcement**:
  - The FDA actively monitors online platforms and imposes penalties on non-compliant entities.

---

2. EU's Approach to Cross-Border E-Pharmacy Services

The European Union (EU) promotes cross-border e-pharmacy services while ensuring regulatory consistency.

- **Guidelines**:
  - Online pharmacies must comply with the **Falsified Medicines Directive (FMD)** to prevent counterfeit drugs.
  - Mandatory display of the EU common logo on all legitimate e-pharmacy websites.
- **Advantages**:
  - Facilitates seamless trade across EU member states.
  - Builds consumer trust through transparency and standardization.

---

3. Examples from Countries Like Australia and Canada

- **Australia**:
  - E-pharmacies operate under the oversight of the **Therapeutic Goods Administration (TGA)**.
  - Emphasis on cold-chain logistics and prescription-only sales.
- **Canada**:
  - Provincial regulations govern e-pharmacies, ensuring alignment with national health standards.
  - Cross-border sales require adherence to both Canadian and recipient country laws.

7.5 Technology in E-Pharmacies

Technology is the backbone of the e-pharmacy industry, enabling these platforms to deliver medicines efficiently, securely, and conveniently. From intuitive digital interfaces to advanced applications of AI, blockchain, and telemedicine integration, technology drives the operational excellence and customer-centric nature of e-pharmacies.

Digital Platforms and Apps

At the core of every e-pharmacy is a digital platform or mobile app that serves as the primary interface for users. These platforms are meticulously designed to provide a seamless user experience while ensuring compliance with healthcare regulations.

1. Features of Digital Platforms and Apps

1. **User-Friendly Interfaces**:
   - Simplified navigation and clear layouts cater to a diverse demographic, including less tech-savvy users.
   - Example: Categorization of products by condition (e.g., diabetes care) or type (e.g., prescription drugs, OTC medicines).
2. **Search Filters**:
   - Advanced search options allow users to filter medications by brand, generic name, price, or availability.
   - Additional filters, such as drug interactions or side effects, enhance decision-making for consumers.
3. **Payment Gateways**:
   - Integration of secure payment gateways ensures smooth and safe financial transactions.
   - Options include credit/debit cards, UPI, mobile wallets, and cash on delivery.

---

2. Examples of Popular E-Pharmacy Apps

1. **India**:
   - **1mg**: Offers a wide range of medicines, lab tests, and health consultations.
   - **PharmEasy**: Known for discounts, chronic care packages, and a robust supply chain network.
   - **Netmeds**: Caters to rural areas with a focus on accessibility and affordability.
2. **Global**:
   - **PillPack (Amazon)**: A US-based e-pharmacy offering personalized medication packaging.
   - **LloydsPharmacy Online Doctor**: Operates in the UK, providing prescriptions alongside telemedicine services.

AI and Machine Learning

Artificial intelligence (AI) and machine learning (ML) play transformative roles in enhancing the efficiency and personalization of e-pharmacies.

---

1. Personalized Medicine Recommendations

AI-driven algorithms analyze user behavior, medical history, and prescription data to offer tailored suggestions.

- **Features**:
  - Recommendations for alternative brands based on availability and price.
  - Alerts about potential drug interactions or contraindications.
- **Example**:
  - A patient purchasing antihypertensive drugs receives recommendations for complementary lifestyle products like low-sodium salt or digital blood pressure monitors.

---

2. Predictive Inventory Management

ML models predict demand patterns and optimize inventory management to prevent stockouts or overstocking.

- **How It Works**:
  - Algorithms analyze historical sales data, seasonal trends, and regional demands to anticipate future requirements.
  - Integration with supply chain systems ensures timely restocking.
- **Benefits**:
  - Reduces wastage and storage costs.
  - Ensures critical medicines are always available, especially during emergencies.

Blockchain

Blockchain technology is revolutionizing supply chain management and ensuring the authenticity of medicines in e-pharmacies.

---

1. Enhancing Supply Chain Transparency

Blockchain provides an immutable ledger that tracks every transaction within the supply chain, from manufacturing to delivery.

- **Applications**:
  - Ensures traceability of medicines, minimizing the risk of counterfeit products entering the supply chain.
  - Enables real-time tracking of shipments for logistics efficiency.

- **Example**:
  - A blockchain-enabled e-pharmacy can instantly verify the origin and transit path of a drug, ensuring its compliance with regulatory standards.

---

2. Verifying Authenticity of Medicines

Counterfeit medicines are a significant challenge for the pharmaceutical industry, and blockchain helps address this issue effectively.

- **How It Works**:
  - Unique digital identifiers, such as QR codes or RFID tags, are assigned to each medicine.
  - Consumers can scan these identifiers to verify the product's authenticity and manufacturing details.
- **Benefits**:
  - Enhances consumer trust in e-pharmacies.
  - Supports regulatory compliance by providing a transparent audit trail.

Integration with Telemedicine

The convergence of e-pharmacies and telemedicine is reshaping healthcare delivery, offering holistic solutions to patients.

---

1. Role in Enabling Seamless Virtual Consultations

E-pharmacies increasingly integrate with telemedicine platforms, creating an end-to-end healthcare ecosystem.

- **Process**:
  - Patients consult licensed doctors via video or chat platforms.
  - Prescriptions generated during consultations are directly linked to the e-pharmacy, enabling immediate fulfillment.
- **Advantages**:
  - Reduces delays in accessing medications post-consultation.
  - Eliminates the need for physical visits, particularly beneficial for rural or immobile patients.

---

2. Prescription Fulfillment

Telemedicine-enabled prescriptions streamline the process of acquiring prescription-only drugs through e-pharmacies.

- **Features**:
  - Automatic prescription uploads to the e-pharmacy's system.
  - Verification by certified pharmacists before order processing.
- **Example**:
  - During the COVID-19 pandemic, telemedicine consultations paired with e-pharmacy services ensured continuous care for chronic patients.

7.6 Market Dynamics of E-Pharmacies

The e-pharmacy sector has experienced significant growth, driven by technological advancements, changing consumer behaviors, and evolving healthcare needs. This section examines the current trends in India's e-pharmacy market and provides projections for the global e-pharmacy market.

Market Size and Growth

1. Current Trends in India's E-Pharmacy Market

India's e-pharmacy market has seen remarkable expansion, influenced by increased internet penetration, smartphone usage, and a shift towards digital healthcare solutions.

- **Market Valuation**:
  - In 2021, the Indian e-pharmacy market was valued at approximately USD 328.42 million.
  - It is projected to reach USD 2,281.6 million by 2028, exhibiting a compound annual growth rate (CAGR) of 34.2% during the forecast period.

    BlueWeave Consulting
- **Growth Drivers**:
  - **Digital Adoption**: The proliferation of internet services and smartphones has facilitated easier access to online pharmacy platforms.
  - **Consumer Convenience**: E-pharmacies offer the ease of home delivery, competitive pricing, and a broader range of products compared to traditional pharmacies.

    - **Regulatory Support**: Government initiatives promoting digital healthcare and telemedicine have created a conducive environment for e-pharmacy growth.
- **Market Trends**:
    - **Increased Demand for Chronic Disease Medications**: There is a growing demand for medications related to chronic diseases, contributing to the expansion of e-pharmacies.
    - **Expansion into Rural Areas**: E-pharmacies are extending their services to rural regions, enhancing healthcare accessibility.

2. Global E-Pharmacy Market Projections

The global e-pharmacy market is on an upward trajectory, with substantial growth anticipated in the coming years.

- **Market Valuation**:
    - In 2023, the global e-pharmacy market was valued at USD 86.2 billion.
    - It is estimated to grow at a CAGR of 13.3% from 2024 to 2032.

      Grand View Research
- **Growth Drivers**:
    - **Rising Internet Penetration**: The increasing number of internet users worldwide facilitates access to online pharmacy services.
    - **Aging Population**: An expanding geriatric population coupled with the growing prevalence of chronic disorders boosts demand for e-pharmacy services.
    - **Technological Advancements**: Integration of artificial intelligence (AI) and machine learning (ML) technologies enhances personalized customer experiences, driving market growth.
- **Regional Insights**:
    - **North America**: Holds a significant share due to advanced healthcare infrastructure and high digital literacy.
    - **Asia-Pacific**: Expected to witness the fastest growth, attributed to increasing digital adoption and supportive regulatory frameworks.

7.7 Key Players in the E-Pharmacy Market

The e-pharmacy sector has experienced significant growth, with several key players emerging both in India and internationally. This section provides an overview of prominent e-pharmacy platforms in India and notable international e-pharmacy companies.

Prominent E-Pharmacy Platforms in India

India's e-pharmacy market has seen the rise of several platforms that have revolutionized access to medicines and healthcare services.

1. Tata 1mg

- **Overview**: Founded in 2015, Tata 1mg is a leading digital healthcare platform in India, offering a wide range of services, including e-pharmacy, online consultations, and lab tests.

  1mg
- **Services**:
  - Delivery of prescription and over-the-counter medicines.
  - Diagnostic services with home sample collection.
  - Telemedicine consultations with licensed doctors.
- **Reach**: Operates in over 100 cities across India, including Delhi, Mumbai, Bangalore, Kolkata, Hyderabad, Gurgaon, Noida, and Pune.

  1mg

2. PharmEasy

- **Overview**: Established in 2014, PharmEasy is one of India's most trusted online pharmacies, providing a comprehensive range of healthcare products and services.

  PharmEasy
- **Services**:
  - Home delivery of medicines and healthcare products.
  - Diagnostic tests with sample collection at home.
  - Online consultations with healthcare professionals.
- **Reach**: Serves over 1,200 cities in India, including major metropolitan areas.

  PharmEasy

3. Netmeds

- **Overview**: Founded in 2010, Netmeds is a prominent online pharmacy in India, offering a wide range of prescription and over-the-counter medicines.

  Netmeds
- **Services**:
  - Delivery of prescription medications and healthcare products.
  - Wellness products and health-related information.
- **Reach**: Provides services across India, ensuring access to quality medicines nationwide.

  Netmeds

International E-Pharmacy Giants

Globally, several e-pharmacy platforms have established significant presence, leveraging technology to enhance healthcare delivery.

1. CVS Pharmacy

- **Overview**: CVS Pharmacy is a leading retail pharmacy chain in the United States, offering both physical stores and online services.

  Expert Market Research
- **Services**:
  - Online prescription refills and home delivery.
  - Over-the-counter medicines and health products.
  - MinuteClinic services for minor health concerns.
- **Reach**: Operates over 9,900 pharmacy locations across the United States.

  Expert Market Research

2. PillPack by Amazon Pharmacy

- **Overview**: PillPack, acquired by Amazon in 2018, is a full-service online pharmacy in the United States.
- **Services**:
  - Pre-sorted medications packaged by dose.
  - Home delivery of prescription medicines.
  - 24/7 customer support from pharmacists.
- **Reach**: Licensed to deliver medications across the United States.

3. LloydsPharmacy

- **Overview**: LloydsPharmacy is a British pharmacy company with both physical stores and an online presence.
- **Services**:
    - Online prescription services and medicine delivery.
    - Health and wellness products.
    - Online doctor consultations for certain conditions.
- **Reach**: Operates extensively across the United Kingdom.

7.8 Competition with Brick-and-Mortar Pharmacies

The rise of e-pharmacies has introduced a transformative shift in the pharmaceutical landscape, creating both synergies and conflicts with traditional brick-and-mortar pharmacies. This dynamic interaction has implications for consumer choices, market competition, and the future of healthcare delivery.

Synergies and Conflicts Between Traditional and Online Pharmacies

The relationship between e-pharmacies and traditional pharmacies is multifaceted, offering opportunities for collaboration while also posing significant challenges.

1. Synergies

E-pharmacies and traditional pharmacies can coexist by leveraging their respective strengths to enhance healthcare access and delivery.

- **Supplementary Services**:
    - E-pharmacies can complement traditional pharmacies by catering to consumers who prefer digital transactions or live in remote areas where physical stores are unavailable.
    - Example: A consumer in a rural area might use an e-pharmacy for specialized drugs not stocked locally, while relying on the local pharmacy for immediate needs.
- **Shared Expertise**:
    - Traditional pharmacies can partner with e-pharmacies to enhance their service offerings, such as enabling online orders with in-store pickups.

    - Example: A hybrid model where local pharmacies fulfill orders placed on e-pharmacy platforms, ensuring faster delivery.
- **Collaborative Models**:
    - Partnerships between traditional pharmacies and e-pharmacies can improve supply chain efficiency, reduce stockouts, and expand the range of available products.

---

2. Conflicts

Despite potential synergies, conflicts between the two models are inevitable, primarily due to differences in their operational frameworks and market strategies.

- **Price Competition**:
    - E-pharmacies often offer significant discounts, enabled by bulk purchasing and reduced overhead costs. This pricing strategy puts pressure on traditional pharmacies, which may struggle to compete.
    - Example: A 10-15% discount on chronic care medications from an e-pharmacy might lure customers away from local stores.
- **Convenience vs. Personal Interaction**:
    - E-pharmacies excel in convenience, offering doorstep delivery and 24/7 access. However, traditional pharmacies provide immediate fulfillment and personal interactions with pharmacists, which many consumers value.
    - Conflict arises when consumers prioritize one over the other, leading to shifts in market share.
- **Regulatory and Ethical Concerns**:
    - Traditional pharmacies often accuse e-pharmacies of violating regulations, such as dispensing prescription drugs without adequate verification. This has led to lobbying efforts to restrict e-pharmacy operations.
    - Example: Associations of traditional pharmacists in India have voiced concerns over the potential misuse of prescription-only medications by e-pharmacies.

Impact on Local Pharmacy Businesses

The advent of e-pharmacies has significantly influenced the operations and viability of local pharmacy businesses, creating a mixed impact.

---

1. Challenges for Local Pharmacies

- **Revenue Loss**:
    - The lower prices and broader product range offered by e-pharmacies have diverted a portion of the customer base from local pharmacies.
    - Example: Consumers with recurring medication needs often shift to e-pharmacies for cost savings and convenience.
- **Reduced Foot Traffic**:
    - As more consumers opt for online orders, foot traffic in traditional pharmacies has declined, particularly in urban areas where e-pharmacy penetration is high.
- **Stock Management**:
    - Local pharmacies often lack the sophisticated inventory management systems used by e-pharmacies, leading to stockouts or inefficiencies.

---

2. Opportunities for Adaptation

Despite these challenges, local pharmacies can adopt strategies to remain competitive and thrive alongside e-pharmacies.

- **Value-Added Services**:
    - Providing personalized consultations, home delivery, and wellness programs can help traditional pharmacies retain customer loyalty.
- **Digital Transformation**:
    - By integrating technology, local pharmacies can adopt hybrid models, offering online ordering options while maintaining their physical presence.
    - Example: Creating a localized app for order placement and scheduling home deliveries.
- **Specialization**:
    - Focusing on niche markets, such as rare medicines or compounding services, can differentiate local pharmacies from e-pharmacies.

The e-pharmacy sector has attracted substantial investments from venture capital (VC) and private equity (PE) firms, alongside supportive government initiatives, fostering its rapid growth and integration into the healthcare ecosystem.

Venture Capital and Private Equity in the E-Pharmacy Sector

1. Investment Trends

- **Increased Funding**: The e-pharmacy market has seen a surge in investments, with VC and PE firms recognizing the potential for scalable growth and significant returns. For instance, in 2021, PharmEasy, a leading Indian e-pharmacy, was in discussions to raise $200 million from investors including Blackstone and Amansa Capital, aiming for a valuation around $6 billion.

  Venture Intelligence News
- **Strategic Acquisitions**: Investors are not only providing capital but also facilitating mergers and acquisitions to consolidate market positions. In April 2024, Advent International invested approximately $297 million in Apollo HealthCo, merging its online pharmacy business with Keimed, a pharmacy distributor, to create a combined entity valued at $2.8 billion.

  Reuters

2. Investment Drivers

- **Digital Transformation**: The shift towards digital healthcare solutions, accelerated by the COVID-19 pandemic, has made e-pharmacies an attractive investment opportunity. The integration of technologies like artificial intelligence and blockchain is reshaping pharmacy services, enhancing efficiency and customer engagement.

  Journal of Hematology & Oncology
- **Market Potential**: The global e-pharmacy market was valued at $86.2 billion in 2023 and is projected to grow at a compound annual growth rate (CAGR) of 13.3% from 2024 to 2032, indicating vast opportunities for investors.

  Grand View Research

Government Initiatives and Funding

1. Policy Support

- **Digital Health Initiatives**: Governments worldwide are implementing policies to promote digital health, including e-pharmacies. For example, the U.S. government has allocated substantial funds to enhance healthcare access through digital platforms, facilitating the growth of e-pharmacies.

McKinsey & Company

- **Regulatory Frameworks**: Establishing clear regulations for e-pharmacies ensures consumer safety and encourages investment by providing a stable operating environment. In India, the government has proposed draft e-pharmacy rules to regulate online sale of medicines, aiming to balance innovation with safety.

2. Financial Incentives

- **Funding Programs**: Some governments offer grants and funding programs to support digital health startups, including e-pharmacies, fostering innovation and market entry. For instance, the Telangana government in India has initiatives to support life sciences and healthcare startups, providing infrastructure and financial assistance.

  Telangana Life Sciences
- **Public-Private Partnerships**: Collaborations between government bodies and private investors facilitate the development of e-pharmacy infrastructure, expanding reach and improving healthcare delivery. These partnerships often focus on enhancing supply chains, digital platforms, and regulatory compliance.

7.9 Case Studies and Success Stories

The evolution of e-pharmacies has been marked by significant milestones, both in India and globally, where innovations and strategic approaches have led to transformative impacts on healthcare. This section explores Indian success stories, highlights global innovations, and identifies lessons learned from pioneers in the e-pharmacy sector.

Indian Success Stories

E-pharmacies in India have made a profound impact, particularly in addressing the challenges of rural healthcare and underserved populations.

---

1. How E-Pharmacies Transformed Rural Healthcare Access

- **Case Study: Netmeds' Outreach in Remote Areas**:
  - **Challenge**: Rural areas in India often face limited access to quality medicines due to inadequate infrastructure and a lack of physical pharmacies.
  - **Solution**: Netmeds expanded its delivery network to rural regions, ensuring essential medicines reached these areas.

- **Outcome**: Increased availability of chronic care medications such as insulin and antihypertensives in remote villages, improving treatment adherence.

- **Telemedicine Integration**:
  - **Example**: PharmEasy collaborated with telemedicine providers to offer consultations in rural areas, ensuring that patients could access prescriptions alongside medications.
  - **Impact**: Reduced the burden on primary healthcare centers by providing an alternative to physical consultations.

---

2. Examples of Successful Platforms Addressing Underserved Populations

- **Tata 1mg's Affordable Healthcare Initiative**:
  - **Objective**: To make healthcare affordable for low-income groups.
  - **Execution**: The platform introduced discounts on generic medications and bundled packages for chronic diseases, such as diabetes and hypertension.
  - **Result**: Enhanced affordability and accessibility for underserved populations, fostering trust and loyalty among customers.
- **Medlife's Focus on Women's Health**:
  - **Initiative**: A targeted campaign to provide discounted prenatal and postnatal care products in semi-urban and rural areas.
  - **Outcome**: Increased access to essential healthcare products for women, improving maternal and child health outcomes.

Global Innovations

International e-pharmacy platforms have demonstrated remarkable advancements in technology, logistics, and cross-border collaborations, setting benchmarks for the industry.

---

1. Innovations in Logistics and AI-Driven Inventory Management

- **Case Study: Amazon Pharmacy (US)**:
  - **Innovation**: Leveraged AI for predictive inventory management, ensuring real-time stock updates and reducing wastage.

   - **Impact**: Enhanced operational efficiency and minimized delays in fulfilling orders, particularly for high-demand medications during the COVID-19 pandemic.
- **DHL's Cold Chain Logistics (Global)**:
   - **Problem**: Temperature-sensitive medicines like vaccines require stringent cold-chain management.
   - **Solution**: Integration of IoT-enabled temperature monitors in logistics, ensuring compliance throughout the supply chain.
   - **Result**: Improved reliability in delivering biologics and other sensitive products across borders.

---

2. Cross-Border Collaborations for Streamlined Delivery

- **Example: LloydsPharmacy and EU Regulations**:
   - **Collaboration**: Worked with European Union regulators to create a standardized framework for cross-border online medicine sales.
   - **Outcome**: Simplified processes for European customers purchasing prescription drugs online, reducing delivery times and regulatory hurdles.
- **Singapore's Integrated Digital Health Network**:
   - **Initiative**: Partnered with neighboring countries to create a seamless network for prescription verification and drug delivery.
   - **Impact**: Enabled patients to access medicines even when traveling across borders, ensuring continuity of care.

Lessons Learned

The journey of e-pharmacies offers valuable insights into effective strategies and potential pitfalls.

---

1. Effective Strategies from Pioneers in the E-Pharmacy Sector

- **Customer-Centric Innovations**:
   - **Example**: PillPack by Amazon focused on pre-sorted medication packaging, catering to elderly patients and those with chronic illnesses.

    - **Lesson**: Addressing specific customer pain points can significantly enhance user satisfaction and loyalty.
- **Technological Adoption**:
    - **Example**: E-pharmacies integrating AI to recommend medicines and detect counterfeit products saw improved trust and operational efficiency.
    - **Lesson**: Leveraging advanced technologies can streamline operations and build consumer confidence.

---

2. Pitfalls and Challenges Encountered

- **Regulatory Non-Compliance**:
    - **Example**: Early entrants in the Indian e-pharmacy market faced backlash for inadequate prescription verification, leading to temporary bans.
    - **Lesson**: Strict adherence to regulatory guidelines is essential to avoid reputational and operational risks.
- **Data Breaches**:
    - **Example**: A major e-pharmacy platform in the US faced lawsuits following a data breach exposing patient health information.
    - **Lesson**: Investing in robust cybersecurity measures is critical to safeguarding consumer trust and avoiding legal repercussions.

CHAPTER 8

Regulatory Affairs

Introduction to Regulatory Affairs

Definition and Scope

What are Regulatory Affairs?

Regulatory affairs is a specialized field within the healthcare and pharmaceutical industries, encompassing the processes and activities required to ensure that products meet all applicable regulations and standards before they reach the market. These products include drugs, medical devices, biologics, cosmetics, and even certain types of food and beverages.

At its core, regulatory affairs is about compliance—ensuring that products adhere to the stringent requirements set forth by national and international authorities. This discipline acts as a bridge between the regulatory agencies that enforce these rules and the industries that must abide by them.

Key Responsibilities of Regulatory Affairs

1. **Product Registration**:
    - Submitting documentation to secure approval for new products.
2. **Compliance Oversight**:
    - Ensuring products meet ongoing standards throughout their lifecycle.
3. **Monitoring Changes in Regulations**:
    - Adapting to evolving regulatory frameworks to maintain compliance.
4. **Post-Marketing Surveillance**:
    - Overseeing safety and efficacy even after products are in the market.

Role in Ensuring Product Safety, Efficacy, and Quality

1. **Safety**:
   - Regulatory affairs ensures that products are free from unacceptable risks. For instance, rigorous clinical trials are conducted to verify that drugs are safe for human use.
   - Example: Monitoring adverse drug reactions through pharmacovigilance programs.
2. **Efficacy**:
   - The primary purpose of any healthcare product is to deliver the intended therapeutic benefit. Regulatory requirements ensure that clinical evidence supports the efficacy claims.
   - Example: Randomized controlled trials (RCTs) are often required to demonstrate a drug's effectiveness.
3. **Quality**:
   - Products must consistently meet high-quality standards. Regulatory affairs ensures adherence to Good Manufacturing Practices (GMP) and Good Laboratory Practices (GLP).
   - Example: A regulatory body might inspect a manufacturing facility to confirm compliance with quality protocols.

Importance in Healthcare and Pharmaceutical Industries

Protecting Public Health

The primary mission of regulatory affairs is to safeguard public health. By ensuring that all healthcare products are safe, effective, and of high quality, regulatory professionals play a crucial role in minimizing risks associated with unsafe or ineffective products.

1. **Examples of Failures**:
   - The thalidomide tragedy in the 1960s, where inadequate drug testing led to birth defects, highlighted the importance of stringent regulatory oversight.
   - As a response, modern regulatory frameworks were designed to prevent such occurrences.
2. **Ensuring Accessibility**:
   - Regulatory processes also focus on timely access to essential medicines and therapies without compromising safety.

Facilitating Global Trade Compliance

1. **Market Access**:
   - In today's globalized economy, healthcare companies often seek to market their products internationally. Regulatory affairs ensures that products meet the unique requirements of each target market.
   - Example: For a pharmaceutical company to sell its products in the EU, compliance with European Medicines Agency (EMA) guidelines is mandatory.
2. **Harmonization of Standards**:
   - Regulatory professionals contribute to global harmonization efforts, such as those led by the International Council for Harmonisation (ICH), ensuring that products can be marketed across multiple regions with minimal duplication of effort.
3. **Competitive Advantage**:
   - Efficient regulatory compliance not only ensures market access but also strengthens a company's reputation and trustworthiness in the industry.

Historical Evolution

The field of regulatory affairs has a rich history, rooted in the need to address public health crises and the increasing complexity of healthcare products.

Origins of Regulatory Systems

1. **Early Regulations**:
   - Regulatory systems date back to the 19th century when governments began to formalize standards for food and medicine safety.
   - Example: The 1906 **Pure Food and Drug Act** in the United States, which laid the groundwork for the FDA.
2. **Catalysts for Change**:
   - Tragic events such as the Elixir Sulfanilamide disaster in 1937, where a toxic solvent in a medicine caused over 100 deaths, spurred the creation of modern drug regulations.
   - The establishment of the FDA in the US and similar agencies globally became a turning point.

Development of Modern Regulatory Frameworks Globally

1. **United States**:
   - Introduction of the **Federal Food, Drug, and Cosmetic Act (1938)** brought significant advancements, requiring safety testing before marketing drugs.
   - The FDA remains one of the most influential regulatory bodies globally.
2. **Europe**:
   - The creation of the **European Medicines Agency (EMA)** in 1995 standardized drug approvals across member states, simplifying market entry for pharmaceutical companies.
3. **India**:
   - The **Drugs and Cosmetics Act, 1940**, governs the Indian pharmaceutical sector, with the **Central Drugs Standard Control Organization (CDSCO)** acting as the regulatory authority.
   - Recent amendments have modernized the system, aligning India's regulations more closely with global standards.
4. **Global Harmonization**:
   - The establishment of the **ICH** and similar organizations has driven harmonization of regulatory requirements, facilitating international trade and collaboration.

8.1 Objectives of Regulatory Affairs

Regulatory affairs serves as the backbone of the healthcare and pharmaceutical industries, ensuring that products meet safety, quality, and efficacy standards. The objectives of regulatory affairs are expansive and vital, aiming to uphold compliance, protect public health, and facilitate market access. Each objective is interconnected, forming a robust framework that ensures both consumer safety and industry growth. This section explores these objectives in-depth, highlighting their significance and practical applications.

Ensuring Product Compliance

At its core, regulatory affairs revolves around compliance—ensuring that healthcare products, ranging from medicines to medical devices, adhere to national and international standards. Compliance is not a mere checkbox exercise but a dynamic process that safeguards public trust and facilitates seamless market operations.

Adherence to National and International Standards

Every country has its unique regulatory framework, tailored to its public health priorities and market needs. Regulatory affairs professionals act as navigators, guiding products through this maze of requirements to ensure compliance.

1. **National Standards**:
   - Each country has a regulatory body that oversees healthcare product compliance.
   - Example: In India, the **Central Drugs Standard Control Organization (CDSCO)** enforces the **Drugs and Cosmetics Act, 1940**, which governs drug approvals, manufacturing practices, and marketing.
2. **International Standards**:
   - For products intended for global markets, adherence to international standards is essential.
   - Example: The **International Council for Harmonisation (ICH)** harmonizes technical requirements for pharmaceuticals, enabling smoother market entry across multiple regions.
3. **Practical Application**:
   - Consider a pharmaceutical company developing a generic drug. To market this product globally, the company must align with:
     - **FDA** guidelines for the US.
     - **EMA** standards for the European Union.
     - Local regulations for emerging markets like Brazil or China.

Preventing Non-Compliant Products from Entering Markets

The consequences of non-compliance are severe, ranging from public health risks to legal penalties and reputational damage for companies. Regulatory affairs professionals play a crucial role in preemptively addressing potential compliance issues.

1. **Key Measures**:
   - Rigorous documentation: Comprehensive dossiers, including preclinical and clinical data, must be submitted for approval.

   - Periodic audits: Manufacturing facilities are inspected to ensure adherence to **Good Manufacturing Practices (GMP)**.
2. **Example**:
   - In 2019, a global recall of a popular blood pressure medication occurred due to contamination with a carcinogenic impurity. This incident highlighted the need for stringent compliance checks during manufacturing.
3. **Proactive Strategies**:
   - Training manufacturing teams on quality standards.
   - Leveraging digital tools to monitor compliance in real-time.

Maintaining Public Safety

The ultimate goal of regulatory affairs is to protect public health by ensuring that only safe, effective, and high-quality products reach the market. This responsibility extends beyond pre-approval compliance to continuous monitoring post-launch.

Monitoring Adverse Effects and Ensuring Corrective Measures

Even with thorough pre-approval testing, unforeseen adverse effects may emerge once a product is widely used. Regulatory frameworks mandate mechanisms to identify and mitigate such risks.

1. **Pharmacovigilance Systems**:
   - Regulatory agencies require companies to establish pharmacovigilance systems to monitor and report adverse drug reactions (ADRs).
   - Example: The **Adverse Event Reporting System (AERS)** by the FDA collects data on drug safety from healthcare providers and consumers.
2. **Corrective Measures**:
   - If significant risks are identified, regulatory authorities may demand actions such as updating product labels, issuing warnings, or recalling the product.
   - Example: The recall of certain batches of a widely used vaccine due to contamination risks showcased the efficiency of regulatory monitoring.

3. **Case Study**:
    - A popular over-the-counter pain reliever was found to cause rare but severe liver damage in certain populations. Regulatory authorities mandated clearer warning labels and lower recommended dosages to mitigate the risk.

Role of Recalls in Mitigating Risks

Recalls are a vital tool in maintaining public safety when defective or harmful products are identified. While recalls may appear as failures, they are actually signs of a robust regulatory system functioning effectively.

1. **Types of Recalls**:
    - **Class I**: High risk; the product poses a serious health hazard (e.g., contaminated medication).
    - **Class II**: Moderate risk; issues like labeling errors or minor contamination.
    - **Class III**: Low risk; cosmetic or manufacturing defects unlikely to cause harm.
2. **Steps in a Recall**:
    - Identification of the issue through reports or routine surveillance.
    - Communication with regulatory authorities.
    - Withdrawal of the product from markets and corrective action.
3. **Real-World Example**:
    - A global pharmaceutical company voluntarily recalled a diabetes medication due to the detection of an impurity. Regulatory authorities facilitated the process to ensure affected patients received guidance and alternative treatments.

Facilitating Market Access

Regulatory affairs not only ensure compliance and safety but also play a pivotal role in enabling companies to bring their products to new markets efficiently. This involves streamlining approval processes and fostering innovation.

Streamlining Product Approvals for New Markets

1. **Understanding Market-Specific Requirements**:
   - Each market has unique submission requirements and approval timelines.
   - Example: The FDA may require additional clinical trial data for US approval, even for products already approved in the EU.
2. **Expedited Approvals**:
   - Many regulatory bodies offer expedited pathways for innovative or life-saving products.
   - Examples:
     - **Fast Track Designation** by the FDA for drugs addressing unmet medical needs.
     - **Conditional Marketing Authorization** by the EMA for medicines treating rare diseases.
3. **Practical Insight**:
   - Companies often hire regulatory consultants or establish in-house teams to navigate complex approval processes and reduce time-to-market.

Encouraging Innovation Through Regulatory Flexibility

1. **Adaptive Frameworks**:
   - Regulatory agencies increasingly adopt flexible approaches to accommodate breakthroughs in technology and medicine.
   - Example: Regulatory pathways for personalized medicine, such as gene and cell therapies, involve ongoing collaboration between regulators and developers.
2. **Support for Emerging Technologies**:
   - Guidelines for digital health tools, wearable devices, and artificial intelligence-based diagnostics.
   - Example: The FDA's **Digital Health Innovation Action Plan** facilitates the approval of software as a medical device (SaMD).
3. **Case Study**:
   - A biotech startup developing a novel cancer therapy received priority review from the FDA, allowing it to launch the product within six months of submission.

8.2 Key Global Regulatory Bodies: United States – Food and Drug Administration (FDA)

The **Food and Drug Administration (FDA)** is one of the most influential regulatory agencies in the world, setting the benchmark for safety, efficacy, and quality in healthcare products. As the regulatory authority of the United States, the FDA's decisions ripple across the global healthcare and pharmaceutical industries. This section provides an in-depth exploration of the FDA's structure, responsibilities, and processes.

Structure of the FDA

The FDA operates as a part of the **Department of Health and Human Services (HHS)**, and its organizational structure is designed to oversee a wide range of products efficiently.

Key Organizational Divisions

1. **Office of the Commissioner (OC)**:
   - The Commissioner of Food and Drugs oversees the entire agency and ensures its alignment with public health goals.
   - Supported by deputy commissioners specializing in regulatory affairs, policy, and scientific development.
2. **Centers and Offices**: The FDA is divided into product-specific centers and support offices:
   - **Center for Drug Evaluation and Research (CDER)**:
     - Focuses on the safety and efficacy of drugs, including generics and biologics.
   - **Center for Biologics Evaluation and Research (CBER)**:
     - Regulates vaccines, blood products, and gene therapies.
   - **Center for Devices and Radiological Health (CDRH)**:
     - Ensures the safety and performance of medical devices.
   - **Center for Food Safety and Applied Nutrition (CFSAN)**:
     - Oversees the safety of food and dietary supplements.
   - **Center for Veterinary Medicine (CVM)**:
     - Regulates animal drugs, feeds, and veterinary devices.

- **Office of Regulatory Affairs (ORA)**:
    - Enforces FDA regulations through inspections and compliance actions.

Regional Offices

To ensure effective implementation, the FDA maintains regional offices across the United States, tasked with inspections, surveillance, and enforcement activities.

Responsibilities of the FDA

The FDA's overarching goal is to protect public health by regulating a diverse array of products, ranging from drugs and devices to cosmetics and food.

1. Pre-Market Approval

Before a product can enter the market, it must undergo rigorous evaluation to ensure it meets the FDA's safety, efficacy, and quality standards.

- **Drugs**:
    - New Drug Applications (NDAs) and Abbreviated New Drug Applications (ANDAs) for generics must demonstrate safety and efficacy through clinical data.
    - Example: Approval of novel cancer therapies under the **Breakthrough Therapy Designation** program.
- **Medical Devices**:
    - Devices are categorized based on risk:
        - **Class I** (low-risk): Exempt from pre-market approval but must adhere to general controls.
        - **Class II** (moderate-risk): Require pre-market notification (510(k)).
        - **Class III** (high-risk): Require extensive pre-market approval (PMA).
- **Biologics**:
    - Vaccines, blood products, and advanced therapies must meet stringent safety and potency requirements.

2. Post-Market Surveillance

The FDA monitors products after they enter the market to ensure continued safety and effectiveness.

- **Adverse Event Reporting**:
  - The FDA's **MedWatch Program** collects data on adverse drug reactions and product defects.
- **Safety Recalls**:
  - Products posing significant risks are recalled, often in collaboration with manufacturers.
  - Example: Recalls of faulty pacemakers or contaminated pharmaceuticals.

3. Inspections and Compliance

The FDA enforces compliance through routine inspections and targeted actions.

- **Good Manufacturing Practices (GMP)**:
  - Inspections ensure facilities comply with GMP standards to prevent contamination or defects.
  - Example: FDA inspectors may visit a pharmaceutical plant to verify production standards.
- **Warning Letters**:
  - Issued for non-compliance, requiring corrective actions within a stipulated timeframe.

4. Regulation of Emerging Technologies

The FDA adapts to technological advancements, ensuring that innovative products meet regulatory standards.

- **Digital Health**:
  - Overseeing software as a medical device (SaMD) under the Digital Health Innovation Action Plan.
  - Example: Approval of AI-powered diagnostic tools for imaging.
- **Gene and Cell Therapies**:
  - Establishing pathways for novel treatments under its regenerative medicine framework.

Processes of the FDA

The FDA employs structured processes to evaluate, approve, and monitor healthcare products.

---

1. Drug Approval Process

The drug approval process is one of the FDA's most rigorous and well-defined procedures.

Stages:

1. **Preclinical Testing**:
   - Drugs are tested in laboratories and on animals to evaluate safety and biological activity.
2. **Investigational New Drug (IND) Application**:
   - Filed to obtain permission for human clinical trials.
3. **Clinical Trials**:
   - Conducted in three phases:
     - **Phase I**: Assess safety and dosage in a small group of volunteers.
     - **Phase II**: Evaluate efficacy and side effects in a larger group.
     - **Phase III**: Confirm effectiveness in a broad population.
4. **New Drug Application (NDA)**:
   - Submitted with comprehensive data from trials for FDA review.
5. **Approval or Rejection**:
   - The FDA reviews the NDA within a standard timeline (typically 10 months for standard applications or 6 months for priority reviews).

---

2. Device Approval Process

The FDA categorizes medical devices by risk, tailoring the approval process accordingly.

- **510(k) Submission**:
  - Used for moderate-risk devices that are "substantially equivalent" to an already marketed device.
- **Pre-Market Approval (PMA)**:
  - Reserved for high-risk devices, requiring clinical evidence of safety and effectiveness.

---

3. Fast-Track and Priority Programs

To accelerate access to critical therapies, the FDA offers expedited pathways.

- **Fast Track**:
  - For drugs addressing serious conditions, allowing early interactions with the FDA.
- **Breakthrough Therapy**:
  - Provides intensive guidance and priority review for transformative therapies.
- **Accelerated Approval**:
  - Approves drugs based on surrogate endpoints, with post-marketing studies required.
- **Priority Review**:
  - Reduces standard review timelines for drugs offering significant improvements over existing treatments.

European Medicines Agency (EMA): Centralized Procedures and Mutual Recognition

The **European Medicines Agency (EMA)** is a pivotal regulatory body in the European Union (EU), ensuring that medicines marketed within the EU are safe, effective, and of high quality. By centralizing certain aspects of drug approval and harmonizing standards across member states, the EMA plays a crucial role in facilitating access to innovative therapies. This section provides an in-depth exploration of the EMA's structure, responsibilities, and processes, with a focus on its **centralized procedures** and **mutual recognition systems**.

Introduction to the EMA

The EMA, established in 1995, is headquartered in Amsterdam, Netherlands. Its mandate is to promote public and animal health by evaluating and supervising medicinal products across the EU. Unlike national regulatory agencies, the EMA operates at the supranational level, coordinating with member states to streamline the drug approval process.

Centralized Procedures

The centralized procedure is a unique aspect of the EMA, allowing a single application to result in a marketing authorization valid across all EU member states, along with Iceland, Liechtenstein, and Norway.

How the Centralized Procedure Works

1. **Eligibility**:
   - Certain medicines must use the centralized procedure:
     - Biologic products, including biosimilars.
     - Advanced therapy medicinal products (ATMPs) like gene and cell therapies.
     - Medicines for rare diseases (orphan drugs).
   - Companies may also voluntarily apply for centralized authorization if the product provides significant innovation.
2. **Application Submission**:
   - A single dossier is submitted to the EMA, following the **Common Technical Document (CTD)** format.
   - The application is reviewed by the **Committee for Medicinal Products for Human Use (CHMP)**, a scientific advisory body composed of experts from EU member states.
3. **Evaluation**:
   - **Scientific Review**:
     - CHMP assesses safety, efficacy, and quality based on preclinical and clinical data.
     - Risk-benefit analysis is central to the evaluation process.
   - **Timelines**:
     - Standard review: 210 days.
     - Accelerated review: 150 days for medicines addressing unmet medical needs.
4. **Decision Making**:
   - CHMP provides a recommendation to the European Commission, which grants the final marketing authorization.
   - The authorization is valid across the EU, enabling uniform market access.
5. **Post-Authorization Requirements**:
   - Continuous monitoring through pharmacovigilance systems.
   - Periodic safety update reports (PSURs) to ensure ongoing evaluation of the product's risk-benefit profile.

Advantages of the Centralized Procedure

1. **Streamlined Access**:
    - A single application leads to EU-wide authorization, reducing administrative burdens for pharmaceutical companies.
2. **Harmonization**:
    - Ensures uniform safety and efficacy standards across all member states.
3. **Encouraging Innovation**:
    - Accelerated pathways and scientific advice foster the development of cutting-edge therapies, particularly for rare diseases and complex conditions.
4. **Public Health Benefits**:
    - Expedited access to new therapies across the EU ensures better health outcomes.

Case Study: Successful Use of the Centralized Procedure

- **COVID-19 Vaccines**:
    - The EMA played a critical role in the rapid approval of COVID-19 vaccines like Pfizer-BioNTech and Moderna through the centralized procedure.
    - Rigorous, transparent evaluations ensured vaccines were available across the EU within months.

Mutual Recognition Procedure (MRP)

The Mutual Recognition Procedure is designed for medicines that are already authorized in one EU member state and wish to gain approval in additional countries.

How the Mutual Recognition Procedure Works

1. **Reference Member State (RMS)**:
    - A product is first approved in a single EU member state, which acts as the RMS.
2. **Application Submission**:
    - The dossier is submitted to other member states where the company seeks marketing authorization, known as **Concerned Member States (CMS)**.

3. **Review Process**:
   - CMS rely on the assessment report provided by the RMS.
   - If there are no objections, the product is authorized in all CMS.
4. **Resolution of Disputes**:
   - In case of disagreements between RMS and CMS, the **Coordination Group for Mutual Recognition and Decentralized Procedures (CMDh)** facilitates resolution.

Decentralized Procedure (DCP)

The decentralized procedure is a variant of the MRP for products that have not yet been approved in any EU member state.

1. **Simultaneous Submission**:
   - Companies submit applications to multiple member states simultaneously.
2. **Harmonized Review**:
   - A consensus is reached among all involved states before authorization is granted.

Advantages of Mutual Recognition and Decentralized Procedures

1. **Flexibility**:
   - Allows companies to tailor their market entry strategies by targeting specific EU countries.
2. **Reduced Duplication**:
   - Avoids repetitive evaluations by leveraging assessments conducted by RMS.
3. **Expanded Market Access**:
   - Facilitates the broader availability of medicines within the EU.

Challenges in MRP and DCP

1. **Harmonization Issues**:
   - Differences in member state preferences or interpretations can delay approvals.

2. **Administrative Complexity**:
   - Coordination among multiple national authorities can be resource-intensive.

Role of EMA in Pharmacovigilance

The EMA's responsibilities extend beyond approvals, ensuring that medicines remain safe and effective after entering the market.

1. **EudraVigilance Database**:
   - A centralized system for collecting and analyzing adverse drug reactions (ADRs) across the EU.
2. **Risk Management Plans (RMPs)**:
   - Companies must submit RMPs detailing how risks will be monitored and mitigated post-authorization.
3. **Recalls and Safety Warnings**:
   - In cases of safety concerns, the EMA collaborates with member states to issue recalls or warnings.

EMA's Role in Global Harmonization

The EMA collaborates with international regulatory bodies to align standards and facilitate global trade.

1. **ICH Guidelines**:
   - The EMA adopts International Council for Harmonisation guidelines, promoting uniform technical standards for pharmaceuticals.
2. **Partnerships**:
   - Regular cooperation with the FDA, WHO, and other global regulators to streamline approvals for innovative therapies.
3. **Case Study**:
   - EMA and FDA collaboration during the COVID-19 pandemic accelerated global vaccine availability.

India: Central Drugs Standard Control Organization (CDSCO)

The **Central Drugs Standard Control Organization (CDSCO)** serves as India's national regulatory authority for pharmaceuticals, medical devices, and cosmetics. Operating under the **Ministry of Health and Family Welfare**, the CDSCO plays a pivotal role in ensuring that healthcare products meet stringent safety, efficacy, and quality standards. As the primary regulatory body in India, it oversees licensing, approvals, and ongoing compliance for a vast array of products in one of the world's fastest-growing healthcare markets.

Structure of the CDSCO

The CDSCO operates through a well-defined structure to handle its multifaceted responsibilities efficiently.

1. Directorate General of Health Services

- The CDSCO functions under the administrative control of the Directorate General of Health Services (DGHS), which is part of the Ministry of Health and Family Welfare.

2. Drug Controller General of India (DCGI)

- The **DCGI** is the head of the CDSCO and is responsible for implementing the **Drugs and Cosmetics Act, 1940**, and its associated rules.
- The DCGI oversees:
    - Approval of new drugs and clinical trials.
    - Setting standards for drugs, cosmetics, and medical devices.
    - Monitoring quality through post-market surveillance.

3. Zonal and Sub-Zonal Offices

- The CDSCO is divided into several zonal, sub-zonal, and port offices to manage regional regulatory activities.
    - **Zonal Offices**: Located in major cities like Mumbai, Kolkata, and Chennai.
    - **Port Offices**: Facilitate import/export regulation of pharmaceuticals.

4. Central Drug Testing Laboratories (CDTLs)

- Laboratories under CDSCO conduct analytical testing to ensure product quality and adherence to standards.

Licensing, Approvals, and Oversight by CDSCO

The CDSCO is responsible for multiple critical functions that span the lifecycle of healthcare products, from pre-market evaluation to post-market surveillance.

---

1. Licensing

Licensing is one of the foundational roles of the CDSCO, ensuring that only authorized entities can manufacture, import, or distribute healthcare products.

Types of Licenses

1. **Manufacturing Licenses**:
   - Issued for the production of pharmaceuticals, medical devices, and cosmetics.
   - Granted at the state level but regulated by the CDSCO for specific categories like new drugs or vaccines.
2. **Import Licenses**:
   - Required for bringing drugs, medical devices, and cosmetics into India.
   - Application involves submitting safety, efficacy, and quality data to the CDSCO for evaluation.
3. **Marketing Licenses**:
   - Companies must obtain marketing authorization before launching a product in India.
   - Includes approval for product labels, advertisements, and package inserts.

---

2. Approvals

The CDSCO oversees a rigorous approval process to ensure products meet Indian regulatory requirements.

Approval of New Drugs

1. **Clinical Trial Approvals**:
   - All new drugs must undergo clinical trials in India unless exempted by global data.
   - Sponsors must file an application with detailed protocols and obtain approval from the DCGI.
   - **Ethics Committees** monitor trial conduct, ensuring adherence to guidelines.
2. **New Drug Application (NDA)**:
   - Manufacturers submit NDAs, including preclinical and clinical data, for evaluation.
   - CDSCO's Subject Expert Committees (SECs) review safety, efficacy, and quality data.

3. **Expedited Approvals**:
   - For drugs addressing unmet medical needs, the CDSCO may offer accelerated pathways.
   - Example: Approval of COVID-19 vaccines like Covaxin and Covishield under emergency use authorization.

Medical Device Approvals

1. **Risk-Based Classification**:
   - Devices are categorized into **Class A** (low-risk) to **Class D** (high-risk), with regulatory stringency increasing with risk level.
2. **Regulatory Pathways**:
   - Premarket clearance is required for Class C and D devices, including clinical evaluations.

---

3. Oversight

The CDSCO enforces regulations throughout the product lifecycle to ensure continued compliance.

Good Manufacturing Practices (GMP)

1. **Implementation of Schedule M**:
   - Manufacturers must adhere to GMP standards outlined in **Schedule M** of the Drugs and Cosmetics Rules, 1945.
2. **Inspections**:
   - Regular audits of manufacturing facilities by CDSCO officials ensure compliance with quality and safety standards.

Post-Market Surveillance

1. **Pharmacovigilance Program of India (PvPI)**:
   - Monitors adverse drug reactions (ADRs) and ensures prompt action when safety concerns arise.
   - Example: PvPI contributed to the recall of contaminated drugs containing NDMA impurities.
2. **Product Recalls**:
   - The CDSCO can mandate recalls of non-compliant or unsafe products.
   - Example: Recalls of certain ranitidine products linked to carcinogenic impurities.

Role in Harmonization and Global Trade

The CDSCO is actively working to align India's regulatory framework with international standards to facilitate global trade and enhance competitiveness.

1. **ICH Guidelines**:
   - India has adopted several ICH guidelines for clinical trials, quality control, and pharmacovigilance.
2. **Global Collaboration**:
   - Partnerships with regulatory bodies like the US FDA and WHO for knowledge sharing and training.

Case Studies

1. Approval of COVID-19 Vaccines

- The CDSCO expedited the approval process for vaccines during the pandemic, balancing safety with urgency.
- Example: Covishield and Covaxin were approved under emergency use authorizations, enabling rapid deployment across the nation.

2. Addressing Substandard Drugs

- In 2022, the CDSCO launched a nationwide campaign to crack down on substandard antibiotics and ensure compliance with GMP standards.

Challenges Faced by the CDSCO

1. **Resource Constraints**:
   - Limited staff and infrastructure for the scale of India's pharmaceutical industry.
2. **Evolving Technologies**:
   - Regulatory gaps in areas like digital health and artificial intelligence-based diagnostics.
3. **Harmonization**:
   - Balancing domestic requirements with international standards remains a challenge.

Other Major Regulatory Agencies

Beyond the regulatory bodies in the United States, European Union, and India, other global agencies play a significant role in shaping pharmaceutical and medical device standards. These include **Japan's Pharmaceuticals and Medical Devices Agency (PMDA)**, the **World Health Organization (WHO)** with its prequalification programs, and the **International Council**

for Harmonisation (ICH), which drives global harmonization efforts. Each of these organizations contributes to enhancing public health and ensuring product quality and safety across borders.

Japan's Pharmaceuticals and Medical Devices Agency (PMDA)

Introduction to PMDA

The **Pharmaceuticals and Medical Devices Agency (PMDA)** is Japan's regulatory authority, responsible for the review, approval, and post-market monitoring of drugs, medical devices, and regenerative medicine products. Established in 2004, PMDA operates under Japan's Ministry of Health, Labour and Welfare (MHLW).

Key Responsibilities of PMDA

1. **Pre-Market Evaluation**
   - PMDA reviews clinical trial applications and new drug applications (NDAs) for safety, efficacy, and quality.
   - Focus on **innovative therapies** such as regenerative medicine and gene therapy products.
2. **Post-Market Surveillance**
   - PMDA monitors adverse drug reactions (ADRs) and medical device failures through Japan's **Pharmacovigilance Program**.
   - Example: Safety updates are regularly issued for newly marketed therapies to mitigate risks.
3. **Scientific Advice and Consultation**
   - PMDA provides developers with scientific advice during the R&D process, enabling efficient regulatory pathways.
   - Particularly supportive of small and medium enterprises (SMEs) working on innovative therapies.

Unique Regulatory Pathways

1. **Sakigake Designation**:
   - An accelerated approval system for breakthrough therapies developed in Japan, similar to the FDA's Fast Track designation.
   - Example: Innovative oncology treatments often benefit from this pathway.

2. **Conditional Early Approval**:
   - Allows approval based on limited clinical data for products addressing serious unmet needs, with additional data collected post-approval.

Global Collaboration

- PMDA collaborates with international regulators like the **FDA**, **EMA**, and **WHO** to align with global standards.
- Actively participates in the **ICH** to harmonize guidelines for drug development and approval.

World Health Organization (WHO): Prequalification Programs

Introduction to WHO's Role

The **World Health Organization (WHO)** is a specialized agency of the United Nations dedicated to global public health. Its **prequalification (PQ) programs** aim to ensure the availability of safe, effective, and quality-assured medicines, vaccines, and diagnostic tools, particularly in low- and middle-income countries.

Key Aspects of WHO Prequalification

1. **Objective**:
   - Facilitate access to quality-assured healthcare products for global health initiatives like malaria, tuberculosis, and HIV/AIDS.
2. **Prequalification Process**:
   - **Assessment**:
     - Evaluation of dossiers submitted by manufacturers, focusing on quality, safety, and efficacy.
   - **Inspection**:
     - On-site inspections of manufacturing facilities to ensure compliance with **Good Manufacturing Practices (GMP)**.
   - **Monitoring**:
     - Post-prequalification monitoring ensures continued compliance with WHO standards.

Impact of Prequalification Programs

1. **Global Health Initiatives**:
   - WHO PQ is critical for procurement by international organizations like **UNICEF** and **Global Fund**.
   - Example: Prequalification of antiretroviral drugs has significantly improved access to HIV/AIDS treatments in resource-poor settings.
2. **Encouraging Industry Standards**:
   - Manufacturers benefit from WHO's feedback, which often aligns with global regulatory expectations, enhancing market access.

Challenges and Future Directions

1. **Capacity Building**:
   - WHO works with national regulatory authorities (NRAs) to strengthen local regulatory systems.
   - Example: Joint inspections with NRAs in Africa aim to boost regional expertise.
2. **Expanding Scope**:
   - Prequalification is evolving to include **biosimilars** and **advanced diagnostics** to address emerging healthcare needs.

International Council for Harmonisation (ICH): Global Harmonization Efforts

Introduction to ICH

The **International Council for Harmonisation of Technical Requirements for Pharmaceuticals for Human Use (ICH)** is a unique initiative that brings together regulatory authorities and industry stakeholders to standardize technical guidelines globally. Established in 1990, ICH aims to streamline drug development, reduce duplication, and ensure the availability of high-quality medicines worldwide.

Key Objectives of ICH

1. **Harmonization of Guidelines**:
   - Align regulatory requirements across regions, reducing redundancy and inefficiencies in the drug development process.

2. **Enhancing Public Health**:
   - Promote the development and approval of safe, effective, and high-quality medicines.

ICH Guidelines

1. **Quality Guidelines (Q Series)**:
   - Focus on Good Manufacturing Practices (GMP), stability testing, and pharmaceutical quality systems.
   - Example: **ICH Q8-Q10** emphasize Quality by Design (QbD), a proactive approach to manufacturing.
2. **Safety Guidelines (S Series)**:
   - Address preclinical safety evaluations, such as carcinogenicity and genotoxicity testing.
   - Example: **ICH S7A** outlines guidelines for safety pharmacology studies.
3. **Efficacy Guidelines (E Series)**:
   - Provide standards for clinical trial design and conduct.
   - Example: **ICH E6 (R2)** is the globally recognized standard for Good Clinical Practice (GCP).
4. **Multidisciplinary Guidelines (M Series)**:
   - Cover topics like the Common Technical Document (CTD) and electronic submissions.
   - Example: **ICH M4** standardizes dossier formats for regulatory submissions globally.

Impact of ICH Harmonization

1. **Streamlined Regulatory Submissions**:
   - By following ICH guidelines, companies can submit standardized applications to multiple regulatory authorities, reducing time and costs.
2. **Facilitating Global Trade**:
   - Harmonized standards enable medicines to move seamlessly across borders.
3. **Fostering Innovation**:
   - Alignment on new technologies like biologics and gene therapies accelerates global access to cutting-edge treatments.

Global Participation

1. **Core Members**:
   - Includes regulatory agencies like the FDA, EMA, and PMDA, along with industry associations.
2. **Observer Status**:
   - Organizations such as WHO and smaller regulatory bodies participate to stay aligned with global practices.

Challenges and Future Directions

1. **Expanding Participation**:
   - Inclusion of emerging economies to ensure universal applicability of guidelines.
2. **Adapting to Innovation**:
   - Developing harmonized standards for advanced therapies, digital health, and AI-driven diagnostics.

8.3 Regulatory Processes: New Drug Applications (NDAs)

The **New Drug Application (NDA)** is the cornerstone of the drug approval process, providing regulatory authorities with comprehensive information to assess the safety, efficacy, and quality of a new pharmaceutical product. This detailed process ensures that only drugs meeting stringent criteria are introduced into the market, safeguarding public health while fostering innovation.

Overview of the NDA Application Process

The NDA submission represents the culmination of years of research, clinical trials, and rigorous data collection. It is the formal mechanism through which a drug sponsor requests regulatory approval to market a new drug.

---

1. Purpose of an NDA

The primary objectives of an NDA are:

- **To demonstrate safety and efficacy**:
  - Data must confirm that the drug provides the intended therapeutic benefits and that its risks are acceptable compared to its benefits.

- **To ensure manufacturing quality**:
    - The production process must consistently yield a drug that meets predetermined standards.
- **To provide labeling information**:
    - Proposed labeling must outline accurate dosing, indications, side effects, and precautions.

---

2. The NDA Pathway

The journey to NDA submission is complex and includes several stages:

1. **Preclinical Studies**:
    - Before human trials, a drug undergoes **in vitro** (test tube) and **in vivo** (animal) studies to evaluate its biological activity, toxicity, and pharmacokinetics.
    - Example: A drug targeting cancer cells might be tested in rodents to determine its safety and initial efficacy.
2. **Investigational New Drug (IND) Application**:
    - Filed with regulatory authorities to gain permission to begin clinical trials in humans.
    - Includes:
        - Preclinical study results.
        - Proposed clinical trial protocols.
        - Manufacturing information.
3. **Clinical Trials**:
    - Conducted in three phases:
        - **Phase I**: Focuses on safety, dosage, and pharmacokinetics in a small group of healthy volunteers.
        - **Phase II**: Explores efficacy and optimal dosing in a larger patient population.
        - **Phase III**: Confirms efficacy and monitors adverse effects in a broad population.
    - Example: A new diabetes drug might undergo trials in thousands of patients to confirm its ability to control blood sugar levels without severe side effects.

4. **NDA Submission**:
   - Once clinical trials are complete, the sponsor compiles all data into an NDA for regulatory review.
5. **Regulatory Review**:
   - The regulatory authority evaluates the NDA for:
     - Clinical benefit-risk assessment.
     - Manufacturing standards compliance.
     - Clear and accurate labeling.
6. **Approval or Rejection**:
   - The regulator either grants marketing authorization or issues a complete response letter (CRL) detailing deficiencies.

---

3. Regulatory Timelines

1. **Standard Review**:
   - Typically takes **10 months**.
2. **Priority Review**:
   - Granted for drugs addressing unmet medical needs or significant therapeutic advances; completed in **6 months**.

Data Requirements for NDAs

The success of an NDA hinges on the quality and comprehensiveness of its data. Regulatory authorities demand robust evidence to support the safety, efficacy, and manufacturing consistency of the drug.

---

1. Clinical Data

1. **Efficacy Data**:
   - Derived from Phase II and Phase III trials, demonstrating the drug's ability to treat or prevent the target condition.
   - Example: A hypertension drug might show statistically significant reductions in blood pressure compared to placebo.
2. **Safety Data**:
   - Reports on adverse events, serious adverse effects, and overall tolerability during clinical trials.
   - Regulators assess whether the benefits outweigh the risks for the intended population.

3. **Pharmacokinetics and Pharmacodynamics (PK/PD)**:
    - Data on the drug's absorption, distribution, metabolism, and excretion (ADME).
    - PK/PD studies ensure that the recommended dosage is both effective and safe.

---

2. Preclinical Data

Preclinical studies provide the foundation for understanding the drug's mechanism of action and potential risks.

1. **Toxicology Studies**:
    - Assess the potential for acute, chronic, reproductive, and carcinogenic toxicity.
    - Example: A study might reveal whether a drug causes organ damage after prolonged use.
2. **Pharmacology Studies**:
    - Explore the biological mechanism of the drug and its impact on target receptors or enzymes.
3. **Animal Models**:
    - Data from animal studies ensure the drug is safe enough to proceed to human trials.

---

3. Manufacturing Data

The manufacturing section of an NDA ensures that the drug can be consistently produced to meet quality standards.

1. **Chemistry, Manufacturing, and Controls (CMC)**:
    - Detailed documentation of the drug's formulation, active pharmaceutical ingredients (APIs), and excipients.
    - Example: For a tablet, CMC data would include the composition of active ingredients and binders.
2. **Good Manufacturing Practices (GMP)**:
    - Facilities must comply with GMP guidelines to ensure product safety and uniformity.
3. **Stability Data**:
    - Stability studies confirm that the drug retains its potency and safety over its shelf life.

---

4. Labeling Data

1. **Proposed Label**:
   - Includes:
     - Indications.
     - Dosage and administration.
     - Warnings and contraindications.
   - Example: The label for an analgesic might warn against use in paticnts with livcr discasc.
2. **Patient Information Leaflet**:
   - Simplified language for non-expert audiences, explaining how to use the drug safely.

Case Study: Successful NDA

Drug: Paxlovid (COVID-19 Treatment)

1. **Preclinical Studies**:
   - Demonstrated antiviral activity against SARS-CoV-2.
2. **Clinical Trials**:
   - Phase III trial showed a **89% reduction in hospitalization and death** among high-risk patients.
3. **NDA Submission**:
   - Pfizer submitted comprehensive data within months, leveraging priority review pathways.
4. **Outcome**:
   - FDA granted emergency use authorization, followed by full approval.

Abbreviated New Drug Applications (ANDAs)

The **Abbreviated New Drug Application (ANDA)** is a regulatory pathway designed specifically for the approval of generic drugs. Unlike the extensive process required for a New Drug Application (NDA), the ANDA streamlines approval by focusing on demonstrating that the generic product is **bioequivalent** to the brand-name drug it aims to replicate. This approach ensures that high-quality, affordable medicines are available to patients without compromising safety or efficacy.

Focus on Generics

Generic drugs are crucial to the healthcare system as they offer cost-effective alternatives to branded medications. The ANDA process enables pharmaceutical manufacturers to introduce generics into the market efficiently, promoting competition and accessibility.

What is a Generic Drug?

A generic drug is a pharmaceutical product that:

1. Contains the same active ingredient(s) as the brand-name drug.
2. Matches the reference drug in:
    - Dosage form (e.g., tablet, capsule).
    - Strength.
    - Route of administration (e.g., oral, intravenous).
    - Intended use.

Key Characteristics of Generics

1. **Therapeutic Equivalence**:
    - A generic must be "therapeutically equivalent" to the reference listed drug (RLD), meaning it provides the same clinical benefit.
2. **Cost Effectiveness**:
    - Generics are typically priced 80–85% lower than their brand-name counterparts.
3. **Regulatory Framework**:
    - Approved under the ANDA pathway, generics bypass the need for extensive clinical trials required for new drugs.

ANDA vs. NDA

1. **Clinical Data**:
    - NDAs require comprehensive clinical trial data to establish safety and efficacy.
    - ANDAs rely on bioequivalence studies to demonstrate similarity to the RLD.
2. **Cost and Time**:
    - ANDAs are less expensive and faster to prepare, often approved within 8–12 months compared to several years for an NDA.

Bioequivalence Studies

The cornerstone of the ANDA process is proving that the generic drug is **bioequivalent** to the RLD. Bioequivalence ensures that the generic performs similarly to the brand-name drug in the body.

What is Bioequivalence?

Bioequivalence refers to the absence of a significant difference in the **rate and extent of absorption** of the active ingredient between the generic and its RLD when administered under similar conditions.

Conducting Bioequivalence Studies

1. **Study Design**:
   - Typically a **crossover study** involving healthy volunteers.
   - Participants receive both the generic and RLD in randomized order, separated by a washout period.
2. **Pharmacokinetic (PK) Parameters**:
   - Key parameters measured include:
     - **Cmax (maximum plasma concentration)**: Indicates the peak level of the drug in the bloodstream.
     - **AUC (area under the curve)**: Reflects the total drug exposure over time.
   - Bioequivalence is established if the 90% confidence interval of the ratio of these parameters (generic vs. RLD) falls within **80–125%**.
3. **Analytical Techniques**:
   - Advanced analytical methods, such as **high-performance liquid chromatography (HPLC)**, are used to quantify drug concentrations in plasma samples.

Waiver of In Vivo Bioequivalence Studies

In certain cases, manufacturers may request a waiver from conducting **in vivo** (human) bioequivalence studies, relying instead on **in vitro** (laboratory-based) testing.

1. **Biopharmaceutics Classification System (BCS)-Based Waivers**:
   - For drugs classified under **BCS Class I** (high solubility and high permeability), in vivo studies may be waived if the dissolution profile of the generic matches the RLD.
   - Example: Simple oral solutions or immediate-release formulations.
2. **Additional Waiver Criteria**:
   - Strength variations within the same formulation:
     - If a bioequivalence study is conducted for one strength, other strengths may qualify for a waiver provided proportional similarity in composition is demonstrated.

Challenges in Bioequivalence

1. **Narrow Therapeutic Index (NTI) Drugs**:
   - For drugs like warfarin or digoxin, even minor variations in plasma levels can lead to significant safety concerns.
   - Stricter bioequivalence criteria may apply.
2. **Complex Generics**:
   - Drugs with complex formulations (e.g., inhalers or extended-release tablets) require additional data to establish equivalence.

ANDA Process in Detail

The ANDA submission involves multiple steps, each requiring meticulous documentation to meet regulatory standards.

---

1. Reference Listed Drug (RLD) Identification

- The generic manufacturer must identify the RLD against which bioequivalence will be established.
- Example: A manufacturer seeking to produce a generic version of Lipitor (atorvastatin) must use Lipitor as the RLD.

---

2. Submission of ANDA

The ANDA dossier includes:

1. **Module 1 (Administrative Information)**:
   - Applicant details and a list of authorized signatories.

2. **Module 2 (Quality and Bioequivalence Summary)**:
    - Concise summaries of key bioequivalence and manufacturing data.
3. **Module 3 (Quality Information)**:
    - Detailed composition, manufacturing process, and stability studies.
4. **Module 5 (Bioequivalence Data)**:
    - Results from bioequivalence studies or evidence supporting a waiver.

---

3. Regulatory Review

1. **FDA Evaluation**:
    - The **Office of Generic Drugs (OGD)** reviews the ANDA to ensure compliance with safety and quality standards.
2. **Deficiency Letters**:
    - If issues are identified, the FDA issues a **Complete Response Letter (CRL)**, and the applicant must address the deficiencies.
3. **Approval**:
    - Upon satisfactory review, the FDA issues approval, allowing the generic drug to enter the market.

Benefits of ANDA and Generics

1. **Affordability**:
    - Generic drugs provide significant cost savings for both healthcare systems and patients.
    - Example: In 2021, generics saved the U.S. healthcare system over $300 billion.
2. **Market Competition**:
    - Increased competition drives innovation and improves accessibility.
3. **Public Health Impact**:
    - Generics expand access to essential medicines, particularly in low- and middle-income countries.

Case Study: ANDA Success

Drug: Atorvastatin (Generic Lipitor)

1. **Background**:
    - Lipitor, a blockbuster cholesterol-lowering drug, faced generic competition after its patent expired.
2. **ANDA Submission**:
    - Multiple manufacturers submitted ANDAs, demonstrating bioequivalence to Lipitor.
3. **Outcome**:
    - The introduction of generics reduced the cost of atorvastatin by over 80%, increasing accessibility worldwide.

Marketing Authorization: Labeling Requirements and Post-Approval Management

Marketing Authorization (MA) is the regulatory approval required to legally market a pharmaceutical product in a specific region or country. It confirms that the product meets the required safety, efficacy, and quality standards set by the regulatory authority. This section delves into two critical aspects of marketing authorization: **labeling requirements** and **renewal and post-approval changes**.

Labeling Requirements

Labeling plays a crucial role in ensuring that healthcare professionals and patients have accurate and essential information about the drug. Regulatory authorities closely scrutinize labeling to ensure that it aligns with the approved marketing authorization dossier and adheres to region-specific guidelines.

---

1. Definition and Purpose of Labeling

Labeling includes all written, printed, or graphic material associated with a pharmaceutical product, such as:

- The **outer carton**.
- The **immediate container** (e.g., blister packs or bottles).
- **Package inserts** or **patient information leaflets**.

The purpose of labeling is to:

1. Ensure the safe and effective use of the drug.

2. Provide accurate information on dosage, administration, contraindications, and adverse effects.
3. Fulfill legal and regulatory requirements for product marketing.

---

2. Key Elements of Drug Labeling

1. **Product Name and Composition**:
   - Includes the **brand name**, **generic name**, and **active pharmaceutical ingredients (APIs)** with their respective strengths.
   - Example: A label for an antibiotic may state, "Amoxicillin 500 mg."
2. **Indications and Usage**:
   - Specifies the approved therapeutic uses of the drug.
   - Example: For an antihypertensive, the indication might read: "For the treatment of primary hypertension."
3. **Dosage and Administration**:
   - Provides detailed instructions on how to take the medication, including frequency and duration.
   - May include adjustments for specific populations (e.g., pediatric, geriatric).
4. **Contraindications**:
   - Lists conditions under which the drug should not be used.
   - Example: "Contraindicated in patients with severe hepatic impairment."
5. **Warnings and Precautions**:
   - Highlights critical safety concerns, such as risks during pregnancy or potential drug interactions.
6. **Adverse Reactions**:
   - Summarizes common and serious adverse effects observed in clinical trials or post-marketing surveillance.
7. **Storage Conditions**:
   - Indicates the appropriate conditions for preserving the drug's stability (e.g., temperature, light, humidity).
8. **Manufacturing and Expiry Details**:
   - Includes the manufacturer's name, batch number, manufacturing date, and expiration date.

9. **Legal and Regulatory Statements**:
    - Displays country-specific regulatory symbols or warnings, such as "Rx-only" for prescription drugs in the U.S.

---

3. Region-Specific Labeling Guidelines

Labeling requirements vary by region, and compliance with local regulations is mandatory.

1. **United States**:
    - Regulated by the **FDA** under the Code of Federal Regulations (CFR).
    - Labels must follow the **Physician Labeling Rule (PLR)** for prescription drugs.
    - Patient leaflets are often mandatory for high-risk drugs.
2. **European Union**:
    - Governed by the **European Medicines Agency (EMA)**.
    - Labels must include information in the official languages of the member states where the drug will be marketed.
    - Summary of Product Characteristics (SmPC) and Patient Information Leaflets (PILs) are critical components.
3. **India**:
    - Regulated by the **Central Drugs Standard Control Organization (CDSCO)** under the **Drugs and Cosmetics Act, 1940**.
    - Labels must include mandatory details such as the drug schedule classification (e.g., Schedule H).
4. **Global Considerations**:
    - Harmonization efforts, such as those by the **ICH**, aim to standardize labeling formats and reduce duplication in multi-region submissions.

Renewal and Post-Approval Changes

Marketing authorization is not a one-time process. Once granted, it requires ongoing compliance and periodic updates to reflect new information about the product.

---

1. Marketing Authorization Renewal

Marketing authorizations are typically valid for a fixed period, such as 5 years, and must be renewed to maintain product availability in the market.

1. **Renewal Process**:
    - Submission of a renewal application before the expiration of the marketing authorization.
    - Includes updates on:
        - **Post-marketing surveillance data**.
        - Changes in manufacturing processes.
        - Ongoing clinical trials or safety studies.
2. **Regulatory Decision**:
    - If no major concerns arise during the renewal review, the marketing authorization may be renewed indefinitely in some regions (e.g., EU).
3. **Challenges in Renewal**:
    - Non-compliance with pharmacovigilance obligations or unresolved safety concerns can lead to rejection or withdrawal.

---

2. Post-Approval Changes

During a product's lifecycle, various modifications may be necessary, ranging from minor adjustments to significant changes that could impact the product's safety or efficacy.

Types of Post-Approval Changes

1. **Administrative Changes**:
    - Changes in the manufacturer's name, address, or contact details.
    - Typically require a simple notification to the regulatory authority.
2. **Quality-Related Changes**:
    - Adjustments in manufacturing processes, facilities, or equipment.
    - Example: Switching to a new production site for APIs.
    - Regulatory authorities may require a **Supplementary New Drug Application (sNDA)** or a **Variation Application** in the EU.

3. **Labeling Changes**:
    - Updates to safety information, dosage instructions, or storage conditions based on new data.
    - Example: Adding a warning about a newly identified drug interaction.
4. **Clinical Changes**:
    - Expanding indications or updating contraindications based on post-marketing studies.
    - Example: Approving a cancer drug for a new tumor type following successful trials.

Regulatory Requirements for Post-Approval Changes

1. **Categorization of Changes**:
    - Changes are categorized as **minor** or **major**, depending on their potential impact on product safety and efficacy.
    - Example:
        - Minor: Change in product packaging design.
        - Major: Introduction of a new manufacturing process.
2. **Approval Timelines**:
    - Minor changes often require simple notifications.
    - Major changes may necessitate a detailed review, with timelines varying by region.

---

3. Pharmacovigilance and Post-Market Surveillance

Regulators require ongoing monitoring of the product's safety and efficacy after market approval.

1. **Periodic Safety Update Reports (PSURs)**:
    - Regular reports summarizing safety data and evaluating the product's risk-benefit profile.
    - Example: A vaccine manufacturer may submit annual PSURs based on global adverse event data.
2. **Risk Management Plans (RMPs)**:
    - Outline strategies to identify, mitigate, and monitor risks associated with the drug.
    - Mandatory for high-risk products or those approved under expedited pathways.

8.4 Regulatory Documentation

Regulatory documentation is the backbone of the pharmaceutical product approval process, serving as a structured repository of all data required to demonstrate the safety, efficacy, and quality of a drug. This section delves into the key types of documentation, the components of a regulatory dossier, and the evolution toward electronic submissions, highlighting their advantages and challenges.

Types of Documentation

Regulatory authorities worldwide require comprehensive documentation to evaluate a drug or medical device for marketing authorization. Two primary formats dominate regulatory submissions: the **Common Technical Document (CTD)** and **non-CTD dossiers**.

---

1. Common Technical Document (CTD) Structure

The **CTD** was introduced by the **International Council for Harmonisation (ICH)** to harmonize regulatory submissions across major markets, including the United States, European Union, and Japan.

Structure of the CTD

The CTD is divided into **five modules**, each addressing a critical aspect of the drug's development:

1. **Module 1: Administrative and Regional Information**
    - Contains region-specific documents such as application forms, product labels, and patient leaflets.
    - Not harmonized; tailored to the requirements of the target regulatory authority.
2. **Module 2: Summaries**
    - High-level summaries of quality, preclinical, and clinical data.
    - Provides an overview of the detailed information in Modules 3, 4, and 5.
3. **Module 3: Quality**
    - Focuses on chemistry, manufacturing, and controls (CMC).
    - Includes details on the drug's formulation, active pharmaceutical ingredients (APIs), and manufacturing processes.

4. **Module 4: Nonclinical Study Reports**
   - Preclinical data, including toxicology, pharmacology, and safety pharmacokinetics.
5. **Module 5: Clinical Study Reports**
   - Clinical trial data demonstrating the drug's safety and efficacy in humans.

Advantages of the CTD

- **Global Standardization**:
  - Accepted by regulatory authorities in over 60 countries, simplifying multi-region submissions.
- **Time Efficiency**:
  - Reduces duplication of effort for sponsors seeking approvals in multiple markets.

---

2. Non-CTD Dossiers

In regions where the CTD is not mandated, submissions follow **non-CTD formats**, which vary by country or regulatory authority.

- **Example: India**:
  - The **Central Drugs Standard Control Organization (CDSCO)** requires a dossier format based on the **Drugs and Cosmetics Rules**, with sections broadly similar to the CTD but structured differently.

Challenges of Non-CTD Dossiers

- Lack of standardization complicates global submissions.
- Increased administrative burden for sponsors managing multiple formats.

Components of a Regulatory Dossier

A regulatory dossier is the compilation of all technical, administrative, and scientific information submitted to authorities for product approval.

---

1. Module 1: Administrative and Product Information

This module contains region-specific information and includes:

- **Application Forms**:
  - Regulatory forms detailing the type of submission (e.g., new drug application, generic application).

- **Product Labels**:
  - Proposed labels, packaging designs, and patient information leaflets.
- **Legal Documents**:
  - Certificates of compliance with Good Manufacturing Practices (GMP) and patent information.

---

2. Module 2: Summaries

Module 2 provides a concise overview of the technical sections to help reviewers navigate the dossier efficiently.

1. **Quality Overall Summary (QOS)**:
   - Summarizes critical aspects of manufacturing, stability, and analytical validation.
2. **Nonclinical Overview**:
   - Key findings from pharmacology, toxicology, and safety studies.
3. **Clinical Overview**:
   - Summarizes clinical trial results, including efficacy, safety, and risk-benefit analysis.

---

3. Modules 3, 4, and 5: Detailed Data

Module 3: Quality

- **Composition**:
  - Details on active and inactive ingredients.
- **Manufacturing Process**:
  - Description of the manufacturing process, process validation, and batch records.
- **Stability Studies**:
  - Data supporting the proposed shelf life and storage conditions.

Module 4: Nonclinical (Preclinical)

- **Pharmacology Studies**:
  - Mechanism of action, target specificity, and dose-response relationships.

- **Toxicology Reports**:
  - Acute, chronic, reproductive, and carcinogenic toxicity studies.

Module 5: Clinical

- **Efficacy Data**:
  - Results from Phase II and Phase III clinical trials.
- **Safety Data**:
  - Adverse event reports, safety monitoring plans, and post-market surveillance strategies.

Electronic Submissions

The transition to electronic submissions has revolutionized regulatory documentation, making it more efficient, transparent, and accessible.

---

1. Electronic Common Technical Document (eCTD)

The **eCTD** is an electronic version of the CTD, allowing sponsors to submit, manage, and archive their regulatory dossiers digitally.

Advantages of eCTD

1. **Streamlined Review**:
   - Facilitates faster review cycles by enabling automated validation and navigation.
2. **Global Adoption**:
   - Mandatory in major markets like the United States (FDA), European Union (EMA), and Japan (PMDA).
3. **Version Control**:
   - Easy tracking of amendments and updates to the dossier.

Implementation:

- Regulatory authorities use validation tools to ensure eCTD submissions comply with technical specifications.
- Sponsors must follow region-specific eCTD guidelines for formatting and metadata.

---

2. Validation Tools and Common Errors

Validation Tools

- Regulatory agencies and sponsors use software tools to validate eCTD submissions for:
  - File integrity.
  - Metadata accuracy.
  - Proper linking between sections.

Common Errors

1. **Incorrect Metadata**:
   - Mislabeling sections or omitting required fields can delay reviews.
2. **Formatting Issues**:
   - Noncompliance with eCTD structure, such as broken hyperlinks or missing bookmarks.
3. **Duplicate Submissions**:
   - Submitting the same data in multiple locations within the dossier.

8.5 Pharmaceutical Regulations in India

Pharmaceutical regulations in India are designed to ensure the safety, efficacy, and quality of drugs and medical devices while protecting public health and fostering industry growth. These regulations, overseen by various guidelines and regulatory bodies, govern the entire lifecycle of a product, from development to post-market surveillance. This section explores the pivotal role of the **Central Drugs Standard Control Organization (CDSCO)**, the framework provided by **Schedule Y** for clinical trials, and other critical guidelines like **Good Manufacturing Practices (GMP)** and **Good Laboratory Practices (GLP)**.

Role of CDSCO

The **Central Drugs Standard Control Organization (CDSCO)** is India's apex regulatory authority for pharmaceuticals and medical devices, operating under the **Ministry of Health and Family Welfare**. It ensures compliance with the **Drugs and Cosmetics Act, 1940**, and its associated rules.

---

1. Approval Process for Drugs and Medical Devices

The CDSCO oversees a comprehensive approval process that spans the lifecycle of pharmaceuticals and medical devices.

Drug Approval

1. **New Drugs**:
   - Drugs containing novel active pharmaceutical ingredients (APIs) or new indications require CDSCO approval.
   - Applicants must submit data from preclinical and clinical trials, along with Chemistry, Manufacturing, and Controls (CMC) information.
   - Example: Approvals for COVID-19 vaccines like Covishield and Covaxin.
2. **Generic Drugs**:
   - Approvals focus on bioequivalence to the reference drug.
   - Streamlined under the Abbreviated New Drug Application (ANDA) pathway.
3. **Biologics and Biosimilars**:
   - Require detailed characterization and clinical data to demonstrate similarity to the innovator product.

Medical Device Approval

1. **Risk-Based Classification**:
   - Devices are categorized into Class A (low risk) to Class D (high risk), with regulatory scrutiny increasing with risk.
2. **Import Licenses**:
   - Foreign manufacturers must obtain CDSCO approval before marketing devices in India.

---

2. Post-Marketing Surveillance

Post-marketing surveillance is critical to monitoring the ongoing safety and efficacy of approved products.

1. **Pharmacovigilance Program of India (PvPI)**:
   - Monitors adverse drug reactions (ADRs) through a network of hospitals and healthcare centers.
   - Example: Withdrawal of ranitidine products following reports of carcinogenic impurities.

2. **Periodic Safety Update Reports (PSURs)**:
   - Mandatory submission by manufacturers to report adverse events and reassess the benefit-risk profile.
3. **Medical Device Monitoring**:
   - Devices are subject to post-market surveillance to identify performance issues or risks.

Schedule Y

Schedule Y, part of the **Drugs and Cosmetics Rules, 1945**, provides a comprehensive framework for the regulation of clinical trials in India. It ensures that trials are conducted ethically and scientifically, protecting the rights and safety of participants.

---

1. Clinical Trial Regulations and Requirements

Schedule Y outlines the processes for conducting clinical trials in India.

Phases of Clinical Trials

1. **Phase I**:
   - Conducted on a small group of healthy volunteers to assess safety and pharmacokinetics.
2. **Phase II**:
   - Evaluates efficacy and optimal dosing in a larger patient population.
3. **Phase III**:
   - Confirms efficacy and monitors adverse effects in a broad population.
4. **Phase IV (Post-Marketing)**:
   - Long-term safety studies conducted after the drug is marketed.

Documentation Requirements

- Investigators must submit a **Clinical Trial Application (CTA)**, including preclinical data, trial protocols, and informed consent forms, to the CDSCO.
- Ethics Committee approval is mandatory.

---

2. Responsibilities of Sponsors, Investigators, and Ethics Committees

Sponsors:

- Responsible for funding, protocol design, and overall trial oversight.
- Must report serious adverse events (SAEs) within prescribed timelines.

Investigators:

- Conduct trials per approved protocols and safeguard participant welfare.
- Maintain accurate records and submit periodic progress reports.

Ethics Committees:

- Ensure trials are ethical and participants' rights are protected.
- Review informed consent processes and trial protocols.

Other Relevant Guidelines

Beyond the approval process and clinical trials, India enforces stringent guidelines to ensure the quality and reliability of pharmaceutical products.

---

1. Good Manufacturing Practices (GMP) Under Schedule M

Schedule M outlines GMP requirements for manufacturing facilities to ensure consistent product quality.

Key Requirements:

1. **Facility Design**:
   - Cleanrooms and proper segregation of manufacturing areas to prevent cross-contamination.
2. **Standard Operating Procedures (SOPs)**:
   - Comprehensive SOPs for manufacturing, quality control, and documentation.
3. **Training**:
   - Regular training for personnel involved in production and quality assurance.

Enforcement:

- Regular audits and inspections by the CDSCO or state-level authorities.

---

2. Good Laboratory Practices (GLP)

GLP standards ensure the reliability and reproducibility of preclinical study data submitted for regulatory approval.

Principles of GLP:

1. **Study Planning**:
    - Clear protocols defining objectives, methods, and analysis.
2. **Documentation**:
    - Maintenance of accurate and complete records.
3. **Quality Assurance**:
    - Independent monitoring to ensure compliance with GLP standards.

Applications:

- Toxicology studies, pharmacokinetics, and other preclinical evaluations.

Challenges in Pharmaceutical Regulation

1. **Evolving Science and Technology**:
    - Regulatory frameworks must adapt to innovations like biosimilars and advanced therapies.
2. **Global Harmonization**:
    - Aligning Indian standards with international guidelines like ICH and WHO.
3. **Resource Constraints**:
    - Limited infrastructure for monitoring clinical trials and post-market surveillance.

CHAPTER 9

Health Insurance

Health Insurance in India

Health insurance plays an indispensable role in securing the health and financial well-being of individuals and families. With rising healthcare costs and the increasing prevalence of lifestyle diseases, the significance of health insurance in India cannot be overstated. This chapter explores the concept of health insurance, its importance in the Indian context, and its historical evolution, offering a comprehensive understanding of this vital financial tool.

Introduction to Health Insurance

When was the last time you thought about the financial implications of a medical emergency? It's a sobering thought—health issues can strike at any time, often with costs that are difficult to bear. This is where **health insurance** steps in as a lifeline, offering financial protection and peace of mind.

Health insurance is not just a policy; it's a promise. A promise that ensures you can focus on recovery without being burdened by spiraling medical expenses. But to appreciate its role fully, we need to start with the basics.

Definition and Scope of Health Insurance

What is Health Insurance?

Health insurance is a type of financial coverage designed to reimburse or directly pay for medical expenses incurred during illness, injury, or other health-related conditions. It operates on a simple principle:

- **Policyholders** pay a periodic premium to the insurance company.
- In return, the insurer provides coverage for eligible medical expenses, which can include hospitalization, outpatient treatments, diagnostic tests, and even preventive care, depending on the policy.

The scope of health insurance varies widely, ranging from individual policies to comprehensive family plans, and can include specialized coverage such as:

- **Critical illness plans** for diseases like cancer or stroke.
- **Maternity coverage** for pregnancy-related expenses.
- **Top-up plans** for additional financial protection beyond basic policy limits.

Difference Between Health Insurance and Other Types of Insurance

While all insurance policies provide financial security, health insurance is distinct in its focus and application. Let's compare it with two other popular types of insurance:

1. **Life Insurance**:
   - Purpose: Provides a lump sum payment to beneficiaries upon the policyholder's death.
   - Key Difference: Focuses on financial stability for dependents, while health insurance addresses the policyholder's medical costs.
2. **General Insurance** (e.g., motor, home insurance):
   - Purpose: Covers losses or damages to assets.
   - Key Difference: Health insurance is about protecting human health, not physical assets.

Importance of Health Insurance in India

India's healthcare system is a mix of public and private providers, with a significant portion of care being out-of-pocket. This reliance on direct payments makes health insurance crucial in mitigating financial strain and ensuring timely access to care.

Rising Healthcare Costs and Financial Security

1. **The Cost Conundrum**:
   - Healthcare costs in India have been rising at an alarming rate. Private hospitalization for a major illness can easily exceed ₹5-10 lakh, a sum that can deplete a family's savings.
   - Example: A single ICU admission for a cardiac condition can cost upwards of ₹2 lakh, excluding post-treatment expenses like medication and rehabilitation.
2. **How Health Insurance Helps**:
   - Protects savings by covering hospitalization, surgeries, and even daily room charges.

  - Reduces financial stress during emergencies, allowing families to focus on recovery rather than expenses.

3. **Impact on the Middle and Lower Classes**:
  - For families with limited income, medical costs often lead to debt or delays in seeking treatment. Health insurance acts as a buffer, ensuring that healthcare remains accessible.

Role in Improving Access to Quality Healthcare

1. **Encouraging Preventive Care**:
  - Many health insurance policies now cover preventive health check-ups, incentivizing regular monitoring of health and early detection of diseases.
  - Example: A policyholder can avail of an annual health check-up, detecting hypertension or diabetes before they escalate into costly complications.
2. **Promoting Private Healthcare Utilization**:
  - Insurance plans often offer cashless hospitalization at network hospitals, making high-quality private healthcare accessible to a wider population.
3. **Reducing Healthcare Inequality**:
  - Government-sponsored schemes like Ayushman Bharat have significantly improved healthcare access for economically weaker sections.

Historical Evolution of Health Insurance in India

To appreciate the current state of health insurance, we must trace its journey. From its humble beginnings to its rapid expansion post-liberalization, health insurance in India reflects the country's socio-economic growth.

Emergence of Health Insurance in India

1. **Pre-Independence Era**:
  - Health insurance, as a concept, was virtually non-existent in colonial India. The focus was on life insurance, catering to the elite.
  - Healthcare during this period relied heavily on public hospitals or out-of-pocket payments.

2. **Post-Independence Developments**:
   - The introduction of the **Employees' State Insurance Scheme (ESIS)** in 1952 marked India's first foray into health insurance.
     - **ESIS Objectives**: Provide affordable healthcare to industrial workers and their dependents.
     - Funded jointly by employers and employees, this scheme remains operational today, covering a specific segment of the workforce.
3. **Growth of Private Health Insurance**:
   - In the 1980s, state-owned insurers like New India Assurance began offering **Mediclaim**, a basic health insurance product aimed at individuals and families.
   - Mediclaim was significant for introducing Indians to the idea of pre-financing healthcare expenses through insurance.

Growth Post-Liberalization of the Insurance Sector

1. **1991 Liberalization Reforms**:
   - Economic liberalization opened India's insurance sector to private players, leading to increased competition and innovation.
   - Private insurers like ICICI Lombard, HDFC ERGO, and Max Bupa introduced tailored products catering to diverse consumer needs.
2. **Formation of the Insurance Regulatory and Development Authority of India (IRDAI)**:
   - Established in 1999, IRDAI brought regulatory oversight and consumer protection to the forefront.
   - Key Contributions:
     - Standardized policies to ensure transparency.
     - Mandated solvency ratios to protect policyholders' interests.
3. **Emergence of Cashless Healthcare**:
   - Collaboration between insurers and hospitals led to the introduction of **cashless hospitalization**, revolutionizing healthcare accessibility.

- Example: A policyholder requiring urgent surgery can receive treatment without paying upfront, with expenses settled directly between the insurer and hospital.

4. **Government-Sponsored Health Schemes**:
    - Schemes like **Rashtriya Swasthya Bima Yojana (RSBY)** launched in 2008 provided health coverage to the unorganized workforce.
    - Recent initiatives like **Ayushman Bharat - Pradhan Mantri Jan Arogya Yojana (PM-JAY)** aim to cover over 500 million Indians, marking a significant leap in healthcare inclusivity.

9.1 Health Insurance Landscape in India

The health insurance landscape in India reflects the country's socio-economic diversity, rapid digital transformation, and evolving healthcare needs. While the sector has seen exponential growth over the years, challenges like low penetration and uneven adoption remain persistent. This section provides an in-depth exploration of the current status, key stakeholders, and market trends shaping the health insurance ecosystem in India.

Current Status

The current state of health insurance in India is a mixed bag of progress and gaps. While urban areas exhibit higher awareness and adoption, rural regions still face significant barriers. A closer look at penetration rates and demographic patterns reveals the challenges and opportunities in this sector.

Penetration Rates and Demographics of Insured Populations

1. **Overall Penetration**:
    - As of recent reports, health insurance penetration in India stands at approximately **37%** of the population. While this represents growth, it still leaves a majority of the population without financial coverage for healthcare.
    - In comparison, developed nations like the USA and Germany have near-universal coverage, highlighting the scope for improvement in India.

2. **Demographic Insights**:
    - **Urban Areas**:
        - Higher penetration due to better awareness, employer-sponsored group policies, and access to private insurers.
        - Example: Large metropolitan cities like Mumbai and Bangalore have significant populations covered under corporate health plans.
    - **Rural Areas**:
        - Limited penetration, largely driven by government schemes like Ayushman Bharat.
        - Challenges include lack of awareness, affordability issues, and limited access to insurers.
3. **Economic Class Divide**:
    - High-income groups tend to purchase comprehensive policies, including critical illness covers.
    - Low-income groups rely heavily on government-sponsored schemes, with limited uptake of private insurance due to cost barriers.

Rural vs. Urban Adoption

1. **Urban Adoption**:
    - Factors Driving Growth:
        - Better healthcare awareness and literacy.
        - Employer-sponsored group insurance policies.
        - Availability of private health insurance providers and TPAs in urban centers.
    - Example: Employees in IT hubs often receive high-coverage group health policies as part of their compensation packages.
2. **Rural Adoption**:
    - Heavily reliant on government initiatives like Ayushman Bharat and Rashtriya Swasthya Bima Yojana.
    - Significant challenges:
        - Lack of digital literacy to access online claim mechanisms.

- Limited healthcare infrastructure to support insurance claims.

- Example: Rural families often rely on local clinics or government hospitals, which may not be covered under private insurance networks.

Key Stakeholders

The health insurance sector in India is a collaborative ecosystem involving insurers, intermediaries, and regulators. Each stakeholder plays a crucial role in ensuring the smooth functioning of the system.

Insurance Companies (Public and Private Players)

1. **Public Insurers**:
    - Companies like **New India Assurance** and **United India Insurance** dominate the market in government-sponsored schemes.
    - Focus Areas:
        - Offering affordable policies with basic coverage.
        - Managing large-scale government health insurance programs.
2. **Private Insurers**:
    - Players like **ICICI Lombard**, **HDFC ERGO**, and **Star Health Insurance** lead the private sector.
    - Focus Areas:
        - Introducing innovative policies like wellness incentives and family floaters.
        - Catering to niche markets with critical illness or top-up plans.
3. **Comparison**:
    - Public insurers emphasize accessibility and affordability.
    - Private insurers focus on customization, customer service, and high-value coverage.

Third-Party Administrators (TPAs)

1. **Role of TPAs**:
    - Act as intermediaries between insurers, policyholders, and healthcare providers.
    - Key Functions:
        - Managing cashless claim settlements.
        - Verifying claims documentation.
        - Maintaining a network of empaneled hospitals.
2. **Significance**:
    - Streamline the claims process, ensuring faster resolutions.
    - Provide customer support to policyholders during hospitalization.
3. **Example**:
    - A policyholder admitted to a network hospital can avail of cashless treatment facilitated by the TPA, reducing out-of-pocket expenses.

Government Agencies and Regulators

1. **Insurance Regulatory and Development Authority of India (IRDAI)**:
    - Regulates the health insurance sector to ensure transparency and consumer protection.
    - Key Initiatives:
        - Standardizing health insurance products for easier comparison.
        - Introducing grievance redressal mechanisms for policyholders.
2. **Government Schemes**:
    - Agencies like the **National Health Authority (NHA)** oversee programs like Ayushman Bharat, ensuring implementation and monitoring.
3. **Significance**:
    - Regulators and government bodies play a critical role in bridging the gap between rural and urban populations, ensuring inclusivity in healthcare coverage.

Market Trends

The health insurance market in India is evolving rapidly, driven by technological advancements and changing consumer preferences. Understanding these trends provides valuable insights into the sector's trajectory.

Growth of the Health Insurance Market

1. **Rapid Expansion**:
   - The market is expected to grow at a compound annual growth rate (CAGR) of **20%**, fueled by increasing awareness and demand.
   - Contributing Factors:
     - Rising middle-class incomes.
     - Post-COVID-19 focus on health security.
2. **Focus on Customization**:
   - Insurers now offer policies tailored to specific demographics, such as senior citizens, women, and individuals with pre-existing conditions.
   - Example: Policies with maternity benefits or diabetes-specific coverage.
3. **Role of Microinsurance**:
   - Affordable plans targeting low-income groups to improve rural penetration.
   - Example: Policies offering coverage for premiums as low as ₹300 annually.

Increasing Adoption of Digital Health Platforms

1. **Digital Transformation in Insurance**:
   - Online platforms now dominate policy purchases, renewals, and claims.
   - Example: Mobile apps by insurers allow users to track claims, access health records, and avail cashless hospitalization.
2. **Role of Telemedicine**:
   - Integration of telehealth services in insurance plans to meet post-pandemic healthcare demands.

- Example: Insurers partnering with telemedicine platforms like Practo or Mfine to offer virtual consultations.

3. **Use of Artificial Intelligence (AI)**:
   - AI-driven tools are transforming underwriting, fraud detection, and claims processing.
   - Example: Algorithms analyze patient history to customize premium calculations.

9.2 Types of Health Insurance Plans

India's health insurance market offers a wide range of policies to cater to the diverse needs of its population. Each plan type is designed with specific objectives, ensuring that individuals, families, and organizations can find solutions tailored to their circumstances. This section explores the key types of health insurance plans, their features, benefits, limitations, and practical applications.

Individual Health Insurance

Coverage Features

An individual health insurance plan provides coverage exclusively for a single person. It reimburses medical expenses incurred due to hospitalization, surgeries, or other healthcare services specified in the policy.

1. **Key Features**:
   - Sum insured: Coverage amount ranges from ₹1 lakh to ₹10 crore, depending on the plan and premium.
   - Includes pre- and post-hospitalization expenses, diagnostic tests, and ambulance charges.
   - Coverage for daycare procedures, such as cataract surgery or chemotherapy.
2. **Eligibility**:
   - Typically offered to individuals aged 18 to 65 years.
   - Children can be covered under family plans or specific child health policies.

Benefits and Limitations

1. **Benefits**:
   - Comprehensive coverage tailored to an individual's needs.
   - Freedom to choose the hospital or healthcare provider within the insurer's network.
   - Tax benefits under Section 80D of the Income Tax Act.
2. **Limitations**:
   - Premiums may be higher compared to shared coverage options like family floaters.
   - Policy exclusions, such as waiting periods for pre-existing conditions, can delay full coverage.
   - Requires separate policies for each family member, which can be costly.

Family Floater Policies

Shared Coverage for Family Members

Family floater plans provide coverage to multiple family members under a single sum insured. The entire family shares the policy limit, offering flexibility and cost efficiency.

1. **Coverage Features**:
   - Includes parents, spouse, and dependent children.
   - Shared sum insured typically ranges from ₹3 lakh to ₹20 lakh.
   - Covers hospitalization, daycare procedures, and critical illnesses (if included in the policy).

Pros and Cons Compared to Individual Policies

1. **Pros**:
   - Cost-effective: One premium covers multiple family members.
   - Flexible: If one family member uses less coverage, the remaining amount is available for others.
   - Convenience: Simplifies policy management with a single plan.

2. **Cons**:
    - High Utilization Risk: If one member uses most of the sum insured, the others may have limited coverage.
    - Age Loading: Premiums may increase if the eldest member is significantly older, as premiums are calculated based on the eldest insured person.

Group Health Insurance

Offered by Employers to Employees

Group health insurance is typically provided by employers as part of employee benefits. It offers collective coverage to employees and, in some cases, their dependents.

1. **Features**:
    - Coverage for employees and sometimes their families.
    - Low or no cost to the employee as premiums are borne by the employer.
    - Immediate coverage without waiting periods for pre-existing conditions.

Customizations and Additional Riders

1. **Customizations**:
    - Employers can choose to include maternity benefits, coverage for pre-existing conditions, or wellness programs.
2. **Additional Riders**:
    - Employees may opt for riders like critical illness cover or top-up plans by paying an extra premium.
3. **Example**:
    - A corporate group policy covering ₹5 lakh per employee, with an optional top-up for an additional ₹10 lakh.

Critical Illness Policies

Specific Coverage for Life-Threatening Illnesses

Critical illness policies focus on severe medical conditions like cancer, heart attack, or kidney failure. They provide financial protection for expensive treatments that regular policies may not fully cover.

1. **Features**:
   - Covers diseases explicitly listed in the policy document.
   - Includes treatment, medication, and rehabilitation costs.

Lump Sum Benefits vs. Regular Reimbursements

1. **Lump Sum Benefits**:
   - Upon diagnosis of a covered illness, a pre-determined lump sum is paid, regardless of the actual expenses.
   - Example: A ₹10 lakh critical illness policy pays the full amount upon a cancer diagnosis.
2. **Regular Reimbursements**:
   - Reimbursement for actual treatment expenses, subject to policy limits.
3. **Practical Application**:
   - Ideal for covering long-term treatment or loss of income during recovery.

Senior Citizen Plans

Special Plans for Individuals Above 60 Years

Senior citizen health insurance caters to the unique needs of the elderly, offering coverage for age-related illnesses and high-risk conditions.

1. **Features**:
   - Entry age: Typically 60 to 80 years.
   - Higher sum insured to account for increased medical costs.
   - Coverage for diseases like arthritis, diabetes, and heart conditions.

Coverage Specifics and Premium Considerations

1. **Specific Coverage**:
   - Routine health check-ups.
   - Coverage for pre-existing conditions after a waiting period.
   - Higher hospitalization expenses.
2. **Premium Considerations**:
   - Premiums are higher due to the increased risk of claims.
   - Insurers may require medical tests before issuing a policy.

3. **Example**:
    - A senior citizen plan with a sum insured of ₹10 lakh and premiums starting at ₹30,000 annually.

Top-Up and Super Top-Up Plans

Additional Coverage for High Medical Costs

Top-up and super top-up plans act as supplementary coverage for existing policies, providing financial protection for expenses exceeding a certain threshold.

1. **Top-Up Plans**:
    - Coverage kicks in once the deductible (the amount not covered by the base policy) is exceeded in a single claim.
    - Example: A ₹10 lakh top-up policy with a ₹3 lakh deductible covers expenses above ₹3 lakh for a single hospitalization.
2. **Super Top-Up Plans**:
    - Unlike top-up plans, super top-up policies aggregate expenses over multiple claims during the policy period.
    - Example: A super top-up plan covers cumulative costs above ₹3 lakh in a policy year.

Differences Between Top-Up and Super Top-Up Policies

1. **Single vs. Cumulative Claims**:
    - Top-up plans apply deductibles to individual claims.
    - Super top-up plans consider cumulative expenses.
2. **Who Should Choose These Plans**:
    - Top-up plans suit individuals expecting a single high-value claim.
    - Super top-up plans benefit those with frequent smaller claims.

9.3 Features and Benefits of Health Insurance

Health insurance is a crucial financial tool that offers comprehensive protection against unforeseen medical expenses. It is not just about safeguarding finances but also about promoting health and wellness. To fully appreciate its value, one must understand the key features and benefits of health insurance policies. These elements determine the coverage, utility, and practical advantages that health insurance offers, ensuring that policyholders can make informed decisions and derive maximum benefit from their plans.

Key Features

The features of a health insurance policy define its structure, coverage, and applicability. They are the foundation upon which policyholders base their selection, aligning their needs with the offerings of the insurer.

Sum Insured and Premium Structures

What Is Sum Insured?

The **sum insured** is the maximum amount that an insurance provider agrees to pay for covered medical expenses during the policy period. It represents the financial safety net a policyholder can rely on in case of medical emergencies.

1. **Determining the Sum Insured**:
    - Factors influencing the sum insured include age, medical history, and geographical location.
    - Example: A young professional may opt for a sum insured of ₹5 lakh, while a family with dependents may require ₹15 lakh or more.
2. **Premium Structures**:
    - Premiums are the periodic payments made by the policyholder to keep the insurance active.
    - Influencing Factors:
        - Higher sum insured results in higher premiums.
        - Add-ons like maternity benefits or critical illness coverage increase the premium.
        - Age-related premiums rise for senior citizens due to higher risk.

Practical Insights:

- Selecting a sum insured requires balancing affordability with adequate coverage.
- Example: For a family living in a metropolitan area with higher healthcare costs, a policy with a higher sum insured is advisable.

Cashless Hospitalization

What Is Cashless Hospitalization?

Cashless hospitalization allows policyholders to receive treatment without paying upfront, as the insurer directly settles bills with the hospital.

1. **How It Works**:
   - The hospital must be part of the insurer's empaneled network.
   - Policyholders present their health insurance card or policy details at the hospital.
   - The insurer's **Third-Party Administrator (TPA)** approves the claim based on policy terms.
2. **Advantages**:
   - Eliminates the need for immediate cash during emergencies.
   - Simplifies the claim process for policyholders.

Real-World Example:

Imagine a policyholder requiring emergency surgery. At a network hospital, the insurer handles the ₹2 lakh bill directly, saving the family from the stress of arranging funds.

Network of Empaneled Hospitals

What Are Network Hospitals?

Network hospitals are healthcare providers that have partnered with the insurer to offer cashless services.

1. **Significance**:
   - Ensures a seamless experience for policyholders.
   - Includes reputed hospitals, offering a wide choice to policyholders.
2. **Key Considerations**:
   - Policyholders should check the network hospitals in their vicinity when choosing a plan.
   - Network size and quality vary across insurers.

Practical Tip:

Always verify the hospital's inclusion in the network before seeking treatment. Policies typically have a list available online or in the policy document.

Waiting Periods for Pre-Existing Conditions

What Are Pre-Existing Conditions?

Pre-existing conditions refer to illnesses or medical conditions diagnosed before purchasing the policy.

1. **Waiting Periods**:
   - Most policies impose a waiting period of **2 to 4 years** for pre-existing conditions.
   - Example: If a policyholder has diabetes at the time of purchase, coverage for diabetes-related complications will only begin after the waiting period.
2. **Implications**:
   - Encourages transparency during policy purchase.
   - Ensures fair risk distribution for insurers.

Practical Insight:

Choose policies with shorter waiting periods if you have known medical conditions. Some insurers offer reduced waiting periods for higher premiums.

Co-Payment Clauses

What Is Co-Payment?

A **co-payment clause** requires the policyholder to bear a percentage of the total medical expenses, with the insurer covering the rest.

1. **How It Works**:
   - A policy with a 10% co-pay means the policyholder pays ₹10,000 for a ₹1 lakh bill, while the insurer covers ₹90,000.
2. **Advantages and Disadvantages**:
   - Advantage: Lowers premiums.
   - Disadvantage: Increases out-of-pocket expenses during claims.

Who Should Opt for Co-Payment?

- Young, healthy individuals may choose co-payment to reduce premiums.
- Families with frequent medical expenses should avoid co-payment clauses.

Benefits

Beyond the structural features, health insurance offers a range of tangible and intangible benefits that significantly enhance its value.

Financial Protection Against Medical Emergencies

Shielding Against Rising Healthcare Costs

1. **Context**:
    - Healthcare inflation in India is among the highest globally, with costs rising by 10-15% annually.
    - Example: A single ICU stay for a critical illness can cost ₹3-5 lakh, excluding follow-up expenses.
2. **How Health Insurance Helps**:
    - Covers hospitalization, surgeries, and diagnostics, ensuring families don't deplete their savings.
    - Provides comprehensive coverage for major medical expenses.

Case Study:

A middle-class family with a ₹10 lakh health insurance policy faced a ₹9 lakh hospitalization bill for a cardiac procedure. The insurance covered the costs, protecting the family from financial distress.

Tax Benefits Under Section 80D of the Income Tax Act

Tax Savings for Policyholders

1. **Eligibility**:
    - Premiums paid for self, spouse, children, and parents qualify for tax deductions under Section 80D.
    - Maximum Deduction Limits:
        - ₹25,000 for individuals below 60 years.
        - ₹50,000 for senior citizens.
        - Additional ₹50,000 for parents aged above 60.
2. **Example**:
    - A 35-year-old paying ₹20,000 for a family floater policy and ₹30,000 for his parents' health insurance can claim a total deduction of ₹50,000.

Practical Insight:

Tax benefits make health insurance an investment, not just an expense. By choosing the right plan, policyholders can secure their health while reducing tax liabilities.

Access to Preventive Healthcare Services

Promoting Wellness and Early Detection

1. **Inclusions in Policies**:
    - Annual health check-ups for early detection of illnesses.
    - Coverage for vaccinations, wellness programs, and dietary consultations.
2. **Why It Matters**:
    - Preventive care reduces the risk of severe illnesses, lowering long-term healthcare costs.
    - Example: Regular screenings for diabetes and hypertension help manage conditions before complications arise.

Innovative Offerings:

Some insurers incentivize healthy behavior by offering discounts on premiums for maintaining fitness goals, tracked via wearable devices.

9.4 Regulatory Framework for Health Insurance in India

A well-defined regulatory framework is the backbone of any sector, and health insurance is no exception. In India, the Insurance Regulatory and Development Authority of India (IRDAI) plays a pivotal role in overseeing and standardizing the industry. This ensures not only the financial stability of insurers but also the protection of consumer rights. This section delves into the regulatory landscape, compliance requirements, and the rights and protections afforded to policyholders in India.

Role of the Insurance Regulatory and Development Authority of India (IRDAI)

The **IRDAI**, established under the IRDA Act of 1999, is the apex body responsible for regulating and promoting the insurance sector in India. Its focus is to ensure a fair and transparent system that benefits both insurers and policyholders.

Guidelines for Health Insurance Providers

The IRDAI issues comprehensive guidelines that govern the operations of health insurance providers, ensuring consumer-centric practices and industry-wide uniformity.

1. **Product Design and Approval**:
    - Insurers must submit all new health insurance products to the IRDAI for approval.
    - Guidelines emphasize clarity, inclusivity, and fairness, particularly regarding exclusions, waiting periods, and age limits.
    - Example: Policies must explicitly define terms like "pre-existing conditions" to prevent ambiguity.
2. **Claim Settlement**:
    - The IRDAI mandates that insurers settle claims within 30 days of receiving complete documentation.
    - Delayed claims attract penalties to ensure timely resolutions.
3. **Premium Regulations**:
    - Insurers cannot increase premiums arbitrarily. Any changes in premium rates must be justified and approved by the IRDAI.
4. **Renewability**:
    - Health insurance policies must offer lifelong renewability unless fraud or non-disclosure is proven.
    - Example: A senior citizen cannot be denied policy renewal due to age-related health conditions.

Standardization of Health Insurance Products

To simplify policy comparison and improve accessibility, the IRDAI has introduced several standardization initiatives.

1. **Standard Definitions**:
    - Common terms like "room rent," "co-payment," and "daycare procedures" are uniformly defined across policies.
    - This eliminates confusion and enables informed decision-making.

2. **Arogya Sanjeevani Policy**:
   - A basic, standardized health insurance product introduced by IRDAI to cater to the masses.
   - Features:
     - Coverage of ₹1 lakh to ₹5 lakh.
     - Uniform terms, premiums, and inclusions across all insurers.
   - Benefits: Simplifies health insurance for first-time buyers, particularly in rural and semi-urban areas.

Compliance Requirements

Insurers in India are required to adhere to strict compliance protocols set by the IRDAI. These ensure operational transparency and protect consumer interests.

Mandatory Disclosures for Insurers

Transparency is a cornerstone of consumer trust. IRDAI mandates insurers to disclose critical information, ensuring that policyholders are fully informed.

1. **Policy Documentation**:
   - Insurers must provide detailed policy documents, including inclusions, exclusions, waiting periods, and claim processes.
   - Example: A health insurance policy must specify the exact diseases or treatments excluded from coverage.
2. **Periodic Updates**:
   - Insurers must regularly update policyholders about changes in network hospitals, premium structures, or regulatory amendments.
3. **Data Reporting**:
   - Insurers are required to submit periodic reports to the IRDAI, detailing claim settlements, grievances, and financial health.

Grievance Redressal Mechanisms

To address consumer complaints efficiently, insurers must establish robust grievance redressal systems.

1. **Internal Grievance Cells**:
   - Insurers must have dedicated teams to handle policyholder complaints.
   - Complaints must be resolved within 15 days, failing which the policyholder can escalate the issue.
2. **IRDAI Grievance Portal**:
   - Policyholders can lodge complaints directly with the IRDAI through the **Integrated Grievance Management System (IGMS)**.
   - Example: A delayed claim settlement can be reported, prompting IRDAI to intervene.
3. **Ombudsman Services**:
   - The **Insurance Ombudsman** offers free dispute resolution services for claims up to ₹20 lakh.
   - Example: A policyholder denied cashless hospitalization can approach the Ombudsman for redressal.

Consumer Rights and Protections

IRDAI emphasizes the importance of safeguarding consumer rights, ensuring that policyholders receive fair treatment and transparent services.

Right to Transparency and Fair Treatment

1. **Clarity in Terms**:
   - Policies must avoid vague or misleading language, ensuring that consumers understand the coverage and limitations.
2. **Non-Discrimination**:
   - Insurers cannot deny policies or claims based on gender, ethnicity, or medical history unless explicitly justified.
3. **Free-Look Period**:
   - Policyholders are entitled to a **15-day free-look period** after purchasing a policy, during which they can cancel it without penalty.

Processes for Claim Settlement Disputes

Despite robust guidelines, disputes in claim settlements are common. The regulatory framework provides multiple avenues for resolution.

1. **Direct Resolution with Insurers**:
   - Policyholders are encouraged to first address disputes with the insurer's grievance cell.
2. **Escalation to IRDAI**:
   - If dissatisfied with the insurer's response, complaints can be filed with the IRDAI through the IGMS.
3. **Ombudsman Intervention**:
   - The Ombudsman's verdicts are binding on insurers but non-binding on policyholders, ensuring fairness.

9.5 Government-Sponsored Health Insurance Schemes

In India, government-sponsored health insurance schemes play a crucial role in bridging the gap between healthcare accessibility and affordability, especially for economically vulnerable populations. These initiatives aim to provide financial protection against the ever-rising costs of healthcare, while also addressing systemic challenges within the health infrastructure. This section explores key national and state-level schemes, social health insurance programs, and their effectiveness in achieving universal health coverage.

Ayushman Bharat - Pradhan Mantri Jan Arogya Yojana (PM-JAY)

Overview and Objectives

PM-JAY, launched in 2018 under the Ayushman Bharat initiative, is one of the world's largest government-funded health insurance schemes. It targets the economically weaker sections of society, providing free healthcare services at a scale unparalleled globally.

1. **Core Objectives**:
   - Reduce out-of-pocket expenditure for families below the poverty line.
   - Promote secondary and tertiary care access in rural and underserved regions.
   - Strengthen India's healthcare infrastructure by incentivizing private-sector participation.

2. **Scope and Scale**:
   - Coverage: Over 500 million individuals.
   - Financial Coverage: ₹5 lakh per family per year for hospitalization costs.

Eligibility and Benefits

1. **Eligibility Criteria**:
   - Determined based on the **Socio-Economic Caste Census (SECC) 2011** data.
   - Targets vulnerable populations, including households without access to a shelter, manual laborers, and landless agricultural workers.
2. **Key Benefits**:
   - **Cashless Treatment**:
     - Covers over 1,500 medical procedures, including surgeries and critical care.
   - **Comprehensive Coverage**:
     - Includes pre- and post-hospitalization expenses, diagnostics, and medication costs.
   - **Portability**:
     - Beneficiaries can avail of services at empaneled hospitals nationwide, ensuring seamless care during inter-state travel.

Challenges and Impact on Healthcare Access

1. **Challenges**:
   - **Operational Hurdles**:
     - Inconsistent implementation across states due to varying administrative capacities.
   - **Awareness Deficit**:
     - Many eligible families remain unaware of their entitlements under PM-JAY.
   - **Fraud and Misuse**:
     - Instances of inflated claims or ineligible beneficiaries accessing benefits.

2. **Impact**:
   - Significant reduction in out-of-pocket expenditure for over 26 million beneficiaries.
   - Increased access to private healthcare facilities for rural populations.
   - Enhanced participation of private hospitals, improving infrastructure in underserved areas.

State-Level Schemes

State governments complement national schemes by implementing localized health insurance initiatives tailored to regional needs.

Rajiv Aarogyasri Scheme (Telangana and Andhra Pradesh)

1. **Overview**:
   - Introduced in 2007, this scheme targets below-poverty-line (BPL) families, offering financial assistance for critical illnesses.
   - Coverage Amount: Up to ₹2 lakh per family annually.
2. **Key Features**:
   - Focus on tertiary care for illnesses like cancer, heart diseases, and kidney failure.
   - Empanelment of both public and private hospitals to expand healthcare reach.
3. **Challenges**:
   - Dependency on private hospitals, leading to underutilization of public health infrastructure.
   - Limited focus on preventive healthcare measures.

Comprehensive Health Insurance Scheme (CHIS) in Kerala

1. **Overview**:
   - Kerala's CHIS integrates with PM-JAY to provide broader coverage, targeting over 3.5 million families.
   - Emphasizes coverage for chronic illnesses prevalent in the region.

2. **Key Features**:
   - Covers advanced treatments like organ transplants.
   - Strong focus on IT-enabled claim processing to minimize fraud.
3. **Challenges**:
   - High operational costs due to Kerala's advanced but expensive healthcare infrastructure.
   - Balancing equitable healthcare access in geographically isolated regions.

Social Health Insurance Programs

Social health insurance programs cater to specific groups, such as formal-sector employees or low-income families, ensuring financial protection for healthcare needs.

Employee's State Insurance Scheme (ESIS)

1. **Overview**:
   - Established in 1952, ESIS targets workers in the organized sector earning below a specific threshold.
   - Funded jointly by employers and employees.
2. **Key Features**:
   - Comprehensive healthcare benefits, including outpatient care, maternity leave, and disability compensation.
   - Operates a network of ESIS hospitals and dispensaries across India.
3. **Challenges**:
   - Outdated infrastructure in ESIS facilities.
   - Limited awareness among eligible workers.

Rashtriya Swasthya Bima Yojana (RSBY)

1. **Overview**:
   - Launched in 2008 to provide insurance to BPL families working in the unorganized sector.
   - Coverage Amount: ₹30,000 per family annually.

2. **Key Features**:
    - Focuses on secondary care and day-care treatments.
    - Utilizes smart cards for efficient claim processing.
3. **Challenges**:
    - Low coverage limit, inadequate for serious medical conditions.
    - Transition issues as many beneficiaries were absorbed into PM-JAY.

Effectiveness and Challenges

While government-sponsored health insurance schemes have expanded access to healthcare for millions, they face persistent challenges that hinder their full potential.

Coverage Gaps and Financial Constraints

1. **Limited Beneficiary Reach**:
    - Many low-income households remain excluded due to outdated data or administrative inefficiencies.
    - Example: PM-JAY relies on SECC 2011 data, which may no longer reflect current poverty demographics.
2. **Insufficient Funding**:
    - State and central governments often face budgetary constraints, affecting scheme sustainability.
    - Example: Delayed reimbursements to hospitals discourage private-sector participation.

Operational Inefficiencies and Fraud Risks

1. **Systemic Inefficiencies**:
    - Fragmented health infrastructure and lack of coordination between central and state authorities slow implementation.
    - Example: Duplicate claim submissions by hospitals due to lack of robust monitoring systems.
2. **Fraud and Abuse**:
    - Inflated claims or billing for services not rendered.
    - Measures like IT-enabled fraud detection systems are being deployed to address these risks.

9.6 Challenges in Health Insurance in India

Despite its growing importance, health insurance in India faces significant challenges that hinder its accessibility and effectiveness. These issues range from low penetration rates to claim settlement difficulties, often exacerbated by a lack of awareness and systemic inefficiencies. This section examines these challenges in detail, shedding light on their root causes and implications.

Low Penetration

One of the most glaring challenges is the low penetration of health insurance in India. Only about 37% of the population is covered by some form of health insurance, leaving a vast majority unprotected.

Awareness Issues and Lack of Education

1. **Limited Awareness**:
   - Many individuals, especially in rural areas, are unaware of the benefits and availability of health insurance.
   - Example: Families living below the poverty line often prioritize immediate financial needs over purchasing health insurance.
2. **Cultural Perceptions**:
   - A significant portion of the population views health insurance as an unnecessary expense rather than a safety net.
   - Lack of trust in insurance providers further discourages adoption.

Socioeconomic Barriers in Rural Areas

1. **Economic Constraints**:
   - Low disposable income in rural households makes health insurance a low priority.
   - Example: A family earning ₹10,000 per month may struggle to pay a premium of ₹5,000 annually.
2. **Inadequate Distribution Networks**:
   - Insurers often focus on urban areas, leaving rural regions underserved.

Affordability

Health insurance premiums are often prohibitively expensive for certain demographics, creating barriers to access.

High Premiums for Certain Demographics

1. **Senior Citizens**:
   - Premiums for senior citizen plans are significantly higher due to the increased risk of claims.
   - Example: A 65-year-old might pay ₹30,000 annually for a policy with ₹5 lakh coverage.
2. **Chronic Illness Coverage**:
   - Policies for individuals with pre-existing conditions like diabetes or heart disease come with higher premiums or exclusions.

Lack of Subsidized Options for the Lower Middle Class

1. **Policy Gaps**:
   - Government schemes cater to the poorest segments, while private insurance is often geared towards higher-income groups.
   - The lower middle class remains under-served, with few affordable options available.

Complexity of Policies

Understanding health insurance policies can be daunting, even for educated consumers.

Difficulties in Understanding Terms, Exclusions, and Conditions

1. **Jargon-Laden Language**:
   - Policies often include technical terms and legal clauses that are hard to decipher.
   - Example: Terms like "co-payment" or "deductible" may confuse first-time buyers.
2. **Hidden Exclusions**:
   - Certain conditions or treatments may not be covered, and policyholders often discover this only during claims.

Misinformation or Lack of Clarity from Agents

1. **Over-Promising**:
   - Insurance agents sometimes provide misleading information to close sales.
   - Example: Agents might omit critical details about waiting periods for pre-existing conditions.

2. **Insufficient Training**:
    - Agents often lack in-depth knowledge, leading to poor guidance for consumers.

Claim Settlement Issues

Claim settlement is a critical aspect of health insurance, but delays and rejections often frustrate policyholders.

Delays in Processing Claims

1. **Bureaucratic Hurdles**:
    - Insurers may require extensive documentation, leading to delays.
    - Example: A policyholder undergoing urgent surgery may face weeks of uncertainty over claim approval.
2. **Overburdened Systems**:
    - A surge in claims, especially during health crises like COVID-19, overwhelms insurers' capacities.

High Rejection Rates for Certain Claims

1. **Policy Ambiguities**:
    - Claims for conditions excluded under fine print are often rejected.
    - Example: A claim for dental surgery might be denied if the policy excludes dental procedures.
2. **Lack of Transparency**:
    - Insurers often fail to clearly communicate reasons for claim rejections.

Fraudulent Practices

Fraudulent activities undermine the integrity of the health insurance sector, increasing costs for both insurers and genuine policyholders.

False Claims by Policyholders

1. **Fabricated Medical Bills**:
    - Some policyholders submit fake bills or inflate expenses to claim higher reimbursements.

2. **Collusion with Hospitals**:
    - In some cases, policyholders and healthcare providers collude to file fraudulent claims.

Unethical Practices by Hospitals or Intermediaries

1. **Overcharging**:
    - Network hospitals may inflate bills for insured patients, knowing that the insurer will cover the costs.
    - Example: Charging ₹10,000 for a diagnostic test that typically costs ₹5,000.
2. **Unnecessary Procedures**:
    - Hospitals may recommend unnecessary treatments to maximize claim amounts.

9.7 Innovations and Trends in Health Insurance

While challenges persist, the health insurance sector is undergoing significant innovation. Advancements in technology, personalization, and wellness integration are reshaping the industry, making it more accessible and consumer-friendly.

Digitization

Technology is revolutionizing every aspect of health insurance, from policy purchase to claim settlement.

Role of Technology in Policy Purchase, Renewal, and Claims

1. **Online Portals**:
    - Consumers can compare policies, purchase plans, and renew coverage online, eliminating the need for intermediaries.
    - Example: Platforms like Policybazaar and insurer websites streamline the buying process.
2. **Faster Claims**:
    - Automation and digital tools reduce the time required for claim approvals and disbursals.

Adoption of Mobile Apps and Online Portals

1. **Features of Mobile Apps**:
    - Instant policy access, premium reminders, and claim tracking.

    - Example: Apps like Star Health and HDFC ERGO enable cashless claims with a few taps.
2. **Integration with Wearables**:
    - Apps integrate with fitness devices to monitor health metrics and offer discounts based on healthy behavior.

Personalized Policies

Personalization is redefining how health insurance is designed and delivered.

Customization Based on Age, Lifestyle, and Health Conditions

1. **Flexible Coverage**:
    - Plans tailored for young professionals, families, or senior citizens.
    - Example: Maternity benefits for women or lifestyle-based plans for fitness enthusiasts.
2. **Affordable Options**:
    - Customization ensures consumers pay only for what they need.

Data-Driven Underwriting Using AI and Machine Learning

1. **Risk Assessment**:
    - AI analyzes medical history and lifestyle data to predict risks more accurately.
    - Example: Smokers might receive tailored plans with higher premiums.
2. **Dynamic Premiums**:
    - Premiums adjusted based on health improvements, incentivizing wellness.

Wellness Programs

Wellness integration is shifting the focus from reactive healthcare to preventive care.

Incentives for Preventive Care

1. **Discounts for Healthy Behavior**:
    - Policyholders achieving fitness goals may receive premium discounts or cashback.

- Example: Achieving 10,000 steps daily might earn a discount on the next renewal.

2. **Coverage for Preventive Check-Ups**:
   - Regular health screenings and vaccinations are covered under many policies.

Integration of Wearable Technology for Monitoring

1. **Health Monitoring**:
   - Wearables track vital signs like heart rate and activity levels.
   - Example: Insurers offer reduced premiums for consistent fitness tracker usage.

Telemedicine and Health Insurance

Telemedicine has gained prominence post-COVID-19, with insurers adapting to the trend.

Coverage for Virtual Consultations and Online Prescriptions

1. **Policy Add-Ons**:
   - Many insurers now cover teleconsultations and digital prescriptions.
   - Example: Online platforms like Practo and Apollo 24/7 partner with insurers to offer seamless services.
2. **Cost-Effective Care**:
   - Reduces the need for physical visits, saving time and money.

Post-COVID-19 Trends in Telehealth Adoption

1. **Mainstream Acceptance**:
   - Insurers increasingly view telemedicine as a core offering, not an optional add-on.
   - Example: During the pandemic, teleconsultations accounted for over 50% of medical interactions.
2. **Future Potential**:
   - Enhanced access to specialists for rural populations, bridging healthcare disparities.

9.8 Case Studies and Real-Life Examples

Case studies and real-life examples provide a ground-level view of how health insurance operates, highlighting both its successes and shortcomings. These stories not only illustrate the practical application of health insurance policies but also reveal gaps that need to be addressed. In this section, we explore success stories, challenges, and lessons learned from the Indian health insurance sector.

Success Stories

The transformative impact of health insurance is best understood through the positive outcomes it delivers. These success stories showcase how policies, both government-sponsored and private, have changed lives.

Impact of Ayushman Bharat in Reducing Out-of-Pocket Healthcare Expenses

1. **Case Study: A Rural Family's Experience with PM-JAY**
    - **Background**: Ramesh, a farmer in Uttar Pradesh, had minimal savings when his wife required emergency surgery costing ₹2.5 lakh. Without Ayushman Bharat - PM-JAY, this expense would have forced him into debt.
    - **Outcome**: Ramesh's family was eligible under PM-JAY. The hospital, part of the empaneled network, offered cashless treatment. The family paid nothing out-of-pocket.
    - **Impact**:
        - Immediate financial relief for the family.
        - Access to quality healthcare, which might have been unattainable otherwise.
2. **National Impact**:
    - Over **26 million beneficiaries** have received free treatment since the scheme's launch.
    - A **30% reduction** in catastrophic health expenditures has been reported in participating states.

Private Insurer Innovations That Improved Customer Satisfaction

1. **Case Study: Digital Claims Simplification by HDFC ERGO**
    - **Problem**: Traditional claim settlement processes often involved lengthy paperwork and delays.
    - **Solution**: HDFC ERGO introduced an **AI-powered claims process**. Policyholders upload documents via a mobile app, and AI validates claims within hours.
    - **Impact**:
        - Claim settlements for routine procedures reduced to **under 48 hours.**
        - Improved customer satisfaction and retention rates.
2. **Case Study: Star Health's Family Floater Plan**
    - **Background**: A family of four in Chennai opted for a family floater plan covering ₹10 lakh.
    - **Outcome**: When the eldest member underwent heart surgery costing ₹8 lakh, the plan covered the expenses, leaving ₹2 lakh for potential future claims in the same year.
    - **Impact**:
        - Affordable premiums for comprehensive family coverage.
        - Flexible benefits tailored to family needs.

Challenges Highlighted

Even with significant advancements, the health insurance sector faces recurring challenges that affect its credibility and effectiveness.

Delayed Claim Settlements Causing Financial Stress

1. **Case Study: Emergency Surgery Claim Delay**
    - **Background**: Seema, a schoolteacher, had health insurance through her employer. When her son required urgent surgery, the claim was delayed by three weeks due to incomplete documentation.
    - **Impact**:
        - Seema had to borrow ₹1 lakh from friends to cover the surgery, creating financial stress despite having valid insurance.

- **Lesson**:
  - Insurers must simplify claim procedures, especially during emergencies.

2. **Industry-Wide Trends**:
   - Claims processing delays are reported in **15-20% of cases**, often due to poor communication between hospitals, TPAs, and insurers.

Instances of Policy Mis-Selling or Denial of Coverage

1. **Case Study: Mis-Selling by an Insurance Agent**
   - **Background**: A retired couple in Delhi was sold a policy marketed as "comprehensive," only to discover later that it excluded pre-existing conditions for four years.
   - **Impact**:
     - When one spouse needed treatment for a pre-existing condition, the claim was denied, leaving the couple feeling betrayed.
   - **Lesson**:
     - Greater emphasis on transparency and ethical sales practices is needed.
2. **Case Study: Denial of Critical Illness Coverage**
   - **Background**: Ravi, a 45-year-old engineer, was diagnosed with cancer but had his claim rejected because the insurer cited a technicality in his policy terms.
   - **Impact**:
     - Ravi's family faced financial ruin, highlighting the need for clearer policy documentation and better grievance redressal systems.

Lessons Learned

Through both successes and challenges, the health insurance sector offers critical lessons that can guide improvements and foster trust among consumers.

Importance of Transparency and Accountability

1. **Transparent Communication**:
   - Insurers must ensure that policyholders fully understand the terms, inclusions, and exclusions of their policies.
   - **Example:** Policies should provide simplified summaries alongside detailed documentation, reducing the risk of misinterpretation.
2. **Accountability in Claim Settlements**:
   - Insurers must streamline claim processes and establish stricter timelines for settlement.
   - **Example**: Incorporating AI-driven validation for routine claims can expedite approvals and reduce grievances.

Need for Consumer Education

1. **Awareness Campaigns**:
   - Governments and insurers should invest in educating consumers about health insurance benefits and processes.
   - **Example:** Public awareness initiatives about government schemes like Ayushman Bharat have boosted enrollment significantly.
2. **Simplification of Policies**:
   - Policies should use straightforward language, making them accessible to individuals across educational backgrounds.
   - **Example:** Creating vernacular versions of policy documents for regional accessibility.

Integration of Technology

1. **Role of Technology**:
   - Digital tools such as mobile apps, AI, and telemedicine services are revolutionizing health insurance.
   - **Example:** Platforms like Policybazaar have simplified the buying process, enabling consumers to compare policies easily.
2. **Preventing Fraud**:
   - AI and blockchain can help detect fraudulent claims and ensure policyholder authenticity, improving trust in the system.

CHAPTER 10

Consumer Protection Laws

Consumer Protection Laws

Consumer protection laws serve as the backbone of a fair and transparent marketplace, ensuring that consumers are safeguarded from exploitation and deceit. As economies grow and trade becomes more complex, these laws play an increasingly vital role in maintaining trust between businesses and consumers. This section introduces the concept of consumer protection laws, their objectives, relevance in the modern economy, and historical evolution, providing a foundation for understanding their importance in today's interconnected world.

Introduction to Consumer Protection Laws

Definition and Purpose

At their core, consumer protection laws are designed to defend the rights and interests of consumers against unfair practices, ensuring a level playing field in the marketplace.

1. **What Are Consumer Protection Laws?**
    - These are legal frameworks that regulate the conduct of businesses, protecting consumers from:
        - Fraudulent or deceptive practices.
        - Unsafe or substandard products.
        - Unethical trade behaviors like price manipulation or false advertising.
2. **Objectives of Consumer Protection Laws**:
    - **Safeguarding Consumer Rights**:
        - Ensuring consumers have access to accurate information about products and services.
        - Protecting them from hazardous goods and unfair terms of trade.

- **Promoting Fair Trade**:
  - Creating an environment where businesses compete ethically.
  - Encouraging transparency and accountability.
- **Ensuring Market Transparency**:
  - Mandating clear labeling, pricing, and quality standards for goods and services.

By establishing trust between consumers and businesses, these laws not only protect individual buyers but also strengthen the overall economy.

Relevance in the Modern Economy

In today's fast-paced, technology-driven world, consumer protection laws have taken on new dimensions, addressing challenges unique to the modern marketplace.

1. **Growth of E-Commerce and Digital Marketplaces**:
   - The rise of online shopping has transformed consumer behavior, but it has also created vulnerabilities:
     - **False Advertising**: Misleading product descriptions or images that differ from delivered goods.
     - **Data Privacy**: Consumers often unknowingly share sensitive personal information with online platforms.
     - **Lack of Recourse**: Difficulty in filing grievances for cross-border or online transactions.

For example, a consumer purchasing a smartphone from an e-commerce platform may encounter issues like receiving counterfeit products or experiencing delays in refunds, necessitating stronger laws to address these concerns.

2. **Increasing Complexity of Products and Services**:
   - Modern products and services are more intricate than ever, spanning from financial instruments to digital applications. This complexity often leaves consumers unable to fully understand what they are purchasing or the potential risks involved.

   Consider the case of financial services: A consumer investing in a mutual fund may not comprehend the associated risks due to ambiguous terms, underscoring the need for legal safeguards.

3. **Global Supply Chains**:
    - The integration of global supply chains means products often pass through multiple jurisdictions, raising questions about accountability for defective or harmful goods.

Historical Perspective

Consumer protection is not a modern concept; its principles have evolved over centuries, shaped by social, economic, and technological changes.

1. **Evolution of Consumer Rights Globally**:
    - Early efforts to protect consumers were primarily focused on **food safety and weights/measures**.
    - The modern consumer protection movement gained momentum in the mid-20th century, spurred by:
        - President John F. Kennedy's declaration of the **Consumer Bill of Rights** in 1962, which emphasized the rights to safety, information, choice, and redress.
        - The establishment of international bodies like the **Organisation for Economic Co-operation and Development (OECD)**, which advocated for global consumer rights.
2. **Evolution of Consumer Rights in India**:
    - Pre-independence, consumer rights were limited to specific industries like food and textiles, with no comprehensive legal framework.
    - Post-independence milestones include:
        - **Essential Commodities Act, 1955**: Ensured fair pricing and availability of essential goods.
        - **Consumer Protection Act, 1986**: The first major legislation to formalize consumer rights, establishing consumer forums for grievance redressal.
3. **Influence of International Frameworks**:
    - The **United Nations Guidelines for Consumer Protection (UNGCP)** have been instrumental in shaping national policies, providing a global blueprint for protecting consumers.

- These guidelines emphasize areas like:
  - Product safety.
  - Consumer education.
  - Access to fair dispute resolution mechanisms.

India has aligned many of its consumer protection initiatives with these global standards, reflecting its commitment to safeguarding consumer rights in a globalized economy.

10.1 Key Principles of Consumer Protection

Consumer protection is built upon foundational principles that aim to safeguard the rights of consumers while ensuring businesses operate ethically and responsibly. These principles create a balance in the marketplace, where consumers are empowered to make informed decisions and businesses are held accountable for their actions. In this section, we will explore these principles in depth, starting with the **rights of consumers** and transitioning to the **responsibilities of businesses**. The journey through these concepts will be thorough, insightful, and enriched with real-world examples.

The Rights of Consumers

At the heart of consumer protection lies a set of core rights that every individual, regardless of their economic status or geographical location, is entitled to. These rights were formalized to ensure that consumers have a voice and agency in a marketplace that often favors powerful corporations.

1. Right to Safety

The **right to safety** ensures that consumers are protected from products and services that may cause harm to their health, safety, or well-being.

1. **Scope**:
   - This right covers both physical safety (e.g., unsafe electronics) and mental well-being (e.g., deceptive financial schemes).
   - It applies to products like medicines, toys, electrical appliances, and even services like food delivery.
2. **Practical Example**:
   - Imagine purchasing a children's toy with small detachable parts that are not labeled as a choking hazard. If the child is harmed due to this oversight, the manufacturer would be held accountable under consumer protection laws.

3. **Ensuring Compliance**:
   - Governments mandate safety standards, like those set by the **Bureau of Indian Standards (BIS)**, to ensure manufacturers comply with safety norms.
   - For instance, electronic appliances must carry certifications such as the BIS mark to indicate their safety.

---

2. Right to Information

The **right to information** empowers consumers to access accurate and comprehensive details about a product or service before making a purchase.

1. **What It Entails**:
   - Clear labeling of ingredients, usage instructions, expiry dates, and pricing.
   - Transparency in advertising and promotional materials.
2. **Real-World Insight**:
   - Consider buying packaged food. The label should disclose nutritional content, allergens, and additives. Without this information, consumers cannot make informed dietary choices.
3. **Impact of Violations**:
   - Misleading advertisements, like promoting a sugary drink as "100% natural," can lead to regulatory penalties under the **Consumer Protection Act, 2019**.

---

3. Right to Choose

The **right to choose** ensures that consumers have the freedom to select from a variety of products and services without being coerced or misled.

1. **Significance**:
   - This right fosters competition among businesses, leading to better quality and pricing.
   - It discourages monopolistic practices that limit consumer options.
2. **Practical Scenarios**:
   - Telecommunication providers must allow consumers to choose from multiple plans without hidden restrictions.
   - Supermarkets offering bundled deals must not mislead consumers into believing the bundle is the only option available.

---

4. Right to Be Heard

The **right to be heard** guarantees that consumer grievances and opinions are taken seriously by businesses and regulatory authorities.

1. **Mechanisms in Place**:
   - Consumer complaint redressal forums at district, state, and national levels provide platforms for grievances.
   - Many businesses now have dedicated customer service departments and ombudsman offices.
2. **Example in Action**:
   - Suppose a defective washing machine is sold, and the retailer refuses to address the issue. The consumer can escalate the matter to a consumer court, ensuring their complaint is addressed.
3. **Encouraging Feedback**:
   - Companies often solicit feedback to improve services, exemplifying the importance of this right in fostering trust.

---

5. Right to Seek Redressal

The **right to seek redressal** provides consumers with a legal avenue to demand compensation or replacement for defective products, substandard services, or unfair practices.

1. **What It Covers**:
   - Refunds, replacements, or monetary compensation for losses incurred due to business negligence.
2. **Legal Support**:
   - The Consumer Protection Act, 2019, streamlines redressal mechanisms, offering online portals like **E-daakhil** for filing complaints.
3. **Practical Example**:
   - A consumer who purchased a smartphone with a manufacturing defect can either demand a replacement or take the case to a consumer court if the seller refuses to cooperate.

---

6. Right to Consumer Education

The **right to consumer education** emphasizes the importance of awareness in protecting consumer interests.

1. **Goals**:
   - Educate consumers about their rights, responsibilities, and the legal framework available to them.
   - Promote informed decision-making in everyday purchases.
2. **Initiatives**:
   - Campaigns like **Jago Grahak Jago** in India aim to spread awareness about consumer rights.
   - Schools and colleges include consumer studies in their curriculum to build foundational knowledge.

Responsibilities of Businesses

While consumers are protected by these rights, businesses also bear significant responsibilities to ensure ethical and fair practices. These responsibilities are essential for maintaining trust and fostering a healthy market environment.

1. Providing Accurate Information

1. **Transparency**:
   - Businesses must provide clear and truthful details about their products or services.
   - Misleading claims or incomplete information can result in penalties and loss of consumer trust.
2. **Examples**:
   - Pharmaceutical companies must disclose side effects and contraindications of drugs.
   - Retailers should provide proper receipts with detailed pricing and tax information.

---

2. Ensuring Product Safety and Quality

1. **Compliance**:
   - Adherence to safety standards and quality certifications is non-negotiable.
   - For example, food manufacturers must meet regulations set by the **Food Safety and Standards Authority of India (FSSAI)**.
2. **Regular Testing**:
   - Businesses should conduct rigorous quality checks to prevent defective or harmful products from reaching the market.

3. **Accountability**:
    - If a product is found unsafe, businesses must initiate recalls and offer replacements or refunds.

---

3. Adhering to Ethical Marketing Practices

1. **Fair Representation**:
    - Advertisements should accurately reflect the product's features and benefits.
    - Overstating capabilities, such as claiming a cosmetic product can "reverse aging," misleads consumers.
2. **Avoiding Exploitation**:
    - Businesses must not exploit vulnerable groups, such as children or the elderly, through targeted marketing strategies.
3. **Ensuring Compliance**:
    - Regulatory bodies like the **Advertising Standards Council of India (ASCI)** monitor marketing practices and penalize false or exaggerated claims.

10.2 Overview of Consumer Protection Legislation in India

India's consumer protection framework has evolved over the years, reflecting changes in market dynamics and consumer behavior. Starting with the foundational **Consumer Protection Act, 1986**, the legal landscape has been significantly upgraded with the enactment of the **Consumer Protection Act, 2019**. These laws, along with supporting regulations, provide a comprehensive framework for safeguarding consumer interests. This section explores these legislations in detail, focusing on their objectives, mechanisms, and impact.

The Consumer Protection Act, 1986

The **Consumer Protection Act, 1986**, was India's first major step toward institutionalizing consumer rights and creating mechanisms for grievance redressal.

Objectives and Scope

1. **Primary Objectives**:
    - Ensure the protection of consumers against unfair trade practices and defective goods.
    - Establish a framework for addressing grievances efficiently.

- Empower consumers to seek redressal through accessible legal mechanisms.

2. **Scope**:
    - The Act applies to all goods and services unless specifically exempted by the central government.
    - It covers consumers purchasing goods or services for personal use, excluding commercial or resale purposes.

Consumer Dispute Redressal Forums

The **Consumer Protection Act, 1986**, introduced a three-tier dispute resolution system to address grievances effectively at the district, state, and national levels.

1. **District Forum**:
    - Jurisdiction: Complaints involving compensation claims up to ₹20 lakh.
    - Structure: A president and two members, one of whom must be a woman.
    - Example: A local complaint about a defective washing machine purchased from a retailer.
2. **State Commission**:
    - Jurisdiction: Appeals from District Forums and cases involving compensation claims between ₹20 lakh and ₹1 crore.
    - Example: Disputes regarding real estate projects affecting multiple consumers in a state.
3. **National Commission**:
    - Jurisdiction: Appeals from State Commissions and cases involving claims exceeding ₹1 crore.
    - Example: A class-action lawsuit against a major corporation for defective automobiles.

The Consumer Protection Act, 2019

The **Consumer Protection Act, 2019**, represents a paradigm shift in consumer protection, addressing gaps in the 1986 Act and introducing provisions for modern commerce.

Key Updates Over the 1986 Act

1. **Expanded Definition of Consumer**:
    - Includes users of goods or services obtained through both offline and online transactions.
    - Covers all digital transactions, reflecting the growing e-commerce market.
2. **Simplified Grievance Mechanisms**:
    - Enhanced accessibility with the introduction of an **E-daakhil portal**, allowing consumers to file complaints online.

Introduction of Central Consumer Protection Authority (CCPA)

1. **Role of CCPA**:
    - Investigates complaints related to unfair trade practices and misleading advertisements.
    - Orders product recalls, refunds, or replacement of defective goods.
    - Penalizes companies for violating consumer rights.
2. **Impact**:
    - A centralized body ensures a uniform approach to addressing systemic issues affecting consumers.

Provisions for E-Commerce and Misleading Advertisements

1. **E-Commerce Platforms**:
    - Obligated to disclose seller information, terms of return, and refund policies.
    - Required to address complaints within a stipulated time.
2. **Misleading Advertisements**:
    - Advertisers can face penalties for false claims, such as promoting unproven health benefits of products.

Related Laws and Regulations

While the Consumer Protection Act forms the backbone of consumer rights in India, several other laws supplement its provisions.

Legal Metrology Act, 2009

1. **Focus**:
   - Ensures accuracy in weights, measurements, and labeling.
   - Mandates clear declarations on packaging, such as net quantity and manufacturing details.
2. **Practical Impact**:
   - Prevents deceptive practices like underweight products or misleading quantity claims.

Drugs and Cosmetics Act, 1940

1. **Objective**:
   - Ensures the safety, quality, and efficacy of drugs and cosmetics sold in India.
2. **Consumer Protection**:
   - Prevents the sale of counterfeit or substandard pharmaceutical products.

Food Safety and Standards Act, 2006

1. **Role**:
   - Regulates the manufacture, storage, and distribution of food products to ensure safety and quality.
   - Provides a framework for recalling unsafe food items.
2. **Relevance**:
   - Protects consumers from food adulteration and contamination.

10.3 Consumer Protection in the Digital Era

The digital age has transformed consumer habits, creating both opportunities and challenges. With the growth of e-commerce and digital platforms, new risks have emerged, necessitating a modern approach to consumer protection.

Challenges in E-Commerce

1. False Advertising and Misleading Product Descriptions

1. **Common Issues**:
   - Discrepancies between advertised and delivered products.

- Use of manipulated reviews or endorsements to mislead consumers.

2. **Example**:
   - An online retailer promoting a "100% cotton" shirt delivers a product made of synthetic fabric.

---

2. Lack of Clear Return and Refund Policies

1. **Consumer Concerns**:
   - Ambiguous return periods or hidden charges.
   - Delays in processing refunds.
2. **Example**:
   - A customer buying an electronic gadget online struggles to return it due to unclear policies.

---

3. Data Privacy Concerns in Online Transactions

1. **Risks**:
   - Personal data theft or misuse by e-commerce platforms.
   - Cybersecurity breaches leading to financial fraud.
2. **Impact**:
   - Erodes consumer trust in digital platforms.

E-Commerce Rules Under the Consumer Protection Act, 2019

Obligations of E-Commerce Platforms

1. **Transparency**:
   - Display comprehensive product information, including prices, seller details, and delivery timelines.
2. **Consumer Rights**:
   - Ensure grievance redressal mechanisms and adhere to refund policies.

Grievance Redressal Mechanisms

1. **Dedicated Support**:
   - Platforms must provide accessible customer service to address complaints promptly.

2. **Escalation Routes**:
   - Consumers can file complaints with regulatory bodies if unsatisfied with platform responses.

Prohibition of Unfair Trade Practices

1. **Accountability**:
   - Platforms face penalties for fraudulent practices like inflating prices during sales.
2. **Impact**:
   - Ensures ethical conduct, building consumer confidence.

Digital Literacy for Consumers

Importance of Educating Consumers About Online Frauds

1. **Awareness Campaigns**:
   - Government initiatives to educate consumers about phishing scams and fake websites.
2. **Practical Tips**:
   - Verifying seller authenticity and reading reviews before purchases.

Role of Government Initiatives Like Digital India

1. **Objective**:
   - Promote digital literacy and build trust in e-commerce ecosystems.
2. **Implementation**:
   - Digital India campaigns include workshops, online resources, and awareness programs.

10.4 Mechanisms for Consumer Redressal

Consumer protection laws are only as effective as the mechanisms available for addressing grievances. While legislation provides the framework, it is the practical accessibility and functionality of redressal mechanisms that ensure justice for consumers. This section explores the various systems in place for consumer grievance redressal in India, starting with traditional forums and extending to modern, digital platforms and alternative dispute resolution mechanisms. By the end, you'll have a comprehensive understanding of how consumers can assert their rights and seek redress for grievances.

The Need for Robust Consumer Redressal Mechanisms

Before diving into the specifics, let's consider a simple question: what happens when a consumer feels wronged by a product or service? Imagine purchasing a high-priced refrigerator, only to find it defective, with the retailer refusing to replace or repair it. Without accessible redressal systems, consumers are left powerless. This is where structured mechanisms, both traditional and digital, step in to ensure fairness, accountability, and timely resolution.

Consumer Dispute Redressal Forums

The **Consumer Protection Act, 1986**, introduced a three-tier system for resolving consumer disputes, designed to address complaints based on their complexity and monetary value. This system, now updated under the **Consumer Protection Act, 2019**, remains the backbone of grievance redressal in India.

Structure and Hierarchy: District, State, and National Commissions

1. **District Consumer Dispute Redressal Commission**:
    - **Purpose**: Handles grievances at the local level for straightforward and lower-value cases.
    - **Composition**:
        - A president (typically a retired judge).
        - Two members, one of whom must be a woman, ensuring representation and fairness.
    - **Example**:
        - A consumer files a complaint regarding a defective washing machine worth ₹10 lakh. This case falls within the District Commission's jurisdiction.
2. **State Consumer Dispute Redressal Commission**:
    - **Purpose**: Addresses more complex cases or appeals from District Commissions.
    - **Composition**:
        - A president (a retired high court judge) and multiple members.
    - **Example**:
        - A real estate buyer disputes the quality of a newly purchased flat and claims damages worth ₹50 lakh. This case is handled at the State Commission level.

3. **National Consumer Dispute Redressal Commission (NCDRC)**:
    - **Purpose**: The apex body for consumer disputes, addressing high-value cases and appeals from State Commissions.
    - **Composition**:
        - Presided over by a retired Supreme Court judge.
    - **Example**:
        - A class-action lawsuit against a multinational company for a defective vehicle model with claims exceeding ₹2 crore is adjudicated here.

Jurisdiction and Monetary Limits for Filing Complaints

- **District Commission**:
    - Jurisdiction: Claims up to ₹1 crore.
    - Ensures swift resolution for local disputes.
- **State Commission**:
    - Jurisdiction: Claims between ₹1 crore and ₹10 crore.
    - Addresses mid-level disputes with broader implications.
- **National Commission**:
    - Jurisdiction: Claims above ₹10 crore.
    - Handles complex, high-stake cases with national or international ramifications.

This tiered structure ensures that complaints are addressed efficiently, based on their scale and complexity, minimizing the burden on higher forums.

Online Grievance Redressal

With the advent of digital technology, consumer grievance redressal has become more accessible and efficient. Recognizing the importance of convenience and speed, the Indian government has launched several online platforms to address consumer complaints.

National Consumer Helpline (NCH)

1. **What It Is**:
    - A toll-free helpline established by the Department of Consumer Affairs to guide consumers on resolving grievances.

2. **How It Works**:
   - Consumers can dial 1800-11-4000 or use the NCH app to register complaints.
   - NCH forwards the complaints to the concerned company or regulator for resolution.
3. **Practical Example**:
   - A consumer facing delivery issues with an e-commerce platform can contact NCH. The helpline mediates between the consumer and the company, often resolving the issue within days.

E-Daakhil Portal for Filing Complaints Online

1. **Purpose**:
   - The **E-daakhil portal** simplifies the process of filing consumer complaints by allowing online submissions.
2. **Features**:
   - Allows submission of complaints with digital evidence.
   - Provides status updates and hearing schedules in real-time.
   - Accessible to consumers across India, reducing the need for physical visits to forums.
3. **Steps to File a Complaint**:
   - **Step 1**: Visit the **E-daakhil portal** and register with valid credentials.
   - **Step 2**: Upload the necessary documents, such as the bill, warranty card, and proof of correspondence with the seller.
   - **Step 3**: Pay the nominal filing fee online.
   - **Step 4**: Track the complaint status and attend virtual hearings, if required.
4. **Practical Example**:
   - A customer purchases a smartphone online, which arrives damaged. Unable to reach a resolution with the seller, they file a complaint through E-daakhil, attaching photos of the damaged phone and the invoice.

Alternative Dispute Resolution (ADR) Mechanisms

While traditional forums and digital platforms are essential, **Alternative Dispute Resolution (ADR)** mechanisms provide an additional layer of efficiency, particularly for disputes that can be settled amicably.

Mediation and Arbitration

1. **Mediation**:
    - **What It Is**:
        - A non-adversarial process where a neutral mediator facilitates a discussion between the parties to arrive at a mutually acceptable solution.
    - **Advantages**:
        - Saves time and cost compared to formal litigation.
        - Preserves relationships, making it ideal for disputes involving ongoing business transactions.
    - **Example**:
        - A hotel guest dissatisfied with services mediates with the hotel management to receive a partial refund and a complimentary stay voucher.
2. **Arbitration**:
    - **What It Is**:
        - A formal process where an arbitrator hears both parties and delivers a binding decision.
    - **Advantages**:
        - Faster resolution with legally enforceable outcomes.
    - **Example**:
        - A contractual dispute between a consumer and a real estate developer over delayed possession is resolved through arbitration.

Advantages of ADR in Resolving Consumer Disputes Quickly

1. **Time-Efficiency**:
    - ADR mechanisms typically resolve disputes within weeks, compared to months or years in traditional forums.
2. **Cost-Effectiveness**:
    - Lower legal costs make ADR accessible to a broader range of consumers.
3. **Confidentiality**:
    - ADR processes are private, ensuring that sensitive business or personal details are not disclosed publicly.

4. **Flexibility**:
   - Parties can select the mediator or arbitrator and schedule proceedings at their convenience.

Conclusion

India's consumer redressal mechanisms provide a robust framework for resolving grievances, combining traditional forums, digital platforms, and ADR mechanisms. The tiered structure of dispute redressal forums ensures accessibility and efficiency, while online initiatives like the E-daakhil portal and NCH cater to the demands of a digital-first world. ADR mechanisms, with their emphasis on speed and cost-effectiveness, complement these systems, offering consumers multiple pathways to justice.

10.5 Challenges in Consumer Protection

Consumer protection, despite its strong legislative framework, faces significant challenges in today's dynamic markets. The rapid evolution of globalized supply chains, digital commerce, and consumer behavior has introduced complexities that traditional systems often struggle to address. This section examines the key challenges, including the intricacies of modern markets, a pervasive lack of awareness among consumers, and delays in justice delivery.

Complexity of Modern Markets

The interconnected nature of today's global economy has transformed consumer markets, introducing new layers of complexity.

Globalized Supply Chains and Cross-Border Trade

1. **Nature of the Challenge**:
   - Products often pass through multiple countries during manufacturing, making it difficult to pinpoint liability for defective goods or safety issues.
   - Example: A smartphone designed in the USA, assembled in China, and sold in India poses a challenge when it malfunctions. Who bears the responsibility— the designer, the assembler, or the retailer?
2. **Implications**:
   - Consumers may face prolonged delays in seeking redressal.
   - Regulatory authorities may lack the jurisdiction to act effectively in cross-border disputes.

Difficulty in Tracing Liability

1. **Complex Distribution Networks**:
   - Many modern products involve partnerships between manufacturers, wholesalers, retailers, and service providers, making accountability a shared and often ambiguous responsibility.
2. **Example**:
   - A defective car part manufactured by a third-party supplier but sold under a prominent automobile brand creates confusion over accountability.
3. **Impact**:
   - Consumers often bear the brunt of such ambiguity, leading to frustration and loss of trust.

Lack of Awareness

Many consumers remain unaware of their rights and the mechanisms available for grievance redressal.

Limited Knowledge of Rights and Redressal Mechanisms

1. **Urban vs Rural Divide**:
   - Urban consumers are more likely to be informed about consumer rights and legal remedies compared to their rural counterparts.
   - Rural areas often lack the resources to disseminate such information effectively.
2. **Consequences**:
   - Cases of exploitation, such as overpricing, poor-quality products, or lack of refunds, go unreported in underserved areas.

Rural and Semi-Urban Consumers Being Disproportionately Affected

1. **Challenges**:
   - Limited access to consumer courts or helplines.
   - Language barriers and inadequate digital literacy exacerbate the problem.

2. **Example**:
    - A rural farmer purchasing defective agricultural equipment may be unaware of their right to demand a replacement or refund.

Delayed Justice

Justice delayed is often justice denied. This adage holds especially true for consumer disputes, where delays can erode trust in the system.

Backlogs in Consumer Courts

1. **Nature of the Problem**:
    - Overburdened consumer courts often struggle with a backlog of cases.
    - Lack of sufficient judges and infrastructure contributes to delays.
2. **Impact**:
    - Consumers waiting years for resolution may abandon their cases, effectively losing their right to redressal.

Limited Resources and Infrastructure

1. **Challenges**:
    - Many forums lack adequate staff, modern technology, or digital systems to streamline proceedings.
    - Rural courts often face even greater resource constraints.
2. **Potential Solutions**:
    - Increased funding for consumer courts.
    - Adoption of technology to expedite case management.

10.6 Global Perspectives on Consumer Protection

India can learn valuable lessons from other countries that have implemented robust consumer protection frameworks. This section explores global best practices and their potential applicability to India.

Comparative Analysis

United States: Role of the Federal Trade Commission (FTC)

1. **Overview**:
   - The FTC enforces consumer protection laws, focusing on areas like deceptive advertising and fraud prevention.
2. **Key Features**:
   - Proactive monitoring of trade practices.
   - Swift actions against violations, including hefty penalties.
3. **Applicability in India**:
   - India's Central Consumer Protection Authority (CCPA) could adopt similar proactive measures to prevent consumer exploitation.

European Union: General Data Protection Regulation (GDPR)

1. **Overview**:
   - GDPR ensures data privacy and protection for EU consumers.
   - Businesses must obtain explicit consent before collecting or processing personal data.
2. **Impact**:
   - Empowered consumers to demand accountability for misuse of personal data.
   - Encouraged businesses to adopt stringent data security measures.
3. **Lessons for India**:
   - Strengthening data protection laws, particularly for e-commerce and digital platforms.

Japan and Australia: Strict Liability and Product Recalls

1. **Japan**:
   - Manufacturers are held strictly liable for defective products, regardless of negligence.
   - Regular audits and product recalls are mandatory.
2. **Australia**:
   - Consumer protection laws mandate prompt compensation or replacement for defective goods.

- The Australian Competition and Consumer Commission (ACCC) actively monitors compliance.

Lessons for India

1. **Adoption of Global Best Practices**:
    - Implementing strict liability laws to ensure consumer confidence in product safety.
    - Enhancing digital privacy standards in line with GDPR.
2. **Harmonizing Indian Laws with International Standards**:
    - Aligning India's consumer protection framework with global trade agreements to boost consumer trust in cross-border transactions.

10.7 Case Studies and Real-Life Examples

Case studies provide a tangible understanding of consumer protection mechanisms in action, illustrating successes and shortcomings.

Successful Consumer Dispute Resolutions

1. **High-Profile NCDRC Case**:
    - A prominent builder was ordered to compensate a group of homebuyers for delayed possession.
    - Outcome: Homebuyers received refunds with interest, setting a precedent for accountability in real estate.

Corporate Accountability

1. **Misleading Advertisements**:
    - A major beverage company was penalized for advertising unverified health benefits.
    - Impact: Reinforced the need for ethical marketing.

Lessons from Failures

1. **Prolonged Delays**:
    - A consumer filing a case against a retailer for defective goods faced delays exceeding five years.

- Lesson: Highlighted the urgency of addressing systemic inefficiencies in consumer courts.

10.8 Future Trends in Consumer Protection

As technology and sustainability reshape commerce, consumer protection must evolve to address new challenges and opportunities.

Integration of Technology

1. **AI and Machine Learning**:
   - Detect patterns of unfair trade practices, such as predatory pricing or counterfeit products.
   - Example: An AI tool flags a surge in complaints about a specific e-commerce platform.
2. **Blockchain**:
   - Ensures transparency in supply chains, allowing consumers to trace product origins and authenticity.

Focus on Sustainability

1. **Ethical Consumption**:
   - Governments and businesses encouraging eco-friendly products.
   - Example: Mandatory labeling of carbon footprints on goods.

Stronger Data Protection Laws

1. **Consumer Privacy**:
   - Enacting stricter regulations on how businesses collect, store, and use consumer data.
   - Example: Mandatory data breach notifications.

CHAPTER 11

Imports and Exports

Trade is the lifeblood of economies. It shapes nations, connects markets, and creates opportunities that transcend borders. When we talk about **imports and exports**, we're referring to the exchange of goods and services across nations—imports bring what we need or want from abroad, while exports showcase what we produce best to the world. This fundamental dynamic forms the bedrock of the global economy. In this chapter, we'll embark on an in-depth exploration of imports and exports, examining their definitions, historical evolution in India, and their significance in driving the nation's economic growth.

Introduction

Let's start by imagining a day in your life. The coffee you sip in the morning may come from Colombia, the smartphone in your hand might be assembled in China, and the software you use could be designed in India. This seamless access to products and services from around the globe is made possible through **international trade**. The interconnectedness of economies, fueled by imports and exports, not only enhances our daily lives but also drives economic progress worldwide.

Overview of Imports and Exports in the Global Economy

Definition and Significance

At its core, international trade involves the buying and selling of goods and services across borders. When a country **imports**, it brings in goods or services from another nation, meeting domestic demand that local production cannot fulfill or offering consumers a wider variety of choices. Conversely, **exports** allow countries to sell their products or services abroad, earning revenue, creating jobs, and showcasing their economic capabilities.

Why does this matter? The exchange of goods and services:

- **Promotes economic growth**: Trade allows nations to specialize in what they do best, increasing productivity and output.
- **Fosters innovation**: Exposure to global competition pushes industries to innovate and improve.
- **Encourages cooperation**: Trade agreements and partnerships build diplomatic and economic ties.

For instance, consider the global supply chain of automobiles. A car may have an engine sourced from Japan, tires manufactured in Germany, and electronics developed in the USA, before being assembled in India. This complexity underscores the vital role of imports and exports in modern economies.

Role of International Trade in Economic Development

Trade has always been a powerful driver of economic development. Let's delve into how it shapes nations:

1. **Efficient Resource Allocation**: Through trade, countries can focus on producing goods where they have a **comparative advantage**—producing efficiently compared to others. For example:
    - India excels in exporting **IT services** due to its skilled workforce and cost advantages.
    - The Middle East capitalizes on its vast **oil reserves** to supply energy to the world.
2. **Technology Transfer**: Imports bring not just products but also knowledge and technology. A country importing high-tech machinery can learn to develop similar capabilities domestically over time.
3. **Job Creation**: Trade generates employment across sectors, from manufacturing to logistics and retail. For example, the rise of **pharmaceutical exports** from India has created thousands of jobs in R&D and production facilities.
4. **Economic Integration**: Nations participating in global trade often enjoy stronger economic ties, reducing the likelihood of conflicts and fostering collaboration. The establishment of organizations like the **World Trade Organization (WTO)** reflects this interconnectedness.

Historical Context of Imports and Exports in India

India's journey in international trade is a fascinating tale of transformation, shaped by its rich history, colonial experience, and post-independence economic policies.

Evolution of India's Trade Policies

1. **Pre-Independence Era**:
    - During the colonial period, India's trade patterns were dictated by British interests. Raw materials like cotton and jute were exported, while finished goods, primarily textiles, were imported from Britain. This exploitative system drained India's resources and stifled industrial growth.
2. **Post-Independence Protectionism (1947–1991)**:
    - After independence, India adopted a **protectionist trade policy** aimed at self-reliance. Key features included:
        - High tariffs and import restrictions to protect domestic industries.
        - A focus on import substitution, encouraging local production of goods that were previously imported.
    - While this strategy nurtured industries like steel and textiles, it also led to inefficiencies and limited integration with global markets.
3. **Economic Liberalization (1991 Onwards)**:
    - Faced with a balance of payments crisis in 1991, India embarked on a path of **economic liberalization**. Key reforms included:
        - Reduction of import tariffs and removal of trade barriers.
        - Promotion of exports through incentives and trade facilitation.
        - Integration with global markets via free trade agreements (FTAs).
    - These reforms transformed India into one of the world's fastest-growing economies, with trade playing a pivotal role.

Transition from Protectionist to Liberalized Trade Regime

The shift from protectionism to liberalization marked a turning point in India's trade story. Let's break it down:

1. **Before 1991**: India's trade policies were inward-looking, prioritizing self-sufficiency over global competitiveness. Import restrictions were so stringent that obtaining foreign goods was a challenge for businesses and consumers alike.
2. **The Liberalization Era**: Post-1991 reforms opened India's economy to the world. Key milestones included:
   - Signing of the **General Agreement on Tariffs and Trade (GATT)** in 1994, leading to India's inclusion in the WTO.
   - Encouragement of foreign direct investment (FDI) to boost trade-related industries.
   - Establishment of **Special Economic Zones (SEZs)** to promote exports.
3. **Impact of Liberalization**:
   - Exports surged, with sectors like **IT services**, **pharmaceuticals**, and **textiles** leading the charge.
   - Imports diversified to include high-tech machinery, electronic goods, and energy resources.

Importance of Imports and Exports for India's Economy

Contribution to GDP

Trade is a significant contributor to India's Gross Domestic Product (GDP). As of recent years:

- **Exports** account for approximately **20% of GDP**, driven by sectors like IT, textiles, and pharmaceuticals.
- **Imports**, particularly of oil and gold, are essential to meet domestic demand and support key industries.

Employment Generation

Trade creates millions of jobs across India. Consider these examples:

- **Export-driven industries**: The **textile sector**, which accounts for a substantial share of India's exports, employs over **45 million workers**.
- **Logistics and supply chains**: Activities like shipping, warehousing, and customs handling create opportunities for skilled and unskilled labor alike.

Integration with Global Markets

India's integration into global markets has brought numerous benefits:

- Access to **advanced technologies** through imports.

- Opportunities for Indian products to reach new markets, such as Africa and Latin America.
- Participation in global supply chains, as seen in the **pharmaceutical sector**, where India is a leading supplier of generic drugs.

11.1 Fundamentals of Imports and Exports

International trade is the backbone of the global economy, facilitating the exchange of goods, services, and ideas across borders. At its essence, trade is about fulfilling needs, leveraging strengths, and creating value through the movement of resources and expertise. This section delves into the fundamentals of **imports and exports**, breaking down their definitions, key concepts, and the various participants involved in this dynamic process.

Definition and Key Concepts

What Are Imports and Exports?

Imports are goods or services brought into a country from abroad. They meet domestic demand for products that are either unavailable, uneconomical, or inefficient to produce locally. For instance:

- India imports **crude oil** to meet its energy requirements.
- Advanced technologies like **semiconductors** are sourced from countries like Taiwan and the USA.

Exports, on the other hand, are goods or services produced domestically and sold to foreign markets. They showcase a country's economic strengths and provide revenue to bolster the local economy. Examples include:

- **Indian IT services**, which are sought after globally for their cost-effectiveness and expertise.
- **Textiles and garments**, a traditional export sector for India.

Together, imports and exports constitute a country's **foreign trade**, driving its interaction with the global economy.

Balance of Trade (BoT) and Balance of Payments (BoP)

1. **Balance of Trade (BoT)**:
    - BoT measures the difference between the value of a country's exports and imports of goods over a specific period.

- **Trade Surplus**: When exports exceed imports, indicating strong production and competitiveness.
- **Trade Deficit**: When imports surpass exports, which may signal dependency on foreign goods or insufficient domestic production.

For example, India often runs a **trade deficit** due to its reliance on oil imports, though it achieves trade surpluses in sectors like IT services and pharmaceuticals.

2. **Balance of Payments (BoP)**:
   - BoP provides a broader picture, encompassing all financial transactions between a country and the rest of the world, including trade, investments, and remittances.
   - BoP is divided into:
     - **Current Account**: Includes goods and services trade, income flows, and transfers.
     - **Capital Account**: Covers investments, loans, and foreign reserves.

Understanding BoT and BoP is crucial for evaluating a country's economic health and its trade relationships.

Tariffs, Quotas, and Trade Barriers

1. **Tariffs**:
   - Tariffs are taxes imposed on imports, making foreign goods more expensive and less competitive compared to domestic products.
   - Example: India imposes **customs duties** on certain imported electronics to promote local manufacturing under the **Make in India** initiative.
2. **Quotas**:
   - Quotas restrict the quantity of specific goods that can be imported or exported within a given timeframe.
   - For instance, quotas on sugar exports help maintain adequate domestic supply and stabilize prices.
3. **Trade Barriers**:
   - These include non-tariff measures like stringent safety standards, certifications, and documentation requirements that can impede the free flow of goods.

    - Example: Some countries impose strict **pesticide residue limits** on agricultural imports, affecting Indian exporters.

These tools are often used to protect domestic industries, generate revenue, or address political and economic concerns.

Types of Goods Traded

Trade isn't limited to tangible goods—it spans a diverse range of products and services, each playing a unique role in the economy.

Raw Materials

- **Definition**: Basic commodities extracted or harvested to produce finished goods.
- **Examples**:
    - Crude oil imported by India.
    - Iron ore exported by Brazil.
- **Importance**:
    - Essential for industrial growth.
    - Raw material imports are often a necessity for countries lacking natural resources.

Intermediate Goods

- **Definition**: Semi-finished products used as inputs in manufacturing final goods.
- **Examples**:
    - Auto components exported by India to Europe.
    - Electronic chips imported by smartphone manufacturers in India.
- **Importance**:
    - Critical for industries like electronics, automotive, and textiles.
    - Trade in intermediate goods often reflects global supply chain integration.

Finished Goods

- **Definition**: End products ready for consumption or use.
- **Examples**:
    - Smartphones imported from China.

    - Pharmaceuticals exported from India.
- **Importance**:
    - Represents consumer preferences and global branding.
    - Finished goods trade drives revenue and innovation.

Services

- **Definition**: Intangible offerings like expertise, technology, and consultancy.
- **Examples**:
    - IT outsourcing services provided by Indian companies like TCS and Infosys.
    - Consulting services imported from global firms like McKinsey.
- **Importance**:
    - Services trade is a growing segment, contributing significantly to India's exports.
    - Encourages intellectual and technological exchange.

Participants in International Trade

International trade involves a wide range of participants, each contributing to the exchange of goods and services.

Governments

- **Role**:
    - Formulating trade policies, negotiating treaties, and ensuring compliance with global norms.
    - Example: India's participation in the **World Trade Organization (WTO)** to advocate for its trade interests.
- **Impact**:
    - Government actions, such as imposing tariffs or entering into free trade agreements, directly influence trade dynamics.

Corporations

- **Role**:
    - Large multinational corporations (MNCs) drive a significant portion of global trade.

  - Example: Companies like **Reliance Industries** import crude oil and export petrochemicals, balancing trade on both fronts.
- **Impact**:
  - Corporations invest in global supply chains, fostering efficiency and innovation.

Small and Medium Enterprises (SMEs)

- **Role**:
  - SMEs often specialize in niche products or services, contributing to both imports and exports.
  - Example: Indian SMEs exporting handicrafts or importing specialized machinery.
- **Challenges**:
  - Limited resources and exposure to global markets.
- **Support**:
  - Government programs like **Make in India** and **Export Promotion Councils** provide assistance to SMEs.

Individuals

- **Role**:
  - While less visible, individuals engage in trade through e-commerce platforms and freelancing services.
  - Example: An Indian freelance graphic designer providing services to clients in the USA.
- **Impact**:
  - The rise of e-commerce platforms like Amazon and Flipkart has enabled cross-border trade for individuals.

11.2 India's Import Landscape

India's import landscape is characterized by a diverse array of goods that cater to its growing industrial, technological, and consumer needs. From energy resources to cutting-edge electronics, imports play a crucial role in meeting domestic demand and supporting various sectors of the economy. This section explores the major goods imported by India, the countries that supply these goods, and the challenges that arise from the country's dependency on imports.

Major Imported Goods

1. **Petroleum and Crude Oil**

   India is one of the largest importers of crude oil globally. With limited domestic reserves, the country depends on imports to meet its energy needs. Crude oil accounts for a significant portion of India's total imports and fuels industries, transportation, and energy production. For instance, India imports crude primarily from Saudi Arabia, Iraq, and the UAE.

2. **Electronic Goods**

   The demand for electronics like smartphones, laptops, and components has surged with India's digital revolution. Most of these are imported from countries like China and South Korea, as domestic manufacturing capabilities in this sector are still developing.

3. **Machinery and Equipment**

   India imports industrial machinery, electrical equipment, and heavy-duty tools to support its infrastructure and industrial growth. These imports are crucial for sectors such as construction, manufacturing, and renewable energy.

4. **Precious Metals (Gold and Silver)**

   Gold is one of India's top imports, driven by cultural and economic factors. Jewelry is an integral part of Indian traditions, and gold serves as a popular investment. Silver, on the other hand, is used in both jewelry and industrial applications.

5. **Chemicals and Pharmaceuticals**

   India imports specialized chemicals for industries like agriculture, pharmaceuticals, and textiles. Active Pharmaceutical Ingredients (APIs) are also heavily imported, primarily from China, to support India's pharmaceutical manufacturing.

Countries of Origin

India's imports are sourced from a variety of trading partners, each contributing to specific sectors.

1. **Key Trading Partners**
   - **China**: The largest supplier of electronics, machinery, and APIs.
   - **UAE and Saudi Arabia**: Major exporters of crude oil and petroleum products.
   - **USA**: Supplies technology, defense equipment, and machinery.

   - **South Korea and Japan**: Key partners for electronics and automobiles.
2. **Regional Trends**
   - The Middle East dominates in energy supplies.
   - Asia, particularly China, leads in consumer goods and electronics.
   - Europe and North America contribute advanced machinery and technology.

Challenges in Imports

1. **Trade Deficits**

   India frequently runs a trade deficit, importing more than it exports. This can lead to economic imbalances and reliance on foreign currencies.
2. **Dependency on Specific Countries**

   Over-reliance on countries like China for critical imports such as APIs and electronics can pose risks to supply chain stability, especially during geopolitical tensions.
3. **Currency Fluctuations**

   The value of the Indian rupee against major currencies like the US dollar impacts import costs. A depreciating rupee increases the cost of imported goods, affecting businesses and consumers alike.

11.3 India's Export Landscape

India's export sector is a vibrant component of its economy, showcasing the country's industrial, agricultural, and technological strengths on the global stage. From textiles to IT services, exports drive economic growth, create employment, and earn valuable foreign exchange.

Major Exported Goods

1. **Textiles and Garments**

   India is a leading exporter of cotton textiles, apparel, and handlooms. These products are prized for their quality and craftsmanship, with major markets in the USA, EU, and Middle East.
2. **Gems and Jewelry**

   The gems and jewelry sector is one of India's largest contributors to exports, with polished diamonds and gold jewelry being highly sought after in global markets like the USA, UAE, and Hong Kong.

3. **Pharmaceuticals and Chemicals**

   India is often referred to as the "pharmacy of the world," supplying generic medicines and APIs to over 200 countries. Its chemical exports include fertilizers, dyes, and specialty chemicals.

4. **Agricultural Products**

   Agricultural exports, including rice, spices, tea, and sugar, are integral to India's trade. Basmati rice and spices like turmeric and cardamom enjoy high demand globally.

5. **Information Technology (IT) Services**

   India's IT services industry, led by companies like TCS, Infosys, and Wipro, is a global leader. Services range from software development to consultancy, catering to markets in the USA, Europe, and Asia.

Export Destinations

1. **Key Markets**
   - **USA**: India's largest export destination, especially for IT services, textiles, and pharmaceuticals.
   - **European Union**: A major buyer of Indian textiles, chemicals, and IT services.
   - **ASEAN Countries**: Growing markets for agricultural products and machinery.
2. **Emerging Markets and Growth Opportunities**
   - Africa and Latin America are expanding markets for pharmaceuticals and processed foods.
   - Middle Eastern countries demand agricultural and construction-related exports.

Government Support for Exports

1. **Incentives and Subsidies**

   The government offers export incentives like the Merchandise Exports from India Scheme (MEIS) and the Service Exports from India Scheme (SEIS) to promote various sectors.

2. **Trade Fairs and Export Promotion Councils**
   - Initiatives like trade fairs and expos help Indian exporters showcase their products globally.
   - Export promotion councils like the Gems and Jewelry Export Promotion Council (GJEPC) and Agricultural and Processed Food Products Export Development Authority (APEDA) support sector-specific growth.

Export Challenges

1. **Global Competition**

   Indian exporters face stiff competition from countries like China, Vietnam, and Bangladesh, especially in textiles and electronics.

2. **Non-Tariff Barriers**

   Issues like strict quality standards, certifications, and import restrictions in certain countries create hurdles for Indian exporters.

3. **Quality and Compliance Issues**

   Ensuring global quality standards and adhering to environmental and labor regulations are ongoing challenges for many sectors.

11.4 Regulatory Framework for Imports and Exports in India

Trade, both domestic and international, operates within a structured framework of rules and regulations. These ensure that the exchange of goods and services across borders is transparent, efficient, and fair. In India, the **regulatory framework for imports and exports** has been meticulously designed to cater to the country's diverse economic landscape and global aspirations. From laws like the Customs Act, 1962, to the policies and procedures of the Directorate General of Foreign Trade (DGFT), every aspect is fine-tuned to facilitate trade while safeguarding national interests. In this section, we'll explore the regulatory backbone that governs India's imports and exports, delving into its laws, policies, key institutions, and compliance mechanisms.

The Customs Act, 1962

Let's begin with the **Customs Act, 1962**, a cornerstone of India's trade regulation. This Act governs the import and export of goods, ensuring compliance with customs duties and procedures. Its significance lies in its dual role—facilitating legitimate trade while curbing illegal practices like smuggling.

Role of Customs Authorities in Trade

The **customs authorities** are the guardians of India's ports and borders. They oversee the movement of goods in and out of the country, ensuring that trade adheres to national laws and international agreements.

1. **Facilitating Trade**: Customs officers play a pivotal role in speeding up the clearance process for imports and exports. Their responsibilities include:

- Verifying the authenticity of documents submitted by traders.
- Calculating and collecting applicable customs duties and taxes.
- Ensuring that goods comply with safety, health, and environmental standards.

2. **Preventing Illegal Activities**: Beyond trade facilitation, customs authorities are tasked with preventing illegal activities like smuggling, counterfeit goods, and the import/export of prohibited items.
3. **Use of Technology**: To streamline operations, customs authorities now rely on tools like:
    - The **Electronic Data Interchange (EDI)** for faster clearance.
    - Risk management systems that flag high-risk consignments for additional scrutiny.

Import/Export Procedures and Documentation

The import/export process involves multiple steps, each requiring specific documentation to ensure legal and regulatory compliance. Here's a step-by-step guide:

1. **Pre-Shipment Stage**:
    - Obtain an **Import-Export Code (IEC)** (explained in detail later) from DGFT.
    - Identify the correct **Harmonized System of Nomenclature (HSN) code** for the goods.
    - Secure necessary permits or certifications, such as phytosanitary certificates for agricultural products.
2. **Shipping and Documentation**:
    - Key documents include:
        - **Commercial Invoice**: Details the value of goods.
        - **Packing List**: Lists the contents of the shipment.
        - **Bill of Lading** or **Airway Bill**: Acts as proof of shipment.
    - Goods are loaded and transported to the port of entry or exit.

3. **Customs Clearance**:
    - Submit the **Bill of Entry** for imports or **Shipping Bill** for exports.
    - Pay applicable duties and taxes.
    - Goods are inspected, cleared, and released for delivery or export.
4. **Post-Clearance Compliance**:
    - Maintain detailed records of imports/exports for future audits.
    - File any claims for duty refunds under relevant schemes.

Foreign Trade Policy (FTP)

The **Foreign Trade Policy (FTP)**, issued by the Ministry of Commerce and Industry, is the guiding document for India's trade regime. It lays out strategies to promote exports, reduce trade deficits, and integrate India into the global economy.

Objectives and Highlights

1. **Core Objectives**:
    - Enhance India's share in global trade.
    - Promote exports from sectors like textiles, pharmaceuticals, and IT.
    - Simplify trade processes to make India a preferred trading partner.
2. **Highlights**:
    - The FTP is typically issued for a five-year period, with periodic updates to address emerging challenges.
    - Key focus areas include:
        - Diversifying export markets.
        - Supporting small and medium enterprises (SMEs) in accessing global markets.
        - Encouraging the adoption of green and sustainable trade practices.

Export Promotion Capital Goods (EPCG) Scheme

The **EPCG Scheme** is a flagship initiative under the FTP, aimed at enhancing India's manufacturing capabilities.

1. **Purpose**:
   - Allow exporters to import capital goods (machinery, tools) at reduced or zero customs duty.
   - Boost the production of goods and services for export markets.
2. **Requirements**:
   - Beneficiaries must commit to achieving a minimum export obligation, calculated as a multiple of the duty saved.
3. **Impact**:
   - The scheme has facilitated the modernization of industries like textiles and engineering, making them more competitive globally.

Duty Exemption and Remission Schemes

1. **Advance Authorization Scheme**:
   - Allows duty-free import of raw materials required for manufacturing export goods.
   - Example: A garment manufacturer can import fabric duty-free under this scheme.
2. **Duty Drawback Scheme**:
   - Refunds duties paid on imported inputs once the final goods are exported.
   - Simplifies cost structures for exporters, improving profitability.

Key Regulatory Bodies

India's trade landscape is supported by a network of regulatory bodies, each playing a distinct role in facilitating and monitoring trade.

Directorate General of Foreign Trade (DGFT)

The **DGFT** is the nodal agency for implementing the Foreign Trade Policy.

- **Functions**:
  - Issues the Import-Export Code (IEC), a mandatory requirement for all traders.
  - Monitors export incentives and schemes like MEIS and SEIS.
  - Addresses trade-related grievances through its helpline and regional offices.

Export Inspection Council (EIC)

The **EIC** ensures that India's exports meet international quality standards.

- **Key Activities**:
    - Certifying products for compliance with foreign regulations.
    - Conducting quality inspections for goods like food products, textiles, and machinery.

Commodity Boards

Commodity boards focus on the development and promotion of specific export-oriented commodities.

1. **Coffee Board**:
    - Promotes the export of Indian coffee to global markets.
    - Supports farmers with quality improvement programs.
2. **Spices Board**:
    - Ensures the global competitiveness of Indian spices through R&D, quality testing, and marketing support.

Compliance Requirements

Compliance is critical for smooth trade operations, ensuring that goods meet legal, safety, and quality standards.

Import-Export Code (IEC)

- **Definition**:
    - The IEC is a 10-digit code issued by the DGFT, mandatory for all importers and exporters.
- **Application Process**:
    - Apply online via the DGFT portal.
    - Submit KYC documents and business details.
    - IEC issuance is typically completed within a few days.

Product Certifications and Standards

1. **Industry-Specific Certifications**:
    - Exporters of food products may require certifications like the **FSSAI license**.
    - Textiles may need eco-labels for markets like the EU.

2. **Global Standards**:
   - Complying with standards like **ISO 9001** or **HACCP** enhances credibility in international markets.

11.5 Processes and Documentation

The movement of goods and services across borders is a meticulous process that requires coordination, compliance, and a range of documentation. For businesses, understanding the detailed steps in the import and export processes, as well as the role of key trade documents, is essential to ensure smooth operations. This section explores these procedures in depth, offering a step-by-step narrative and insights into technological integration that has revolutionized global trade.

Steps in Import Process

Importing goods into India involves several steps, each requiring careful planning and adherence to regulations. Let's break down the process.

Supplier Identification and Trade Agreement

The first step in the import process is identifying a reliable supplier and finalizing a trade agreement. This stage involves:

- Researching suppliers based on product quality, pricing, and compliance with Indian standards.
- Drafting a detailed contract that outlines terms like product specifications, delivery schedules, payment terms, and incoterms (e.g., FOB, CIF).

For example, a company importing electronic components might negotiate FOB (Free on Board) terms, where the supplier is responsible for shipping the goods to the port of origin.

Application for IEC

The **Import-Export Code (IEC)** is a mandatory requirement for importers in India. Without this unique 10-digit code issued by the DGFT, businesses cannot engage in international trade.

- **Steps to Apply**:
  1. Register on the DGFT online portal.
  2. Submit necessary documents such as PAN, Aadhaar, and bank details.
  3. Pay the application fee.

- The process is entirely digital, and the IEC is typically issued within a few working days.

Customs Clearance and Duties

Once goods arrive at the port of entry, customs clearance is required. This involves:

- Filing a **Bill of Entry** with detailed information about the shipment.
- Submission of supporting documents, including the commercial invoice, packing list, and certificate of origin.
- Payment of applicable customs duties, calculated based on the product's HSN code and declared value.
- Inspection and verification by customs officers to ensure compliance with import regulations.

Goods are released for delivery only after clearance is granted.

Delivery and Warehousing

The final stage in the import process involves:

- Arranging transportation from the port to the importer's warehouse.
- Ensuring proper warehousing conditions, particularly for sensitive goods like pharmaceuticals or perishables.

For example, companies importing vaccines must store them in temperature-controlled warehouses to maintain efficacy.

Steps in Export Process

Exporting goods involves a similar series of steps, though the focus shifts to market research, documentation, and compliance with the destination country's regulations.

Market Research and Buyer Identification

Before exporting, businesses must:

- Conduct market research to identify demand for their products.
- Shortlist potential buyers using platforms like trade fairs, export promotion councils, and online marketplaces.
- Establish communication and finalize a sales agreement detailing product specifications, payment terms, and shipping conditions.

Export Documentation

Documentation is the backbone of the export process, ensuring that goods reach their destination legally and efficiently. Essential documents include:

- **Commercial Invoice**: Specifies the value of goods sold.
- **Packing List**: Details the contents of the shipment.
- **Bill of Lading (or Airway Bill)**: Serves as proof of shipment and ownership transfer.

Customs Clearance and Freight Forwarding

1. **Customs Clearance**:
    - Submit a **Shipping Bill** to the customs authorities for export approval.
    - Provide additional documents like the certificate of origin and insurance certificate.
2. **Freight Forwarding**:
    - Engage a freight forwarder to handle logistics, ensuring that goods are transported to the destination port or airport efficiently.

Payment Mechanisms

Securing payment is a critical aspect of the export process. Common mechanisms include:

- **Letter of Credit (LC)**: A bank guarantees payment to the exporter upon fulfilling terms of the sales contract.
- **Advance Payment**: The buyer pays before shipment, providing security to the exporter.
- **Open Account**: Payment is made after delivery, usually for trusted buyers.

Key Documents in Trade

Trade documentation ensures the legality, safety, and financial security of international transactions. Below are the key documents every importer and exporter should be familiar with:

1. **Commercial Invoice**:
    - A detailed record of the transaction, including the buyer, seller, product description, quantity, and price.
    - It serves as the primary document for customs valuation.

2. **Certificate of Origin**:
   - Certifies the country of manufacture of the goods.
   - Often required to qualify for preferential tariffs under free trade agreements.
3. **Insurance Certificate**:
   - Protects against potential losses or damage to goods during transit.
   - Mandatory under certain trade terms like CIF (Cost, Insurance, and Freight).
4. **Shipping Bill**:
   - Submitted to customs authorities for export clearance.
   - Contains information about the shipment, including value, destination, and mode of transport.

Technological Integration

Technology has revolutionized the import and export processes, reducing paperwork, improving efficiency, and enhancing transparency.

Role of Electronic Data Interchange (EDI)

EDI enables the digital exchange of trade-related documents between businesses, customs, and other stakeholders.

- **Benefits**:
  - Faster processing of customs clearance.
  - Reduced errors and duplication of data entry.
  - Improved tracking of shipments.

For example, India's **ICEGATE portal** allows traders to file customs documents electronically, streamlining the import/export process.

Single-Window Systems for Documentation

India has implemented a **single-window system** to simplify trade documentation. Through this platform:

- Importers and exporters can submit all required documents to multiple regulatory agencies at once.
- The system integrates with various departments, reducing delays and manual intervention.

11.6 Role of Free Trade Agreements (FTAs)

Free Trade Agreements (FTAs) are pivotal tools for fostering international trade by reducing barriers, opening markets, and strengthening economic ties between nations. For a country like India, with its growing economy and significant global trade ambitions, FTAs play a crucial role in shaping trade relationships and enhancing competitiveness in the global market. This section delves into the importance of FTAs, India's key agreements, and the benefits and challenges associated with them.

Importance of FTAs

Reducing Tariffs and Trade Barriers

FTAs primarily aim to lower or eliminate **tariffs**—taxes imposed on imports and exports—and other trade barriers, making goods and services more affordable and accessible in partner countries.

- **Tariff Reductions**: For example, under the **India-ASEAN Free Trade Agreement**, tariffs on a significant percentage of goods were either reduced or eliminated, encouraging trade in sectors like textiles, electronics, and agricultural products.
- **Non-Tariff Barriers**: FTAs also address non-tariff barriers, such as restrictive standards or lengthy customs procedures, simplifying the trade process.

By reducing costs, FTAs make Indian goods more competitive in foreign markets and provide Indian consumers with a wider variety of affordable imports.

Enhancing Market Access

FTAs provide Indian businesses with preferential access to the markets of partner countries, helping them expand their customer base.

- **Examples of Market Access**:
    - **Pharmaceuticals**: Through agreements with developed economies, Indian pharmaceutical companies gain entry into high-value markets like Japan and the European Union.
    - **Agricultural Products**: Indian tea, rice, and spices have found new markets in ASEAN countries due to favorable trade terms.

FTAs often include provisions for service sectors, allowing Indian IT, education, and healthcare providers to operate in partner economies with reduced restrictions.

Boosting Bilateral and Multilateral Trade

FTAs serve as a platform for strengthening trade relationships between two or more countries.

- **Bilateral Agreements**: These focus on partnerships between two nations, such as the **India-Sri Lanka Free Trade Agreement**, which has significantly boosted trade between the two neighbors.
- **Multilateral Agreements**: These involve multiple countries and have a broader impact. For instance, the **India-ASEAN Free Trade Agreement** connects India to a dynamic regional bloc, enhancing trade and investment opportunities.

By fostering trust and economic cooperation, FTAs often pave the way for broader diplomatic and strategic partnerships.

India's Key FTAs

India has entered into several important FTAs, each with specific objectives and outcomes.

Comprehensive Economic Partnership Agreement (CEPA) with Japan

Signed in 2011, the **India-Japan CEPA** is one of India's most comprehensive FTAs.

- **Key Features**:
    - Elimination of tariffs on over 90% of trade items, including auto parts, electronics, and textiles.
    - Enhanced access for Indian services, such as IT and engineering, in the Japanese market.
    - Collaboration in areas like infrastructure development and technology transfer.
- **Impact**:
    - Increased trade in sectors like pharmaceuticals, where India is a leading exporter to Japan.
    - Strengthened ties between two major Asian economies.

India-ASEAN Free Trade Agreement

The **India-ASEAN FTA**, signed in 2009, has been instrumental in boosting trade between India and the 10 ASEAN member countries.

- **Scope**:
  - Reduction or elimination of tariffs on goods ranging from agricultural produce to industrial products.
  - Provisions for the trade in services and investments.
- **Impact**:
  - Significant growth in exports of Indian goods like textiles, machinery, and pharmaceuticals to ASEAN markets.
  - Increased imports of electronics and raw materials from ASEAN nations.

Regional Comprehensive Economic Partnership (RCEP) Negotiations

The **RCEP** is a multilateral trade agreement involving ASEAN countries and six additional partners, including China, Japan, and Australia.

- **India's Position**:
  - India participated in the negotiations but opted out in 2019, citing concerns about potential negative impacts on domestic industries, particularly agriculture and manufacturing.
  - Despite its withdrawal, RCEP remains a point of discussion as India evaluates its trade strategy in the region.
- **Potential Benefits**:
  - Joining RCEP could provide access to one of the largest trading blocs in the world.
  - It could integrate Indian businesses into global supply chains.

Benefits and Challenges

Benefits for Exporters and Importers

FTAs bring a host of benefits to Indian businesses engaged in international trade.

- **For Exporters**:
  - Preferential access to partner markets reduces costs and enhances competitiveness.
  - FTAs often include streamlined customs procedures, saving time and resources.

- **For Importers**:
    - Reduced tariffs make raw materials and finished goods more affordable.
    - Access to high-quality imports improves the efficiency of Indian industries.

For instance, the **India-South Korea CEPA** allows Indian businesses to import advanced machinery at lower costs, boosting domestic production.

Challenges in Negotiating Favorable Terms

While FTAs offer numerous advantages, they also present challenges.

1. **Balancing Domestic and International Interests**:
    - Negotiating FTAs requires balancing the interests of domestic industries with the need to open up markets. For example, Indian farmers often express concerns about cheap agricultural imports under FTAs.
2. **Competitiveness of Indian Goods**:
    - Indian exporters face stiff competition from countries like Vietnam and China, which often have lower production costs.
3. **Complex Negotiations**:
    - FTAs involve lengthy and complex negotiations to address issues like tariff schedules, intellectual property rights, and dispute resolution mechanisms.
4. **Implementation Challenges**:
    - Even after an FTA is signed, ensuring compliance and creating awareness among businesses can be difficult, particularly for small and medium enterprises.

11.7 Trade Facilitation Initiatives in India

Trade facilitation encompasses the various efforts and strategies implemented to streamline the movement of goods and services across borders. For a country like India, with its growing global trade ambitions, robust trade facilitation initiatives are essential to reduce costs, enhance competitiveness, and attract investments. This section explores the key trade facilitation measures in India, focusing on procedural simplification, infrastructure development, financial support, and the role of Special Economic Zones (SEZs).

Simplification of Procedures

One of the critical elements of trade facilitation is simplifying the procedural requirements that businesses face in importing and exporting goods. India has made significant progress in this area by embracing technology and regulatory reforms.

Automation of Customs Clearance

Customs clearance is often seen as a bottleneck in international trade. To address this, India has implemented several automation initiatives to reduce manual intervention and accelerate the process.

1. **Electronic Data Interchange (EDI)**:
   - Customs clearance processes are now conducted through EDI systems like **ICEGATE** (Indian Customs EDI Gateway).
   - Benefits include faster documentation processing, reduced errors, and enhanced transparency.
2. **Risk Management Systems**:
   - Automated risk-based screening allows low-risk shipments to pass through with minimal checks, focusing manual inspections on high-risk consignments.
3. **Faceless Assessment**:
   - Introduced to eliminate regional biases and delays, this initiative enables customs officers from any location to process documents electronically.

Implementation of the Goods and Services Tax (GST) for Seamless Trade

The introduction of the **Goods and Services Tax (GST)** in 2017 was a landmark reform in India's trade landscape. GST replaced a complex web of indirect taxes with a unified system, significantly improving trade facilitation.

1. **Streamlined Tax Structure**:
   - GST subsumed multiple taxes like central excise, VAT, and service tax, reducing compliance burdens for businesses.
2. **E-Way Bill System**:
   - A digital mechanism to track the movement of goods in real-time, ensuring faster transportation and reduced paperwork.

3. **Impact on Cross-Border Trade**:
   - Harmonization of taxes across states has minimized logistical delays and made Indian goods more competitive in global markets.

Infrastructure Development

Efficient infrastructure is the backbone of trade facilitation, enabling the swift and cost-effective movement of goods. India has prioritized the development of world-class logistics and transport networks to support its trade ecosystem.

Ports and Shipping Connectivity

1. **Modernization of Ports**:
   - Initiatives under the **Sagarmala Project** focus on enhancing the capacity and efficiency of India's ports.
   - Key features include automated cargo handling, dredging for deeper berths, and the establishment of dedicated freight corridors.
2. **Expansion of Shipping Connectivity**:
   - India has strengthened its shipping networks to connect with major global trade routes, reducing transit times for exports and imports.

Inland Container Depots (ICDs) and Logistics Hubs

1. **Role of ICDs**:
   - Located inland, ICDs act as extensions of ports, enabling businesses in remote areas to access customs clearance and shipping facilities.
2. **Development of Logistics Hubs**:
   - Multi-modal logistics parks and warehouses are being developed across India to streamline cargo storage and distribution.
   - These hubs integrate road, rail, and air transport, reducing costs and improving efficiency.

Financial Support

Access to affordable financing is a critical enabler for businesses engaged in international trade. The government has introduced various financial schemes to support exporters and small and medium enterprises (SMEs).

Export Credit Guarantee Schemes

1. **Purpose**:
   - Protect exporters from payment risks, such as buyer insolvency or political instability in the importing country.
2. **Key Schemes**:
   - **Export Credit Guarantee Corporation of India (ECGC)** provides insurance cover to exporters and financial institutions.
   - Specialized schemes for SMEs ensure that small businesses can participate in global trade without fear of financial losses.

Financial Assistance for SMEs

1. **Export Development Fund**:
   - Offers grants and subsidies to SMEs for marketing, participation in international trade fairs, and adopting global standards.
2. **Interest Subvention Schemes**:
   - Provide reduced interest rates on loans for export-related activities.
3. **Technology Upgradation Support**:
   - Financial incentives encourage SMEs to invest in modern machinery and technology to meet international quality standards.

Special Economic Zones (SEZs)

Special Economic Zones (SEZs) are designated areas designed to boost exports and attract investments by offering a favorable business environment. These zones have become a cornerstone of India's trade facilitation strategy.

Role in Boosting Exports

1. **Export-Oriented Ecosystem**:
   - SEZs are equipped with state-of-the-art infrastructure, streamlined regulatory processes, and access to global markets.
   - Industries like IT, textiles, and pharmaceuticals have thrived within SEZs, contributing significantly to India's export revenue.

2. **Notable SEZs**:
   - The **Santacruz Electronics Export Processing Zone (SEEPZ)** in Mumbai focuses on electronics and jewelry exports.
   - The **Kandla SEZ** in Gujarat is one of India's oldest and most successful SEZs.

Incentives for Businesses Operating in SEZs

1. **Tax Benefits**:
   - Businesses in SEZs enjoy tax holidays on profits from exports, along with exemptions from customs duties.
2. **Ease of Doing Business**:
   - SEZs offer simplified compliance procedures, faster approvals, and a single-window clearance system for regulatory requirements.
3. **Attracting FDI**:
   - SEZs have been instrumental in attracting foreign direct investment (FDI) by providing a secure and business-friendly environment.

11.8 Global Trends and India's Trade Position

International trade is in a constant state of flux, influenced by geopolitical shifts, technological advancements, and global economic cycles. For India, understanding and responding to these trends is vital to maintaining its position in the global trade landscape. This section examines the evolving global trade dynamics, India's trade competitiveness, and the profound impact of events like the COVID-19 pandemic.

Global Trade Dynamics

Global trade dynamics encompass the patterns and policies that dictate how goods and services flow across borders. In recent decades, globalization, regionalism, and geopolitical tensions have significantly reshaped these dynamics.

Impact of Globalization and Regionalism

1. **Globalization**:
   - The increasing interconnectedness of economies has led to:
     - The rise of **global value chains (GVCs)**, where products are manufactured across multiple countries.
     - Increased accessibility of goods and services, fostering competition and innovation.

   Example: An iPhone's components are sourced from multiple countries, including the USA, South Korea, and China, before being assembled in China and distributed worldwide.

2. **Regionalism**:
   - Alongside globalization, regional trade agreements like the **European Union (EU)** and **ASEAN** have emerged as significant drivers of trade.
   - Regionalism has created challenges for countries outside such agreements, as they face higher tariffs or restricted access.

   India's **withdrawal from the Regional Comprehensive Economic Partnership (RCEP)** highlights its cautious approach to regionalism, focusing instead on bilateral trade deals.

Shifts in Trade Patterns Due to Geopolitical Tensions

1. **US-China Trade War**:
   - The ongoing trade tensions between the USA and China have disrupted traditional trade routes and opened opportunities for other nations, including India, to fill supply gaps.
   - Example: India's exports of electronics and textiles to the USA have seen a boost as companies diversify their supply chains away from China.

2. **Russia-Ukraine Conflict**:
   - The conflict has disrupted global energy and agricultural supply chains, leading to increased prices and a reevaluation of trade partnerships.
   - India has sought to balance its imports of oil and fertilizers while exploring new markets for exports like wheat.

3. **Technology and Trade**:
   - Geopolitical concerns over technology, such as restrictions on Huawei and the race for semiconductor dominance, have created new trade battlegrounds.
   - India's push to become a hub for electronics and semiconductors is a strategic response to these trends.

India's Trade Competitiveness

India's trade competitiveness is a mix of established strengths and persistent challenges, shaped by its industrial capabilities and policy environment.

Strengths in Key Sectors

1. **Information Technology (IT)**:
   - India is the world's largest exporter of IT services, contributing significantly to its trade surplus in services.
   - Companies like TCS, Infosys, and Wipro have a strong presence in markets like the USA, EU, and Asia.
2. **Pharmaceuticals**:
   - Known as the "pharmacy of the world," India exports affordable generic drugs to over 200 countries.
   - During the COVID-19 pandemic, India's supply of vaccines and medicines underscored its importance in global healthcare.
3. **Textiles**:
   - India is a leading exporter of cotton, handlooms, and ready-made garments.
   - Markets like the USA and Europe value Indian textiles for their quality and craftsmanship.

Weaknesses in High-Value Manufacturing

1. **Electronics**:
   - Despite being a major importer of electronic goods, India's domestic manufacturing in this sector remains limited.
   - The government's **Production-Linked Incentive (PLI) scheme** aims to address this gap by encouraging investments in local production.

2. **Machinery and Automobiles**:
   - India lags behind countries like Germany and Japan in exporting high-value machinery and automobiles.
   - A lack of advanced R&D facilities and supply chain inefficiencies contribute to this weakness.
3. **Dependence on Imports**:
   - India's reliance on imports for critical sectors like energy, electronics, and capital goods impacts its trade balance and exposes it to global price fluctuations.

Impact of COVID-19

The COVID-19 pandemic was a seismic event for global trade, causing unprecedented disruptions and forcing nations to rethink their trade strategies. India, too, faced significant challenges and opportunities during this period.

Disruption of Supply Chains

1. **Initial Impact**:
   - Lockdowns and restrictions on movement disrupted production and transportation, leading to delays in shipments and unfulfilled orders.
   - Key sectors like textiles, automotive, and electronics were particularly hard-hit due to their dependence on global supply chains.
2. **Shift in Consumer Behavior**:
   - The pandemic accelerated the adoption of e-commerce and digital services, boosting demand for IT exports and consumer electronics.
3. **Opportunities in Pharmaceuticals**:
   - India's ability to ramp up the production of essential medicines, personal protective equipment (PPE), and vaccines positioned it as a reliable supplier during the crisis.

Shift Towards Self-Reliance (Atmanirbhar Bharat)

1. **Vision of Self-Reliance**:
   - The Indian government launched the **Atmanirbhar Bharat** initiative to reduce dependence on imports and boost domestic production.

2. **Focus Areas**:
    - o Electronics: Encouraging local manufacturing of smartphones, semiconductors, and other electronic components.
    - o Renewable Energy: Expanding domestic production of solar panels and equipment to reduce reliance on Chinese imports.
    - o Defense: Promoting indigenous production of defense equipment to meet strategic needs.
3. **Impact on Trade**:
    - o While self-reliance aims to strengthen India's manufacturing base, it also raises concerns about protectionism and its potential impact on foreign investments and global trade partnerships.

11.9 Challenges and Opportunities in International Trade

International trade is a dynamic domain, offering immense potential while posing significant challenges. For a country like India, which aspires to be a major global trading hub, navigating these challenges and leveraging opportunities is crucial. This section explores the hurdles India faces in its international trade journey and the avenues that can propel its trade growth.

Challenges

Trade Deficits and Dependency on Imports

India often experiences trade deficits, where the value of imports exceeds that of exports. This imbalance arises due to several factors:

1. **High Dependency on Imports**:
    - o **Energy Imports**: Crude oil constitutes a significant portion of India's import bill. Despite efforts to diversify energy sources, reliance on oil-producing nations like Saudi Arabia and Iraq remains high.
    - o **Electronics and Machinery**: India imports a substantial amount of electronic components, semiconductors, and industrial machinery, mainly from China and South Korea, due to inadequate domestic production.
2. **Economic Impact**:
    - o Persistent trade deficits lead to pressure on foreign exchange reserves and a weakening of the Indian rupee.

- Heavy import dependency in critical sectors leaves the economy vulnerable to global price fluctuations and geopolitical disruptions.

Compliance with International Quality Standards

1. **Stringent Quality Norms**:
    - Exporters often face non-tariff barriers such as stringent quality and safety standards in developed markets.
    - For example, Indian agricultural exports like mangoes and basmati rice often face scrutiny for pesticide residues in the European Union.
2. **Lack of Standardization**:
    - Small and medium enterprises (SMEs), which form the backbone of India's export sector, often lack the resources to adhere to global standards like ISO certifications or HACCP for food safety.
3. **Impact on Market Access**:
    - Failure to meet compliance standards can result in the rejection of shipments, leading to financial losses and reputational damage.

Impact of Global Economic Slowdowns

1. **Reduced Demand**:
    - During global recessions or crises, demand for non-essential goods declines. For instance, luxury goods and textiles often face reduced demand during economic slowdowns.
2. **Volatility in Global Markets**:
    - Economic crises, such as the 2008 financial crisis or the COVID-19 pandemic, disrupt global supply chains and reduce trade volumes.
3. **Export-Driven Industries**:
    - Sectors like IT services, pharmaceuticals, and textiles, heavily reliant on foreign markets, experience slower growth during global downturns.

Opportunities

Expanding Markets in Africa and Latin America

1. **Emerging Markets**:
   - African and Latin American countries present untapped potential for Indian exports, especially in sectors like pharmaceuticals, textiles, and agriculture.
   - For example, Indian generic drugs are gaining traction in African countries due to their affordability and quality.
2. **Bilateral Engagements**:
   - India has actively pursued trade agreements and partnerships with these regions, fostering stronger economic ties.
   - Initiatives like the **India-Africa Forum Summit** have strengthened trade in critical areas like renewable energy and healthcare.
3. **Strategic Positioning**:
   - India's position as a supplier of affordable goods and services aligns well with the developmental needs of these regions, creating opportunities for sustained trade growth.

Diversification of Export Products

1. **Value-Added Exports**:
   - Moving beyond traditional exports like textiles and agricultural products, India can focus on high-value goods such as electronics, chemicals, and machinery.
   - Government initiatives like the **Production-Linked Incentive (PLI) scheme** encourage the manufacturing of high-tech products domestically.
2. **Pharmaceutical Innovations**:
   - Beyond generic drugs, India can explore exporting biologics, vaccines, and high-end pharmaceutical formulations to developed markets.
3. **Cultural and Creative Exports**:
   - India's rich cultural heritage offers opportunities to export handicrafts, traditional medicines, and entertainment content, catering to niche global markets.

Leveraging Digital Trade and E-Commerce

1. **Growth of E-Commerce Platforms**:
   - Platforms like Amazon, Flipkart, and Alibaba provide Indian businesses, especially SMEs, with access to international consumers without the need for physical presence in foreign markets.
2. **Government Support**:
   - Initiatives like the **Digital India program** aim to integrate digital technologies into the trade ecosystem, enabling exporters to leverage online marketplaces and streamline operations.
3. **Cross-Border Digital Trade**:
   - With India's strong IT infrastructure, services such as software development, digital marketing, and content creation are poised for exponential growth in global markets.
4. **Blockchain and Trade**:
   - Technologies like blockchain can revolutionize trade logistics by enhancing transparency and reducing fraud in international transactions.

11.10 Case Studies

Case studies offer a lens into real-world applications, illustrating the successes and challenges faced by India in its international trade endeavors. Through these narratives, we gain insights into the strategies that have propelled India forward and the obstacles that require resolution. This section delves into India's triumphs in pharmaceuticals and IT services while reflecting on lessons learned from challenges in electronics and agriculture.

Success Stories

How India Became a Leading Exporter of Generics in the Pharmaceutical Sector

India's pharmaceutical industry is often referred to as the "pharmacy of the world," a title earned through decades of strategic growth and innovation.

1. **Key Factors for Success**:
   - **Cost Efficiency**: Indian pharmaceutical companies leverage economies of scale and low production costs to produce affordable generics.

- **Regulatory Expertise**: Firms like Sun Pharma, Dr. Reddy's, and Cipla have mastered the art of navigating complex regulatory landscapes in markets like the USA and Europe.
- **R&D Investments**: Continuous investment in research and development has enabled India to reverse-engineer patented drugs and develop bioequivalent generics.

2. **Major Milestones**:
   - India supplies over **50% of Africa's demand for generics** and is a major contributor to the **global vaccine supply chain**.
   - During the COVID-19 pandemic, Indian companies played a pivotal role in producing and exporting vaccines, such as Covishield.
3. **Global Recognition**:
   - India is the largest exporter of generic medicines, accounting for **20% of the global volume**.

Growth of IT Services Exports in Global Markets

India's IT services sector is another remarkable success story, demonstrating the power of leveraging human capital and technological expertise.

1. **Genesis of the Industry**:
   - The IT revolution in India began in the late 1980s, with firms like **Infosys**, **TCS**, and **Wipro** pioneering outsourced IT services.
2. **Drivers of Growth**:
   - **Skilled Workforce**: A large pool of English-speaking, tech-savvy professionals enabled India to dominate global IT services.
   - **Cost Advantage**: Competitive labor costs made Indian IT services attractive to businesses worldwide.
   - **Special Economic Zones (SEZs)**: Government-supported IT hubs like Bengaluru, Hyderabad, and Pune facilitated infrastructure and policy support.
3. **Global Footprint**:
   - Indian IT firms provide services ranging from software development to cloud computing and AI solutions to clients in the USA, EU, and Australia.

- Exports from the sector have reached over **$150 billion annually**, contributing significantly to India's trade surplus in services.

Lessons from Challenges

Impact of Import Dependency on Electronics

India's heavy reliance on imports for electronic goods and components is a cautionary tale, highlighting the risks of insufficient domestic capacity.

1. **Extent of Dependency**:
   - India imports over **80% of its electronic components**, primarily from China.
   - Critical items include semiconductors, mobile phone components, and consumer electronics.
2. **Consequences**:
   - **Trade Deficits**: Electronics account for a significant portion of India's import bill, exacerbating the trade deficit.
   - **Vulnerability to Disruptions**: Geopolitical tensions and supply chain disruptions, as seen during the COVID-19 pandemic, exposed India's dependency risks.
3. **Corrective Measures**:
   - The government's **Production-Linked Incentive (PLI) scheme** aims to boost domestic manufacturing of electronics.
   - Investments in semiconductor fabrication plants are being prioritized to reduce import dependency.

Trade Barriers Faced by Indian Agricultural Products

India's agricultural exports, despite their potential, have faced significant barriers in international markets.

1. **Non-Tariff Barriers**:
   - Stringent pesticide residue standards in the EU and USA often lead to the rejection of Indian shipments.
   - Exporters of fresh produce like mangoes and grapes frequently encounter compliance issues.
2. **Structural Challenges**:
   - Lack of modern storage facilities and cold chains affects the quality of perishable exports.

- Fragmented supply chains result in inconsistencies in product quality.

3. **Lessons Learned**:
   - Investments in cold storage and logistics are critical to maintaining the quality of exports.
   - Adopting international certifications, like GlobalGAP, can enhance acceptance in global markets.

Conclusion

Recap of the Importance of Imports and Exports for India's Economic Growth

Imports and exports form the foundation of India's integration with the global economy. While imports meet critical domestic needs—such as crude oil and advanced machinery—exports showcase India's industrial and service capabilities on the world stage. Trade contributes significantly to GDP, creates jobs, and drives technological advancements.

Emphasis on Balancing Trade Policies

A balanced approach to trade policies is essential for addressing challenges like trade deficits and import dependency while enhancing competitiveness in global markets. Key priorities include:

- Encouraging domestic production through initiatives like **Make in India**.
- Strengthening trade partnerships via Free Trade Agreements (FTAs).
- Enhancing compliance with global standards to boost export acceptance.

Vision for India's Future in Global Trade

India's future in global trade hinges on its ability to adapt to evolving dynamics. By leveraging **innovation**, **sustainability**, and **strategic partnerships**, India can:

- Diversify its export portfolio to include high-value goods and cutting-edge technologies.
- Capitalize on emerging markets in Africa, Latin America, and Southeast Asia.

- Build resilient supply chains to mitigate risks from global disruptions.

With a forward-looking trade strategy, India is well-positioned to achieve its goal of becoming a $5 trillion economy while solidifying its role as a key player in the global trading system.

CHAPTER 12

Food Safety and Standards Authority of India (FSSAI)

Introduction

In the rapidly evolving world of food production and consumption, ensuring the safety and quality of what we eat has never been more critical. Food safety is not merely about hygiene or regulatory compliance; it is a cornerstone of public health, consumer trust, and economic stability. At the heart of India's food safety framework lies the **Food Safety and Standards Authority of India (FSSAI)**, a statutory body tasked with overseeing and regulating the vast, intricate web of the country's food supply chain. From the farm to the fork, FSSAI has become synonymous with the nation's commitment to safe and nutritious food.

In this chapter, we will delve deep into the origins, objectives, and importance of FSSAI, exploring how it addresses public health concerns, fosters trust among consumers, and aligns India's food safety standards with global norms. Through a structured narrative, we aim to build a comprehensive understanding of this vital institution.

Overview of FSSAI

To appreciate the role of FSSAI in India's food ecosystem, it is essential to understand its foundation, purpose, and broader objectives. FSSAI is not merely a regulatory body; it embodies a vision for transforming India into a nation where food safety is a shared responsibility among producers, regulators, and consumers.

Definition and Establishment

The **Food Safety and Standards Authority of India (FSSAI)** is a statutory body established under the **Food Safety and Standards Act, 2006 (FSSA)**. Officially operational since 2011, FSSAI was created to bring coherence to a previously fragmented regulatory system, where multiple laws governed different aspects of food safety.

Before FSSAI, India relied on an array of overlapping and often conflicting regulations:

- **The Prevention of Food Adulteration Act, 1954 (PFA)** focused on preventing adulteration but lacked a holistic approach.
- Laws like the **Fruit Products Order (FPO)** and the **Meat Food Products Order (MFPO)** targeted specific food categories but operated in silos.

FSSAI was envisioned as a single, unified authority to:

1. **Establish Scientific Standards**: Develop evidence-based food safety standards applicable across the country.
2. **Streamline Regulatory Mechanisms**: Replace overlapping laws with a cohesive framework.
3. **Enhance Consumer Awareness**: Promote education and participation in food safety initiatives.

The authority operates under the Ministry of Health and Family Welfare and works collaboratively with state governments, food businesses, and consumers to uphold food safety standards.

Objectives and Vision for Food Safety in India

FSSAI's vision extends beyond regulatory oversight—it aims to create a culture where food safety is intrinsic to how food is produced, processed, transported, and consumed. Its key objectives include:

1. **Protecting Public Health**: Foodborne illnesses are a significant public health concern. By enforcing strict safety standards, FSSAI seeks to minimize contamination, adulteration, and the spread of foodborne pathogens.
2. **Ensuring Fair Practices**: FSSAI promotes fair trade practices by preventing fraudulent activities like mislabeling, counterfeit products, and misleading claims.
3. **Harmonizing Standards**: India's food industry is a critical player in the global supply chain. FSSAI works to align domestic standards with international benchmarks, such as those set by the **Codex Alimentarius Commission**, ensuring that Indian food products meet global quality expectations.

4. **Fostering Innovation**: The authority encourages innovation in food production and processing by creating a regulatory environment that balances safety with growth.
5. **Educating Stakeholders**: From consumers to food business operators (FBOs), FSSAI's initiatives aim to spread awareness about food safety, empowering individuals and organizations to make informed decisions.

The ultimate vision of FSSAI can be encapsulated in its tagline: **"Safe and Nutritious Food for All."**

Importance of Food Safety and Standards

Implications for Public Health and Consumer Trust

Food safety is not just about ensuring the absence of harmful contaminants; it is a fundamental determinant of public health. Contaminated or substandard food can lead to:

- **Acute Health Issues**: Such as food poisoning, gastrointestinal infections, and outbreaks of diseases like cholera or typhoid.
- **Chronic Conditions**: Long-term exposure to toxins, such as pesticides or heavy metals, can result in conditions like cancer, developmental disorders, and organ damage.

For instance, consider the infamous **adulteration of milk with urea** or **synthetic dyes in sweets**—both pose severe health risks but were rampant before stricter regulations were enforced. FSSAI's stringent standards and regular inspections have significantly curtailed such practices.

From a consumer perspective, trust in the food supply chain is paramount. When consumers know their food adheres to safety and quality standards, it fosters confidence, which is essential for sustaining demand and supporting the economy. Conversely, scandals involving contaminated or unsafe food can erode trust, disrupt markets, and have far-reaching economic consequences.

Role in Economic Stability

The food sector is a vital contributor to India's GDP and a significant employer. FSSAI's role in ensuring consistent quality standards directly impacts:

1. **Exports**: Indian food exports, including spices, tea, and processed foods, are highly sought after. Aligning with global safety standards enhances their acceptance in international markets.

2. **Domestic Markets**: A well-regulated food sector attracts investment, promotes innovation, and ensures equitable growth.

Role in Aligning with Global Food Safety Norms

Globalization has interconnected food supply chains, making it imperative for national standards to harmonize with international regulations. FSSAI's role in this context includes:

1. **Adopting International Standards**: FSSAI actively incorporates guidelines from the **Codex Alimentarius Commission**, which sets global standards for food safety. For instance:
   - Pesticide residue limits in agricultural produce.
   - Nutritional labeling requirements.
2. **Facilitating Export Readiness**: By ensuring that Indian food products meet international safety norms, FSSAI helps exporters avoid rejections and enhances India's reputation as a reliable supplier of high-quality food products.
3. **Engaging with Global Agencies**: FSSAI collaborates with organizations like the **World Health Organization (WHO)** and **Food and Agriculture Organization (FAO)** to address emerging challenges, such as antimicrobial resistance and foodborne illnesses.
4. **Training and Capacity Building**: To meet global standards, FSSAI conducts training programs for food businesses, enabling them to adopt best practices in food safety and quality management.

A Holistic Approach to Food Safety

FSSAI's comprehensive approach to food safety encompasses three critical pillars:

1. **Regulation and Enforcement**: Setting scientifically robust standards and ensuring compliance through inspections, penalties, and recalls.
2. **Education and Awareness**: Initiatives like the **"Eat Right India" campaign** encourage healthier food choices and promote understanding of food safety standards.
3. **Innovation and Collaboration**: By working with industry stakeholders, research institutions, and consumers, FSSAI fosters a culture of innovation while maintaining safety and quality.

12.1 Historical Background

The journey of food safety regulations in India has been one of gradual evolution, reflecting the country's changing socio-economic landscape, public health priorities, and global integration. From the patchwork of pre-FSSAI regulations to the establishment of a unified authority under the **Food Safety and Standards Act, 2006**, the evolution of food safety frameworks has been driven by the need to ensure the health and trust of Indian consumers. This section traces the history of food safety regulations in India, exploring the pre-FSSAI era and the factors that led to the formation of the **Food Safety and Standards Authority of India (FSSAI).**

Evolution of Food Safety Regulations in India

Pre-FSSAI Regulatory Framework

Before the establishment of FSSAI, food safety in India was governed by multiple laws and regulations, each addressing specific aspects of food production, processing, and distribution. While these regulations were well-intentioned, their fragmented nature often resulted in inefficiencies, overlaps, and gaps in enforcement.

1. **The Prevention of Food Adulteration Act, 1954 (PFA)**:
    - One of the earliest laws aimed at ensuring food safety in India.
    - Focused primarily on combating **adulteration**, a widespread problem that posed significant health risks.
    - Defined standards for food items, specified permissible limits for contaminants, and penalized offenders.
    - Limitation: It lacked a comprehensive approach, focusing mainly on end-product testing rather than preventive measures.
2. **Fruit Products Order (FPO), 1955**:
    - Governed the manufacture and distribution of fruit-based products like juices, squashes, and jams.
    - Emphasized quality control during production.
    - Limitation: Applied only to a narrow category of food items, creating regulatory silos.
3. **Milk and Milk Products Order (MMPO), 1992**:
    - Regulated milk production and distribution to ensure hygienic practices and prevent contamination.

- Important in a country where milk is a staple food and a critical component of the diet.
- Limitation: Did not integrate with broader food safety standards.

4. **Meat Food Products Order, 1973**:
   - Ensured hygienic practices in the production and distribution of meat and poultry products.
   - Limitation: Focused on specific sectors, leading to a lack of unified enforcement across food categories.
5. **Other Regulations**:
   - Essential Commodities Act, 1955 (focused on price control and availability rather than safety).
   - Solvent Extracted Oil, De-oiled Meal, and Edible Flour Control Order, 1967.

The fragmentation of these regulations led to challenges such as:

- **Overlapping Jurisdictions**: Multiple agencies were responsible for enforcement, creating confusion and inefficiencies.
- **Regulatory Gaps**: Emerging food safety risks, such as pesticide residues or heavy metal contamination, were inadequately addressed.
- **Inconsistent Standards**: Each law operated in isolation, leading to a lack of uniformity in food safety standards.

Need for a Unified Authority

The growing complexity of the food supply chain and the emergence of new challenges necessitated a unified approach to food safety. Key drivers for the establishment of a single authority included:

1. **Changing Consumption Patterns**:
   - Rapid urbanization and globalization brought a shift towards processed and packaged foods, increasing the need for comprehensive safety standards.
2. **Public Health Concerns**:
   - High-profile cases of food adulteration and contamination highlighted the inadequacies of the existing framework. For example:
     - The use of **metanil yellow** (a non-edible dye) in turmeric.
     - Adulteration of milk with **urea** and synthetic substances.

   - Foodborne illnesses became a growing concern, necessitating preventive measures rather than reactive enforcement.

3. **Global Trade and Standards**:
   - India's integration into global markets required alignment with international food safety standards, such as those set by the **Codex Alimentarius Commission.**
   - Export rejections due to non-compliance with international norms underscored the need for harmonized standards.

4. **Consumer Awareness**:
   - Increasing consumer demand for safe, nutritious, and transparently labeled food products created pressure for regulatory reforms.

Formation of FSSAI

Food Safety and Standards Act, 2006

Recognizing the need for a comprehensive and unified food safety framework, the Indian government enacted the **Food Safety and Standards Act (FSSA), 2006**. This landmark legislation aimed to:

- Replace the fragmented pre-FSSAI regulations with a single, cohesive law.
- Establish the **Food Safety and Standards Authority of India (FSSAI)** as the apex body for regulating food safety.

Key Features of the FSSA, 2006:

1. **Single Authority**: The Act consolidated food-related laws and brought them under one umbrella, ensuring consistency in enforcement.
2. **Scientific Standards**: Emphasized evidence-based standards for food safety, developed in consultation with experts and stakeholders.
3. **Preventive Approach**: Shifted the focus from reactive enforcement (detecting and penalizing violations) to preventive measures (ensuring safety throughout the supply chain).
4. **Consumer-Centric Provisions**: Introduced mechanisms for consumer grievance redressal and encouraged public participation in food safety initiatives.
5. **Integration with International Standards**: Mandated FSSAI to align domestic food standards with global benchmarks, facilitating trade and export growth.

Structure and Key Milestones Since Its Inception

Structure of FSSAI:

FSSAI operates under the Ministry of Health and Family Welfare and comprises:

- **Chairperson and Chief Executive Officer (CEO)**: Oversee the authority's operations and ensure the implementation of its mandate.
- **Scientific Panels**: Develop and review food safety standards for specific categories.
- **Advisory Committees**: Provide policy recommendations and facilitate stakeholder engagement.
- **State Food Authorities**: Collaborate with FSSAI to enforce food safety standards at the local level.

Key Milestones:

1. **Operationalization in 2011**: FSSAI became fully functional, replacing the fragmented regulatory framework.
2. **Introduction of Packaging and Labeling Standards (2011)**: Established clear guidelines for food labeling, including nutritional information and allergen declarations.
3. **Launch of the Eat Right India Campaign (2018)**: A flagship initiative to promote healthier food choices and raise awareness about food safety.
4. **COVID-19 and Food Safety (2020)**: FSSAI issued guidelines to ensure the safety of food supply chains during the pandemic, emphasizing hygiene and sanitation.

12.2 Organizational Structure of FSSAI

The organizational structure of the **Food Safety and Standards Authority of India (FSSAI)** has been meticulously designed to address the multifaceted challenges of ensuring food safety across a vast and diverse nation like India. This structure is a combination of centralized oversight, regional and state-level integration, and specialized committees for scientific and advisory functions. By aligning governance, regulatory enforcement, and scientific expertise, FSSAI operates as a cohesive and efficient body dedicated to upholding food safety standards.

Governance and Hierarchy

Role of the Chairperson and Chief Executive Officer (CEO)

At the helm of FSSAI's governance are the Chairperson and the Chief Executive Officer (CEO), whose roles are integral to the authority's functioning and strategic direction.

1. **Chairperson**:
   - The Chairperson serves as the highest-ranking official in FSSAI, appointed by the **Central Government**.
   - Responsibilities include:
     - Providing overall leadership and strategic vision for FSSAI's objectives.
     - Representing FSSAI in policymaking discussions with government ministries, international organizations, and industry stakeholders.
     - Overseeing the development and implementation of food safety regulations and policies.
2. **Chief Executive Officer (CEO)**:
   - The CEO, also appointed by the Central Government, handles the day-to-day operations and administration of FSSAI.
   - Key duties include:
     - Coordinating with state food authorities to ensure uniform enforcement of food safety standards.
     - Supervising various divisions within FSSAI, including licensing, compliance, and risk communication.
     - Acting as the bridge between the Chairperson and FSSAI's operational teams.

Together, the Chairperson and CEO ensure that FSSAI operates as a dynamic, responsive, and effective regulatory authority.

Regional Offices, State-Level Authorities, and Their Integration

FSSAI's centralized governance is complemented by a robust network of **regional offices** and **state food authorities**, ensuring effective enforcement and oversight at the ground level.

1. **Regional Offices**:
   - FSSAI has set up regional offices across the country to oversee regulatory activities in their respective zones.
   - Functions include:
     - Issuing licenses to food business operators (FBOs).
     - Conducting inspections and audits of food manufacturing units.
     - Facilitating communication between the central authority and state-level authorities.
2. **State-Level Authorities**:
   - Each state has its own **State Food Safety Commissioner**, responsible for implementing FSSAI's regulations within the state.
   - State-level food inspectors and officers play a critical role in:
     - Monitoring compliance with food safety standards.
     - Investigating cases of food adulteration and contamination.
     - Organizing awareness campaigns for consumers and FBOs.
3. **Integration Mechanisms**:
   - To ensure seamless coordination, FSSAI has established:
     - A **centralized data-sharing system** to track inspections, compliance reports, and incidents of non-compliance.
     - Regular training programs for state-level officials to keep them updated on regulatory changes and best practices.

This hierarchical integration ensures that FSSAI's policies and standards are uniformly enforced across the country, bridging the gap between central planning and local implementation.

Committees and Advisory Bodies

FSSAI's governance is strengthened by a network of committees and advisory bodies that provide scientific, technical, and strategic guidance. These bodies play a crucial role in ensuring that the authority's policies are evidence-based, transparent, and aligned with global standards.

Scientific Panels for Food Standards and Risk Assessments

The backbone of FSSAI's regulatory framework is its **Scientific Committee** and **Scientific Panels**, which develop food safety standards and conduct risk assessments.

1. **Scientific Committee**:
    - Composed of experts from various fields, including nutrition, toxicology, microbiology, and public health.
    - Responsibilities:
        - Reviewing and approving standards proposed by the scientific panels.
        - Ensuring that food safety regulations are scientifically robust and consistent with international norms.
2. **Scientific Panels**:
    - FSSAI has multiple specialized panels, each focusing on a specific category of food products or safety concerns. Examples include:
        - **Panel on Food Additives and Flavourings**: Evaluates the safety of additives used in processed foods.
        - **Panel on Pesticide Residues**: Sets maximum permissible limits for pesticide residues in agricultural produce.
        - **Panel on Genetically Modified Organisms (GMOs)**: Assesses the safety of genetically engineered foods.
    - Functions:
        - Conducting risk assessments based on scientific data.
        - Developing and updating standards for contaminants, toxins, and residues.
        - Providing recommendations for new food safety challenges, such as emerging pathogens or novel foods.

Central Advisory Committee (CAC) and Its Functions

The **Central Advisory Committee (CAC)** is a pivotal body within FSSAI, facilitating coordination and collaboration between various stakeholders.

1. **Composition**:
   - The CAC includes representatives from:
     - State food authorities.
     - Industry associations.
     - Consumer organizations.
     - Academic and research institutions.
2. **Functions**:
   - **Policy Coordination**: The CAC acts as a platform for discussing and aligning food safety policies across states and regions, ensuring uniform implementation.
   - **Stakeholder Engagement**: By including industry and consumer representatives, the CAC ensures that all voices are heard in the policymaking process.
   - **Feedback Mechanisms**: Collects feedback from state authorities and stakeholders on the practical challenges of enforcing food safety standards, which is then used to refine policies.
3. **Meeting Schedule**:
   - The CAC meets periodically to review progress, discuss emerging food safety issues, and propose actionable solutions to the central authority.

12.3 Functions and Responsibilities of FSSAI

Ensuring the safety and quality of the food we consume every day is no small feat. It requires a meticulous, multi-layered approach that combines science, enforcement, and education. This is where the **Food Safety and Standards Authority of India (FSSAI)** comes in. As the apex food regulatory body, FSSAI's responsibilities extend across every aspect of the food supply chain, from setting standards to licensing food businesses and educating the public. Let's explore how FSSAI fulfills its diverse responsibilities, step by step.

Development of Food Standards

Scientific Basis for Setting Standards

Food standards are the backbone of any regulatory framework. They provide a clear, measurable benchmark against which food safety and quality can be assessed. For FSSAI, developing these standards is both an art and a science.

1. **Why Standards Matter**: Imagine a jar of honey on a supermarket shelf. How do you know it's pure? Without clear standards, terms like "pure" or "natural" would be meaningless. Standards ensure that food products meet specific criteria for quality, safety, and authenticity.
2. **Scientific Process Behind Standards**: FSSAI relies on a rigorous scientific process to set these benchmarks:
    - **Data Collection**: Scientific panels within FSSAI gather data from research studies, food testing labs, and international guidelines.
    - **Risk Analysis**: For example, when setting permissible limits for pesticide residues, FSSAI considers factors like:
        - Average dietary consumption.
        - Toxicity of the pesticide.
        - Residue levels found in similar foods globally.
    - **Stakeholder Review**: Draft standards are shared with industry experts, consumer groups, and academic bodies for feedback. This ensures that the standards are practical and scientifically sound.
3. **Global Alignment**: FSSAI actively aligns its standards with international benchmarks like those of the **Codex Alimentarius Commission**, ensuring that Indian food products are globally competitive.

Collaboration with Stakeholders and Scientific Bodies

FSSAI's approach is far from insular. Collaboration is a cornerstone of its operations.

1. **Industry Collaboration**: FSSAI engages with food manufacturers and retailers to ensure the standards are implementable. For instance:
    - When setting standards for trans fats in packaged foods, FSSAI worked with industry stakeholders to gradually reduce the permissible levels, giving businesses time to adapt.
2. **Scientific Expertise**: FSSAI's scientific panels include experts in toxicology, nutrition, microbiology, and food engineering. These experts provide insights on emerging food safety challenges, such as the safety of genetically modified foods.

3. **Consumer Representation**: Consumer organizations are involved to voice public concerns and ensure that standards protect consumer interests. This inclusive approach builds trust in FSSAI's processes.

Licensing and Registration

Every food business in India, whether a roadside tea stall or a multinational food corporation, must be licensed or registered with FSSAI. This system ensures accountability across the food supply chain.

Eligibility Criteria and Application Process

1. **Who Needs a License?**

   The size and nature of the business determine whether it requires:

   - A **license** (for larger entities like food manufacturers, importers, and restaurants).
   - A **registration** (for smaller operators like local vendors or petty retailers).
2. **Application Process**:
   - **Step 1: Online Application**: FBOs must submit an application through the **FSSAI Food Licensing and Registration System (FoSCoS)** portal, detailing:
     - The nature of their business.
     - Manufacturing or processing methods.
     - Compliance with hygiene and safety norms.
   - **Step 2: Inspection**: Once the application is filed, food safety officers conduct inspections to ensure the premises meet FSSAI's standards.
   - **Step 3: License Issuance**: Upon successful inspection, the FBO receives its license or registration certificate.
3. **Renewal and Upgradation**: Licenses need to be renewed periodically, and businesses can upgrade their registration as they expand.

Role of FSSAI in Monitoring Compliance

Once licensed, businesses remain under FSSAI's watchful eye.

1. **Regular Inspections**: Food safety officers conduct surprise inspections to check compliance with hygiene standards, labeling norms, and storage conditions.

2. **Penalties for Non-Compliance**: FSSAI has the authority to impose fines, revoke licenses, or initiate legal proceedings against violators. For instance:
   - A sweet manufacturer found using non-edible dyes could face penalties ranging from financial fines to closure of operations.
3. **Supportive Role**: While enforcement is strict, FSSAI also provides guidance to help FBOs meet compliance requirements. Training sessions and manuals are regularly issued to educate businesses on best practices.

Surveillance and Enforcement

Monitoring the vast food ecosystem in India requires robust surveillance and swift enforcement mechanisms.

Mechanisms for Market Surveillance

1. **Sampling and Testing**: FSSAI conducts regular market surveys, collecting samples of products for laboratory analysis. Key focus areas include:
   - Detecting adulterants like **formalin in fish** or **artificial ripening agents in fruits**.
   - Verifying nutritional claims on packaged foods.
2. **Hotspot Surveillance**: Certain regions or product categories with a history of violations are subjected to increased scrutiny. For instance:
   - Milk adulteration in urban centers.
   - Contaminants in street food.
3. **Special Drives**: FSSAI launches targeted campaigns, such as:
   - Testing sweets during festive seasons.
   - Inspecting imported food items at customs points.

Handling of Non-Compliance and Penalties

1. **Identifying Non-Compliance**: Violations are categorized based on severity:
   - Minor infractions, like improper labeling, may require corrective actions.
   - Serious breaches, like the presence of harmful toxins, lead to recalls and penalties.

2. **Recall Mechanisms**: When unsafe products reach the market, FSSAI initiates recalls to prevent harm. The process involves:
   - Alerting consumers and retailers.
   - Coordinating with manufacturers to remove the product from shelves.
3. **Imposing Penalties**: FSSAI's enforcement powers include:
   - Fines ranging from ₹1 lakh to ₹10 lakh for severe violations.
   - Suspension or cancellation of licenses for repeat offenders.

Risk Assessment and Communication

Prevention is always better than cure. FSSAI's risk assessment and communication strategies aim to identify potential hazards before they become public health crises.

Identifying Potential Food Safety Hazards

1. **Data-Driven Risk Analysis**: FSSAI uses data from food testing labs, consumer complaints, and scientific research to predict and mitigate risks. For example:
   - An uptick in pesticide residues in vegetables might prompt FSSAI to issue guidelines for farmers.
2. **Emerging Challenges**:
   - **Microbial Contaminants**: FSSAI monitors pathogens like **Salmonella** in poultry or **E. coli** in water.
   - **Chemical Hazards**: Heavy metals like lead in spices or arsenic in rice are priority areas for risk management.

Public Awareness Campaigns and Consumer Education

1. **Awareness Initiatives**: Campaigns like **"Eat Right India"** educate consumers about safe eating habits, balanced nutrition, and recognizing authentic products.
2. **Digital Tools**: Mobile apps like **Food Safety Connect** allow consumers to:
   - Check FSSAI licenses of food outlets.
   - Report unsafe food products.
3. **Grievance Redressal**: FSSAI operates a consumer helpline and online portal for lodging complaints about unsafe or mislabeled products.

12.4 Key Regulations Under FSSAI

The Food Safety and Standards Authority of India (FSSAI) is built upon a strong regulatory foundation designed to ensure that the food consumed by millions of people is safe, nutritious, and free from harmful contaminants. At the heart of this framework lies the **Food Safety and Standards Act, 2006**, supported by a range of specific regulations that address various aspects of food production, labeling, and quality control. These regulations aim to harmonize standards, enhance consumer trust, and make compliance easier for food business operators (FBOs). Let's dive into the details of these key regulations and their real-world implications.

Food Safety and Standards Act, 2006

Scope and Jurisdiction

The **Food Safety and Standards Act, 2006**, often abbreviated as FSSA, is the cornerstone of India's food safety framework. It consolidates and replaces multiple older laws, creating a unified regulatory system that oversees every aspect of the food supply chain.

1. **Comprehensive Coverage**: FSSA applies to **all stages of food handling**, including:
    - Production.
    - Processing.
    - Distribution.
    - Sale and import.
2. **Who Falls Under Its Jurisdiction?** The Act covers every entity in the food ecosystem, from large-scale manufacturers to small roadside vendors. Even home-based food businesses come under its purview if they sell their products commercially.
3. **Focus Areas**:
    - **Public Health**: Protecting consumers from foodborne illnesses.
    - **Consumer Rights**: Ensuring food quality and accurate labeling.
    - **Trade Facilitation**: Promoting compliance with global food safety standards for export competitiveness.

Provisions for Food Safety Management

The Act emphasizes a **preventive approach** to food safety, focusing on managing risks before they escalate into public health issues. Key provisions include:

1. **Food Safety Management Systems (FSMS)**:
    - Businesses are required to implement FSMS based on internationally recognized standards like HACCP (Hazard Analysis and Critical Control Points).
    - FSMS involves identifying potential hazards in the production process and implementing measures to mitigate them.
2. **Food Safety Audits**:
    - Regular audits by trained food safety officers ensure compliance.
    - For example, a food processing unit must demonstrate that its cleaning protocols, ingredient sourcing, and storage methods meet safety standards.
3. **Mandatory Licensing and Registration**:
    - No food business can operate without obtaining a license or registration from FSSAI, ensuring accountability across the supply chain.

Major Regulations and Guidelines

The FSSA is implemented through a series of regulations, each targeting specific areas of food safety and quality. These regulations provide detailed guidance to FBOs and serve as benchmarks for compliance.

Food Safety and Standards (Licensing and Registration) Regulations

1. **Purpose**:
   These regulations ensure that all food businesses, regardless of size, are registered or licensed, creating a formalized ecosystem.
2. **Two-Tier System**:
    - **Registration**: For small businesses like local vendors or petty retailers.
    - **Licensing**: For medium to large-scale businesses, including manufacturers, importers, and exporters.

3. **Process Highlights**:
   - Online applications through the **FoSCoS portal**.
   - Inspections by food safety officers to verify compliance.
   - Renewal requirements to maintain validity.
4. **Impact**:
   - Formalization of small-scale food vendors, increasing their credibility.
   - Enhanced traceability of food products, aiding enforcement and recall mechanisms.

Food Safety and Standards (Packaging and Labeling) Regulations

Packaging and labeling are not just about aesthetics; they play a critical role in consumer safety and informed choices.

1. **Packaging Standards**:
   - Materials used in packaging must not contaminate the food.
   - For example, plastics used for milk packaging must meet FSSAI-approved specifications to prevent chemical leaching.
2. **Labeling Requirements**:
   - Mandatory details include:
     - Product name.
     - Nutritional information (e.g., calories, fats, vitamins).
     - Ingredients list in descending order of quantity.
     - Expiry or "Best Before" date.
     - FSSAI license number and logo.
   - Allergens like nuts or gluten must be clearly indicated.
3. **Innovations**:
   - Introduction of **front-of-pack labels** for high-fat, high-sugar, and high-salt products to encourage healthier choices.

Food Safety and Standards (Contaminants, Toxins, and Residues) Regulations

Contamination and residues are among the most significant threats to food safety. These regulations define limits for contaminants, ensuring that food products are safe for consumption.

1. **Permissible Limits**:
    - **Pesticides and Heavy Metals**: For example, the maximum residue limit (MRL) for pesticides in vegetables is set to minimize exposure.
    - **Naturally Occurring Toxins**: Aflatoxins in grains and nuts must not exceed specified limits.
2. **Regular Monitoring**:
    - Sampling by food inspectors ensures compliance. For instance, random checks of packaged spices ensure they are free from harmful lead residues.
3. **Consumer Safety**:
    - These regulations have led to recalls of products with unsafe contamination levels, protecting public health.

Food Safety and Standards (Fortification of Foods) Regulations

Food fortification addresses nutrient deficiencies in the population by enriching staple foods with essential vitamins and minerals.

1. **Fortified Products**:
    - Commonly fortified foods include:
        - Milk and edible oil (Vitamin A and D).
        - Rice and wheat flour (Iron, Folic Acid, Vitamin B12).
        - Salt (Iodine and Iron).
2. **Mandatory and Voluntary Fortification**:
    - While fortification is voluntary for most products, FSSAI has made it mandatory for certain items like edible oil to combat widespread vitamin deficiencies.
3. **Logo for Fortified Foods**:
    - The **"+" logo** on packaging indicates fortified food, making it easier for consumers to identify healthier options.

Food Safety and Standards (Organic Foods) Regulations

With growing consumer demand for organic products, these regulations provide a framework for certifying and labeling organic foods.

1. **Certification Standards**:
   - Organic foods must comply with the standards set by agencies like **India Organic** or **Participatory Guarantee System (PGS)-India**.
   - Certification ensures that the product is free from synthetic fertilizers, pesticides, and genetically modified organisms (GMOs).
2. **Labeling**:
   - Organic products must carry a certification logo, along with the statement "Organic" to distinguish them from conventional products.
3. **Consumer Trust**:
   - These regulations help consumers identify genuine organic products, preventing fraud and misrepresentation.

12.5 FSSAI's Role in Ensuring Food Safety

Ensuring food safety in a country as vast and diverse as India is a monumental task, requiring meticulous oversight, effective systems, and consistent innovation. The **Food Safety and Standards Authority of India (FSSAI)** takes a comprehensive approach to maintain food safety standards, leveraging inspection systems, state-of-the-art laboratories, and targeted strategies to combat adulteration. This section explores the mechanisms FSSAI employs to guarantee that the food we consume is safe, nutritious, and free from harmful contaminants.

Inspection and Audit Systems

Role of Food Safety Officers (FSOs)

At the frontline of food safety enforcement are the **Food Safety Officers (FSOs)**, whose responsibilities are critical to FSSAI's regulatory framework.

- **Primary Duties**:
   - Inspecting food manufacturing, processing, and retail establishments.
   - Ensuring compliance with FSSAI regulations on hygiene, storage, and labeling.
   - Sampling food products for testing and initiating action in case of violations.

- **Key Contributions**:
    - FSOs serve as the first line of defense against foodborne hazards. For instance, during festivals, FSOs intensify inspections of sweet shops and street food vendors to ensure the quality of products sold during high-demand periods.
- **Challenges**:
    - Covering vast jurisdictions with limited resources often places FSOs under significant pressure. Nevertheless, their role remains indispensable in safeguarding public health.

Procedures for Audits and Inspections

FSSAI has developed a standardized system for audits and inspections to ensure consistency and transparency.

1. **Pre-Inspection Preparation**:
    - FSOs review the license or registration details of the food business.
    - A checklist of applicable standards is prepared based on the nature of the business (e.g., dairy, bakery, or seafood processing).
2. **On-Site Inspection**:
    - **Physical Observation**: Hygiene, cleanliness, and equipment conditions are assessed.
    - **Documentation Review**: Records of raw materials, processing methods, and quality control measures are verified.
    - **Sample Collection**: Food samples are collected for lab testing as per FSSAI's **sampling protocols** (discussed below).
3. **Post-Inspection Actions**:
    - **Compliance Reports**: FSOs prepare detailed reports highlighting areas of compliance and non-compliance.
    - **Follow-Up**: Businesses are given time to rectify minor issues, while severe violations may result in penalties, license suspension, or legal action.

Food Testing and Laboratories

Testing and analysis are central to FSSAI's food safety strategy, ensuring that food products meet the established safety and quality standards.

FSSAI-Accredited Labs and Their Functions

FSSAI operates a network of accredited laboratories across India, each equipped to handle specific types of food testing.

- **Categories of Labs**:
    1. **Primary Labs**: Handle routine testing of food samples.
    2. **Referral Labs**: Focus on advanced testing and verifying disputed results.
    3. **National Food Laboratories**: FSSAI's flagship labs, located in Kolkata and Ghaziabad, conduct high-priority tests and research.
- **Key Functions**:
    - Testing for **adulterants** and **contaminants** (e.g., pesticide residues in vegetables or heavy metals in fish).
    - Verifying nutritional claims on food labels.
    - Identifying microbial contamination in perishable items like dairy and meat products.
- **Quality Assurance**:
    - Labs operate under strict accreditation standards, such as **ISO/IEC 17025**, ensuring accuracy and reliability of results.

Sampling Protocols and Analysis Methods

Food sampling is a meticulously designed process to ensure that test results are representative and legally valid.

1. **Sampling Protocols**:
    - FSOs collect samples randomly but systematically, ensuring no prior bias.
    - Samples are divided into three parts:
        - One for testing.
        - One for the food business operator (FBO) for reference.
        - One retained for dispute resolution.
    - Chain of custody is maintained to prevent tampering.

2. **Analysis Methods**:
    - **Chemical Analysis**: Detects contaminants like artificial dyes or toxic chemicals.
    - **Microbiological Testing**: Identifies harmful pathogens like *E. coli* or *Salmonella.*
    - **Nutritional Testing**: Verifies the accuracy of claims like "low-fat" or "high-protein" on product labels.

Addressing Food Adulteration

Adulteration, the intentional addition of inferior or harmful substances to food, remains one of the biggest challenges to food safety in India. FSSAI tackles this issue with a combination of identification, enforcement, and technology.

Identifying and Eliminating Adulterants

1. **Common Adulterants**:
    - **Milk**: Water, detergent, or synthetic milk compounds.
    - **Spices**: Lead chromate in turmeric or brick powder in chili powder.
    - **Vegetables and Fruits**: Artificial ripening agents like calcium carbide.
2. **Detection and Action**:
    - FSSAI conducts **special drives** during peak adulteration seasons, such as festivals, to identify and seize adulterated products.
    - Penalties for adulteration include:
        - Fines ranging from ₹1 lakh to ₹10 lakh.
        - Imprisonment for severe violations impacting public health.

Use of Rapid Detection Technologies

FSSAI leverages modern technology to enhance its ability to detect adulteration and contamination.

- **Rapid Analytical Kits**:
    - Tools like the **Milk Adulteration Detection Kit** allow FSOs and even consumers to quickly test milk for water, urea, and detergents.

- **AI and Machine Learning**:
  - Advanced tools are being developed to predict adulteration trends based on historical data and supply chain analysis.
- **Mobile Labs**:
  - FSSAI has introduced mobile food testing labs, or **Food Safety on Wheels**, which can conduct on-the-spot testing in remote areas and marketplaces.

12.6 FSSAI and Consumer Awareness

Consumer awareness is a critical pillar of food safety, as informed consumers are empowered to make healthier choices and demand higher standards from the food industry. The **Food Safety and Standards Authority of India (FSSAI)** has launched numerous initiatives to educate the public, promote healthy eating habits, and address grievances. This section explores FSSAI's role in enhancing consumer awareness and trust.

Initiatives to Educate Consumers

Eat Right India Campaign

The **Eat Right India campaign** is one of FSSAI's flagship initiatives aimed at transforming India's food environment.

- **Purpose**:
  - Encourage consumers to eat safe, healthy, and sustainably.
  - Spread awareness about food safety, balanced diets, and the risks of adulteration.
- **Key Components**:
  - **Eat Right Mela**: Interactive events that combine entertainment and education about food safety.
  - **Eat Right Schools**: Programs designed to instill healthy eating habits in children through fun activities and quizzes.
  - **Eat Right Campus**: Certification programs for workplaces, hospitals, and educational institutions that implement safe and healthy food practices.
- **Impact**:
  - Raised awareness among millions of consumers about food safety and healthy eating habits.
  - Fostered collaboration between consumers, food businesses, and regulators.

Food Safety Mobile Apps and Digital Platforms

FSSAI has embraced digital technology to make food safety accessible to every consumer.

- **Mobile Apps**:
  - **Food Safety Connect**:
    - Provides consumers with a platform to verify the FSSAI license of food outlets.
    - Enables users to report unsafe or adulterated food products.
  - **Eat Right App**:
    - Offers tips on healthy eating, nutrition, and food safety practices.
- **Digital Platforms**:
  - FSSAI's official website includes educational materials, videos, and resources for consumers.
  - **Social Media Campaigns**: Regular updates, infographics, and videos shared on platforms like Twitter and Instagram.

Role in Promoting Healthy Eating Habits

Fortification and Its Benefits

FSSAI has been a strong advocate of **food fortification** to combat malnutrition and micronutrient deficiencies in India.

- **Fortified Foods**:
  - Commonly fortified products include rice, wheat flour, salt, milk, and edible oil.
  - Fortification adds essential nutrients like Vitamin A, Vitamin D, Iron, Folic Acid, and Iodine to these staples.
- **Consumer Awareness**:
  - The **"+F" logo** helps consumers identify fortified products easily.
  - Educational campaigns explain the health benefits of consuming fortified foods.

Reducing Trans Fats and Promoting Balanced Diets

- **Eliminating Trans Fats**:
  - FSSAI aims to reduce industrial trans fats in food to less than **2% by 2022**.

    - Campaigns like **"Heart Attack Rewind"** highlight the dangers of trans fats and encourage healthier alternatives.
- **Promoting Balanced Diets**:
    - Educational initiatives focus on the importance of portion control, eating seasonal fruits and vegetables, and reducing sugar, salt, and fat intake.

Grievance Redressal Mechanisms

Consumer Complaints and Their Resolution

FSSAI provides multiple channels for consumers to report food safety violations or register complaints about substandard products.

- **Complaint Handling**:
    - Consumers can lodge complaints through FSSAI's helpline or **Food Safety Connect** app.
    - Complaints are forwarded to the appropriate Food Safety Officer for investigation.

Role of FSSAI Helpline and Online Portals

- **Helpline**:
    - A toll-free number allows consumers to report issues and seek guidance on food safety.
- **Online Portals**:
    - The **FSSAI Grievance Portal** offers a user-friendly interface for tracking complaint statuses and resolutions.

12.7 FSSAI and Industry Collaboration

FSSAI recognizes that food businesses are key partners in ensuring food safety. Through collaboration, training, and support, the authority fosters an environment where compliance becomes an enabler rather than a burden.

Support for Food Businesses

Simplification of Licensing and Registration Processes

- FSSAI has streamlined licensing through the **FoSCoS portal**, enabling food businesses to apply, renew, and track their licenses online.

- Training sessions help businesses understand the requirements and benefits of compliance.

Training Programs for Food Business Operators (FBOs)

- **Food Safety Training and Certification (FoSTaC)**:
    - Mandatory training for FBOs to improve hygiene and safety standards.
    - Over **150 training modules** tailored to various types of food businesses.

Promoting Innovation and Entrepreneurship

Initiatives to Support Start-Ups in Food Technology

- FSSAI provides guidance on regulatory requirements, helping start-ups navigate the licensing process smoothly.

Encouraging Sustainable Practices

- FSSAI promotes environmentally friendly practices, such as reducing food wastage and adopting eco-friendly packaging.

Partnerships with International Organizations

Collaboration with WHO, FAO, Codex Alimentarius, and Others

- FSSAI aligns its standards with international benchmarks to ensure Indian food products are competitive globally.
- It works with organizations like the **World Health Organization (WHO)** and **Food and Agriculture Organization (FAO)** to address emerging food safety challenges.

12.8 Challenges and Limitations of FSSAI

Despite its achievements, FSSAI faces several challenges that limit its effectiveness.

Enforcement Challenges

Addressing Regional Disparities

- Uneven enforcement across states due to varying capacities of state food authorities.

Resource Constraints

- Limited manpower and infrastructure hinder comprehensive monitoring.

Regulatory Gaps and Ambiguities

Overlapping Jurisdictions

- Confusion between FSSAI and other regulatory bodies like the Bureau of Indian Standards (BIS) leads to delays.

Need for Updates

- Emerging issues like genetically modified foods and novel food products require new standards.

Balancing Consumer Safety with Industry Growth

Managing Industry Pushback

- Stricter norms often face resistance from large food manufacturers.

Supporting Small-Scale FBOs

Ensuring that compliance costs remain affordable for small businesses is a significant challenge.

CHAPTER 13

Goods and Services Tax (GST)

Introduction to Goods and Services Tax (GST) and its Impact on Pharmaceuticals Export Promotion Council of India (PHARMEXCIL)

The introduction of the Goods and Services Tax (GST) in India marked a paradigm shift in the country's indirect taxation framework. Launched on July 1, 2017, GST aimed to consolidate a fragmented tax structure into a unified system that could simplify compliance, reduce inefficiencies, and enhance the ease of doing business. For the pharmaceutical sector, a critical contributor to India's economy, this reform carried transformative potential, addressing long-standing challenges while presenting new opportunities. To fully appreciate GST's impact, particularly in the context of the Pharmaceuticals Export Promotion Council of India (PHARMEXCIL), one must delve into the intricacies of its framework, its historical context, and its implications for the sector.

Overview of the GST Framework in India

Definition and Purpose of GST

At its core, GST is a **comprehensive, destination-based tax** that subsumes multiple indirect taxes previously levied by the central and state governments. It operates on the principle of **value addition**, where tax is levied at each stage of the supply chain but with credit provided for the tax paid on inputs. This ensures that the tax burden is borne by the final consumer while eliminating cascading effects, where tax is levied on tax.

The primary objectives of GST are to:

1. Simplify the taxation process by replacing multiple indirect taxes with a single, unified tax.
2. Eliminate inefficiencies caused by overlapping state and central taxes.

3. Reduce tax evasion through improved transparency and compliance mechanisms.
4. Create a seamless, common national market by removing interstate tax barriers.

For the pharmaceutical industry, these objectives translated into potential benefits like easier compliance, lower transaction costs, and a more transparent tax structure. However, the journey to GST was neither quick nor simple—it required years of debate, negotiation, and preparation.

Transition from Pre-GST Tax Regimes to GST in India

Before GST, India's indirect tax system was characterized by a complex web of taxes levied at multiple levels. Central taxes like **excise duty**, **service tax**, and **central sales tax (CST)** coexisted with state taxes such as **value-added tax (VAT)**, **entry tax**, and **octroi**. Each of these taxes came with its own set of rules, rates, and compliance requirements, leading to inefficiencies and higher costs.

Challenges of the Pre-GST System

1. **Cascading Taxes**: A major drawback of the old system was the "tax on tax" phenomenon. For example, excise duty was levied on the manufacturing cost, which already included VAT paid on raw materials. This cascading effect inflated the final price of goods, including pharmaceuticals, making them less competitive internationally.
2. **Interstate Barriers**: The movement of goods across state borders was fraught with logistical challenges due to the imposition of CST and entry taxes. Pharmaceutical companies faced delays and increased costs, especially when distributing medicines to remote areas.
3. **Compliance Complexity**: Pharmaceutical exporters, particularly small and medium enterprises (SMEs), struggled to navigate the multiple tax regimes, each requiring separate filings and documentation. This often led to errors, delays, and penalties.

The GST Era

The introduction of GST addressed these challenges by:

- **Subsuming Multiple Taxes**: GST replaced over 17 central and state taxes, simplifying the taxation landscape.
- **Uniform Taxation**: The tax was levied uniformly across the country, removing barriers to interstate trade.

- **Input Tax Credit (ITC)**: Businesses could claim credits for the GST paid on inputs, reducing the cascading effect and lowering costs.

The pharmaceutical sector, being highly regulated and price-sensitive, stood to benefit significantly from this streamlined structure.

Importance of GST in the Pharmaceutical Sector

The pharmaceutical industry plays a pivotal role in India's economy, contributing over USD 25 billion in exports annually and supplying affordable medicines to over 200 countries. For an industry of this scale and complexity, GST offered solutions to long-standing inefficiencies while aligning with global trade practices.

Streamlining of Indirect Taxes

The most immediate benefit of GST was the elimination of overlapping taxes that had previously burdened the sector. Consider the example of a pharmaceutical company manufacturing paracetamol tablets:

- Under the pre-GST system, the company would pay **excise duty** on manufacturing, **VAT** on sales, and **CST** if the goods were sold interstate. Each tax was calculated independently, leading to higher cumulative costs.
- Under GST, a single tax replaced all these levies, and the company could claim **input tax credits** for the GST paid on raw materials like APIs, excipients, and packaging.

This shift not only simplified calculations but also reduced costs, enabling manufacturers to price their products more competitively.

GST as a Catalyst for Enhancing Exports

For pharmaceutical exporters, GST introduced several advantages that directly impacted their global competitiveness:

1. **Zero-Rated Exports**: Under GST, exports are classified as zero-rated supplies, meaning that exporters do not have to pay GST on their output. They can also claim refunds for the GST paid on inputs, improving cash flow and reducing operational costs.
2. **Improved Supply Chain Efficiency**: The removal of interstate taxes and the introduction of the **e-way bill** system streamlined the movement of goods across borders. Pharmaceutical companies could now distribute medicines and vaccines more efficiently, ensuring timely delivery to export markets.
3. **Harmonization with International Practices**: GST brought India closer to the tax frameworks of developed economies, making it

easier for Indian exporters to comply with global trade standards. This alignment enhanced the credibility of Indian pharmaceutical products in international markets.

Role of PHARMEXCIL in Navigating GST Reforms for Exporters

The transition to GST, while beneficial in the long term, posed initial challenges for exporters, particularly in understanding the new system, adapting processes, and managing compliance. PHARMEXCIL stepped in as a crucial facilitator during this period.

Advocacy and Representation

PHARMEXCIL worked closely with the government to ensure that the pharmaceutical sector's unique needs were addressed in the GST framework. This included:

- Advocating for lower GST rates on essential medicines and APIs.
- Highlighting the need for faster refund mechanisms for exporters.
- Proposing clarifications on ambiguous GST provisions related to pharmaceuticals.

Capacity Building and Training

Recognizing the steep learning curve associated with GST, PHARMEXCIL organized numerous workshops, webinars, and training sessions for its members. These programs covered:

- Basics of GST compliance, including registration and filing.
- Procedures for claiming input tax credits and export refunds.
- Best practices for adapting supply chains to the GST regime.

Resolving Member Concerns

PHARMEXCIL established dedicated helpdesks and support teams to address member grievances related to GST. Whether it was clarifying procedural requirements or liaising with tax authorities on behalf of exporters, PHARMEXCIL played a hands-on role in ensuring a smooth transition.

13.1 Overview of GST and its Applicability in Pharmaceuticals

The Goods and Services Tax (GST) is a transformative indirect tax regime designed to unify and streamline taxation across India. By eliminating the inefficiencies of the pre-GST tax structure, it has simplified compliance and enhanced transparency for businesses, including the pharmaceutical sector. Understanding GST's unique structure, its applicability to pharmaceutical products, and the compliance requirements for exporters is essential to fully appreciate its impact on the industry.

Definition of GST and Its Unique Structure

What is GST?

GST is a **comprehensive, destination-based indirect tax** levied on the supply of goods and services. Its primary objectives are to:

1. Replace multiple taxes with a unified system.
2. Eliminate the cascading effect of taxes.
3. Promote ease of doing business by simplifying compliance.

Under GST, taxes are collected at each stage of value addition, but businesses can claim **input tax credits (ITC)** for the tax paid on inputs. This ensures that the burden of taxation is ultimately borne by the end consumer.

Tax Slabs Under GST

To accommodate the diversity of goods and services, GST is levied at different rates categorized into **five tax slabs**:

- **0%**: Applicable to essential items, including unprocessed food and certain life-saving medicines.
- **5%**: Levied on essential goods such as basic formulations and APIs.
- **12%**: Applicable to a broader range of pharmaceutical products, including finished formulations and over-the-counter drugs.
- **18%**: Levied on services like contract manufacturing and certain specialized pharmaceuticals.
- **28%**: Reserved for luxury items; rarely applicable to pharmaceutical products.

These tax slabs allow the government to balance revenue generation with the affordability of essential goods, a critical consideration in the pharmaceutical sector.

Dual GST Model: CGST, SGST, and IGST

India's GST system follows a **dual structure** to accommodate the federal nature of governance:

1. **Central GST (CGST)**: Levied by the central government on intra-state supplies.

2. **State GST (SGST)**: Levied by state governments on intra-state supplies.
3. **Integrated GST (IGST)**: Levied by the central government on inter-state supplies and imports.

For example:

- A pharmaceutical manufacturer selling within a state will pay CGST and SGST.
- An exporter shipping goods to another country will pay IGST, which is eligible for a refund under the zero-rated supply provisions.

Applicability of GST to Pharmaceutical Products

The pharmaceutical industry is diverse, encompassing APIs, formulations, vaccines, herbal products, and more. GST's applicability varies across these categories, depending on their nature and use.

Taxation on Active Pharmaceutical Ingredients (APIs), Formulations, and Vaccines

1. **Active Pharmaceutical Ingredients (APIs)**: APIs, the raw materials used to manufacture medicines, attract a GST rate of **18%**. While this is higher than the rate for finished formulations, manufacturers can claim ITC for the tax paid on APIs, reducing the overall cost burden.
2. **Finished Formulations**: Formulated medicines such as tablets, capsules, and syrups are taxed at **5%** or **12%**, depending on their category. This relatively lower rate ensures affordability while maintaining revenue for the government.
3. **Vaccines**:Vaccines, being critical to public health, are taxed at **5%**. This preferential rate is intended to encourage their widespread distribution and accessibility.

Exemptions for Life-Saving Drugs

Certain life-saving drugs are **exempt from GST**, ensuring they remain affordable for patients. These include medicines for:

- Cancer treatment.
- HIV/AIDS.
- Tuberculosis.
- Rare diseases.

The exemption covers both domestic supplies and imports, highlighting the government's commitment to making essential healthcare accessible.

GST Compliance Requirements for Pharmaceutical Exporters

For exporters in the pharmaceutical sector, GST compliance involves several key steps to ensure smooth operations and avoid penalties.

Registration Under GST

- **Who Needs to Register?**

  All businesses with an annual turnover exceeding **₹20 lakh** (₹10 lakh for special category states) must register for GST. Exporters, regardless of turnover, are also required to register to avail of benefits such as ITC and export refunds.
- **GST Identification Number (GSTIN)**: Upon registration, businesses are assigned a unique GSTIN, which must be quoted on all invoices and returns.

Maintenance of Documentation and Invoicing

Accurate documentation is critical for GST compliance, especially for exporters. Key requirements include:

1. **Tax Invoices**: Invoices must include details such as GSTIN, invoice number, date, HSN (Harmonized System of Nomenclature) codes for goods, tax rate, and amount.
2. **Export Documentation**: Exporters must maintain the following:
   - Bill of Export.
   - Shipping bill or airway bill.
   - Bank realization certificate (BRC) or foreign inward remittance certificate (FIRC) for claiming refunds.
3. **Returns Filing**: Exporters are required to file periodic GST returns, including:
   - **GSTR-1**: Details of outward supplies, including exports.
   - **GSTR-3B**: Summary of monthly transactions and tax payments.
   - **RFD-01**: For claiming refunds on zero-rated exports.
4. **E-Way Bills**: For goods transported within India, exporters must generate e-way bills for consignments exceeding ₹50,000 in value. These bills ensure compliance with GST during interstate and intrastate movement.

13.2 PHARMEXCIL's Role in GST Implementation

The introduction of GST was a transformative yet challenging reform for the Indian pharmaceutical sector. Transitioning to this unified tax regime required significant adjustments in processes, pricing structures, and compliance mechanisms. PHARMEXCIL played a pivotal role in ensuring that pharmaceutical exporters navigated these changes smoothly, addressing industry concerns, and fostering collaboration between stakeholders. This section delves into PHARMEXCIL's contributions during the GST transition, its support initiatives for exporters, and its collaborative efforts with government bodies.

Advocacy During the Transition to GST

Engagement with Policymakers to Address Industry Concerns

The pharmaceutical sector faced unique challenges during the transition to GST. As an industry heavily regulated on quality and pricing, concerns regarding tax rates, refunds, and compliance complexities were prominent. PHARMEXCIL stepped in as a vocal advocate for the sector, ensuring that the industry's concerns were addressed by policymakers.

1. **Representation of Industry Needs**: PHARMEXCIL engaged extensively with the GST Council and the Ministry of Finance to present the industry's perspective. Specific areas of focus included:
   - The need for lower tax rates on essential medicines.
   - Ensuring timely refunds for exporters to maintain cash flow.
   - Simplifying compliance for small and medium enterprises (SMEs) in the pharmaceutical sector.
2. **Highlighting the Sector's Sensitivity**: PHARMEXCIL emphasized the critical role of the pharmaceutical sector in public health, advocating for tax structures that would not increase the cost burden on consumers. This engagement ensured that life-saving drugs and vaccines received preferential tax treatment under GST.
3. **Advocacy for Export-Oriented Benefits**: Recognizing the export-driven nature of the pharmaceutical industry, PHARMEXCIL pushed for provisions like zero-rated exports and streamlined refund mechanisms to support exporters in competing globally.

Proposals for GST Rate Rationalization for Pharmaceuticals

PHARMEXCIL actively contributed to the discussion on GST rates for pharmaceutical products, aiming to strike a balance between government revenue needs and the affordability of medicines.

1. **Tax Slabs for Pharmaceuticals**: PHARMEXCIL's proposals ensured:
    - A **5% GST rate** for essential drugs, including formulations and vaccines.
    - Zero-rated status for exports to maintain global competitiveness.
    - Exemptions for life-saving medicines, ensuring affordability for critical healthcare needs.
2. **Special Considerations for APIs**: PHARMEXCIL advocated for the rationalization of GST on APIs, initially taxed at 18%. The council argued that high tax rates on raw materials would increase the cost of formulations, ultimately impacting consumers and exporters. This advocacy led to discussions on reducing tax rates for specific APIs to encourage domestic manufacturing and reduce import dependency.

Support for Exporters in Adapting to GST

Workshops and Seminars on GST Compliance

For many exporters, particularly SMEs, adapting to the GST regime posed significant challenges due to its procedural requirements and documentation complexities. PHARMEXCIL addressed this by organizing workshops and seminars tailored to the pharmaceutical sector.

1. **Capacity-Building Initiatives**: These programs provided exporters with hands-on training on:
    - GST registration and compliance procedures.
    - Filing GST returns, including GSTR-1, GSTR-3B, and refund applications.
    - Managing input tax credits and e-way bills.
2. **Sector-Specific Focus**: The workshops were customized to address industry-specific issues, such as:
    - GST compliance for contract manufacturing and clinical trials.

- Tax implications for exporters dealing in APIs, formulations, and herbal medicines.

3. **Collaboration with Experts**: PHARMEXCIL invited tax consultants, legal experts, and government officials to lead these sessions, ensuring that members received accurate and actionable guidance.

Dissemination of Updates on GST Rules and Notifications

GST rules and notifications are frequently updated, often requiring businesses to adapt quickly. PHARMEXCIL played a crucial role in keeping its members informed:

1. **Timely Communication**: The council regularly disseminated updates on GST-related changes through newsletters, webinars, and email alerts. These updates included:
    - Changes in tax rates or exemptions.
    - New procedural requirements, such as modifications to e-invoicing norms.
    - Clarifications on ambiguous GST provisions.
2. **Guidance Documents**: PHARMEXCIL developed detailed guides and FAQs tailored to the pharmaceutical sector, covering topics such as:
    - Claiming GST refunds for zero-rated exports.
    - Handling composite and mixed supplies under GST.
3. **Helpdesk for Members**: The council established a dedicated helpdesk to address member queries related to GST. This service provided personalized support, enabling exporters to resolve issues promptly and avoid penalties.

Collaboration with Government Bodies

Partnership with the Central Board of Indirect Taxes and Customs (CBIC)

PHARMEXCIL worked closely with the CBIC, the apex body overseeing GST implementation, to address the pharmaceutical sector's unique challenges:

1. **Joint Awareness Programs**: PHARMEXCIL collaborated with CBIC to conduct awareness campaigns, ensuring that exporters understood the benefits and obligations under GST.

2. **Resolution of Operational Issues**: The council facilitated discussions between its members and CBIC officials to resolve issues such as:
   - Delays in GST refunds for exporters.
   - Technical glitches in filing returns on the GST Network (GSTN).
3. **Feedback Mechanisms**: PHARMEXCIL regularly shared industry feedback with CBIC, helping the government refine GST processes and policies for the pharmaceutical sector.

Contributions to GST Council Discussions on the Pharmaceutical Sector

As a key stakeholder, PHARMEXCIL actively participated in GST Council discussions, representing the interests of pharmaceutical exporters and ensuring that the sector's needs were considered in policy decisions.

1. **Data-Driven Recommendations**: PHARMEXCIL presented detailed reports on the impact of GST on the pharmaceutical sector, supported by data on pricing, export trends, and compliance costs.
2. **Advocacy for Simplified Refund Mechanisms**: The council pushed for faster processing of GST refunds for exporters, emphasizing the importance of cash flow in maintaining global competitiveness.
3. **Long-Term Policy Suggestions**: PHARMEXCIL provided input on aligning GST policies with broader government initiatives, such as the "Make in India" program and the promotion of domestic API manufacturing.

13.3 GST and Pharmaceutical Exports

The introduction of the Goods and Services Tax (GST) marked a significant milestone for India's pharmaceutical exporters. It redefined how exports were taxed, managed, and incentivized, addressing inefficiencies while introducing new compliance frameworks. This section explores the impact of GST on export pricing and competitiveness, highlights its benefits for exporters, examines the challenges faced, and presents case studies showcasing its practical implications for the pharmaceutical sector.

Impact of GST on Export Pricing and Competitiveness

The GST regime has profoundly influenced the cost structure and competitiveness of Indian pharmaceutical exports. By eliminating inefficiencies in the pre-GST tax system, it has streamlined pricing and boosted global competitiveness.

Removal of Cascading Taxes

Under the pre-GST tax system, the pharmaceutical supply chain was plagued by **cascading taxes**—a scenario where tax was levied on tax. For example:

- Excise duty was charged on the manufacturing cost, which already included VAT on raw materials.
- Interstate sales attracted Central Sales Tax (CST) without credit for taxes paid earlier in the supply chain.

GST addressed these issues by subsuming all indirect taxes and introducing a **seamless input tax credit (ITC) mechanism**. This eliminated the cascading effect, reducing the overall tax burden and making Indian pharmaceuticals more price-competitive globally.

Example:

A manufacturer producing APIs paid VAT on raw materials and excise duty on the finished product under the old tax regime. Under GST, the manufacturer can offset the GST paid on raw materials against the GST liability on the finished product, reducing costs.

Availability of Input Tax Credits (ITC) for Exporters

GST's ITC mechanism allows exporters to claim refunds for the GST paid on inputs, including:

- Active pharmaceutical ingredients (APIs).
- Packaging materials.
- Utility expenses like electricity and water (where GST is applicable).

This provision ensures that taxes paid during production do not inflate export prices, enhancing the global appeal of Indian pharmaceuticals. The availability of ITC also improves cash flow for exporters, enabling them to reinvest in their operations.

Benefits for Exporters Under the GST Regime

Zero-Rated Exports and Refund of Accumulated ITC

One of the most significant advantages of GST for exporters is the **zero-rated export policy**. Under this provision:

- No GST is charged on goods or services exported from India.
- Exporters are eligible for refunds on the GST paid on inputs used in the production of exported goods.

Exporters can choose between two refund mechanisms:

1. **Export under Bond or Letter of Undertaking (LUT)**: Allows for zero GST payment at the time of export, with a refund claim for ITC on inputs.
2. **Export with Payment of IGST**: Involves paying IGST on exports and subsequently claiming a refund for the amount paid.

This flexibility ensures that exporters can manage their tax liabilities efficiently.

Simplification of Export Documentation Under GST

The GST regime has significantly simplified export documentation, reducing the compliance burden on exporters. Key improvements include:

- **Unified Returns Filing**: Exporters now file a single set of returns, eliminating the need for separate filings under multiple tax authorities.
- **Digital Submission**: The introduction of e-invoicing and the GST Network (GSTN) has enabled digital submission of invoices and refund applications, reducing paperwork and processing times.
- **E-Way Bill System**: Ensures seamless movement of goods across state borders, minimizing delays and logistical costs.

These changes have streamlined export operations, allowing pharmaceutical exporters to focus on expanding their global footprint.

Challenges Faced by Exporters

Despite its benefits, the GST regime has posed certain challenges for pharmaceutical exporters, particularly in terms of procedural complexities and cash flow management.

Delay in GST Refunds and Working Capital Issues

One of the most common complaints among exporters is the **delay in processing GST refunds**. These delays can have significant consequences:

- **Strained Cash Flow**: Refunds often account for a substantial portion of an exporter's working capital. Delays in receiving these funds can hinder operations, particularly for small and medium enterprises (SMEs).
- **Increased Financing Costs**: Exporters may need to rely on external financing to bridge cash flow gaps, increasing their cost of doing business.

Complexity in Availing Exemptions and Refunds for Deemed Exports

Deemed exports, such as supplies to Export Oriented Units (EOUs) or Special Economic Zones (SEZs), are eligible for GST exemptions or refunds. However, exporters often face challenges in:

- Understanding eligibility criteria.
- Navigating procedural requirements for claiming refunds.
- Dealing with discrepancies in documentation, leading to rejections or delays.

These complexities underscore the need for enhanced clarity and streamlined processes to fully realize the benefits of GST for exporters.

Case Studies of GST Impact on Specific Pharmaceutical Exporters

Success Stories of Improved Efficiency

Case 1: Large-Scale Vaccine Exporter

A leading vaccine manufacturer in India reported significant improvements in efficiency under the GST regime. By leveraging the ITC mechanism, the company reduced production costs by 10%, allowing it to offer competitive pricing in international tenders. Additionally, the adoption of e-invoicing under GST streamlined documentation, reducing the time required to file refund claims from weeks to days.

Case 2: SME Exporting APIs

An SME producing APIs for Southeast Asian markets benefited from the zero-rated export policy. By exporting under an LUT, the company avoided the upfront payment of IGST, preserving its cash flow. The timely processing of ITC refunds enabled the SME to invest in expanding its production capacity, boosting its export volume by 20%.

Instances of Procedural Bottlenecks

Case 1: Delayed Refunds

A mid-sized pharmaceutical exporter faced delays of up to six months in receiving GST refunds due to discrepancies in submitted invoices. The lack of clarity on reconciliation procedures led to multiple follow-ups with tax authorities, increasing administrative overheads and affecting the company's liquidity.

Case 2: Challenges in Deemed Exports

A supplier to SEZs struggled with documentation requirements for claiming GST exemptions. Ambiguities in the rules regarding the classification of deemed exports resulted in the rejection of its claims, forcing the company to reapply and endure further delays.

13.4 GST's Influence on Pharmaceutical Supply Chains

The Goods and Services Tax (GST) has profoundly impacted supply chains across industries, including the pharmaceutical sector. By introducing a unified taxation system, GST has streamlined operations, reduced costs, and improved efficiency. These changes are especially significant for pharmaceutical supply chains, which require precision, transparency, and regulatory compliance at every step. This section explores the effects of GST on domestic and global supply chains, highlights its role in enhancing integration with international markets, and examines PHARMEXCIL's contributions to optimizing supply chains under the GST regime.

Effects on Domestic Supply Chains

Uniform Taxation Across States

Before the implementation of GST, India's pharmaceutical supply chains were fragmented by state-specific taxes, such as VAT, CST, and entry taxes. These taxes created inefficiencies, increased costs, and hindered the seamless movement of goods.

1. **Removal of Interstate Tax Barriers**: GST replaced state-specific taxes with a single, uniform tax structure, enabling pharmaceutical companies to distribute products more efficiently across the country. For example:
    - Manufacturers in Gujarat can now supply medicines to Tamil Nadu without incurring CST or entry taxes, significantly reducing transaction costs.
2. **Centralized Warehousing**: Under the old tax regime, companies maintained multiple warehouses in different states to minimize interstate taxes. GST's uniform taxation allows companies to consolidate their warehouses, reducing infrastructure costs and improving inventory management.
3. **Simplified Tax Compliance**: GST has streamlined tax compliance by requiring pharmaceutical companies to file a single set of returns through the GST Network (GSTN), irrespective of the states they operate in.

Reduction in Logistics Costs and Time

Logistics plays a critical role in pharmaceutical supply chains, where timely delivery can mean the difference between life and death. GST has introduced several efficiencies in this domain:

1. **Elimination of Checkpoints**: Pre-GST, state borders were notorious for delays caused by tax checkpoints. GST's unified framework eliminated the need for such checkpoints, reducing transit times by 20–30%.
2. **Lower Fuel Costs**: Faster transit translates to reduced fuel consumption, lowering logistics costs. For pharmaceutical companies with extensive distribution networks, this has been a game-changer.
3. **Efficiency in Cold Chain Logistics**: Products like vaccines and biologics require temperature-controlled transportation. GST's streamlined processes have improved the reliability of cold chain logistics, ensuring better compliance with quality standards.

Integration of Supply Chains with Global Markets

Improved Transparency and Traceability

GST's emphasis on digital compliance and documentation has enhanced transparency and traceability across pharmaceutical supply chains. Key improvements include:

1. **E-Invoicing**:
   The mandatory implementation of e-invoicing under GST ensures that every transaction is digitally recorded, reducing the scope for tax evasion and errors.
2. **Traceability of Raw Materials and Finished Products**: The ITC mechanism under GST allows companies to trace the origin and movement of raw materials, intermediates, and finished products. This is particularly critical for pharmaceutical exports, where traceability is often a regulatory requirement.
3. **Enhanced Reporting Standards**: The GST system aligns with international best practices, making it easier for Indian pharmaceutical companies to meet the documentation requirements of foreign regulators.

Harmonization with International Tax Systems

By replacing India's fragmented tax structure with a unified system, GST has brought the country closer to international tax frameworks, simplifying trade for exporters. Benefits include:

1. **Easier Customs Processes**: GST's integration with customs duties has streamlined import and export procedures. Exporters can now file a single GST return that covers both domestic and international transactions.
2. **Alignment with Free Trade Agreements (FTAs)**: The simplified tax structure under GST aligns better with the terms of FTAs, allowing Indian exporters to leverage preferential trade agreements more effectively.
3. **Improved Competitiveness**: By reducing costs and enhancing transparency, GST has made Indian pharmaceutical products more competitive in global markets, particularly in price-sensitive regions like Africa and Southeast Asia.

Role of PHARMEXCIL in Optimizing Supply Chains

PHARMEXCIL has played a vital role in helping pharmaceutical companies optimize their supply chains under the GST regime. Its efforts focus on advocacy, capacity building, and technical guidance.

Advocacy for GST Concessions on Raw Materials

1. **Lower GST Rates for APIs**: Active pharmaceutical ingredients (APIs) are the backbone of drug manufacturing. Initially taxed at 18%, APIs were a significant cost factor for manufacturers. PHARMEXCIL's advocacy led to discussions on reducing GST rates for critical APIs, aligning with the government's "Make in India" initiative to boost domestic production.
2. **Exemptions for Essential Inputs**: PHARMEXCIL has consistently pushed for GST exemptions on essential raw materials and intermediates used in life-saving drugs. These efforts aim to reduce manufacturing costs and ensure affordability.
3. **Support for Import Substitution**: By advocating for concessional GST rates on domestically produced inputs, PHARMEXCIL has encouraged local sourcing, reducing dependence on imports and strengthening supply chain resilience.

Guidance on ITC Management to Reduce Costs

1. **Workshops on ITC Optimization**: PHARMEXCIL regularly conducts training sessions to educate exporters on effectively managing input tax credits. These workshops cover:
    - Identifying eligible credits.
    - Avoiding common mistakes in claiming ITC.
    - Maximizing refund claims for zero-rated exports.
2. **Advisory Services for Complex Transactions**: Pharmaceutical supply chains often involve composite and mixed supplies, such as bundled products or services. PHARMEXCIL provides tailored advice to its members on handling such transactions under GST, minimizing tax liabilities.
3. **Advocacy for Simplified Refund Mechanisms**: Recognizing the importance of timely refunds for exporters, PHARMEXCIL has advocated for faster processing of GST refunds. Its efforts have led to improvements in refund timelines and reduced procedural bottlenecks.

13.5 Addressing Sector-Specific Challenges Under GST

The implementation of the Goods and Services Tax (GST) brought significant advantages to India's pharmaceutical sector, but it also introduced sector-specific challenges that required targeted interventions. These challenges stemmed from non-uniformity in tax rates, complexities in taxing pharmaceutical services, and ambiguity in the classification of composite and mixed supplies. PHARMEXCIL has played a pivotal role in addressing these issues, advocating for policy changes and providing practical solutions to its members. This section explores these challenges and the measures taken to overcome them.

Non-Uniformity in GST Rates for APIs and Formulations

The Issue of Disparity in Tax Rates

One of the major challenges faced by the pharmaceutical sector under GST was the **disparity in tax rates** between Active Pharmaceutical Ingredients (APIs) and finished formulations:

- APIs, the raw materials used to produce medicines, were taxed at **18%**, significantly higher than the **5% or 12%** levied on finished formulations.

- This discrepancy led to a higher cost of production for manufacturers, as the tax credit mechanism could not fully offset the input tax burden, particularly for exporters.

For example, a manufacturer producing paracetamol tablets from APIs would pay 18% GST on the raw material but only charge 5% GST on the final product. This created a mismatch in input-output tax credits, increasing operational costs.

PHARMEXCIL's Proposals for Rate Alignment

Recognizing the impact of this disparity, PHARMEXCIL actively engaged with policymakers to propose a more rational tax structure:

1. **Lowering GST Rates on APIs**: PHARMEXCIL advocated for reducing the GST on APIs from 18% to 5%, aligning it with the rate on essential formulations. This proposal aimed to:
    - Reduce production costs.
    - Encourage domestic manufacturing of APIs, supporting the government's "Make in India" initiative.
    - Enhance the competitiveness of Indian formulations in global markets.
2. **Differentiating Critical and Non-Critical APIs**: To balance revenue considerations, PHARMEXCIL suggested a dual-rate structure, with lower GST rates for APIs used in life-saving drugs and higher rates for non-essential APIs.
3. **Encouraging Domestic API Production**: The council emphasized the need for tax incentives to reduce dependency on imported APIs, particularly from China. These recommendations aligned with the government's Production Linked Incentive (PLI) scheme for the pharmaceutical sector.

Taxation of Pharmaceutical Services

The GST regime expanded the tax net to include services provided by the pharmaceutical sector, such as **clinical trials, contract manufacturing**, and **research and development (R&D)**. However, ambiguities in classification and valuation posed challenges for compliance.

Clinical Trials

Clinical trials, a critical component of drug development, involve activities like testing drugs on human subjects to assess their safety and efficacy. Under GST:

- These services were initially taxed at **18%**, leading to higher costs for pharmaceutical companies.
- Exported clinical trial services qualified as zero-rated supplies, but procedural complexities in claiming refunds created hurdles for service providers.

PHARMEXCIL's Response:

- Advocated for exemptions or reduced tax rates on clinical trial services conducted within India to promote the country as a global hub for clinical research.
- Conducted workshops to guide service providers on documentation requirements for claiming GST refunds on exported services.

Contract Manufacturing

Contract manufacturing involves outsourcing the production of pharmaceutical products. Under GST:

- Contract manufacturing services were taxed at **18%**, significantly higher than the rate on finished goods (5% or 12%).
- This mismatch led to cost escalation and disputes over classification.

PHARMEXCIL's Response:

- Sought clarifications on the distinction between "job work" and "manufacturing services" under GST, advocating for uniform tax treatment.
- Recommended that GST on contract manufacturing be aligned with the rate applicable to the final product.

Research and Development (R&D) Services

Pharmaceutical R&D services, including drug discovery and formulation development, faced similar challenges:

- Taxation at 18% increased the cost of innovation, deterring investment in new drug development.
- Exported R&D services required meticulous documentation for claiming GST refunds, adding to administrative burdens.

PHARMEXCIL's Response:

- Advocated for tax incentives or exemptions for R&D services to encourage domestic innovation.
- Provided member companies with detailed guidelines on managing GST compliance for R&D projects.

Complexities in Handling Composite and Mixed Supplies

Understanding Composite and Mixed Supplies

The GST regime introduced the concepts of **composite supplies** and **mixed supplies**, which posed classification challenges for the pharmaceutical sector:

- **Composite Supply**: Two or more goods/services supplied together, where one is a principal supply. GST is charged at the rate applicable to the principal supply.
    - Example: A bundled package of a drug and its administration service.
- **Mixed Supply**: Two or more independent goods/services supplied together, with GST charged at the highest applicable rate.
    - Example: A promotional kit containing medicines and unrelated items like water bottles.

Challenges Faced by Pharmaceutical Companies

1. **Classification Ambiguity**: Companies often struggled to determine whether a supply was composite or mixed, leading to disputes and penalties.
2. **Higher Tax Burdens**: Incorrect classification of a composite supply as mixed resulted in higher GST liability.
3. **Documentation Requirements**: The need for detailed invoicing and record-keeping added to compliance costs.

Clarifications Provided by PHARMEXCIL to its Members

PHARMEXCIL played a crucial role in helping pharmaceutical companies navigate these complexities:

1. **Detailed Guidelines**: Issued advisories explaining the distinction between composite and mixed supplies, using real-world examples relevant to the pharmaceutical sector.
2. **Case-Specific Support**: Provided member companies with personalized advice on classifying complex transactions to ensure accurate GST filings.
3. **Advocacy for Simplification**: Engaged with the GST Council to propose simpler rules for classifying bundled supplies, reducing the scope for disputes and errors.

13.6 GST and Trade Policy Alignment

The introduction of the Goods and Services Tax (GST) has not only streamlined taxation but also significantly influenced India's trade policies.

By aligning with existing export schemes and complementing broader trade objectives, GST has created a more conducive environment for Indian pharmaceutical exports. This section examines the synergy between GST and India's export policies, explores how it supports export growth targets, and highlights PHARMEXCIL's role in integrating GST benefits with export schemes.

Synergy Between GST and India's Export Policies

Alignment with Foreign Trade Policy (FTP)

India's **Foreign Trade Policy (FTP)** is designed to promote exports by providing incentives, simplifying processes, and ensuring global competitiveness. GST integrates seamlessly with the objectives of the FTP, creating a cohesive framework for boosting pharmaceutical exports.

1. **Zero-Rated Exports**: Under GST, exports are treated as **zero-rated supplies**, meaning:
    - No GST is charged on export transactions.
    - Exporters are eligible for refunds of the GST paid on inputs, ensuring that tax is not embedded in the cost of exported goods.
    - This aligns with the FTP's goal of minimizing tax burdens on exporters.
2. **Export Promotion Capital Goods (EPCG) Scheme**: GST compliance is integrated with the EPCG scheme, allowing pharmaceutical exporters to import capital goods without paying GST, provided they fulfill export obligations. This has facilitated investment in advanced manufacturing technologies.
3. **Export-Oriented Units (EOUs) and SEZs**: The GST regime complements FTP benefits for EOUs and Special Economic Zones (SEZs), ensuring seamless tax exemptions and ITC refunds. This synergy has strengthened India's position as a global pharmaceutical hub.

Leveraging GST for Achieving Export Growth Targets

The pharmaceutical sector, contributing over **USD 25 billion annually** to India's export economy, relies on a competitive pricing structure to maintain its global leadership. GST has played a pivotal role in enabling this by:

1. **Eliminating Cascading Taxes**: By allowing input tax credits across the supply chain, GST reduces production costs, enabling exporters to price their products competitively in international markets.

2. **Streamlined Logistics**: The uniform tax structure and the e-way bill system have enhanced supply chain efficiency, ensuring timely delivery of pharmaceutical products to global markets.
3. **Ease of Compliance**: GST's digital framework simplifies compliance, making it easier for exporters to claim benefits under trade policies like Duty Drawback and Advance Authorization schemes.

PHARMEXCIL's Role in Integrating GST Benefits with Export Schemes

PHARMEXCIL has been instrumental in ensuring that pharmaceutical exporters fully leverage GST benefits while aligning with India's export policies. Its initiatives focus on advocacy, capacity building, and practical support for exporters.

Duty Drawback Schemes and GST Linkage

1. **Understanding Duty Drawback Under GST**: The Duty Drawback scheme allows exporters to claim refunds on customs duties and GST paid on inputs. Under GST, PHARMEXCIL has worked to:
    - Clarify the applicability of Duty Drawback alongside ITC refunds.
    - 'Advocate for exporters' ability to claim benefits without duplication or procedural delays.
2. **Resolving Transitional Issues**: The transition from the pre-GST tax regime created confusion regarding the overlap of GST and Duty Drawback benefits. PHARMEXCIL played a crucial role in:
    - Engaging with the Ministry of Commerce and Industry to address exporters' concerns.
    - Issuing detailed advisories on navigating the new system.
3. **Enhancing Accessibility**: By collaborating with customs authorities, PHARMEXCIL has streamlined the process for pharmaceutical exporters to claim Duty Drawback benefits, ensuring faster disbursements.

Market Access Initiative (MAI) and GST Compliance

The **Market Access Initiative (MAI)** is a flagship scheme under the FTP, designed to promote Indian exports by providing financial assistance for market penetration, branding, and participation in international trade events. GST compliance is a critical aspect of utilizing MAI benefits, and

PHARMEXCIL has actively supported its members in this regard.

1. **Promoting Awareness**: PHARMEXCIL organizes workshops and webinars to educate exporters on:
    - The interplay between GST compliance and eligibility for MAI funding.
    - The importance of accurate invoicing and GST filing for claiming MAI benefits.
2. **Facilitating MAI Applications**: Exporters often face challenges in linking GST documentation with MAI applications. PHARMEXCIL provides hands-on guidance to ensure that:
    - GST-compliant invoices and returns are properly aligned with MAI requirements.
    - Exporters can seamlessly claim reimbursements for international marketing activities.
3. **Addressing Procedural Bottlenecks**: Delays in processing MAI claims due to GST-related discrepancies can impact exporters' cash flow. PHARMEXCIL acts as a liaison between exporters and government bodies, resolving these issues efficiently.

Recap of GST's Transformative Role in the Pharmaceutical Sector

GST has revolutionized the pharmaceutical industry by addressing long-standing inefficiencies and aligning the sector with international best practices. Its transformative effects are evident in three key areas:

1. **Simplification of Tax Processes**: The unification of multiple indirect taxes into a single GST framework has significantly reduced compliance complexity for pharmaceutical companies. Businesses now navigate a streamlined system with fewer procedural redundancies and better transparency.
2. **Enhanced Efficiency**: The removal of cascading taxes and interstate barriers has improved supply chain efficiency, enabling pharmaceutical products to reach domestic and international markets faster. Innovations like the e-way bill system and digital invoicing have further streamlined operations.
3. **Cost Reduction**: By allowing seamless input tax credits (ITC) and eliminating double taxation, GST has reduced the overall cost of production. This has made Indian pharmaceutical products more competitive in global markets, contributing to export growth and reinforcing India's position as a leading pharmaceutical exporter.

Acknowledgment of PHARMEXCIL's Contributions to Easing GST Transitions

PHARMEXCIL's proactive and adaptive approach has been instrumental in helping the pharmaceutical sector navigate the complexities of GST. Key contributions include:

1. **Advocacy and Policy Support**: PHARMEXCIL worked tirelessly to represent the industry's concerns during the GST transition, advocating for rate rationalizations, streamlined refund mechanisms, and incentives for exporters.
2. **Capacity Building for Exporters**: Through workshops, webinars, and advisory services, PHARMEXCIL empowered exporters to comply with GST requirements effectively. Its efforts ensured that even small and medium enterprises (SMEs) could adapt to the new regime without significant disruptions.
3. **Collaboration with Policymakers**: By acting as a bridge between the government and the industry, PHARMEXCIL played a vital role in refining GST processes and resolving sector-specific challenges. Its contributions have ensured that the pharmaceutical sector operates smoothly within the framework of the Goods and Services Tax (GST). By addressing industry concerns, PHARMEXCIL has facilitated a more streamlined tax regime that minimizes operational disruptions and enhances compliance.

Key outcomes of this collaboration include:

1. **Resolution of GST Rate Issues**: PHARMEXCIL actively advocated for lower tax rates on life-saving drugs, essential medicines, and raw materials, ensuring affordability for consumers and viability for manufacturers.
2. **Clarity on Input Tax Credit (ITC)**: It worked with policymakers to resolve ambiguities surrounding ITC claims, enabling pharmaceutical companies to offset their tax liabilities more effectively and maintain competitive pricing.
3. **Simplification of Export Refunds**: PHARMEXCIL contributed to refining the GST refund process for exporters, ensuring timely disbursement of refunds for zero-rated supplies, which is critical for maintaining liquidity in export-driven industries.
4. **Special Provisions for Contract Manufacturing**: The council's efforts led to better recognition of the unique challenges in contract manufacturing, with policy adjustments to address cascading taxes and streamline supply chain operations.

5. **Promotion of Ease of Doing Business**: By voicing the industry's concerns, PHARMEXCIL helped the government introduce measures that simplify compliance, such as e-invoicing, digital reporting mechanisms, and grievance redressal systems.

Through these initiatives, PHARMEXCIL has not only supported the growth of the pharmaceutical sector but also contributed to India's emergence as a global pharmaceutical hub, ensuring that the GST regime aligns with the sector's operational and strategic needs. Its role as a mediator and advocate underscores its importance in shaping policies that balance government objectives with industry requirements.

CHAPTER 14

The Manufacture and Licensing of Medicinal Products

Introduction

When discussing the manufacture and licensing of medicinal products, it is vital to appreciate how these processes serve as the foundation of modern healthcare systems worldwide. From the initial conception of a drug to its eventual use by a patient, the journey is marked by meticulous planning, stringent regulations, and a commitment to safety and efficacy. This introduction sets the stage for understanding the complexities and significance of these interconnected processes, beginning with definitions and their broader implications, moving through their historical evolution, and concluding with their role in today's healthcare landscape.

Definition and Scope

Manufacturing medicinal products involves far more than simply assembling ingredients into a final form. It is a multifaceted process that integrates science, engineering, quality assurance, and compliance with regulatory requirements. But what exactly constitutes the manufacture of medicinal products? Broadly, it includes all activities related to the preparation, processing, packaging, and labeling of pharmaceutical goods. This process begins with sourcing raw materials and active pharmaceutical ingredients (APIs) and extends through formulation, quality testing, and final packaging.

Consider a common pain reliever like paracetamol. Its manufacture involves several stages: the precise weighing of active and inactive ingredients, blending them to form a homogenous mixture, compressing the mixture into tablets, and finally coating, labeling, and packaging the finished product. Each of these steps is governed by protocols designed to ensure the product's consistency, safety, and efficacy. This detailed orchestration ensures that every tablet delivers the promised therapeutic benefit without unintended harm.

Licensing, on the other hand, acts as a gatekeeper for these manufactured products. Why is licensing so important? Without it, there would be no uniform standard to ensure that a drug is safe for consumption, effective in treating the condition it claims to address, and manufactured under hygienic conditions. Licensing encompasses the evaluation of manufacturing facilities, processes, and products before they can enter the market. It ensures that companies adhere to Good Manufacturing Practices (GMP) and comply with regulatory standards.

Through licensing, regulators provide an additional layer of scrutiny. Consider the case of vaccines. During the COVID-19 pandemic, the accelerated development of vaccines highlighted the importance of licensing. Despite the urgency, regulatory bodies such as the US FDA and EMA ensured that vaccines underwent rigorous evaluations for safety and efficacy before granting emergency use authorizations. Licensing reassures the public that medicines meet a baseline of reliability, even in unprecedented situations.

Historical Perspective

The journey toward modern manufacturing and licensing practices is steeped in history, marked by incremental advancements and transformative events. Initially, the preparation of medicines was an artisanal craft. Apothecaries and early chemists prepared remedies based on local knowledge, often relying on rudimentary methods and anecdotal efficacy. These practices, while innovative for their time, lacked standardization and were prone to errors.

The industrial revolution catalyzed significant changes. By the late 19th century, pharmaceutical companies began to emerge, leveraging advancements in chemistry and engineering to produce medicines on a larger scale. However, the absence of regulations led to several public health crises. One notable example is the tragic case of diethylene glycol poisoning in the 1930s, where an improperly tested solvent used in a sulfa drug formulation caused over 100 deaths in the United States. This incident underscored the urgent need for regulatory oversight and led to the enactment of the US Federal Food, Drug, and Cosmetic Act in 1938.

Globally, regulatory frameworks continued to evolve throughout the 20th century. In Europe, the formation of the European Medicines Agency (EMA) in 1995 marked a significant milestone in harmonizing regulations across member states. Meanwhile, organizations like the World Health Organization (WHO) provided international guidance, emphasizing the need for Good Manufacturing Practices (GMP) and quality control standards.

In India, the journey began with the establishment of the Drugs and Cosmetics Act of 1940, which laid the foundation for regulating medicinal products. Over the years, amendments to the Act have expanded its scope, aligning Indian regulations with global standards. The establishment of the Central Drugs Standard Control Organization (CDSCO) further strengthened India's regulatory framework, enabling the country to become a leading exporter of generic medicines.

The historical evolution of these frameworks is a testament to the increasing recognition of the risks associated with unregulated medicines. Each regulatory milestone reflects a lesson learned from past challenges, reinforcing the importance of vigilance and standardization in safeguarding public health.

Relevance in Modern Healthcare

In today's world, where diseases are becoming increasingly complex and patient populations are growing, the role of manufacturing and licensing has never been more critical. These processes form the backbone of pharmaceutical innovation, ensuring that life-saving drugs reach those who need them most.

Manufacturing and licensing contribute significantly to public health by enabling access to high-quality medicines. Imagine a scenario without these systems in place. Patients would face inconsistent drug quality, unreliable efficacy, and increased risks of adverse reactions. Thanks to stringent manufacturing protocols and licensing requirements, such scenarios are largely mitigated, fostering trust in the healthcare system.

Furthermore, these processes enhance global drug availability and affordability. India, often referred to as the "pharmacy of the world," exemplifies this dynamic. By adhering to global manufacturing standards and obtaining necessary licenses, Indian pharmaceutical companies supply affordable generics to developing countries, addressing critical healthcare gaps. The availability of generic antiretroviral drugs, for instance, has been instrumental in combating the HIV/AIDS epidemic in Africa.

The role of licensing extends beyond quality assurance. It drives innovation by creating a structured pathway for new drug development. Pharmaceutical companies invest heavily in research and development (R&D), knowing that successful licensing will allow them to recoup costs through market exclusivity and sales. This system incentivizes the discovery of novel therapies while maintaining rigorous safety standards.

Licensing also ensures preparedness during public health emergencies. The rapid approval of COVID-19 vaccines under emergency use authorizations showcased how regulatory systems can adapt without compromising safety. Manufacturing facilities worldwide scaled up production, supported by licenses that ensured adherence to quality standards. This coordinated effort highlighted the symbiotic relationship between manufacturing and licensing in addressing global crises.

14.1 Regulatory Framework

The manufacture and licensing of medicinal products operate within a robust regulatory framework designed to ensure the safety, efficacy, and quality of medicines worldwide. Regulatory frameworks, established by national and international bodies, provide the legal and procedural guidelines for manufacturers and licensors to follow. This ensures consistency in quality and protects public health by preventing the distribution of substandard or unsafe drugs. This section explores the global regulatory landscape, delves into country-specific regulations, and examines the legal basis for licensing medicinal products.

Global Regulatory Landscape

Regulating medicinal products on a global scale requires cooperation between international bodies and national authorities. International organizations like the World Health Organization (WHO), International Council for Harmonisation of Technical Requirements for Pharmaceuticals for Human Use (ICH), US Food and Drug Administration (US FDA), and European Medicines Agency (EMA) play pivotal roles in setting standards and facilitating harmonization across countries.

The WHO acts as a global custodian of public health, issuing guidelines on Good Manufacturing Practices (GMP) and drug quality standards. Its Prequalification Programme ensures that essential medicines meet international standards before being distributed in low-income countries. For example, antimalarial drugs certified under this program are widely used in malaria-prone regions.

The ICH focuses on harmonizing technical requirements for pharmaceuticals across the US, EU, and Japan. Its guidelines are categorized into three primary areas: quality (Q), safety (S), and efficacy (E). The ICH Q7 guideline, for instance, provides GMP standards for active pharmaceutical ingredients, while ICH E6 outlines principles for Good Clinical Practice

(GCP). These guidelines minimize redundant testing, lower development costs, and expedite the licensing process for global markets.

The US FDA, a key regulatory authority, ensures that all drugs sold in the United States are safe and effective. The FDA's rigorous drug approval process includes preclinical evaluations, clinical trials, and a detailed review of manufacturing facilities. Similarly, the EMA oversees drug approval for the European Union, emphasizing centralized procedures that allow a single application to cover all EU member states. This centralized approach facilitates faster market access for innovative therapies.

Harmonization efforts like those spearheaded by the ICH have simplified the regulatory landscape for manufacturers targeting multiple markets. However, challenges persist in aligning regional requirements, particularly in areas like post-marketing surveillance and biosimilar approvals.

Country-Specific Regulations

Despite global harmonization efforts, regulatory frameworks still vary significantly across countries, reflecting differences in legal systems, public health priorities, and economic conditions. Understanding these distinctions is critical for manufacturers seeking licenses in multiple regions.

India: In India, the manufacture and licensing of medicinal products are governed by the Drugs and Cosmetics Act, 1940, and its associated rules. The Central Drugs Standard Control Organization (CDSCO) acts as the national regulatory authority, overseeing drug approval, quality control, and compliance. Manufacturing licenses are issued by state-level authorities under the CDSCO's guidance. Indian regulations are particularly stringent on generic drug manufacturing, with Indian companies supplying a significant proportion of the world's generics.

United States: The FDA's regulatory framework is among the most comprehensive globally. Manufacturers must submit a New Drug Application (NDA) for innovative drugs or an Abbreviated New Drug Application (ANDA) for generics. The process involves preclinical studies, phased clinical trials, and inspections of manufacturing facilities. The FDA's emphasis on post-marketing surveillance ensures that adverse events are tracked and addressed promptly.

European Union: The EMA coordinates the evaluation and supervision of medicinal products across member states. Its centralized procedure allows a single marketing authorization to be valid throughout the EU. However, manufacturers can also opt for decentralized or mutual recognition procedures for products intended for specific member states.

Japan: The Pharmaceuticals and Medical Devices Agency (PMDA) regulates the licensing of medicinal products in Japan. The PMDA collaborates with the Ministry of Health, Labour, and Welfare (MHLW) to ensure that drugs meet quality, safety, and efficacy standards. Japan places a strong emphasis on pharmacovigilance and post-marketing studies.

Each region's licensing procedures have unique requirements, such as documentation formats, clinical trial standards, and timelines. For instance, while the FDA and EMA accept the Common Technical Document (CTD) format for drug submissions, India requires additional local clinical data for certain categories of drugs. These variations necessitate tailored approaches by manufacturers seeking multi-country licenses.

Legal Basis for Licensing

The legal foundation for licensing medicinal products is established through national acts, regulations, and guidelines that outline the obligations of manufacturers and the penalties for non-compliance.

In **India**, the Drugs and Cosmetics Act, 1940, serves as the cornerstone of pharmaceutical regulation. It defines the standards for manufacturing, importing, and selling drugs, as well as the penalties for violations. For example, manufacturing a drug without a valid license can result in imprisonment of up to five years and fines. The Act also empowers regulatory authorities to inspect manufacturing facilities, seize non-compliant products, and revoke licenses.

In the **United States**, the Federal Food, Drug, and Cosmetic Act governs drug manufacturing and licensing. It grants the FDA authority to approve new drugs, regulate manufacturing practices, and enforce compliance through inspections and penalties. Companies found guilty of non-compliance face severe consequences, including product recalls, monetary fines, and criminal charges.

The **European Union** relies on a combination of EU directives and regulations to govern medicinal products. The EMA enforces compliance through rigorous pre- and post-authorization evaluations. Companies failing to meet EU standards may face marketing suspensions, legal penalties, and reputational damage.

Globally, non-compliance with licensing regulations has led to significant public health crises and economic losses. The thalidomide disaster of the 1960s, where inadequate testing resulted in widespread birth defects, prompted stricter licensing laws worldwide. Similarly, the heparin contamination incident of 2008 highlighted the need for stringent oversight in manufacturing and supply chains.

Enforcement mechanisms include regular inspections, market recalls, and penalties for violations. Regulatory bodies also maintain adverse event reporting systems to monitor drug safety post-approval. For example, India's pharmacovigilance program collects and analyzes data on adverse drug reactions, enabling swift corrective actions.

14.2 Manufacturing of Medicinal Products

The manufacturing of medicinal products represents a critical stage in the journey from drug discovery to patient use. It involves highly regulated processes designed to ensure that every product meets stringent safety, efficacy, and quality standards. This section provides a detailed examination of the manufacturing process, Good Manufacturing Practices (GMP), quality assurance and control, types of facilities, and the challenges manufacturers face.

Manufacturing Process Overview

The manufacturing process for medicinal products is a complex sequence of activities that transforms raw materials into finished products ready for distribution and use. It requires precision, consistency, and strict adherence to regulatory standards.

Steps from Raw Materials to Finished Products

1. **Procurement of Raw Materials**: The process begins with sourcing high-quality raw materials, including active pharmaceutical ingredients (APIs) and excipients. Suppliers are often audited to ensure compliance with regulatory standards.
2. **Weighing and Mixing**: Ingredients are measured with precision to ensure consistency in dosage. Advanced mixers and granulators are used to achieve uniformity.
3. **Formulation**: Depending on the product type, the formulation process involves blending ingredients to create tablets, capsules, syrups, or injectable solutions.
4. **Processing and Manufacturing**: Tablets, for example, undergo compression, while liquid formulations require filtration and sterilization. Technologies such as freeze-drying are used for sensitive products like biologics.

5. **Packaging**: Products are packed into bottles, blister packs, or vials. Packaging must protect the product while meeting labeling requirements.
6. **Final Quality Checks**: Before distribution, finished products undergo rigorous quality control testing to ensure compliance with specifications.

Key Technologies and Methodologies in Modern Manufacturing

- **Continuous Manufacturing**: A shift from batch processes to continuous systems enhances efficiency and reduces waste.
- **Automation and Robotics**: Automating repetitive tasks minimizes human error and ensures precision.
- **3D Printing**: Emerging technologies like 3D printing enable the production of personalized medicine with precise dosages tailored to individual patients.
- **Single-Use Systems**: These disposable technologies reduce contamination risks, particularly in biologics manufacturing.

Good Manufacturing Practices (GMP)

GMP is a cornerstone of pharmaceutical manufacturing, ensuring that products are consistently produced and controlled according to quality standards.

Core Principles and Importance of GMP

- **Documentation**: Detailed records of every step in the manufacturing process are mandatory to ensure traceability.
- **Validation**: Processes, equipment, and facilities must be validated to confirm they consistently produce high-quality products.
- **Personnel Training**: Employees must be trained in GMP principles and their specific responsibilities.
- **Hygiene and Sanitation**: Facilities and equipment must be regularly cleaned to prevent contamination.

Implementation and Certification Processes

- Manufacturers must establish GMP-compliant processes and conduct regular internal audits.
- Certification is provided by national and international regulatory bodies after thorough inspections.

- Examples include WHO GMP certification and the EU GMP standards, both of which are prerequisites for exporting medicines to many countries.

Quality Assurance and Control

Quality assurance (QA) and quality control (QC) are essential in maintaining the integrity of medicinal products throughout the manufacturing process.

Role of Quality Assurance in Maintaining Product Integrity

- QA ensures that all manufacturing processes comply with established protocols and regulatory requirements.
- It encompasses the design and monitoring of processes to prevent defects before they occur.

Methods and Techniques for Quality Control

- **Analytical Testing**: Techniques such as High-Performance Liquid Chromatography (HPLC) and Mass Spectrometry are used to verify the chemical composition of products.
- **Microbiological Testing**: Ensures that products, particularly injectables, are free from microbial contamination.
- **Stability Testing**: Evaluates how environmental factors like temperature and humidity affect product efficacy over time.
- **Visual Inspections**: Finished products are visually examined for defects in appearance, labeling, or packaging.

Types of Manufacturing Facilities

The type of facility used for manufacturing plays a crucial role in compliance and efficiency.

Dedicated vs. Multi-Product Facilities

- **Dedicated Facilities**: Designed for a single product or product category, reducing cross-contamination risks. These are often used for products like vaccines or biologics.
- **Multi-Product Facilities**: Capable of manufacturing multiple products but require rigorous cleaning and validation processes between production cycles.

Importance of Facility Design and Layout in Compliance

- Facilities must be designed to prevent cross-contamination and ensure smooth workflow.

- Segregation of areas for raw material storage, manufacturing, and packaging is mandatory.
- Advanced HVAC systems are required to maintain air quality and control particulate matter.

Challenges in Manufacturing

Pharmaceutical manufacturing faces numerous challenges that require innovative solutions.

Supply Chain Issues

- Sourcing APIs and raw materials can be disrupted by geopolitical tensions or natural disasters.
- Dependence on imports for APIs has been a significant issue in countries like India.

Technology Integration

- Transitioning to advanced manufacturing technologies requires significant investment and training.
- Legacy systems often pose compatibility challenges with modern technologies.

Regulatory Hurdles

- Navigating the regulatory requirements of multiple markets can delay product launches.
- Non-compliance with GMP or QC standards can lead to product recalls and reputational damage.

Case Studies of Common Manufacturing Pitfalls and Solutions

- **Case 1**: A major recall of a batch of vaccines due to contamination during filling highlighted the importance of aseptic techniques. The manufacturer implemented automation to reduce manual intervention.
- **Case 2**: A shortage of raw materials during the COVID-19 pandemic disrupted global supply chains. Manufacturers diversified their sourcing to mitigate future risks.

The manufacturing of medicinal products is a highly sophisticated process requiring meticulous attention to detail at every stage. By adhering to GMP, implementing robust QA and QC systems, and navigating challenges effectively, manufacturers can ensure that their products meet the highest standards of safety and efficacy.

14.3 Licensing of Medicinal Products

Licensing of medicinal products is a critical process that ensures drugs meet safety, efficacy, and quality standards before reaching the market. It serves as a regulatory checkpoint, safeguarding public health while providing pharmaceutical companies the legal right to manufacture, market, and distribute their products. This section delves into the importance of licensing, the types of licenses required, detailed procedures, post-licensing obligations, and common barriers that companies face during the process.

Importance of Licensing

Licensing plays a foundational role in the pharmaceutical industry, ensuring that every medicinal product released to the public meets stringent regulatory standards.

Ensuring Product Safety and Efficacy

Licensing evaluates a product's safety profile and therapeutic benefits based on preclinical and clinical trial data. It ensures that medicines are effective in treating their intended conditions while minimizing risks. Without licensing, substandard or harmful products could reach consumers, leading to serious health consequences.

For instance, thalidomide, a drug introduced in the 1960s without thorough regulatory oversight, caused severe birth defects in thousands of children. This incident underscored the importance of licensing frameworks that require comprehensive safety testing.

Regulatory Oversight and Market Authorization

Licensing ensures that manufacturers comply with established guidelines, such as Good Manufacturing Practices (GMP). Regulatory bodies like the US FDA, EMA, and CDSCO oversee the licensing process, granting market authorization only to products that pass rigorous scrutiny. This oversight builds trust among healthcare providers and patients, ensuring that approved medicines consistently meet quality standards.

Market authorization also enables regulators to monitor products post-launch, identifying and addressing adverse events, thereby maintaining a safety net even after the product is on the market.

Types of Licenses

The licensing of medicinal products encompasses several categories, each tailored to specific stages of the product lifecycle.

Manufacturing License

This license permits the production of medicinal products. It ensures that manufacturing facilities comply with GMP and that the processes used are consistent, controlled, and capable of producing high-quality medicines. Regulatory bodies inspect facilities before granting this license.

Marketing Authorization

This license allows the product to be marketed and sold. It involves a detailed review of the drug's safety, efficacy, and quality through data submitted in a Common Technical Document (CTD) format. Marketing authorization is granted by agencies like the US FDA or EMA.

Distribution License

This license governs the storage and transportation of medicinal products. It ensures that supply chain operations maintain product integrity, particularly for temperature-sensitive items like vaccines.

Licenses for APIs vs. Finished Formulations

Licensing requirements differ for active pharmaceutical ingredients (APIs) and finished formulations. While APIs require documentation of their purity, stability, and manufacturing process, finished formulations must also include bioavailability and bioequivalence data.

For example, in India, the CDSCO mandates separate licenses for manufacturing APIs and formulations, each requiring detailed technical dossiers and facility inspections.

Licensing Procedures

The process of obtaining a license for medicinal products involves multiple steps, each designed to ensure compliance with regulatory standards.

Steps Involved in Obtaining a Manufacturing License

1. **Application Submission**: Manufacturers submit an application to the relevant authority (e.g., CDSCO, US FDA).
2. **Facility Inspection**: Regulators inspect the manufacturing site to verify GMP compliance.
3. **Document Review**: The application must include detailed process descriptions, equipment specifications, and quality control measures.
4. **Approval or Rejection**: If the facility meets all requirements, the license is granted. Otherwise, deficiencies must be addressed before reapplication.

Submission Requirements

- **Dossiers**: These include manufacturing details, stability data, and specifications.
- **Clinical Trial Data**: For marketing authorization, regulators review data from preclinical and clinical studies to assess the drug's safety and efficacy.
- **Environmental Impact Assessments**: Required in some regions to ensure that manufacturing practices do not harm the environment.

Post-Licensing Obligations

Licensing does not end with market entry; manufacturers are required to adhere to several ongoing obligations to maintain compliance.

Periodic Reviews and Renewals

Regulatory authorities conduct periodic reviews to ensure continued compliance with licensing conditions. Licenses often have fixed validity periods, requiring renewal applications that demonstrate adherence to quality standards.

Compliance Monitoring and Adverse Event Reporting

Manufacturers must implement pharmacovigilance systems to monitor adverse drug reactions and report them to regulatory bodies. This real-world data helps regulators reassess the product's risk-benefit profile and take corrective actions if needed, such as updating labeling or restricting use.

For instance, the EMA's EudraVigilance system collects and evaluates adverse event reports from across Europe, enabling swift regulatory interventions.

Common Barriers to Licensing

The licensing process, while essential, is often fraught with challenges that can delay product launches or increase costs.

Regulatory Complexities and Delays

Different regions have varying requirements, creating a complex web of regulations that manufacturers must navigate. For instance, while the US FDA focuses heavily on clinical trial design, the EMA requires detailed risk management plans. Harmonization efforts like ICH guidelines have reduced some disparities but have not eliminated them entirely.

Approval timelines can also be a significant barrier. A typical new drug application in the US takes 10-12 months for review, and delays are common if additional data or clarifications are requested.

Issues with Documentation and Facility Compliance

Incomplete or inaccurate documentation is a leading cause of licensing delays. For example, if stability data is insufficient or missing, regulators may reject the application outright. Similarly, manufacturing facilities that fail to meet GMP standards during inspections must undergo costly upgrades and re-inspections.

Case Examples of Barriers

1. **Data Deficiencies**: A generic drug manufacturer faced a two-year delay in obtaining FDA approval due to inconsistencies in bioequivalence data.
2. **Facility Non-Compliance**: An Indian pharmaceutical company had its EU license suspended after failing to address deficiencies in its sterilization processes.

Key Components in Licensing Applications

The licensing process for medicinal products is meticulous and demands detailed documentation to ensure compliance with regulatory requirements. A comprehensive application includes technical dossiers, safety and efficacy data, environmental assessments, and evidence of validated manufacturing processes. These components collectively demonstrate that the product is safe, effective, and manufactured according to stringent quality standards.

Technical Documentation

Technical documentation forms the backbone of a licensing application, providing regulators with a detailed understanding of the product and its manufacturing process.

Quality Dossiers (Common Technical Document - CTD Format)
The CTD format is a globally accepted standard that organizes technical data into five modules:

1. **Module 1**: Administrative and product information (region-specific requirements).
2. **Module 2**: Summary documents, including overviews of quality, nonclinical, and clinical data.

3. **Module 3**: Quality documentation, including information on the manufacturing process, raw materials, and finished product specifications.
4. **Module 4**: Nonclinical study reports, focusing on pharmacology and toxicology data.
5. **Module 5**: Clinical study reports, detailing trial results.

The CTD format streamlines the submission process for multiple regions, reducing redundancy and expediting reviews.

Stability Data, Specifications, and Batch Records

- **Stability Data**: Stability studies assess how environmental factors like temperature, humidity, and light affect the product's quality over time. These studies support the determination of shelf life and storage conditions.
- **Specifications**: Detailed criteria for raw materials, in-process controls, and finished products ensure consistency in quality. For example, specifications for a tablet might include acceptable ranges for weight, hardness, and dissolution rate.
- **Batch Records**: Comprehensive records of each manufacturing batch provide traceability and demonstrate adherence to the approved process. These records include information on raw material lot numbers, processing conditions, and quality control test results.

Safety and Efficacy Data

Regulators require robust evidence that a medicinal product is safe and effective for its intended use.

Preclinical and Clinical Trial Results

- **Preclinical Studies**: Conducted in laboratories and on animal models, these studies evaluate the pharmacological effects, toxicity, and safety margins of the product. For example, acute toxicity studies determine the lethal dose in animal models, providing a baseline for clinical trials.
- **Clinical Trials**: Divided into phases, these trials assess the product's safety and efficacy in humans:
    - **Phase 1**: Focuses on safety, involving a small group of healthy volunteers.
    - **Phase 2**: Evaluates efficacy and optimal dosing in patients with the target condition.

- **Phase 3**: Confirms efficacy and monitors adverse reactions in a larger population.
- **Phase 4**: Post-marketing surveillance to track long-term effects and rare side effects.

Detailed reports of these trials, including study protocols, statistical analyses, and adverse event data, must be included in the application.

Requirements for Bioequivalence Studies

For generic drugs, bioequivalence studies are essential to demonstrate that the generic version performs similarly to the branded product. These studies compare parameters such as:

- **Cmax (Maximum Plasma Concentration)**: The peak drug concentration in the bloodstream.
- **AUC (Area Under the Curve)**: The total drug exposure over time.

Regulatory agencies like the FDA and EMA have specific thresholds (e.g., 80%-125% for key parameters) that must be met for bioequivalence approval.

Environmental Impact Assessments

Environmental sustainability is increasingly important in licensing applications, reflecting a broader commitment to public health and ecological well-being.

Evaluating the Ecological Footprint of Manufacturing

- Assessments examine the impact of manufacturing processes on air, water, and soil quality. For example, emissions from chemical synthesis or the disposal of pharmaceutical waste must comply with local and international environmental standards.
- Companies may be required to adopt pollution control measures, such as effluent treatment plants, to minimize environmental harm.

Regulatory Mandates for Sustainability

- Many regulatory bodies now require an Environmental Impact Assessment (EIA) as part of the licensing process. For instance, the European Union mandates that pharmaceutical companies adhere to the EU Environmental Liability Directive.
- Sustainability initiatives, such as reducing carbon footprints and transitioning to green chemistry, are increasingly rewarded with expedited reviews or incentives.

Validation and Certification

Validation and certification ensure that the manufacturing process consistently produces high-quality products and complies with market requirements.

Process Validation Protocols

- **Prospective Validation**: Conducted before production begins, ensuring that the process parameters achieve desired outcomes.
- **Concurrent Validation**: Performed during routine production to confirm consistency.
- **Retrospective Validation**: Applied to products already in distribution, using historical batch data to verify process reliability.

Process validation includes:

- Equipment qualification (Installation, Operational, and Performance Qualification - IQ/OQ/PQ).
- Validation of critical steps like sterilization or lyophilization.

Certifications Needed for Export and Local Market Access

- **Certificate of Pharmaceutical Product (CPP)**: Issued by the regulatory authority of the manufacturing country, confirming that the product complies with GMP and is authorized for marketing.
- **Good Manufacturing Practices (GMP) Certification**: Required by most importing countries as proof of compliance with international quality standards.
- **WHO Prequalification**: Ensures that products meet WHO standards, enabling procurement by UN agencies and global health initiatives.

The key components of licensing applications provide a comprehensive framework for regulators to assess the safety, efficacy, and quality of medicinal products. By meticulously addressing each component, manufacturers can navigate the complex regulatory landscape and achieve market authorization efficiently.

14.4 International Trade and Export Licensing

The global trade of medicinal products plays a pivotal role in ensuring access to essential medicines across borders. International trade and export licensing are governed by complex regulatory frameworks that vary from country to country. These processes require manufacturers to comply with additional requirements, certifications, and harmonized standards to ensure the safety, efficacy, and quality of products in international markets. This section explores licensing for export markets, the role of export promotion bodies, and challenges in harmonizing regulatory standards across countries.

Licensing for Export Markets

Exporting medicinal products requires manufacturers to fulfill stringent requirements that extend beyond domestic licensing. These additional regulations aim to ensure that exported products meet the importing country's safety and quality standards.

Additional Requirements for Exporting Medicinal Products When exporting medicinal products, manufacturers must meet the following requirements:

1. **Export Licenses**: Issued by the regulatory authority of the manufacturing country, these licenses confirm that the product complies with local and international standards.
2. **Documentation**: Exporters must provide detailed dossiers, including information about the product's composition, manufacturing process, and quality control measures.
3. **Importing Country Requirements**: Regulations vary widely between countries. For example, the US FDA mandates compliance with its specific guidelines, while the EU requires adherence to its directives and standards.
4. **Pharmacovigilance**: Exporters must establish a pharmacovigilance system to monitor adverse effects in the importing country.

Certification Needs

Key certifications required for export include:

- **Certificate of Pharmaceutical Product (CPP)**: Issued by the regulatory authority of the exporting country, the CPP confirms that the product is authorized for sale and complies with Good Manufacturing Practices (GMP). It is a prerequisite for entering many international markets.
- **WHO Prequalification**: This certification ensures that products meet WHO standards, enabling their inclusion in global procurement programs, such as those run by UNICEF or the Global Fund.
- **Free Sale Certificate (FSC)**: Confirms that the product is freely sold in the manufacturing country, assuring importing countries of its safety and efficacy.

For example, Indian pharmaceutical companies exporting generic drugs to Africa often require both CPPs and WHO prequalification to meet the standards of local regulatory authorities.

Role of Export Promotion Bodies

Export promotion bodies provide essential support to pharmaceutical manufacturers, enabling them to navigate complex international markets and regulatory requirements.

Support from Organizations Like PHARMEXCIL

The Pharmaceuticals Export Promotion Council of India (PHARMEXCIL) is a key organization supporting Indian pharmaceutical exporters. Its roles include:

1. **Market Intelligence**: Providing exporters with detailed reports on market trends, demand patterns, and regulatory updates for various countries.
2. **Trade Fairs and Delegations**: Organizing participation in international trade fairs and delegations to promote Indian pharmaceutical products.
3. **Training Programs**: Conducting workshops on export documentation, compliance, and best practices.

For instance, PHARMEXCIL's support has helped Indian companies expand their presence in markets like Southeast Asia and Latin America, where regulatory landscapes are evolving rapidly.

Assistance with International Trade Agreements and Compliance

Export promotion bodies also assist manufacturers in leveraging international trade agreements, such as:

- **Bilateral and Multilateral Agreements**: Helping exporters benefit from reduced tariffs or simplified customs procedures under trade pacts like the ASEAN Free Trade Area (AFTA) or Comprehensive and Progressive Agreement for Trans-Pacific Partnership (CPTPP).
- **Regulatory Compliance Support**: Providing guidance on meeting the specific requirements of countries under these agreements.

For example, PHARMEXCIL has collaborated with Indian embassies to streamline regulatory approvals in countries like South Africa, ensuring faster market access for Indian generics.

Harmonization Challenges

While efforts to harmonize regulatory standards aim to simplify international trade, significant challenges remain due to varying requirements and practices across countries.

Differences in Regulatory Standards Across Countries

Each country's regulatory framework reflects its unique public health priorities, leading to inconsistencies in licensing requirements:

1. **Clinical Trial Data Requirements**: Some countries, like the US, require extensive clinical trial data, while others may rely on bioequivalence studies for generics.
2. **GMP Standards**: Although GMP principles are broadly consistent, specific guidelines for facility inspections and documentation vary.
3. **Post-Market Surveillance**: Expectations for adverse event reporting and monitoring differ significantly, complicating compliance for exporters.

For instance, exporting a single product to both the US and EU may require separate submissions tailored to FDA and EMA standards, increasing the time and cost of market entry.

Efforts to Streamline Licensing for Global Trade

To address these challenges, several initiatives have been launched to harmonize regulatory processes:

1. **ICH Guidelines**: The International Council for Harmonisation has developed common technical requirements for pharmaceuticals, simplifying submissions for multiple markets.
2. **Mutual Recognition Agreements (MRAs)**: Agreements between countries or regions, such as the EU-US MRA, enable mutual acceptance of GMP inspections, reducing duplication.
3. **WHO Collaborative Procedure**: This program accelerates the registration of WHO-prequalified products in participating countries, benefiting global health initiatives.

While these efforts have made significant progress, achieving full harmonization remains an ongoing challenge. Differences in language, infrastructure, and economic priorities continue to hinder a seamless global licensing process.

International trade and export licensing are indispensable for ensuring the global availability of high-quality medicinal products. By meeting additional requirements, leveraging support from export promotion bodies, and addressing harmonization challenges, manufacturers can successfully navigate the complexities of international markets. These efforts not only benefit exporters but also contribute to improving global health by making essential medicines accessible to those in need.

14.5 Emerging Trends in Manufacturing and Licensing

As the pharmaceutical industry evolves, manufacturing and licensing processes are undergoing transformative changes driven by advancements in technology, evolving regulations, and a growing emphasis on sustainability. These trends are reshaping how medicinal products are developed, produced, and brought to market, ensuring that the industry remains agile and responsive to global challenges.

Technological Advancements

The integration of advanced technologies into pharmaceutical manufacturing and licensing is revolutionizing the industry, improving efficiency, reducing errors, and enhancing transparency.

Role of AI, Machine Learning, and Blockchain in Manufacturing

- **Artificial Intelligence (AI)**: AI is transforming pharmaceutical manufacturing by optimizing production processes, predicting equipment failures, and ensuring consistent product quality. For example, AI-driven algorithms can analyze vast amounts of data to identify the most efficient manufacturing conditions or predict potential deviations before they occur.
- **Machine Learning (ML)**: ML models are being used to enhance drug formulation and predict outcomes in manufacturing. They can identify patterns in historical data to improve yield rates and minimize waste.
- **Blockchain Technology**: Blockchain is being adopted to improve supply chain transparency and prevent counterfeit medicines. By maintaining an immutable ledger, blockchain ensures that every step of the manufacturing and distribution process is traceable. For instance, Pfizer and IBM have piloted blockchain solutions to track medicines from production to end-users, reducing fraud and ensuring authenticity.

Automation in Quality Control and Process Monitoring

- **Robotics and Automation**: Automated systems are replacing manual processes in quality control laboratories, ensuring precision in testing and reducing human errors. Robotic arms are used for sample handling, while automated analyzers conduct tests with minimal intervention.
- **Real-Time Monitoring**: Sensors and IoT (Internet of Things) devices provide real-time monitoring of production environments, ensuring that conditions such as temperature, humidity, and pressure remain within acceptable ranges. This approach minimizes the risk of product defects and ensures compliance with regulatory standards.

Evolving Regulations

Regulatory frameworks are adapting to keep pace with advancements in drug development and public health demands, leading to new challenges and opportunities for manufacturers and licensors.

Changes Driven by New Drug Types (e.g., Biologics, Gene Therapy)

- **Biologics**: The rise of biologics, such as monoclonal antibodies and vaccines, has introduced new complexities in manufacturing and licensing. Regulatory agencies require additional data on stability, immunogenicity, and batch-to-batch consistency.
- **Gene Therapy**: Gene therapy products, which offer potential cures for genetic disorders, have unique regulatory requirements. Agencies like the US FDA have issued specific guidelines for the development, testing, and approval of these products. For instance, products like Luxturna (for retinal dystrophy) required extensive data on long-term efficacy and safety.
- **Advanced Therapy Medicinal Products (ATMPs)**: The EU's focus on ATMPs highlights the need for specialized manufacturing environments and accelerated approval pathways for innovative therapies.

Impact of Pandemics and Public Health Emergencies on Regulatory Policies

- The COVID-19 pandemic demonstrated how regulatory bodies can adapt to public health crises. Emergency Use Authorizations (EUAs) allowed vaccines and therapeutics to reach the market faster while maintaining safety standards. For example, the US FDA and EMA provided expedited pathways for COVID-19 vaccines, prioritizing clinical trial data reviews and rolling submissions.

- Regulatory agencies are also enhancing collaboration during emergencies. Initiatives like the WHO's COVAX program streamlined global vaccine distribution by prequalifying products and coordinating supply chains.

Focus on Sustainability

Sustainability is becoming a critical focus in pharmaceutical manufacturing, with regulators and companies striving to minimize environmental impact while maintaining efficiency.

Green Manufacturing Practices

- **Reducing Waste**: Companies are adopting process intensification techniques to reduce material and energy use. Continuous manufacturing, for instance, minimizes waste compared to traditional batch processes.
- **Solvent Recovery and Recycling**: Advanced solvent recovery systems are being used to recycle and reuse solvents in the manufacturing process, reducing chemical waste.
- **Biodegradable Packaging**: Pharmaceutical companies are exploring sustainable packaging options, such as biodegradable blister packs and recycled materials, to minimize plastic waste.

Regulatory Incentives for Sustainable Operations

- Regulatory agencies are introducing policies that encourage sustainable practices. For example, the EU's Green Deal includes provisions to reduce emissions from pharmaceutical manufacturing and incentivizes companies adopting green technologies.
- Certifications such as ISO 14001 for environmental management systems are becoming increasingly important for market access. Manufacturers with these certifications demonstrate their commitment to sustainability and gain a competitive edge.

14.6 Challenges and Practical Considerations

The manufacture and licensing of medicinal products involve numerous challenges that can impact timelines, costs, and regulatory compliance. These hurdles require manufacturers and licensors to adopt proactive strategies to mitigate risks while ensuring the delivery of safe and effective medicines to the market. This section examines the critical challenges in manufacturing and licensing, along with illustrative case studies and lessons learned.

Manufacturing Challenges

The pharmaceutical industry faces significant challenges in maintaining high-quality standards while managing cost pressures and sourcing reliable raw materials.

Cost Pressures and Maintaining High-Quality Standards

Manufacturing medicinal products demands substantial investment in infrastructure, technology, and workforce training. High-quality standards must be maintained throughout production to meet stringent regulatory requirements. However, these demands often lead to escalating costs:

- **Infrastructure Costs**: Setting up and maintaining GMP-compliant facilities requires significant capital investment. For example, sterile manufacturing facilities need advanced HVAC systems, cleanrooms, and automated equipment, all of which increase operational costs.
- **Labor Costs**: Hiring and retaining skilled personnel trained in GMP and quality assurance practices adds to expenses.
- **Regulatory Compliance**: Frequent audits, validation procedures, and documentation requirements contribute to ongoing operational costs.

Balancing these expenses while keeping the final product affordable is particularly challenging for manufacturers of generic drugs. For example, Indian generic manufacturers face intense competition in pricing while adhering to the high standards demanded by global markets such as the US and EU.

Issues in Raw Material Procurement and Sourcing

- **Supply Chain Vulnerabilities**: The pharmaceutical supply chain heavily relies on global sourcing of active pharmaceutical ingredients (APIs). Disruptions caused by geopolitical tensions, natural disasters, or pandemics can delay production. For instance, during the COVID-19 pandemic, the dependence on China for APIs led to supply shortages for many Indian manufacturers.
- **Quality Concerns**: Ensuring the quality and consistency of raw materials is another challenge. Poor-quality APIs can lead to product recalls, regulatory action, and reputational damage.
- **Cost Fluctuations**: Variability in the cost of raw materials, driven by market demand or trade restrictions, adds to manufacturing complexities.

To mitigate these risks, companies are increasingly diversifying their supply chains and investing in local API manufacturing capabilities.

Licensing Bottlenecks

Obtaining licenses for medicinal products is a time-intensive process that involves navigating complex regulatory landscapes and bureaucratic hurdles.

Long Approval Timelines and Bureaucratic Hurdles

- **Extended Review Periods**: Regulatory bodies often require extensive documentation and detailed analyses, leading to long approval timelines. For example, a New Drug Application (NDA) with the US FDA typically takes 10-12 months for review, while delays can extend this period further.
- **Bureaucratic Challenges**: Manufacturers face hurdles such as inefficiencies in communication with regulators, inconsistent feedback, and repeated requests for additional data, which prolong the licensing process.

For small and medium enterprises (SMEs), these delays can result in financial strain, as they rely on timely product launches to recoup R&D investments.

Managing Changing Regulatory Requirements

- **Dynamic Regulations**: Licensing requirements frequently evolve due to scientific advancements, new safety concerns, or public health crises. Manufacturers must stay updated and adapt to these changes.
- **Regional Variations**: Divergent regulatory standards across countries add complexity for manufacturers seeking multi-country licenses. For instance, while the US FDA and EMA share similarities in their requirements, differences in post-marketing surveillance expectations can complicate compliance for global products.

Proactive engagement with regulatory agencies and participation in harmonization initiatives, such as those led by the ICH, can help manufacturers navigate these challenges.

Case Studies

Real-world examples provide valuable insights into the challenges faced by pharmaceutical companies and the strategies they employed to overcome them.

Case Study 1: Manufacturing Disruptions Due to Supply Chain Issues

- **Scenario**: A generic drug manufacturer in India faced production delays when API imports from China were disrupted due to geopolitical tensions. This led to shortages of critical medicines in domestic and export markets.

- **Resolution**: The company diversified its API sourcing by developing partnerships with suppliers in Europe and establishing an in-house API manufacturing unit. This reduced its dependence on a single source and ensured continuity in production.

Lessons Learned

- Diversifying supply chains can mitigate risks associated with geopolitical or logistical disruptions.
- Investing in local production capabilities enhances resilience and reduces costs over time.

Case Study 2: Licensing Delays for an Innovative Drug

- **Scenario**: A biotechnology company developing a novel gene therapy experienced licensing delays due to evolving regulatory requirements. Regulators requested additional clinical data and long-term safety monitoring, which extended the review period by two years.
- **Resolution**: The company collaborated with regulators to design post-marketing surveillance plans and provided interim data from ongoing clinical trials. This proactive approach demonstrated the product's safety and efficacy, leading to eventual approval.

Lessons Learned

- Early and continuous engagement with regulatory agencies can streamline the approval process.
- Flexibility in adapting to regulatory feedback is crucial for overcoming licensing challenges.

Case Study 3: Quality Failures Leading to Product Recalls

- **Scenario**: A multinational pharmaceutical company faced a global recall of a blood pressure medication after impurities were detected in the API, leading to regulatory scrutiny and financial losses.
- **Resolution**: The company implemented enhanced quality assurance measures, including supplier audits and real-time monitoring systems. It also worked with regulators to establish stricter impurity limits and prevent future occurrences.

Lessons Learned

- Rigorous quality assurance systems are essential for maintaining product integrity and avoiding regulatory actions.
- Collaboration with regulators during crises can restore trust and minimize long-term impacts.

Successful Licensing Stories

Licensing is a complex process that requires meticulous planning, comprehensive documentation, and adherence to regulatory guidelines. Several companies have demonstrated exemplary practices in obtaining licenses efficiently and effectively.

Examples of Companies Excelling in Obtaining Licenses

1. **Sun Pharmaceutical Industries (India)**
    - Sun Pharma successfully navigated US FDA and EMA requirements to launch multiple generic drugs in international markets.
    - Their ability to submit detailed and accurate Common Technical Document (CTD) dossiers and conduct high-quality clinical trials was instrumental in meeting regulatory expectations.
2. **Moderna (USA)**
    - During the COVID-19 pandemic, Moderna expedited the licensing process for its mRNA-based COVID-19 vaccine by leveraging Emergency Use Authorizations (EUAs).
    - The company's transparent collaboration with regulatory bodies and comprehensive safety data from clinical trials enabled swift approvals in multiple countries.

Factors Contributing to Their Success

- **Robust Regulatory Knowledge**: Companies that excel in licensing invest in expert teams with a thorough understanding of regulatory requirements across regions.
- **Early Engagement with Regulators**: Open communication with regulatory agencies helps address concerns proactively and speeds up the review process.
- **Investment in Quality Assurance**: High-quality manufacturing and data integrity are critical for gaining the trust of regulatory bodies.

Manufacturing Excellence

Excellence in pharmaceutical manufacturing is marked by adherence to Good Manufacturing Practices (GMP), innovative technologies, and a commitment to quality.

Highlighting State-of-the-Art Manufacturing Facilities

1. **Roche's Biologics Manufacturing Facility (Singapore)**
   - This facility uses single-use bioreactor technology, which enhances flexibility and reduces contamination risks.
   - Real-time monitoring systems ensure consistent quality and efficiency.
2. **Dr. Reddy's Laboratories (India)**
   - Dr. Reddy's has established GMP-compliant facilities with advanced automation and robotics for tablet production, ensuring uniformity and precision.
   - Their integrated supply chain model reduces production costs while maintaining high standards.

Best Practices for Compliance and Innovation

- **Continuous Manufacturing**: Transitioning from batch to continuous processes increases efficiency and reduces waste.
- **Automated Quality Control**: Robotics and AI-driven systems minimize human error and ensure consistent product quality.
- **Sustainability**: Companies adopting green manufacturing practices, such as solvent recovery and energy-efficient processes, demonstrate leadership in environmental responsibility.

Lessons from Non-Compliance

Regulatory failures often lead to severe consequences, including product recalls, financial losses, and damage to reputations. These case studies illustrate the importance of compliance and proactive risk management.

Case Studies of Regulatory Failures

1. **Ranbaxy Laboratories (India)**
   - Ranbaxy faced a $500 million fine from the US FDA for data falsification and GMP violations in 2013.
   - The company's failure to maintain data integrity and address inspection findings resulted in a ban on exporting products to the US.
2. **Valsartan Contamination Scandal (Global)**
   - Several manufacturers recalled valsartan, a common hypertension medication, due to the presence of carcinogenic impurities in the API.

  - The root cause was traced to inadequate quality control during manufacturing processes.

Impact of Non-Compliance on Businesses and Consumers

- **For Businesses**: Non-compliance can lead to financial penalties, loss of market access, and long-term damage to brand reputation. For instance, Ranbaxy's inability to meet US FDA standards significantly reduced its global market share.
- **For Consumers**: Regulatory failures undermine patient trust and can lead to serious health risks, as seen in the valsartan contamination case, where patients were exposed to harmful impurities over prolonged periods.

Key Takeaways from Case Studies

- **Proactive Compliance**: Companies that prioritize compliance from the outset avoid costly delays and penalties.
- **Investment in Quality Systems**: Ensuring robust quality assurance and control mechanisms is non-negotiable for regulatory success.
- **Collaboration with Regulators**: Open communication and transparency during the licensing process foster trust and expedite approvals.

14.7 Conclusion

The manufacture and licensing of medicinal products form the backbone of the pharmaceutical industry, ensuring that patients receive safe, effective, and high-quality medicines. This concluding section synthesizes the key insights from the previous chapters and provides recommendations for addressing challenges while embracing emerging opportunities.

Summary of Key Points

Recap of the Importance of Manufacturing and Licensing

Manufacturing and licensing are integral to the pharmaceutical value chain, guaranteeing that products meet stringent safety and efficacy standards before reaching consumers. The manufacturing process transforms raw materials into finished products through precise, regulated procedures, while licensing acts as a safeguard, ensuring that these products comply with national and international regulations. Together, they uphold public health, build consumer trust, and drive the growth of the pharmaceutical industry.

Key Challenges and Emerging Opportunities

While the pharmaceutical sector has made significant advancements, it faces persistent challenges, including:

- Cost pressures in maintaining high-quality standards during manufacturing.
- Complex licensing requirements, varying across regions, leading to delays and financial strain.
- Supply chain vulnerabilities, especially in sourcing APIs and managing distribution.

Despite these hurdles, emerging trends offer promising opportunities:

- Technological advancements, such as AI, blockchain, and continuous manufacturing, are revolutionizing efficiency and quality.
- Evolving regulatory frameworks are adapting to new therapies like biologics and gene therapies, paving the way for innovation.
- Sustainability initiatives in manufacturing align with global environmental goals, creating competitive advantages for early adopters.

The Way Forward

Recommendations for Businesses and Regulators

To navigate the evolving landscape of pharmaceutical manufacturing and licensing, businesses and regulators must work collaboratively:

- **For Businesses**:
    - Invest in cutting-edge technologies to streamline manufacturing processes and enhance compliance.
    - Develop robust supply chains with diversified sourcing to mitigate risks.
    - Foster a culture of quality by prioritizing GMP adherence and continuous employee training.
- **For Regulators**:
    - Simplify and harmonize licensing processes across regions to reduce redundancy and accelerate approvals.
    - Provide clear and transparent guidelines for emerging therapies and technologies.
    - Strengthen collaboration with industry stakeholders to anticipate challenges and co-create solutions.

Emphasis on Innovation, Compliance, and Collaboration

Innovation must remain at the forefront of the pharmaceutical industry, driving the development of novel therapies and efficient manufacturing techniques. Compliance with global standards ensures the safety and efficacy of products, reinforcing public trust in medicines. Collaboration between manufacturers, regulators, and global health organizations is critical to addressing challenges such as pandemics, supply chain disruptions, and environmental concerns.

Closing Reflection

The manufacture and licensing of medicinal products represent a delicate balance of science, regulation, and business strategy. By embracing innovation, adhering to stringent compliance standards, and fostering collaboration across stakeholders, the pharmaceutical industry can continue to deliver life-saving medicines to patients worldwide while adapting to the challenges of a rapidly changing world. The future of healthcare depends on the resilience and adaptability of these foundational processes, ensuring that no patient is left behind in the quest for better health.

CHAPTER 15

Pharmaceuticals Export Promotion Council of India (PHARMEXCIL)

Introduction

The pharmaceutical industry is often referred to as the "lifeline industry" because of its critical role in improving health outcomes, increasing life expectancy, and ensuring the well-being of populations globally. While individual companies are central to drug development and production, the broader ecosystem relies on organizations and councils that enable trade, promote standards, and foster collaboration across borders. One such organization is the **Pharmaceuticals Export Promotion Council of India (PHARMEXCIL)**. Established as a bridge between India's pharmaceutical industry and the global market, PHARMEXCIL has played an indispensable role in ensuring that Indian pharmaceutical products achieve widespread acceptance and success internationally.

Overview of PHARMEXCIL

Definition and Purpose of PHARMEXCIL

At its core, the **Pharmaceuticals Export Promotion Council of India (PHARMEXCIL)** serves as the official agency under the Ministry of Commerce and Industry, Government of India, tasked with promoting Indian pharmaceutical exports. But what does this really mean? Imagine a large, vibrant marketplace where products from across the globe compete for attention. For Indian pharmaceutical products, PHARMEXCIL is both the ambassador and the advocate, ensuring that these products not only stand out but also comply with stringent global quality standards. Its purpose extends beyond mere promotion; it provides strategic direction, regulatory guidance, and a unified voice for the Indian pharmaceutical export community.

Through trade fairs, policy advocacy, and capacity-building programs, PHARMEXCIL has cemented its role as an essential player in India's economic and healthcare diplomacy. It is responsible for ensuring that India's pharmaceutical exports remain competitive, comply with international regulations, and address the evolving needs of diverse global markets.

Establishment: History and Foundation Year

The story of PHARMEXCIL is deeply interwoven with the evolution of India's pharmaceutical industry. Established in **2004**, PHARMEXCIL was born out of the recognition that India's burgeoning pharmaceutical sector required a dedicated body to promote exports systematically. Before its establishment, pharmaceutical exports were often fragmented, with individual companies navigating international markets without adequate governmental support or cohesive representation.

Why was 2004 the turning point? In the early 2000s, India's pharmaceutical industry was undergoing a transformation driven by the **TRIPS agreement (Trade-Related Aspects of Intellectual Property Rights)**, which required adherence to global patent laws. This new compliance burden created both opportunities and challenges for Indian manufacturers. Recognizing the need to address these challenges, the Government of India founded PHARMEXCIL as a platform to support exporters, educate them about evolving international regulations, and enable them to compete on the global stage.

Since its inception, PHARMEXCIL has grown exponentially, representing over **4,000 member companies** spanning a wide array of pharmaceutical categories, including **active pharmaceutical ingredients (APIs)**, **formulations**, **herbal products**, **nutraceuticals**, and **biopharmaceuticals**.

Role in India's Pharmaceutical Sector

PHARMEXCIL is more than a promotional body; it is a cornerstone of India's pharmaceutical growth story. To understand its role, let us consider the multiple ways it supports the industry:

1. **Market Intelligence and Research:** Imagine a pharmaceutical company planning to expand into Latin America. Where does it start? PHARMEXCIL provides detailed market intelligence reports, helping exporters identify high-demand products, regulatory requirements, and market entry strategies. These reports are often

based on painstaking research, ensuring accuracy and practical utility.

2. **Regulatory Support:** International markets have diverse regulatory landscapes. PHARMEXCIL acts as a guide, assisting companies in understanding and meeting the requirements of organizations like the **U.S. FDA**, **EMA (European Medicines Agency)**, and **WHO**. By organizing workshops and consultations, PHARMEXCIL demystifies complex regulations and reduces the barriers to market entry.
3. **Advocacy:** Exporters often face trade barriers like tariffs, non-tariff restrictions, or import bans. PHARMEXCIL represents Indian exporters in global forums and negotiates with foreign governments to resolve trade disputes. For example, when Indian generic drugs faced skepticism in certain African markets, PHARMEXCIL launched campaigns to demonstrate their quality and efficacy.
4. **Promotion of Indian Pharmaceuticals:** PHARMEXCIL organizes **international trade fairs**, **buyer-seller meets**, and **pharma expos**. These events are designed to showcase India's capabilities and foster partnerships. For instance, its flagship event, the **International Pharma and Healthcare Exhibition (iPHEX)**, attracts participants from over **120 countries** annually.

By integrating these functions, PHARMEXCIL has become an indispensable pillar of India's pharmaceutical ecosystem.

Importance in Global Pharmaceutical Trade

Contributions to India's Export Economy

To appreciate the significance of PHARMEXCIL, one must consider the staggering scale of India's pharmaceutical exports. As of **2023**, India is the **largest supplier of generic medicines globally**, accounting for approximately **20% of global generics exports**. This dominance didn't happen overnight. Behind this success lies a well-coordinated effort, with PHARMEXCIL playing a central role.

Consider the case of **antiretroviral drugs (ARVs)** used to treat HIV/AIDS. India supplies over **70% of the global demand for ARVs**, a feat made possible by PHARMEXCIL's consistent advocacy for Indian pharmaceutical companies in international markets. By facilitating partnerships with global organizations like **UNICEF** and **WHO**, PHARMEXCIL ensured that Indian manufacturers could meet both the quality expectations and supply demands of these agencies.

Furthermore, PHARMEXCIL has been instrumental in reducing India's trade deficit. Pharmaceutical exports generated over **USD 25 billion** in revenue in **2022-2023**, contributing significantly to India's foreign exchange reserves. Every dollar earned in exports reflects the cumulative efforts of countless stakeholders, coordinated through PHARMEXCIL's strategic interventions.

Position in Global Pharmaceutical Exports

Where does India stand globally, and how has PHARMEXCIL influenced this position? India ranks among the top **five exporters of pharmaceuticals worldwide**, alongside giants like the United States, China, and Germany. This achievement is especially noteworthy given India's unique challenges, including a vast population, resource constraints, and the need for affordable healthcare solutions.

Real-world examples highlight the impact of PHARMEXCIL's initiatives. Consider the **COVID-19 pandemic**: when global supply chains were disrupted, PHARMEXCIL facilitated the export of **hydroxychloroquine**, **paracetamol**, and **vaccines** to over **150 countries**. These efforts not only reinforced India's reputation as the "pharmacy of the world" but also showcased its commitment to global health.

PHARMEXCIL's efforts have also helped India penetrate niche markets. For example:

- In **Africa**, Indian generic drugs are a lifeline for millions of patients.
- In **Eastern Europe**, Indian APIs dominate the supply chain for local manufacturers.
- In **Latin America**, herbal medicines and nutraceuticals from India are gaining popularity.

15.1 Historical Background

The historical context of PHARMEXCIL provides a fascinating insight into how India's pharmaceutical industry transitioned from a primarily domestic-focused sector to a global powerhouse. The establishment of PHARMEXCIL is not merely a bureaucratic event but a significant milestone that reflects India's strategic intent to capitalize on its growing pharmaceutical capabilities. This section explores the initiatives that led to the council's formation, its legal framework, and the milestones that have shaped its journey over the years.

Formation and Legal Framework

Initiatives That Led to the Creation of PHARMEXCIL

In the late 1990s and early 2000s, India's pharmaceutical industry was experiencing a period of rapid growth. Indian pharmaceutical companies were making inroads into global markets with cost-effective generics, active pharmaceutical ingredients (APIs), and formulations. However, this growth brought with it significant challenges, including compliance with international regulations, addressing trade barriers, and maintaining competitive pricing. To address these issues, the Government of India identified the need for a specialized body that could promote exports and support the industry in navigating the complexities of international trade.

The foundation for PHARMEXCIL was laid through a series of consultations between industry leaders, policymakers, and trade experts. The primary goal was to create an organization that could act as a bridge between Indian pharmaceutical companies and global markets. By 2004, this vision materialized with the establishment of PHARMEXCIL under the Ministry of Commerce and Industry.

Role of the Ministry of Commerce and Industry

The Ministry of Commerce and Industry played a pivotal role in the creation and operationalization of PHARMEXCIL. Recognizing the pharmaceutical sector as a critical component of India's export economy, the ministry provided the necessary institutional backing and resources to ensure the council's success. PHARMEXCIL was designated as the official export promotion council for pharmaceuticals, giving it a mandate to represent India's pharmaceutical exporters on a global platform.

The ministry continues to guide PHARMEXCIL by providing policy direction, funding for promotional activities, and support for international trade negotiations. This collaborative relationship has enabled the council to address both the micro-level needs of individual exporters and the macro-level challenges faced by the industry.

Regulatory Framework Under Which PHARMEXCIL Operates

PHARMEXCIL operates under the Foreign Trade Policy of India, which provides a legal framework for export promotion councils. As a non-profit organization, it is governed by the Companies Act, ensuring transparency and accountability in its operations. The council is also subject to oversight by the Ministry of Commerce and Industry, which ensures alignment with national trade policies and objectives.

The regulatory framework empowers PHARMEXCIL to:

- Organize trade fairs and buyer-seller meets.

- Provide financial assistance under export promotion schemes.
- Represent Indian exporters in international trade forums.
- Disseminate information on market trends, regulatory changes, and export opportunities.

This framework has been instrumental in enabling PHARMEXCIL to effectively fulfill its mandate.

15.2 Milestones in Development

Key Achievements Since Its Inception

Since its establishment in 2004, PHARMEXCIL has achieved several milestones that highlight its contribution to India's pharmaceutical sector. One of its earliest successes was the organization of the International Pharma and Healthcare Exhibition (iPHEX), which has since become a flagship event. This exhibition provides a platform for Indian pharmaceutical companies to showcase their products and capabilities to an international audience, fostering collaborations and business opportunities.

Another notable achievement was PHARMEXCIL's role in securing international recognition for Indian generic drugs. By actively engaging with regulators and stakeholders in key markets, the council helped establish the credibility of Indian pharmaceutical products, particularly in regions like Africa, Latin America, and Southeast Asia.

During the COVID-19 pandemic, PHARMEXCIL's efforts were critical in maintaining the global supply chain for essential medicines. The council facilitated the export of life-saving drugs and vaccines, ensuring that Indian manufacturers could meet global demands despite logistical challenges.

Expansion in Member Base and Global Reach

Over the years, PHARMEXCIL's member base has grown significantly, reflecting the increasing participation of Indian pharmaceutical companies in global trade. From a few hundred members at its inception, the council now represents over 4,000 companies, including small and medium enterprises, multinational corporations, and public-sector undertakings.

PHARMEXCIL's global reach has also expanded considerably. Initially focused on traditional markets like the United States and Europe, the council has successfully opened new avenues in emerging markets such as Africa, Latin America, and the Middle East. These regions now account for a substantial portion of India's pharmaceutical exports, demonstrating the effectiveness of PHARMEXCIL's strategies.

The council has also played a key role in fostering public-private partnerships, enabling Indian companies to participate in international projects and initiatives. For example, PHARMEXCIL has facilitated collaborations with organizations like the World Health Organization and the United Nations, enhancing the global visibility of Indian pharmaceutical products.

15.3 Organizational Structure

The organizational structure of PHARMEXCIL is designed to ensure efficient governance, promote industry participation, and facilitate effective decision-making. It reflects the council's commitment to representing the diverse stakeholders of India's pharmaceutical export industry while maintaining a high level of transparency and accountability. This section explores the governance and leadership framework of PHARMEXCIL, as well as the membership structure that forms its backbone.

Governance and Leadership

Board of Directors and Key Leadership Positions

The governance of PHARMEXCIL is spearheaded by a **Board of Directors**, which acts as the central decision-making body. The board consists of senior representatives from the pharmaceutical industry, government officials, and domain experts. This diverse composition ensures that the council's policies and initiatives address the varied needs of its stakeholders while aligning with national trade objectives.

The board is led by a **Chairperson**, who is elected from among the members of the council. The Chairperson plays a pivotal role in providing strategic direction, representing the council in high-level discussions, and ensuring that its objectives are met. Supporting the Chairperson is the **Vice-Chairperson**, who assists in operational and policy-related matters.

Other key leadership positions include:

- **Executive Director:** Responsible for overseeing the day-to-day operations of the council, the Executive Director acts as a bridge between the board and the council's staff. This role involves implementing the board's decisions, managing administrative functions, and coordinating with external stakeholders.
- **Secretary-General:** Focused on regulatory and compliance aspects, the Secretary-General ensures that PHARMEXCIL operates within

the legal framework and fulfills its obligations to both the government and its members.

The board also appoints specialized committees to handle specific functions such as export promotion, market research, and capacity building. These committees are composed of experts with deep knowledge in their respective areas, enabling the council to deliver targeted and impactful initiatives.

Decision-Making Processes and Hierarchies

The decision-making processes within PHARMEXCIL are hierarchical yet inclusive. Major policy decisions are made by the Board of Directors, often in consultation with industry stakeholders and government representatives. These decisions are then translated into actionable plans by the Executive Director and the operational teams.

To ensure that the council remains responsive to the needs of its members, PHARMEXCIL frequently organizes consultative meetings and forums. These platforms allow members to voice their concerns, propose ideas, and provide feedback on the council's initiatives.

The hierarchical structure ensures accountability at every level:

- The **Board** sets the overall strategy and monitors its implementation.
- The **Executive Team** manages the execution of initiatives, guided by the board's directives.
- **Regional Offices** act as the council's local representatives, facilitating member engagement and addressing region-specific challenges.

This layered yet collaborative approach allows PHARMEXCIL to function efficiently while staying attuned to the dynamic needs of the pharmaceutical export sector.

Membership

Eligibility Criteria for Membership

Membership in PHARMEXCIL is open to entities involved in the pharmaceutical export industry, provided they meet certain eligibility criteria. These include:

1. **Legal Registration:** The entity must be registered under applicable laws in India, such as the Companies Act, the Societies Registration Act, or other relevant statutes.

2. **Export Activity:** The applicant must be actively engaged in the export of pharmaceutical products, services, or related items.
3. **Compliance:** The entity must adhere to all regulatory requirements, both domestic and international, and maintain high ethical standards in its operations.

Applicants are required to submit documentation such as proof of registration, export performance data, and financial statements. Once approved, members gain access to a wide range of benefits and services.

Categories of Members

PHARMEXCIL categorizes its members based on their role in the pharmaceutical export ecosystem. These categories include:

1. **Manufacturers:** Companies that produce active pharmaceutical ingredients (APIs), formulations, herbal products, or other pharmaceutical goods. These members benefit from initiatives aimed at showcasing Indian manufacturing capabilities on global platforms.
2. **Exporters:** Entities primarily engaged in the export of pharmaceutical products, including trading houses and distributors. Exporters rely on PHARMEXCIL for market intelligence, trade facilitation, and advocacy in resolving trade disputes.
3. **Service Providers:** Organizations that offer services such as clinical research, contract manufacturing, regulatory consulting, or quality testing. These members benefit from networking opportunities and access to global clients through PHARMEXCIL events.
4. **Affiliate Members:** Academic institutions, industry associations, and research organizations that contribute to the pharmaceutical sector indirectly. These members engage with PHARMEXCIL for knowledge sharing, collaborations, and capacity-building programs.

This categorization allows the council to tailor its services and initiatives to the specific needs of each group, ensuring maximum impact and relevance.

Benefits of Being a Member

Membership in PHARMEXCIL offers a plethora of benefits, making it a valuable asset for entities involved in pharmaceutical exports. Some key advantages include:

1. **Market Intelligence:** Members receive access to detailed reports on market trends, export opportunities, and regulatory updates. These insights help them identify growth areas and mitigate risks.
2. **Trade Facilitation:** PHARMEXCIL assists members in navigating complex international trade regulations, resolving trade barriers, and

participating in global tenders. This support is particularly valuable for small and medium enterprises (SMEs) looking to expand their export footprint.

3. **Promotional Activities:** Members can showcase their products and services at international trade fairs, buyer-seller meets, and roadshows organized by PHARMEXCIL. These events provide a platform for networking and building business relationships.
4. **Advocacy:** The council represents its members' interests in discussions with government bodies, international trade organizations, and regulatory authorities. This advocacy ensures that the voice of Indian pharmaceutical exporters is heard at the highest levels.
5. **Capacity Building:** Through workshops, training programs, and webinars, PHARMEXCIL helps members enhance their skills and stay updated on global best practices.
6. **Financial Assistance:** Members can avail of financial support under export promotion schemes such as the Market Access Initiative (MAI) and the Market Development Assistance (MDA) program.

By fostering a supportive ecosystem for its members, PHARMEXCIL not only enhances their competitiveness but also contributes to the growth of India's pharmaceutical export industry as a whole.

15.4 Objectives and Mandate

The Pharmaceuticals Export Promotion Council of India (PHARMEXCIL) operates with a clear and comprehensive mandate: to elevate the global standing of Indian pharmaceutical products and ensure the sector thrives in an increasingly competitive and regulated global environment. Its objectives are centered around promoting exports, supporting the domestic industry, and fostering collaboration with government agencies and international organizations. This section delves into the specific goals and strategies of PHARMEXCIL, examining how they align with its broader mission.

Promotion of Pharmaceutical Exports

Strategies to Increase Exports Globally

The primary objective of PHARMEXCIL is to expand the footprint of Indian pharmaceutical products in international markets. To achieve this, the council employs a multi-faceted strategy that includes market intelligence, targeted promotions, and strategic partnerships.

1. **Market Research and Intelligence**: PHARMEXCIL conducts detailed studies on global pharmaceutical trends, demand patterns, and regulatory requirements. These studies help Indian exporters identify high-potential markets, understand the competitive landscape, and tailor their strategies accordingly.
2. **Trade Shows and Exhibitions**: The council organizes and participates in international trade fairs and exhibitions, such as iPHEX and CPhI Worldwide. These events provide a platform for Indian exporters to showcase their products, network with potential buyers, and secure new business opportunities.
3. **Buyer-Seller Meets**: PHARMEXCIL facilitates interactions between Indian exporters and international buyers through focused buyer-seller meets. These events, often held in target markets, help bridge the gap between supply and demand, fostering long-term partnerships.
4. **Digital Platforms**: In response to evolving trade dynamics, PHARMEXCIL has embraced digital tools to promote exports. Online marketplaces, virtual trade fairs, and digital marketing campaigns enable exporters to reach global buyers more efficiently.
5. **Export Incentives**: The council advocates for and facilitates access to government export incentives under schemes like the Market Access Initiative (MAI) and the Market Development Assistance (MDA) program. These incentives reduce financial barriers for exporters, particularly small and medium enterprises.

Target Markets and Focus Regions

While Indian pharmaceuticals have a strong presence in established markets like the United States and Europe, PHARMEXCIL recognizes the importance of diversifying export destinations. The council has identified several focus regions based on their growth potential and strategic importance:

1. **Africa**: With its rising demand for affordable medicines, Africa remains a key focus area. Indian pharmaceutical companies supply a significant portion of generic medicines used in African healthcare systems, including antiretroviral drugs for HIV treatment.
2. **Latin America**: Countries like Brazil, Mexico, and Argentina offer opportunities for Indian APIs, formulations, and herbal products. PHARMEXCIL has facilitated market entry by addressing regulatory challenges and promoting Indian products at regional trade fairs.

3. **Middle East and Southeast Asia**: These regions are emerging as hubs for pharmaceutical innovation and trade. PHARMEXCIL works to strengthen India's presence by organizing promotional events and forging partnerships with local distributors.
4. **Commonwealth of Independent States (CIS)**: The CIS region, including Russia and Ukraine, is a growing market for Indian pharmaceutical products. PHARMEXCIL has focused on enhancing regulatory understanding and market penetration in these countries.

Supporting Indian Pharmaceutical Industry

Assistance in Regulatory Compliance

One of the most significant challenges for Indian pharmaceutical exporters is navigating the complex regulatory requirements of international markets. PHARMEXCIL provides comprehensive support in this area through:

1. **Regulatory Guidance**: The council organizes workshops, webinars, and one-on-one consultations to educate exporters about regulatory frameworks like the U.S. FDA, EMA, and WHO GMP standards.
2. **Documentation Support**: PHARMEXCIL assists members in preparing the necessary documentation for regulatory approvals, including dossiers, certificates of analysis, and quality compliance reports.
3. **Resolution of Trade Barriers**: When exporters face issues like import bans or tariff barriers, PHARMEXCIL intervenes by negotiating with foreign regulators and governments to resolve these challenges.
4. **Regulatory Updates**: The council disseminates regular updates on changes in global pharmaceutical regulations, ensuring that Indian exporters stay ahead of the curve.

Capacity Building for Small and Medium Enterprises

Recognizing the vital role of small and medium enterprises (SMEs) in India's pharmaceutical sector, PHARMEXCIL has implemented several capacity-building initiatives to enhance their competitiveness:

1. **Training Programs**: PHARMEXCIL conducts skill development programs on topics like quality assurance, export procedures, and intellectual property rights. These programs are designed to address the specific needs of SMEs.

2. **Access to Export Financing**: The council collaborates with financial institutions to provide SMEs with access to export financing and credit facilities, enabling them to expand their operations.
3. **Mentorship and Networking**: Through mentorship programs, PHARMEXCIL connects SMEs with experienced exporters who provide guidance on market entry, regulatory compliance, and business strategies.
4. **Cluster Development**: PHARMEXCIL supports the formation of pharmaceutical clusters, where SMEs can collaborate on research, production, and export activities. These clusters enhance efficiency and reduce costs, making SMEs more competitive globally.

Collaboration with Government and Agencies

Policy Advocacy and Recommendations

PHARMEXCIL serves as a vital link between the pharmaceutical industry and the government, advocating for policies that promote exports and address industry challenges. Its advocacy efforts include:

1. **Export-Friendly Policies**: The council provides recommendations to the Ministry of Commerce and Industry on trade policies, tax incentives, and export promotion schemes. These inputs ensure that the policy framework aligns with the needs of exporters.
2. **Resolution of Industry Issues**: PHARMEXCIL represents the industry in discussions with government bodies to resolve issues like pricing controls, import restrictions, and intellectual property disputes.
3. **Global Trade Agreements**: The council participates in negotiations for trade agreements, ensuring that India's pharmaceutical sector benefits from favorable terms and reduced barriers to entry.

Collaboration with Indian and International Bodies

PHARMEXCIL actively collaborates with various organizations to strengthen India's pharmaceutical export ecosystem. These collaborations include:

1. **Indian Institutions**: The council works with bodies like the Indian Pharmacopoeia Commission, the Drugs Controller General of India, and the Confederation of Indian Industry to enhance industry standards and competitiveness.
2. **International Organizations**: PHARMEXCIL engages with global agencies such as the WHO, UNICEF, and WTO to promote Indian

pharmaceuticals and address regulatory challenges. For example, it has partnered with the WHO to improve the availability of quality-assured generic medicines in developing countries.

3. **Bilateral Partnerships**: The council facilitates partnerships between Indian exporters and foreign governments, trade bodies, and pharmaceutical companies. These collaborations have opened doors to new markets and strengthened India's global presence.

15.5 Services Offered by PHARMEXCIL

The Pharmaceuticals Export Promotion Council of India (PHARMEXCIL) serves as a critical support system for Indian pharmaceutical exporters by offering a comprehensive range of services. These services address the various challenges faced by exporters, from navigating complex regulatory requirements to identifying new market opportunities. Each service is tailored to meet the specific needs of exporters, ensuring that they remain competitive in an ever-evolving global market. This section explores these services in detail, highlighting their practical applications and impact.

Export Assistance

Guidance on Export Documentation and Procedures

Exporting pharmaceutical products requires adherence to detailed documentation and procedures that vary across countries. PHARMEXCIL provides exporters with step-by-step guidance to simplify these processes:

- **Documentation Support**: Exporters receive assistance in preparing critical documents such as invoices, packing lists, bills of lading, certificates of origin, and product-specific regulatory documents.
- **Customs Procedures**: The council educates members on customs formalities, ensuring smooth clearance of goods at ports and avoiding delays caused by incomplete or incorrect documentation.
- **Export Compliance**: PHARMEXCIL advises exporters on country-specific requirements, such as labeling, packaging standards, and regulatory declarations.

For example, a company exporting to the European Union must comply with stringent documentation related to product safety, efficacy, and quality. PHARMEXCIL's guidance ensures that such requirements are met efficiently.

Financial Support and Subsidies

To ease the financial burden on exporters, PHARMEXCIL facilitates access to government schemes and subsidies:

- **Market Access Initiative (MAI)**: Under this scheme, exporters can receive financial assistance for participating in international trade fairs, exhibitions, and buyer-seller meets.
- **Market Development Assistance (MDA)**: Small and medium enterprises (SMEs) can avail of subsidies for travel, participation fees, and promotional activities in overseas markets.
- **Export Credit Facilities**: PHARMEXCIL collaborates with banks and financial institutions to provide exporters with favorable credit terms, ensuring they have the liquidity needed to fulfill large orders.

This financial support is particularly valuable for smaller companies looking to expand their global reach without overstretching their resources.

Market Intelligence

Reports on International Markets

PHARMEXCIL equips its members with detailed reports on international markets, helping them identify opportunities and make informed business decisions. These reports include:

- **Demand Analysis**: Insights into high-demand pharmaceutical products in specific regions.
- **Competitive Landscape**: Data on key competitors, pricing strategies, and market shares.
- **Regulatory Overview**: Information on the legal and regulatory requirements of target markets.

For instance, a report on the African pharmaceutical market might highlight the increasing demand for generic antiretroviral drugs and outline the regulatory pathways for entering this market.

Analysis of Trade Trends and Opportunities

The council monitors global trade trends to help exporters stay ahead of the curve. This includes:

- **Trade Data Analysis**: Trends in export and import volumes, value, and growth rates across regions.
- **Emerging Markets**: Identification of untapped or underserved markets where Indian pharmaceuticals can gain a competitive edge.

- **Policy Updates**: Implications of trade agreements, tariffs, and international sanctions on pharmaceutical exports.

By providing such insights, PHARMEXCIL enables exporters to adapt their strategies to changing market conditions.

Regulatory Support

Assistance with International Regulatory Approvals

Navigating the regulatory requirements of different countries is one of the most significant challenges for pharmaceutical exporters. PHARMEXCIL provides end-to-end support to help members secure necessary approvals:

- **Dossier Preparation**: Assistance in compiling technical dossiers required for product registration in foreign markets.
- **Regulatory Pathways**: Guidance on the processes for obtaining approvals from agencies like the U.S. FDA, European Medicines Agency (EMA), and World Health Organization (WHO).
- **Compliance Audits**: Pre-inspection audits to ensure compliance with international quality standards, minimizing the risk of rejection or delays.

For example, PHARMEXCIL helps companies prepare for inspections by the U.S. FDA by organizing training sessions and mock audits.

Guidance on Good Manufacturing Practices (GMP)

Compliance with GMP is essential for exporting pharmaceutical products. PHARMEXCIL supports its members by:

- **Training Programs**: Organizing workshops and webinars on GMP standards and best practices.
- **Gap Analysis**: Conducting assessments to identify areas where companies need to improve their manufacturing processes to meet international standards.
- **Certification Support**: Assisting in obtaining GMP certifications, which are often prerequisites for entering regulated markets.

These services ensure that Indian pharmaceutical manufacturers consistently produce high-quality products that meet global standards.

Business Matchmaking and Networking

Trade Delegations and Exhibitions

PHARMEXCIL organizes trade delegations and participates in international exhibitions to promote Indian pharmaceuticals. These events serve as platforms for showcasing products, building relationships, and exploring new business opportunities:

- **International Pharma and Healthcare Exhibition (iPHEX)**: A flagship event organized by PHARMEXCIL, iPHEX attracts buyers, regulators, and stakeholders from across the globe.
- **Participation in Global Trade Shows**: The council facilitates Indian companies' participation in prominent international events like CPhI Worldwide and Arab Health.

Such initiatives enable exporters to connect with potential buyers, distributors, and partners in target markets.

Facilitating Buyer-Seller Meets

To directly connect Indian exporters with international buyers, PHARMEXCIL organizes buyer-seller meets. These events are tailored to specific markets and product categories:

- **Sector-Specific Meets**: Events focused on APIs, herbal medicines, or formulations.
- **Regional Meets**: Meets organized in target markets like Africa, Latin America, and Southeast Asia.
- **Virtual Platforms**: Online buyer-seller meets to bridge geographic barriers and enable continuous engagement.

These matchmaking efforts have resulted in numerous long-term partnerships and expanded market access for Indian exporters.

15.6 Key Initiatives and Programs

PHARMEXCIL has been instrumental in driving the global success of Indian pharmaceutical exports through a variety of well-planned and impactful initiatives. These programs are designed to address the multifaceted challenges faced by exporters, ranging from market entry to regulatory compliance. This section delves into the council's key initiatives and programs, highlighting their design, execution, and outcomes.

International Trade Fairs and Exhibitions

Organization and Participation in Global Events

Trade fairs and exhibitions are among the most effective platforms for showcasing products, building relationships, and exploring new markets. PHARMEXCIL organizes and participates in several global events, acting as a bridge between Indian exporters and international buyers. The council ensures that Indian pharmaceutical companies have a strong presence at these events, creating opportunities for visibility and networking.

- **Organized Events**: PHARMEXCIL's flagship event, the International Pharma and Healthcare Exhibition (iPHEX), is one of the most significant platforms for the Indian pharmaceutical industry. It brings together buyers, regulators, and industry leaders from over 120 countries, showcasing India's capabilities in manufacturing, innovation, and quality assurance.
- **Participatory Support**: The council facilitates the participation of its members in international exhibitions such as CPhI Worldwide, Arab Health, and Africa Health. These events are strategically chosen based on their relevance to target markets and product segments.

Prominent Trade Fairs and Their Outcomes

The impact of PHARMEXCIL's trade fair initiatives is evident in the tangible outcomes achieved by Indian exporters. For example:

- At iPHEX, Indian companies have secured multi-million-dollar deals with global buyers, expanding their footprint in markets like Latin America, Southeast Asia, and Africa.
- Participation in CPhI Worldwide has helped Indian companies establish long-term partnerships with European buyers, particularly for APIs and generic formulations.
- Trade fairs in Africa have opened new opportunities for Indian companies in supplying life-saving drugs for diseases like malaria and HIV.

These events not only boost exports but also enhance India's reputation as a reliable supplier of high-quality pharmaceuticals.

Market Access Programs

Strategies for Entering Emerging Markets

Emerging markets like Africa, Latin America, and Southeast Asia offer immense potential for Indian pharmaceutical products. PHARMEXCIL's market access programs are tailored to help exporters tap into these opportunities while addressing the unique challenges posed by each market.

- **Customized Market Entry Strategies**: PHARMEXCIL provides exporters with detailed insights into market demand, regulatory requirements, and competitive dynamics. For example, in Africa, the focus is on affordability and essential medicines, whereas in Latin America, the emphasis is on APIs and herbal products.

- **Government-to-Government Engagements**: PHARMEXCIL collaborates with Indian embassies and trade missions to facilitate market entry by addressing local policy barriers and fostering bilateral agreements.

Addressing Non-Tariff Barriers and Trade Restrictions

Non-tariff barriers, such as stringent regulatory requirements, import quotas, and local manufacturing mandates, often hinder exports. PHARMEXCIL actively works to resolve these challenges:

- **Negotiations with Foreign Governments**: The council represents Indian exporters in discussions with foreign regulators to advocate for fair and transparent trade practices.
- **Capacity Building for Compliance**: Training programs and workshops help exporters meet the technical standards and documentation requirements of target markets.
- **Awareness Campaigns**: In regions where Indian generics face skepticism, PHARMEXCIL conducts campaigns to highlight their quality, efficacy, and affordability.

These efforts have significantly reduced trade barriers and expanded access to key markets.

Capacity Building

Training Programs for Pharmaceutical Professionals

To remain competitive in global markets, Indian exporters must continually enhance their knowledge and skills. PHARMEXCIL's capacity-building initiatives focus on equipping professionals with the expertise needed for successful exports:

- **Regulatory Training**: Workshops on international regulations such as U.S. FDA, EMA, and WHO GMP help exporters navigate complex approval processes.
- **Export Readiness Programs**: These programs cover practical topics like preparing export documentation, managing logistics, and understanding tariff structures.
- **Technical Skill Development**: Training on quality control, supply chain management, and innovative manufacturing techniques ensures that Indian pharmaceutical products meet global standards.

Seminars and Workshops on Export Readiness

PHARMEXCIL organizes regular seminars and workshops to foster a culture of continuous learning:

- **Focused Topics**: Topics such as intellectual property rights, international trade policies, and emerging market trends are addressed by industry experts.
- **Interactive Sessions**: These workshops encourage interaction between participants and facilitators, enabling exporters to clarify doubts and share experiences.
- **Real-World Scenarios**: Case studies and role-playing exercises simulate real-world challenges, helping participants develop practical solutions.

These initiatives have empowered exporters, particularly SMEs, to confidently enter and sustain themselves in competitive markets.

Digital Initiatives

Use of Technology in Export Promotion

Recognizing the transformative potential of technology, PHARMEXCIL has embraced digital solutions to promote exports more effectively:

- **Online Marketplaces**: The council has developed digital platforms where Indian exporters can showcase their products to a global audience, simplifying the process of connecting with buyers.
- **Digital Marketing Campaigns**: Targeted campaigns using social media, email marketing, and online advertising help Indian pharmaceutical companies reach international buyers in a cost-effective manner.
- **Data Analytics**: PHARMEXCIL uses analytics tools to study trade data, identify trends, and provide actionable insights to its members.

Online Platforms for Networking and Trade Facilitation

In addition to physical events, PHARMEXCIL has invested in virtual platforms to foster networking and trade facilitation:

- **Virtual Trade Fairs**: These events replicate the experience of physical trade fairs, allowing exporters and buyers to interact through video calls, chat rooms, and virtual booths.
- **Webinars and E-Conferences**: These platforms enable knowledge sharing on topics like regulatory updates, market trends, and export strategies.

- **Member Portals**: PHARMEXCIL's member portal provides a one-stop solution for accessing reports, registering for events, and connecting with potential buyers.

These digital initiatives have been particularly valuable during disruptions like the COVID-19 pandemic, ensuring that trade promotion activities continue without interruption.

15.7 PHARMEXCIL's Role in Shaping Policies

PHARMEXCIL's role extends beyond promoting pharmaceutical exports; it also actively contributes to the policy-making process to create a favorable environment for Indian exporters. As the official representative of the pharmaceutical export sector, the council engages with government bodies, trade organizations, and international stakeholders to advocate for policies that enhance the global competitiveness of Indian pharmaceuticals. This section explores how PHARMEXCIL influences national and international trade policies, facilitates ease of doing business, and resolves trade disputes.

Policy Advocacy

Inputs on National Export Policies

PHARMEXCIL plays a pivotal role in shaping India's export policies by providing informed and practical recommendations to the Ministry of Commerce and Industry. Its policy advocacy efforts focus on ensuring that government strategies align with the needs of the pharmaceutical export sector.

- **Data-Driven Recommendations**: PHARMEXCIL uses its extensive market research and industry data to identify barriers to export growth. For instance, high tariffs in certain markets or cumbersome documentation requirements can hinder exporters. The council compiles these insights into detailed reports, which it submits to policymakers.
- **Focus on Export Incentives**: The council has been instrumental in advocating for export promotion schemes such as the Market Access Initiative (MAI) and the Market Development Assistance (MDA) program. These programs provide financial support to exporters, enabling them to compete in global markets effectively.
- **Sector-Specific Policies**: PHARMEXCIL's inputs are often tailored to the unique needs of various pharmaceutical sub-sectors, such as

active pharmaceutical ingredients (APIs), herbal products, and biopharmaceuticals. For example, the council has recommended policies to reduce import dependency on APIs by promoting domestic production under the "Make in India" initiative.

Recommendations for Improving Ease of Doing Business

Ease of doing business is a critical factor in fostering export growth. PHARMEXCIL collaborates with government agencies to streamline processes and reduce bureaucratic hurdles for exporters.

- **Simplifying Export Procedures**: The council has proposed measures to reduce the complexity of export documentation and customs procedures. Initiatives such as digitizing export clearance processes and integrating regulatory approvals into single-window systems are examples of PHARMEXCIL's influence.
- **Regulatory Harmonization**: By advocating for uniform regulatory standards across states, PHARMEXCIL ensures that pharmaceutical exporters face fewer inconsistencies and delays in obtaining certifications and approvals.
- **Tax Reforms**: PHARMEXCIL has been a vocal proponent of tax reforms that benefit exporters, such as GST refunds and duty drawback schemes. These reforms improve cash flow and reduce costs for exporters, particularly small and medium enterprises (SMEs).

Influence on Trade Agreements

Contributions to Bilateral and Multilateral Trade Agreements

Trade agreements play a significant role in determining market access, tariffs, and regulatory requirements for pharmaceutical exports. PHARMEXCIL provides expert inputs during the negotiation of bilateral and multilateral agreements, ensuring that the interests of Indian pharmaceutical exporters are safeguarded.

- **Bilateral Trade Agreements**: PHARMEXCIL collaborates with the Ministry of Commerce and Industry to identify opportunities for enhancing pharmaceutical trade in bilateral agreements. For example, its inputs have been critical in securing favorable terms for Indian generics in agreements with African and Latin American countries.
- **Multilateral Forums**: In global trade forums such as the World Trade Organization (WTO), PHARMEXCIL represents the Indian pharmaceutical sector's perspective on issues like intellectual

property rights, trade barriers, and market access. Its advocacy ensures that trade agreements reflect the importance of affordable and quality medicines for global healthcare.

Addressing Trade Disputes and Fostering Collaboration

Trade disputes can disrupt exports and strain international relationships. PHARMEXCIL plays a proactive role in resolving such disputes and fostering collaboration between stakeholders.

- **Dispute Resolution**: The council acts as a mediator between Indian exporters and foreign regulators or governments. For instance, when Indian pharmaceutical products face import bans or excessive scrutiny, PHARMEXCIL engages with the concerned authorities to address the issues and restore market access.
- **Collaboration with Foreign Bodies**: PHARMEXCIL fosters partnerships with international trade organizations, regulatory agencies, and industry associations. These collaborations not only facilitate smoother trade relations but also enhance the global reputation of Indian pharmaceuticals.
- **Case Studies of Success**: One notable example is PHARMEXCIL's intervention in the African market, where skepticism about Indian generics led to restrictive policies. The council conducted awareness campaigns, showcasing the quality and affordability of Indian medicines, and successfully reopened these markets to Indian exporters.

Contributions to India's Pharmaceutical Sector

The impact of PHARMEXCIL on India's pharmaceutical sector is profound and multi-faceted. Its initiatives and programs have not only elevated India's status as a global pharmaceutical powerhouse but have also contributed significantly to the country's economic growth. This section explores how PHARMEXCIL has boosted export volumes, promoted Indian pharma globally, and solidified India's reputation as the "Pharmacy of the World."

15.8 Boosting Export Volumes

Statistical Analysis of Export Growth Due to PHARMEXCIL

PHARMEXCIL has been instrumental in driving the exponential growth of India's pharmaceutical exports over the past two decades. The sector's contribution to India's foreign trade has consistently increased, reflecting the success of PHARMEXCIL's initiatives.

- **Export Statistics**: In 2004, the year of PHARMEXCIL's establishment, India's pharmaceutical exports stood at approximately **USD 3.5 billion**. By **2022-2023**, this figure had surpassed **USD 25 billion**, a nearly sevenfold increase. This growth has been fueled by strategic market penetration, increased regulatory compliance, and robust promotion efforts spearheaded by PHARMEXCIL.
- **Geographical Reach**: Indian pharmaceutical products are now exported to over **200 countries**, including highly regulated markets like the United States and the European Union, as well as emerging markets in Africa, Latin America, and Southeast Asia. The diversification of export destinations has reduced dependence on specific regions and increased market resilience.
- **Sectoral Contributions**: PHARMEXCIL's targeted support for various sub-sectors has ensured balanced growth:
    - **Active Pharmaceutical Ingredients (APIs)**: India is the world's largest producer of APIs, accounting for **20% of global production by volume**.
    - **Generic Medicines**: Indian generics constitute nearly **40% of the generic drugs supplied to the U.S. market** and a substantial share of global supplies.
    - **Vaccines**: India supplies over **60% of the world's vaccines**, with PHARMEXCIL playing a key role in promoting vaccine exports to developing countries through partnerships with global organizations like UNICEF and WHO.

Key Products Driving Exports

India's pharmaceutical exports are dominated by a few key product categories, each of which has been a focus area for PHARMEXCIL:

- **Generic Drugs**: The affordability and quality of Indian generics have made them a preferred choice in both developed and developing markets. Products like antiretroviral drugs for HIV treatment and anti-malarial medicines have been particularly successful.
- **Vaccines**: India's position as the world's largest vaccine supplier has been strengthened through PHARMEXCIL's efforts to highlight the country's manufacturing capabilities and regulatory compliance.
- **APIs and Intermediates**: India has established itself as a reliable supplier of APIs, particularly for antibiotics, anti-inflammatory drugs, and cardiovascular medicines. PHARMEXCIL's advocacy for

increased domestic production under the "Make in India" initiative has further boosted this segment.

- **Herbal and Traditional Medicines**: Ayurvedic and herbal products have found a niche in international markets, thanks to PHARMEXCIL's promotional efforts and quality assurance initiatives.

Promoting Indian Pharma Globally

Branding India as the "Pharmacy of the World"

India's identity as the "Pharmacy of the World" is a result of sustained efforts by PHARMEXCIL to showcase the country's capabilities on a global stage. This branding has been built on several pillars:

- **Quality Assurance**: PHARMEXCIL has worked tirelessly to ensure that Indian pharmaceutical products meet the highest international standards. By facilitating compliance with regulatory requirements such as U.S. FDA and EMA approvals, the council has enhanced global trust in Indian medicines.
- **Affordability**: Indian pharmaceuticals are known for their cost-effectiveness. PHARMEXCIL has emphasized this aspect in its promotional campaigns, positioning India as a vital player in improving global healthcare access.
- **Global Collaborations**: Partnerships with international organizations like WHO, UNICEF, and WTO have bolstered India's reputation. During the COVID-19 pandemic, PHARMEXCIL played a key role in coordinating the export of vaccines and essential medicines to over **150 countries**, cementing India's status as a global health leader.

Success Stories of Indian Companies Entering Global Markets

PHARMEXCIL's initiatives have enabled numerous Indian pharmaceutical companies to achieve remarkable success in international markets. A few notable examples include:

- **Sun Pharmaceutical Industries**: With support from PHARMEXCIL in navigating regulatory approvals, Sun Pharma has become the largest Indian pharmaceutical company in the U.S., offering a wide range of generic and specialty medicines.
- **Dr. Reddy's Laboratories**: Leveraging PHARMEXCIL's market intelligence and trade facilitation programs, Dr. Reddy's has established a strong presence in Russia, the U.S., and Latin America.

- **Serum Institute of India**: As the world's largest vaccine manufacturer, Serum Institute has benefited from PHARMEXCIL's efforts to promote Indian vaccines globally. Its pivotal role in supplying COVID-19 vaccines is a testament to this collaboration.
- **Cipla**: Cipla's entry into African markets, driven by its affordable HIV medications, was facilitated by PHARMEXCIL's advocacy and capacity-building programs.

These success stories highlight the transformative impact of PHARMEXCIL's initiatives on the global competitiveness of Indian pharmaceutical companies.

15.9 Challenges Faced by PHARMEXCIL

While PHARMEXCIL has played a pivotal role in driving the growth of India's pharmaceutical exports, it faces several challenges that test its ability to sustain momentum and meet the evolving needs of the industry. These challenges arise from external trade barriers, increasing global competition, and internal limitations within the organization. This section examines these challenges in detail and explores potential strategies to address them.

Trade Barriers

Regulatory Hurdles in Export Destinations

One of the most significant challenges faced by PHARMEXCIL is helping Indian exporters navigate the complex and varying regulatory landscapes of global markets. Many export destinations have stringent requirements that can be daunting, especially for small and medium enterprises (SMEs).

- **Stringent Approval Processes**: Markets like the United States and the European Union require extensive documentation and testing, including bioequivalence studies, stability data, and Good Manufacturing Practices (GMP) compliance. These processes are time-consuming and costly, often delaying market entry for Indian products.
- **Frequent Policy Changes**: Exporters often face uncertainty due to changing regulations in target markets. For example, sudden modifications to import policies or labeling requirements can lead to disruptions in supply chains and financial losses.
- **Lack of Harmonization**: The absence of uniform regulatory standards across countries increases the burden on exporters, who

must tailor their submissions to meet the unique requirements of each market.

Non-Tariff Barriers Impacting Market Access

Non-tariff barriers, which include restrictions other than tariffs, pose another significant challenge for Indian pharmaceutical exporters:

- **Quality Perception Issues**: Despite meeting international standards, Indian generics sometimes face skepticism about their quality and efficacy in certain markets.
- **Local Manufacturing Requirements**: Some countries impose mandates requiring pharmaceuticals to be manufactured locally to reduce dependency on imports. These policies can limit market access for Indian exporters.
- **Customs Delays and Bureaucratic Red Tape**: Lengthy customs clearance processes in certain countries increase costs and delay the delivery of life-saving medicines.

PHARMEXCIL must continuously engage with foreign regulators and policymakers to resolve these trade barriers and advocate for fair trade practices.

Competition from Other Countries

Analysis of Competitors Like China, EU, and the US

India's pharmaceutical sector faces intense competition from other global players, each with its own strengths:

- **China**:
  China's dominance in the production of bulk drugs and active pharmaceutical ingredients (APIs) poses a significant challenge. With large-scale, cost-efficient manufacturing facilities, China often undercuts Indian exports in price-sensitive markets.
- **European Union (EU)**: The EU has a well-established pharmaceutical industry known for innovation, quality, and brand recognition. Indian generics face stiff competition from European patented drugs, particularly in high-income markets.
- **United States**: The U.S. pharmaceutical industry excels in research and development, producing high-value biologics and specialty medicines. Although Indian generics have a strong foothold in the U.S. market, domestic companies remain dominant in niche and high-margin segments.

Strategies to Maintain Competitiveness

To address this competition, PHARMEXCIL has implemented several strategies:

- **Focus on Innovation**: Encouraging Indian companies to invest in R&D and move up the value chain by producing biosimilars, complex generics, and specialty medicines.
- **Cost Competitiveness**: Advocating for policies that reduce input costs, such as incentivizing domestic production of APIs under the "Make in India" initiative, to decrease reliance on imports from China.
- **Strengthening Regulatory Expertise**: Providing exporters with advanced training on regulatory compliance to accelerate approvals and reduce entry barriers in regulated markets.
- **Market Diversification**: Promoting Indian pharmaceuticals in untapped regions such as Africa, Latin America, and Southeast Asia to reduce dependency on traditional markets like the U.S. and Europe.

Internal Challenges

Limitations in Resources and Outreach

As a non-profit organization, PHARMEXCIL operates within resource constraints that limit its ability to scale its services and initiatives:

- **Limited Funding**: The council's financial resources are often stretched thin, especially when organizing large-scale international events or expanding digital initiatives.
- **Regional Outreach Gaps**: While PHARMEXCIL has regional offices, they may not be accessible to exporters in remote areas. This can lead to underrepresentation of certain regions and their specific challenges.

Addressing Member Grievances and Inefficiencies

Maintaining member satisfaction while addressing their diverse needs is another challenge for PHARMEXCIL:

- **Varied Expectations**: Large pharmaceutical companies may prioritize global regulatory compliance, whereas SMEs often need support with basic export procedures. Balancing these expectations can be difficult.
- **Operational Delays**: Members sometimes report delays in receiving support for documentation, financial assistance, or dispute resolution, which can impact their export timelines.

- **Feedback Mechanisms**: Although PHARMEXCIL organizes forums for member interaction, the feedback mechanisms may not always be comprehensive, leading to unresolved grievances.

To address these challenges, PHARMEXCIL is working on enhancing its digital infrastructure, increasing member engagement, and collaborating more closely with government agencies to secure additional funding.

15.10 Case Studies and Success Stories

The impact of PHARMEXCIL's efforts can best be understood through real-world examples and success stories that highlight its effectiveness in promoting Indian pharmaceutical exports. These cases not only showcase the tangible outcomes of PHARMEXCIL's initiatives but also demonstrate its ability to address challenges and create opportunities for growth. This section presents notable export breakthroughs, testimonials from member companies, and the regional impact of PHARMEXCIL's work.

Prominent Success Stories

Notable Instances of Export Breakthroughs Facilitated by PHARMEXCIL

1. **Expanding Indian Generics in the African Market**: In the early 2010s, several African countries were hesitant to adopt Indian generics due to misconceptions about their quality. PHARMEXCIL launched an awareness campaign targeting healthcare regulators and stakeholders across the continent. By organizing trade delegations, buyer-seller meets, and showcasing Indian pharmaceutical standards, PHARMEXCIL successfully opened the market for Indian exporters. Today, India supplies over **40% of generic drugs used in Africa**, especially for diseases like HIV, malaria, and tuberculosis.
2. **Facilitating Vaccine Exports During COVID-19**: During the COVID-19 pandemic, PHARMEXCIL played a pivotal role in coordinating vaccine exports to over **150 countries**. It worked closely with the Serum Institute of India and Bharat Biotech to streamline regulatory approvals and logistics. These efforts not only strengthened India's reputation as the "Pharmacy of the World" but also positioned Indian vaccines as a critical component of global healthcare responses.
3. **Breakthrough in the Latin American Market**: Entering Latin America has always been challenging due to strict regulatory

requirements and market-specific barriers. PHARMEXCIL's targeted efforts, including trade fairs in Brazil and Mexico and collaborations with local regulatory authorities, enabled Indian companies like Dr. Reddy's Laboratories to establish a strong foothold in the region. The Latin American market now accounts for a significant share of India's pharmaceutical exports.

4. **Biopharmaceutical Success in Developed Markets**: Biocon, a leader in biopharmaceuticals, benefited from PHARMEXCIL's support in navigating U.S. FDA and EMA regulations for its biosimilar products. PHARMEXCIL facilitated training and mock audits, ensuring compliance with international standards. Today, Biocon is a recognized name in biosimilars, with a substantial presence in the U.S. and Europe.

Member Testimonials

Feedback from Pharmaceutical Companies

The success of PHARMEXCIL's initiatives is often reflected in the positive feedback from its member companies. A few testimonials highlight the council's contributions:

1. **Cipla Ltd.** "PHARMEXCIL's guidance during our entry into the Middle East was invaluable. Their market intelligence reports and buyer-seller meets provided us with the insights and connections we needed to expand successfully."
2. **Sun Pharmaceutical Industries** "Participating in international trade fairs like iPHEX, organized by PHARMEXCIL, has been a game-changer for us. These platforms allowed us to showcase our capabilities to a global audience and secure multi-million-dollar contracts."
3. **Serum Institute of India** "The support provided by PHARMEXCIL during the pandemic was extraordinary. Their coordination with government bodies and international organizations ensured that our vaccines reached countries in need without delays."
4. **Small and Medium Enterprises (SMEs)** "As an SME, navigating regulatory requirements was always a challenge for us. PHARMEXCIL's training sessions and documentation support simplified the process and enabled us to start exporting to new markets."

Regional Impact

Growth in Exports from Specific Regions of India

PHARMEXCIL's efforts have had a significant regional impact, promoting pharmaceutical exports from various parts of India. Some regions have emerged as key hubs for pharmaceutical production and export due to PHARMEXCIL's targeted initiatives.

1. **Hyderabad (Telangana)**: Often referred to as the "Bulk Drug Capital of India," Hyderabad has seen remarkable growth in API exports. PHARMEXCIL's support in organizing industry-specific trade fairs and addressing regulatory challenges has been instrumental in this success. The region now contributes a significant share to India's overall pharmaceutical exports.
2. **Ahmedabad and Baroda (Gujarat)**: Gujarat has become a hub for formulations and generic drugs. PHARMEXCIL's facilitation of buyer-seller meets with European and African buyers has boosted exports from this region. Companies based in Gujarat have reported steady growth in export volumes and market reach.
3. **Mumbai and Pune (Maharashtra)**: Maharashtra has emerged as a leader in biopharmaceuticals and vaccines. PHARMEXCIL's assistance with compliance training and international regulatory submissions has played a critical role in the success of companies like Serum Institute and Wockhardt.
4. **Baddi (Himachal Pradesh)**: Known for its manufacturing units, Baddi has benefited from PHARMEXCIL's efforts to promote SMEs. Training programs and export readiness workshops conducted in the region have empowered small-scale manufacturers to enter global markets.
5. **Chennai (Tamil Nadu)**: Tamil Nadu has seen growth in the export of herbal and traditional medicines. PHARMEXCIL's promotion of these products in Southeast Asia has opened new avenues for exporters in the region.

15.11 Conclusion

As we reach the culmination of this exploration of PHARMEXCIL's remarkable journey, it is evident that the Pharmaceuticals Export Promotion Council of India has been a cornerstone of India's emergence as a global pharmaceutical powerhouse. Through its tireless efforts, the council has addressed critical challenges, opened doors to new markets, and reinforced

India's identity as the "Pharmacy of the World." This conclusion reflects on PHARMEXCIL's impact, underscores the importance of continued innovation, and envisions its future contributions to the pharmaceutical industry.

Summary of PHARMEXCIL's Impact

Overview of Key Contributions to Indian Pharma Exports

PHARMEXCIL's contributions have been integral to the exponential growth of India's pharmaceutical exports over the past two decades. Its initiatives have empowered Indian companies to navigate complex international markets, comply with stringent regulatory standards, and build lasting relationships with global stakeholders.

- **Export Growth**: PHARMEXCIL has facilitated a nearly sevenfold increase in pharmaceutical exports, from approximately USD 3.5 billion in 2004 to over USD 25 billion in 2023. These exports now reach over 200 countries, including highly regulated and emerging markets.
- **Promotion of Indian Pharmaceuticals**: By organizing trade fairs, buyer-seller meets, and digital platforms, PHARMEXCIL has elevated the visibility of Indian pharmaceuticals on the global stage. Key products such as generics, APIs, and vaccines now dominate international markets.
- **Support for SMEs**: PHARMEXCIL has been a lifeline for small and medium enterprises, offering them financial support, regulatory guidance, and training programs that enable them to compete with global giants.
- **Policy Advocacy**: The council's role in shaping export-friendly policies, resolving trade disputes, and contributing to trade agreements has enhanced the global competitiveness of Indian pharmaceuticals.
- **Regional Impact**: From Hyderabad's dominance in APIs to Gujarat's leadership in generics and Maharashtra's success in biopharmaceuticals, PHARMEXCIL has contributed to regional growth, ensuring a balanced and inclusive expansion of India's pharmaceutical sector.

These achievements collectively underline PHARMEXCIL's pivotal role in transforming India into a trusted and indispensable player in the global pharmaceutical supply chain.

Call for Continued Innovation

Importance of PHARMEXCIL in Maintaining India's Global Leadership

The global pharmaceutical landscape is evolving rapidly, driven by advancements in biotechnology, personalized medicine, and complex generics. To maintain its leadership, India must stay ahead of these trends, and PHARMEXCIL will continue to play a crucial role in this journey.

- **Fostering Innovation**: The council must encourage Indian companies to invest in research and development, particularly in areas like biosimilars, cell and gene therapies, and artificial intelligence-driven drug discovery.
- **Sustainability and Ethics**: With increasing scrutiny on environmental and social practices, PHARMEXCIL can lead the way in promoting sustainable manufacturing processes and ethical trade practices.
- **Digital Transformation**: Embracing technology is imperative. PHARMEXCIL's efforts to digitize trade facilitation, enhance market intelligence through analytics, and expand virtual networking platforms will be critical to its success.
- **Strengthening Global Partnerships**: As global health challenges like pandemics and antimicrobial resistance grow, PHARMEXCIL must deepen collaborations with international organizations, ensuring India's pharmaceutical sector remains a key contributor to global health solutions.

By driving these initiatives, PHARMEXCIL can help Indian exporters adapt to changing market dynamics, sustain competitiveness, and capture emerging opportunities.

Final Thoughts

Vision for PHARMEXCIL's Role in the Future of the Pharmaceutical Industry

PHARMEXCIL's vision for the future must encompass both continuity and change. While continuing to build on its legacy of export promotion, the council must also evolve to address emerging challenges and opportunities in the pharmaceutical sector.

The future of the global pharmaceutical industry will demand greater innovation, sustainability, and collaboration. PHARMEXCIL's ability to anticipate these needs, advocate for industry-friendly policies, and provide targeted support to its members will define its relevance and success. By fostering an ecosystem that encourages innovation, promotes equity, and ensures quality, PHARMEXCIL can lead the next phase of growth for India's pharmaceutical exports.

As the pharmaceutical industry becomes increasingly interconnected with advancements in technology and healthcare delivery, PHARMEXCIL's role as a catalyst for transformation will remain indispensable. The journey so far is a testament to its achievements, and the road ahead is filled with opportunities to further elevate India's position in the global pharmaceutical landscape.

www.ingramcontent.com/pod-product-compliance
Lightning Source LLC
Chambersburg PA
CBHW071222230926
51849CB00001B/9
* 9 7 8 9 3 4 9 5 6 2 8 9 9 *